READING GROUP CHOICES

2015

*Selections for lively
book discussions*

**READING
GROUP**
Choices

Reading Group Choices' goal is to join with publishers, bookstores, libraries, trade associations, and authors to develop resources to enhance the shared reading group experience. *Reading Group Choices* is distributed annually to bookstores, libraries, and directly to book groups. Titles from previous issues are posted on ReadingGroupChoices.com. Books presented here have been recommended by book group members, librarians, booksellers, literary agents, publicists, authors, and publishers. All submissions are then reviewed to ensure the discussibility of each title. Once a title is approved for inclusion, publishers are asked to underwrite production costs, so that copies of *Reading Group Choices* can be distributed for a minimal charge. For additional copies, please call your local library or bookstore, or contact us by phone or email. Quantities are limited. For more information, please visit our website at **ReadingGroupChoices.com.**

For further information, contact:
Reading Group Choices
info@ReadingGroupChoices.com
ReadingGroupChoices.com

PRAISE FOR *READING GROUP CHOICES*

"Selecting a book is one of the hardest and most important decisions a group has to make each month. With Reading Group Choices as their guide, online and in print, groups can't go wrong." —**Julie Robinson, owner, Literary Affairs and founder of The Beverly Hills Literary Escape**

"Reading Group Choices is the next best thing to having your own professional facilitator, librarian or bookseller as a part of your reading group. Highly recommended." —**Jill A. Tardiff, Women's National Book Association, National Reading Group Month Chair**

"Reading Group Choices continues to be a first-rate resource that book groups anticipate to guide them through the choices to find books that are discussible, enjoyable, and enrich their time together." —**Donna Paz Kaufman, Paz & Associates, The Bookstore Training Group**

"We have learned over the years that displays are a great way to encourage circulation at our small, rural library. One of our best displays is based on the wonderful literary guide published by Reading Group Choices! *Patrons cannot wait to get their . . . copies and start reading."* —**Gail N., Sandusky District Library**

"Let's get ready to rumble! The latest Reading Group Choices *book has just arrived on my desk, and I'll be using this to help select the book group titles for next year. . . . I have to say that I've kept every single one of these collections. I go back and look at the older editions to find books my group may have missed."* —**Kaite S., Book Group**

"I'm a reader's advisor at a public library and we have a service that obtains books for over 100 local clubs. I can attest to the wonderful resource that Reading Group Choices *is to our staff and patrons. We always order multiple copies of your annual booklet to share and they get a lot of use. Thank you for your great website and resource for book clubs everywhere."* —**Connie R., The Sullivan Book Group**

Welcome to READING GROUP Choices

When I look back, I am so impressed again with the life-giving power of literature. If I were a young person today, trying to gain a sense of myself in the world, I would do that again by reading, just as I did when I was young.
—**Maya Angelou** (1928-2014)

Dear Readers,

We are proud to introduce another collection of wonderful books to inspire your book club toward meaningful and lively discussions.

Since April, when I purchased Reading Group Choices, I have received emails from our reading group members with kind words about what we provide, as well as thank you notes for the contests and drawings they have won. In all of these messages, I have noticed a pattern: each person commented on how much they love reading, or how excited they are to read a certain book, or how much they are looking forward to their next reading group discussion. When I email the Favorite Books Contest winners and Spotlight Clubs, and drop the random drawing winners' packages in the mail each month, it feels like giving gifts; I know our readers will be as excited about the books they have won as I was when I first received them. At Reading Group Choices, we strive to recommend books and provide resources that prompt people to send these unnecessary thank yous. We are happy to hear what books are next on your list, and we are glad that many come from our own guide and website each year.

The 2015 edition once again provides over 50 book recommendations for your group. It includes books by authors and publishers we have featured before, as well as books by debut authors and independent presses from Minnesota to Pennsylvania to North Carolina. There are nonfiction and fiction selections, and some books will be published in 2015, so when you plan your group's list for the year, you can plan ahead! Also, many of these books will be included in contests on our website this fall and winter so be sure to check the site on the first of each month and sign up for our monthly newsletter to find out what's new.

Heartfelt gratitude goes to Charlie Mead, and Donna Paz Kaufman and Mark Kaufman of Paz & Associates. Donna and Mark founded Reading Group Choices in 1994. Charlie and his late wife, Barbara, purchased the business in 2005 and carried on Reading Group Choices from 2005 to 2014. I now have the honor to continue Reading Group Choices' mission to provide fantastic literary resources for book clubs and individuals. I would like to personally thank Charlie, without whose guidance, assistance and encouragement this edition would not have been possible.

As always, we would like to thank you, our readers, for supporting and inspiring us. Thank you as well to our many talented authors, our independent bookseller partners, and our friends in the publishing industry.

Please visit us online at ReadingGroupChoices.com, Facebook, Twitter, Pinterest, Instagram, and through our downloadable app.

Here's to another year of happy reading!

M. m

Mary Morgan
Reading Group Choices

Contents

ABOUT A GIRL

Lindsey Kelk

Tess Brookes has always been a girl with a plan. But when the plan goes belly up, she's forced to reconsider. After accidently answering her roommate Vanessa's phone, she decides that since being Tess isn't going so well, she might try being Vanessa. With nothing left to lose, she accepts Vanessa's photography assignment to Hawaii—she used to be an amateur snapper, how hard can it be? Right? But Tess is soon in big trouble. And the gorgeous journalist on the shoot with her, who is making it very clear he'd like to get into her pants, is an egotistical monster. Far from home and in someone else's shoes, Tess must decide whether to fight on through, or 'fess up and run…

International Praise for *About a Girl*:

"Fans of the I Heart series will instantly fall for this gorgeously funny and romantic read." —Closer

"Perfect for your summer holiday!" —Bella

"Kelk has a hilarious turn of phrase and a sparkling writing style…" —**Daily Express**

ABOUT THE AUTHOR: **Lindsey Kelk** was a children's book editor and is now a magazine columnist and author of *I Heart New York, I Heart Hollywood, I Heart Paris, I Heart Vegas, I Heart London* and *The Single Girl's To-Do List*. When she isn't writing or watching more TV than is healthy, Lindsey likes to wear shoes, shop for shoes and judge the shoes of others. She loves living in New York but misses Sherbet Fountains, London, and drinking Gin & Elderflower cocktails with her friends. Not necessarily in that order.

April 2015 | Trade Paperback | Fiction | 416 pp | $14.99 | ISBN 9780007591411
Harper | harpercollins.com | lindseykelk.com

1. Tess and Charlie have been best friends for a decade but when they sleep together it seems to completely derail their friendship. Do you think that two friends can go back to being "just friends" after sleeping together? How do you think their relationship has been affected by their actions?

2. Tess has been in love with Charlie for as long as they have been friends. Why do you think he never realized?

3. Why do you think Tess decided to take over her roommate's identity? How was this action out of character for someone like Tess? Is there a psychological reason behind this decision?

4. Why do you think that Tess is drawn towards Nick though she is in love with Charlie? Who did you think she should be with? Who would you pick for yourself?

5. How do you think Tess handles her confession when she comes clean about who she really is? If you were Tess, how do you think you would have handled it? How about if you were Kekipi? If you were Nick, what would you have done?

6. What do you think that Tess has learned from her experience pretending to be someone else?

7. In the end Tess must make a choice between her old life and her new. Which do you think Tess should choose? Which would you choose?

ACROSS A GREEN OCEAN

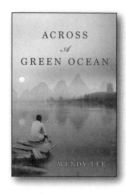

Wendy Lee

After his father's death, Michael Tang finds himself in possession of a letter sent to his dad from a long-ago friend in China. Without a word to his mother or sister, he empties his bank account and maxes out his credit cards to make the long journey to a remote part of that enormous country. Once there, he's confronted with the man his father once was, and how the choices he made long ago continue to echo throughout all of their lives. His mother, Ling, never expected to be so lonely. After the sudden loss of her husband, she worries she's somehow driven her children away—Emily, to long hours and a childless marriage, Michael to a country whose language he doesn't even speak. Though in many ways they are living the lives Ling and her husband sacrificed so much to give them, Ling has to wonder: was it all worth it? As an immigration lawyer, Emily sees people at their worst. But it's not until a case ends horribly that she starts to question every choice she's made—every one, that is, except the one her husband hopes she'll reconsider.

"As haunting as it is inspiring. Lee creates characters who are each, at times, profoundly flawed and deeply moving. I will not soon forget them."
—**Katrina Kittle, author of *The Blessings of the Animals***

"An emotionally-charged story about fear of censure and how it conceals truths that isolate us even as we crave understanding from the ones we love."
—**Janie Chang, author of *Three Souls***

About the Author: **Wendy Lee** is the author of *Happy Family*, which was named one of the top ten first novels of 2008 by *Booklist* and received an honorable mention from the Association of Asian American Studies. She has taught writing at the Asian American Writers Workshop and served as a mentor with the nonprofit organization Girls Write Now. She lives in Astoria, New York.

February 2015 | Trade Paperback | Fiction | 352 pp | $15.00 | ISBN 9781617734878
Kensington Books | kensingtonbooks.com | wendyleebooks.com

CONVERSATION STARTERS

1. Ling is afraid that her children's relationship is doomed to "older sibling–younger sibling rivalry or worse, indifference." What kind of siblings are Emily and Michael? How has their relationship changed over the years?

2. Describe Emily and Julian's marriage. Do they have more issues other than the fact that Julian wants children and Emily doesn't? In explaining their marital problems, Emily says, "We've never had to struggle for anything together, against anything, except our parents' expectations . . . and that's not enough to keep two people together." What part does this play in the dissolution of their marriage?

3. Michael is constantly testing his relationship with David, from going on a trip without telling him to almost cheating on him. Why does Michael feel the need to push these boundaries? Will Michael and David's relationship last?

4. How does Gao Hu remind Emily of her own father? Why did she become an immigration lawyer, and how much of it has to do with her parents? Are these good reasons to pursue a career?

5. In considering her husband, Ling reflects that she knows "how delicate his stomach was; how loud his snores at night; how his discarded socks looked like cow dung . . . If knowing the most intimate details of someone's life wasn't really knowing that person, then what was?" Does knowing these kinds of things about someone mean that you truly know them? How is this different from understanding someone?

6. While visiting Liao's home, Michael thinks that maybe Liao, rather than his own father, is the lucky one. Even though he spent fifteen years in a labor camp, what does Liao have in his life that Han did not? What do people lose through the immigration process?

7. In a sense, Han Tang will always remain an enigmatic person to his wife and children. What kind of closure do they find on their own? How does this help them continue with their lives?

8. A reason many people immigrate to another country is to make a better life for their children. To many immigrants, this "better life" means traditional spouses, children, and job security—none of which Emily or Michael have by the end of the novel. Is this a betrayal of their parents' sacrifices? What do the children of immigrants owe their parents?

AFTER I'M GONE

Laura Lippman

When Felix Brewer meets Bernadette "Bambi" Gottschalk at a Valentine's Dance in 1959, he charms her with wild promises, some of which he actually keeps. Thanks to his lucrative—if not all legal—businesses, she and their three girls live in luxury. But on the 4th of July, 1976, Bambi's comfortable world implodes when Felix, newly convicted and facing prison, vanishes. Though Bambi has no idea where her husband—or his money—might be, she suspects one woman does: his mistress, Julie. When Julie disappears ten years to the day that Felix went on the lam, everyone assumes she's left to join him—until her remains are eventually found. Now, twenty-six years after Julie went missing, Roberto "Sandy" Sanchez, a retired Baltimore detective working cold cases for extra cash, is investigating her murder. What he discovers is a tangled web stretching over three decades that connects five intriguing women. And at the center is the missing man Felix Brewer. Somewhere between the secrets and lies connecting past and present, Sandy will find the truth. And when he does, no one will ever be the same.

"Despite the murder at its center, this is less a suspenseful whodunit than a masterly novel of character, with secrets skillfully and gradually revealed. Revel in the pace and pleasures of this book [...] that should add to Lippman's literary luster." —**Library Journal** (**starred review**)

"Lippman is a bet you just can't lose." —**Kirkus Reviews** (**starred review**)

ABOUT THE AUTHOR: Since her debut in 1997, **Laura Lippman** has been heralded for her thoughtful, timely crime novels set in her beloved hometown of Baltimore. She is the author of twenty works of fiction. She lives in Baltimore, New Orleans, and New York City with her family.

August 2014 | Trade Paperback | Fiction | 352 pp | $14.99 | ISBN 9780062083418
William Morrow Paperbacks | harpercollins.com | lauralippman.net

CONVERSATION STARTERS

1. We begin the novel with Felix Brewer's point of view as he goes on the lam, yet we don't return to Felix until the very last chapter, in which we see Felix through the eyes of his housekeeper, Consuelo. Why do you think the author chose to begin and end the story this way? Is this novel about Felix? Why or why not?

2. Young Bambi describes herself as a prize, and she certainly knows how to manage the game. What is it about Felix that draws her in so quickly and completely? Do you think his absence for much of their adult life influenced her feelings for him positively or negatively?

3. When Sandy reminisces about his first date with his departed wife, Mary, he recalls, "He was poised, as if on a tightrope, and things were either going to go very wrong or very right, no in-between" (34). Do you think this kind of perspective is borne out by events in the novel?

4. One of the benefits of a novel with multiple point-of-view characters is that we see each person's views. Compare Felix's perspective of his relationships to Bambi and Julie in the first chapter to the reality these women express. How else does the author use this technique to explore the complexity of other characters' relationships?

5. This novel revolves around two "father figure" older male characters: Felix, whose absence anchors the story, and Sandy, around whose investigation the story unfolds. Discuss these two characters. What do you think the novel has to say about the total of our successes and shortcomings at the end of life?

6. On page 145, Sandy admits with some surprise that "the things [he] thought he remembered best were the things he was getting wrong." But he also wonders if, as long as they were loving, it really mattered whether his memories were inaccurate. What do you think? How else do memories play a role in the mystery of *After I'm Gone*?

7. After the truth is revealed, Bambi muses, "It would be nice if at least one of us got what we wanted. . .At least our kids seem to have" (312). Do any of the characters get what they want? At what cost?

8. This novel explores what happens to the Brewer women and Julie after Felix's disappearance. As we ride along on their journey, what did you come to think of these five women? Did your opinion of them, and their actions, change throughout the novel? If so, how? If not, why not?

THE ART OF ARRANGING FLOWERS

Lynne Branard

A moving and eloquent novel about love, grief, renewal—and the powerful language of flowers.

Ruby Jewell knows flowers. In her twenty years as a florist she has stood behind the counter at the Flower Shoppe with her faithful dog, Clementine, resting at her feet. A customer can walk in, and with just a glance or a few words, Ruby can throw together the perfect arrangement for any occasion.

Whether intended to rekindle a romance, mark a celebration, offer sympathy, or heal a broken heart, her expressive floral designs mark the moments and milestones in the lives of her neighbors. It's as though she knows just what they want to say, just what they need.

Yet Ruby's own heart's desires have gone ignored since the death of her beloved sister. It will take an invitation from a man who has flown to the moon, the arrival of a unique little boy, and concern from a charming veterinarian to reawaken her wounded spirit. Any life can be derailed, but the healing power of community can put it right again.

"I devoured this book...There is art and beauty in this story that will linger after the final scene." —**Debbie Macomber**, **#1** *New York Times* **bestselling author of** *Rose in Bloom* **and** *Starry Night*

"An expertly penned and tender tale about the blossoming of hearts amidst the storms of loss and grief." —**Richard Paul Evans**, **#1** *New York Times* **and** *USA Today* **bestselling author**

ABOUT THE AUTHOR: **Lynne Branard** is a pseudonym for *New York Times* bestselling author Lynne Hinton. She has written more than a dozen books, including *Friendship Cake*, *Pie Town*, and *Welcome Back to Pie Town*.

June 2014 | Trade Paperback | Fiction | 320 pp | $15.00 | ISBN 9780425272718
Berkley | us.penguingroup.com | lynnehinton.com

CONVERSATION STARTERS

1. Regarding missing a flower delivery, Lucy says "that's just a mistake that cannot be forgiven." Why do flowers symbolize something so paramount that missing a delivery would be a disaster? What crucial roles do flowers play in relationships—both romantic and nonromantic—between people?

2. Ruby makes it clear that she has never been in a serious romantic relationship, though we hear undeniably erotic descriptions of plants as "stems of short, curved, tender blades," and "white with little narrow lips of purple." Do you think Ruby expresses her sensuality through her trade? Do you think her passion for flowers is a stand-in for other longings?

3. Nora and Jimmy are both alcoholics, and their relationship is rooted in the recovery process. How do Ruby and Dan forge a similar (platonic) bond, and what fuels that bond?

4. Jimmy tells Ruby that she has a reputation for "fixing hearts." And much later, Nora echoes that the whole town has expressed that sentiment. In "fixing" others' hearts, how might Ruby have neglected her own? Can empathy overextend into self-neglect?

5. Dan says that "When I was in space and saw the stars . . . I felt as if I were seeing something of myself . . . I felt as if I were somehow connected to these great beings." Have you ever felt that kind of ineffable connection that Dan describes? Was it with a person, or a place, or a thing—like Dan's stars?

6. Will says, "Sometimes I worry that everybody I love will die." Many of the characters are either at death's door or have suffered the tragic loss of a loved one. How do they find ways not to live in the constant fear that Will expresses?

7. What is the symbolic significance of Clementine's encounter with the porcupine and Ruby's interference—and subsequent injury? How is that a watershed moment in Ruby's life?

8. The Greeks had four words for love: eros, agape, philia, and storge (in short: romantic love, spiritual love, friendship, and familial love). How do we see these different types of love manifested in Creekside?

AS CLOSE AS SISTERS

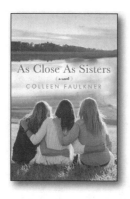

Colleen Faulkner

Since the age of twelve, McKenzie Arnold has spent every summer at Albany Beach, Delaware with her best friends Aurora, Janine, and Lilly. The seaside house teems with thirty years of memories—some wonderful, others painful—and secrets never divulged beyond its walls. This summer may be the last they spend together, as Janine contemplates selling her family cottage. For now, all four enjoy morning beach walks and lazy evenings on the porch celebrating Lilly's longed-for pregnancy and offering support during McKenzie's greatest crisis. It's a time for laughter and recriminations, a time to forge a new understanding of a long-ago night when Aurora sealed their bond with one devastating act. And as the days gradually shorten, events will unfold in ways that none of them could have predicted, to make this the most momentous summer of all. In a deeply moving novel filled with heartbreak and warmth, Colleen Faulkner explores the complex ties between four very different women as they move through life together, and apart.

"This deeply moving story of maternal love and renewal will touch your heart. It's a celebration of the capacity of the human heart to heal itself and embrace change, beautifully written with rare insight." —**Susan Wiggs, # 1 New York Times bestselling author**

"Be prepared to weep tears of sorrow as well as tears of joy. This is a novel you won't soon forget." —**Holly Chamberlin**

ABOUT THE AUTHOR: **Colleen Faulkner** lives in Delaware where her family settled more than three hundred years ago. She comes from a long line of storytellers and spends her days, when she's not writing, running the family farm, reading, and traveling the world. She's still married to her high school sweetheart and has four children and two grandchildren.

October 2014 | Trade Paperback | Fiction | 288 pp | $15.00 | ISBN 9780758255716
Kensington Books | kensingtonbooks.com | colleenfaulknernovels.blogspot.com

CONVERSATION STARTERS

1. Would McKenzie, Janine, Lilly, and Aurora have continued to be friends beyond middle school had it not been for Buddy's death? Why did they grow closer together, rather than further apart?

2. What do you think of the way McKenzie is handling her terminal diagnosis? Do you think it's realistic? If you were McKenzie, how would you respond differently?

3. Do you think that Janine has recovered from the sexual abuse by her father or does that abused child still live in her? Did what Aurora did to Buddy really save Janine?

4. What are your thoughts on McKenzie's relationship with her ex-husband, Jared? Is he a good father?

5. Do you think it's odd that Janine chose to be a police officer like her father? Do you think it gives her the control she didn't have as a child? Is law enforcement something that's "in your blood"?

6. Why do you think Lilly was a part of the group? What does she add? Is she in the inner circle? Were you surprised by her secret that only McKenzie knew about? Is it always better to share secrets with those you love?

7. Do you think Aurora is a brave woman? Is she selfish or unselfish? Do you think her strength is real or a facade? Do you know someone with similar characteristics?

8. Did you think McKenzie's daughters, Mia and Maura, behave selfishly? Did you think they'd be okay after their mother's death?

9. If you could choose two of these women to spend a girls' weekend at a beach house with, which two would it be? Why?

10. Do you think what happens to Aurora is an accident? Why or why not?

BEFORE WE MET

Lucie Whitehouse

If you loved *Gone Girl* and *The Husband's Secret*, *Before We Met* should be your next read.

Hannah has always been wary of commitment, but when she meets Mark, a fellow Brit, one hot New York summer, her ideas change. Within months, they are married, and she has moved back to London to be with him, leaving her life in New York behind. But when Mark fails to return from a business trip, her certainty about their marriage starts to crack. Why don't his colleagues know about the trip? Who is the woman who keeps calling his office? And why has Hannah's bank account been emptied? Hannah's questions will uncover secrets that throw into doubt everything she has believed about her husband, secrets that lead her to a place of violence and fear. Can you ever really know what happened before you met?

"Loved Gone Girl? *This is the Brit version . . . You won't want to put it down."* —*Glamour UK*

"Whitehouse's writing keeps you glued to the page . . . A gripping tale about ties that bind." —**Holly Chamberlin**

"Nail-biting [and] spine-tingling." —*The Observer,* **Thriller of the Month**

"A crackerjack premise that will hook readers from the first page . . . A gripping cat-and-mouse read." —**Booklist**

ABOUT THE AUTHOR: **Lucie Whitehouse** was born in Warwickshire, England in 1975, studied classics at the University of Oxford, and now lives in Brooklyn, New York, with her husband and daughter. She is the author of *The House at Midnight* and *The Bed I Made.*

September 2014 | Trade Paperback | Fiction | 288 pp | $15.00 | ISBN 9781620407646
Bloomsbury USA | bloomsbury.com/us

CONVERSATION STARTERS

1. At the beginning of the novel, Hannah feels useless for having left her high-powered life in New York and embarrassed by her unemployment and domesticity. Hannah's feelings of displacement and insecurity fuel her search for Mark's mistress, but as the lies unfold, her embarrassment blooms into regret. Discuss Hannah's choice to leave her old life. Do you feel that it was an act of weakness or strength?

2. Hannah is distraught and furious that Mark, the man she married, could keep such egregious secrets from her. And yet Mark insists that he only kept them "to save [their] marriage" (271). What is fundamentally different about the way they view marital bonds? Discuss the nature of Mark and Hannah's marriage. How does their dynamic change as Hannah begins to learn more about Mark's past?

3. Tom's uncompromising honesty is refreshing, but often hurtful. Explore the function of Tom's blunt, no-nonsense approach to life. In what ways does it both contrast and complement Hannah's flighty yet headstrong nature? Why is Hannah so afraid of Tom's disapproval?

4. Hannah kicks herself for never pushing Mark about his past or taking it upon herself to learn anything about him. Do you think Hannah, swept up in her new found love, was negligent or naïve? Or do you think she was justified in taking Mark at his word?

5. When Hannah is unsure if Mark is having an affair, she feels guilty for rifling through his belongings and accosting his friends and coworkers. Even when asking about Nick, she is careful to be respectful of Mark's feelings. Hannah is wary of overstepping Mark's boundaries but also hurt that he would withhold information from her. Where is the line between being entitled to the truth and invading someone's privacy?

6. When Hannah goes to see Nick and Mark's parents, she sees a side of Mark's life he had decided to leave behind forever. Discuss the disparities between Mark's memories of his childhood and the version Hannah sees in person. How is this trip enlightening for Hannah?

7. Because of Mark's expert manipulation of the truth, Hannah is in a constant state of unearthing devastating secrets. What were some of the most suspenseful or surprising moments for you? What techniques does Whitehouse use to build suspense?

BLOOD WILL OUT

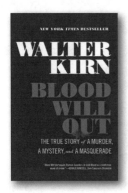

The True Story of a Murder, a Mystery, and a Masquerade

Walter Kirn

New York Times Bestseller

Hailed by critics as "one of the best true-crime books . . . and also one of the best memoirs" (*Seattle Times*) in recent memory, Walter's unbelievable "Hitchcockian psychological thriller" (Amy Tan) of his fifteen-year friendship with grifter-turned-murderer "Clark Rockefeller" is a one-of-a-kind study in criminal psychology, credulity, and the relationship between a writer and his subject. Both a memoir of being duped by a real-life Mr. Ripley and an investigation into the crimes of a true psychopath, *Blood Will Out* exposes the dance between con and mark that beats at the heart of the American dream.

"One of the most honest, compelling and strangest books about the relationship between a writer and his subject ever penned by an American scribe." —**Los Angeles Times**

"[A] tight, gripping book....[T]his bit of noir, from Mr. Kirn about Clark Rockefeller, is just right." —**The New York Times**

"[E]quals Truman Capote's In Cold Blood *as a nonfiction novel of crime."* —**San Francisco Chronicle**

ABOUT THE AUTHOR: **Walter Kirn** is the author of *Thumbsucker* and *Up in the Air*, both made into major films. His work has appeared in *GQ, New York, Esquire,* and *The New York Times Magazine.*

March 2014 | Hardcover | Nonfiction | 272 pp | $25.95 | ISBN 9780871404510
March 2015 | Trade Paperback | Nonfiction | 272 pp | $15.95 | ISBN 9781631490224
Liveright | wwnorton.com | walterkirn.com

CONVERSATION STARTERS

1. Do you think there is anything beneath Clark's ever-shifting façades? Does he have a genuine "personality?"

2. How does Clark's life, which is built around the telling of lies, differ from the author's life as a novelist?

3. On page 61 the author writes, "'You can't cheat an honest man,' goes the old saying, the notion being that falling for a charlatan requires moral softness in the victim." Do you think there is a tacit complicity between con and mark?

4. How do various locales inform the narrative? What does the American West, New York City, or Hollywood represent to Clark and the author?

5. How do literature and the media influence Clark's invented personalities? Do you think our general saturation in pop culture helped or hurt his attempts at hoodwinking others?

6. Did the fact that Clark pretended to be a member of one of America's wealthiest families make his ruse more believable? Would he have been just as successful pretending to be a member of the middle class?

7. How does Clark's proposal of the theory (142) that reality is a "computer program" and life is "an illusion" aid him in his schemes?

8. Clark is constantly performing an act for those around him. In what ways is the author playing a part? Is he ever aware of his role?

9. The author says that Clark "spoke from inside my own American mind." How was Christian Gerhartsreiter able to manipulate Americans through his position as a secret outsider?

10. Clark tells Walter that the key to manipulating people is "Vanity, vanity, vanity." Can you think of examples where this is true in the book?

11. How does the author's story of the time he got lost in the woods during a snowstorm inform his relationship with Clark?

12. What methods does Clark use to take advantage of the idea of "Faith in strangers, rewarded in full measure?"

13. Do you think it's possible for Clark to feel remorse?

14. Do you think Clark would have fooled you if you'd come across him?

BRIDGET JONES: MAD ABOUT THE BOY

Helen Fielding

What do you do when your girlfriend's sixtieth birthday party is the same day as your boyfriend's thirtieth? Is it better to die of Botox or die of loneliness because you're so wrinkly? Is it morally wrong to have a blow-dry when one of your children has head lice? Is sleeping with someone after two dates and six weeks of texting the same as getting married after two meetings and six months of letter writing in Jane Austen's day?

Fourteen years after landing Mark Darcy, Bridget's life has taken her places she never expected. But despite the new challenges of single parenting, online dating, wildly morphing dress sizes, and rediscovering her sexuality, she is the same irrepressible and endearing soul we all remember. Studded with witty observations about the perils and absurdities of our times—and why one should never, ever text while drunk—*Mad About the Boy* is both outrageously comic and genuinely moving. As we watch her dealing with heartbreaking loss and rediscovering love and joy, Bridget invites us to fall for her all over again.

"Sharp and humorous. . . . Snappily written, observationally astute. . . . Genuinely moving." —The New York Times Book Review

"Helen has always had a sharp eye for the obsessions and neuroses of our times, a talent much in evidence here—her [Bridget's] liability rests very much on her believability." —**Anna Wintour, editor in chief of** *Vogue*

ABOUT THE AUTHOR: **Helen Fielding** is the author of *Bridget Jones's Diary* and *Bridget Jones: The Edge of Reason,* and was part of the screenwriting team on the movies of the same names. *Bridget Jones: Mad About the Boy* is her fifth novel. She has two children and lives in London and sometimes Los Angeles.

June 2014 | Trade Paperback | Fiction | 496 pp | $15.95 | ISBN 9780345806345
Anchor | randomhouse.com

CONVERSATION STARTERS

1. Who is "the boy"? Is it who you thought it would be?

2. How did you react when you read about Mark Darcy's fate?

3. Age is a major theme in this novel. Why does Bridget feel the struggles more acutely than some of her contemporaries?

4. Bridget's friends deal with aging in different ways. Talitha believes in Botox while Bridget notes that Woney has not done any of this "rebranding" (66). Why do these characters make these decisions?

5. Dating rules have changed dramatically since Bridget's last appearance. How well does she adapt?

6. Bridget is adapting Hedda Gabbler, a story about "the perils of trying to live through men" (17). What is Fielding's intent with this parallel?

7. In what ways did Daniel change from the previous books? And how did he stay the same?

8. Why does Roxster tell Bridget he "hearts" her? (250). Does he really mean "love," or is this something else?

9. Mr. Wallaker tells Bridget, ". . . other people's lives are not always as perfect as they appear, once you crack the shell" (323). How does Bridget finally learn this lesson? What earlier opportunities did she have to learn it?

10. On page 361, Tom tells Bridget about a survey: "It proves that the quality of someone's relationships is the biggest indicator of their long-term emotional health—not so much the 'significant other' relationship, as the measure of happiness is not your husband or boyfriend but the quality of the other relationships you have around you." How does this bode for Bridget?

11. At the carol concert, Mr. Wallaker looks at Bridget in a certain way and she realizes she loves him. What finally brings her around?

12. What is the significance of the owl?

13. Bridget's last entry ties up the story in a cozy, comforting way. What do you imagine will happen next?

THE CIRCLE

Dave Eggers

Set on an idyllic, green-lawned campus in California, the Circle is a place where dreams come true. It's where nearly all of the world's information is stored and communicated, and through its remarkable ability to synthesize personal data in one place it has completely revolutionized the way individuals interface online. It's also where Mae Holland, a young ingenue longing for a job with purpose, lands a prime seat among the Circle's assiduous, yet aboundingly energetic, team. Although she starts off low in the ranks in the Customer Experience (CE) department, answering floods of email queries from Circle users, Mae quickly assimilates into the Circle's culture of socializing, product perks, and inspirational messages literally etched into her new surroundings: "Dream," "Imagine," "Innovate," "Let's Do This." Compared with her hometown in Colorado, the world of the Circle is endlessly more vast and infinitely better than anything Mae has ever imagined. But soon Mae finds herself facing truths about her family, her colleagues, and herself that perhaps were best kept unknown, and her shattering conclusion leaves the reader questioning how fine a line can be drawn between private and public, education and indoctrination, and—ultimately—good and evil.

"Simply a great story, with a fascinating protagonist, sharply drawn supporting characters and an exciting, unpredictable plot . . . As scary as the story's implications will be to some readers, the reading experience is pure pleasure." —**Hugo Lindgren, *The New York Times Magazine***

ABOUT THE AUTHOR: **Dave Eggers** grew up near Chicago and graduated from the University of Illinois at Urbana-Champaign. He is the founder of *McSweeney's*, an independent publishing house in San Francisco. His work has been nominated for the National Book Award, the Pulitzer Prize, and the National Book Critics Circle Award. Eggers lives in Northern California with his family.

April 2014 | Trade Paperback | Fiction | 512 pp | $15.95 | ISBN 9780345807298
Vintage | randomhouse.com | mcsweeneys.net

CONVERSATION STARTERS

1. How does Mae's behavior during her first days at work foreshadow what happens to her over the course of the novel? In what ways is she an "ideal" employee?

2. The wings of the Circle are named after different regions of the world and time periods, such as Old West, the Renaissance, the Enlightenment, Machine Age, the Industrial Revolution. What do these names say about the company's vision of historical innovation versus its future-looking work? Is there an inherent hierarchy in these names, despite their apparent equality?Age is a major theme in this novel. Why does Bridget feel the struggles more acutely than some of her contemporaries?

3. In what ways does Annie motivate Mae in terms of the level of success that can be achieved at the Circle? Does Mae consider Annie's position the product of Annie's ambition, or something she imbibed from the company's ethos? How does knowing first about their professional relationship shape your understanding of their shared past?

4. For a company that thrives on order and efficiency, the Circle also seems to endorse loose and extravagant socializing. What do these two seemingly opposite values say about what working for them entails? How does Mae's value set evolve to accommodate these expectations?

5. Mae's first serious blunder on the job is failing to respond to and attend Alistair's Portugal brunch. How does the meeting in Dan's office set the tone for Mae's pushing the Circle's networks on others?

6. Among the Three Wise Men—Ty, Bailey, and Stenton—who has a vision of what the Circle can—and should—do that seems most viable? In the end, is this trifecta of power able to prevent tyranny? What might the novel's conclusion say about man's reaction to power—even when humanity is apparently subsumed under technology?

7. We see Mae involved with three very different men throughout the novel: Mercer, Francis, and Kalden. While they are on the surface wildly different, what might you say are traits they share that reveal what Mae is looking for in a relationship—and how do they satisfy these needs in their own ways? Does Mae ever seem truly happy?

CLAIRE OF THE SEA LIGHT

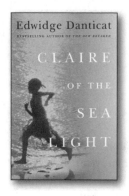

Edwidge Danticat

A *New York Times Book Review* and *Washington Post* Notable Book, an NPR "Great Read," a *Christian Science Monitor* Best Fiction Book, and a *Library Journal* Top Book

Just as her father makes the wrenching decision to send her away for a chance at a better life, Claire Limyè Lanmè—Claire of the Sea Light—suddenly disappears. As the people of the Haitian seaside community of Ville Rose search for her, painful secrets, haunting memories, and startling truths are unearthed. In this stunning novel about intertwined lives, Edwidge Danticat crafts a tightly woven, breathtaking tapestry that explores the mysterious bonds we share—with the natural world and with one another.

"Haunting. . . . Writing with lyrical economy and precision, Ms. Danticat recounts her characters' stories in crystalline prose that underscores the parallels in their lives." —**The New York Times**

"Hypnotic. . . . Danticat creates rich and varied interior lives for her characters. . . . Heartbreaking." —**The New York Times Book Review**

ABOUT THE AUTHOR: **Edwidge Danticat** is the author of numerous books, including *Brother, I'm Dying,* a National Book Critics Circle Award winner and National Book Award finalist; *Breath, Eyes, Memory,* an Oprah Book Club selection; *Krik? Krak!,* a National Book Award finalist; *The Farming of Bones,* an American Book Award winner; and *The Dew Breaker,* a PEN/Faulkner Award finalist and winner of the inaugural Story Prize. The recipient of a MacArthur Fellowship, she has been published in *The New Yorker, The New York Times,* and elsewhere. She lives in Miami.

July 2014 | Trade Paperback | Fiction | 256 pp | $15.00 | ISBN 9780307472274
Vintage | knopfdoubleday.com/imprint/vintage/

CONVERSATION STARTERS

1. The opening chapter of *Claire of the Sea Light* moves backward chronologically through each of Claire's birthdays, ultimately returning to the present day of the narrative. How does this structure contribute to the book's sense of time overall, and to its weaving of past and present as more characters are introduced?

2. What does it mean that Albert Vincent is both the town of Ville Rose's undertaker and mayor? How are these roles reflected in his relationship with Claire Narcis, Nozias's wife and Claire's mother, when she works for him preparing bodies for burial? On page 61 the author writes, "'You can't cheat an honest man,' goes the old saying, the notion being that falling for a charlatan requires moral softness in the victim." Do you think there is a tacit complicity between con and mark?

3. That Claire visits her mother's grave on her birthdays brings poignantly to the fore the notion that life and death are intertwined. In what other ways does that happen in the book? Do ghosts—or chimè—have a positive or negative influence over the living?

4. The sea opens and closes the book, offering powerful images of its destructive and restorative force: the fisherman Caleb is drowned at the book's beginning, and at the book's end, Max Junior is spat back from the sea that had "taken [him] this morning" (237). What roles does the sea play in the fates of all the characters in the book? What other myths, stories, and fables come to your mind by this book's evocation of water?

5. At one point in the story, Nozias recalls another watery scene, when he and wife Claire Narcis went night fishing, and Claire slipped into the moonlit water to observe a school of shimmering fish. It is from this moment that their daughter, and Danticat's book, get their name. How does this important memory shape your impression of Claire Narcis, including in what we learn about her by the book's conclusion?

6. Although this is fiction, Danticat vividly evokes present-day Haitian culture and society, including its poverty (5), gangs, and restavèk children—the child-servitude that Nozias fears for Claire. How do these realities affect your reading of the book and the sense of authenticity of Claire's story? Of Bernard's?

CRAZY RICH ASIANS

Kevin Kwan

In an over-the-top, modern-day romance comedy of manners, Kevin Kwan brilliantly captures a world of unimaginable wealth and unrestrained consumption.

Nick Young, born in Singapore, and Rachel Chu, his Chinese American girlfriend, are academics contentedly living in New York City. When Nick invites Rachel to go home with him for the wedding of his best friend, she looks forward to the adventure and to taking their relationship to a new level. She doesn't know, however, that her handsome boyfriend is the scion of one of Singapore's richest families—and long-regarded as the most eligible bachelor in a close-knit network of upper-crust families. From his haughty, suspicious mother to embittered ex-girlfriends and wanna-be-wives, to cousins and friends obsessed with the latest fashions and their lavish homes, Rachel finds herself facing challenges and intrigues beyond her wildest imaginings.

Kwan, who grew up among the Singaporean elite, brings a unique sensibility and sharp satirical eye to a delightful and revealing insider's view of the cultural and social implications of the rise of Asian wealth.

"A dizzily shopaholic comedy. . . . Wickedly delectable. . . . Offers refreshing nouveau voyeurism to readers who long ago burned out on American and English aspirational fantasies. . . . Hilarious." —**Janet Maslin, The New York Times**

"[An] instant favorite. . . . Opulence and zaniness reign." —**O, The Oprah Magazine**

ABOUT THE AUTHOR: **Kevin Kwan** was born and raised in Singapore. He currently lives in Manhattan. *Crazy Rich Asians* is his first novel.

May 2014 | Trade Paperback | Fiction | 544 pp | $15.00 | ISBN 9780345803788
Anchor | randomhouse.com

CONVERSATION STARTERS

1. Compare how Nick's mother (21–28, 56) and Rachel's mother (31–34, 68) react to hearing about their trip to Singapore. What do their reactions reveal about each of them as mothers? What qualities, if any, do they share? What is the significance of the "Chinese Way" (68) in the mothers' approach to courtship and marriage? Compare this with Rachel and Sophie's conversation about marriage later in the book (278–79).

2. Does Nick's description—"It's like any big family. I have loudmouthed uncles, eccentric aunts, obnoxious cousins, the whole nine yards" (67)—match the way most of us view our own families? Why doesn't he tell Rachel more about the background and status of his family before their trip?

3. What does Rachel's view of Asian men reveal about the complications of growing up Asian in America (90)? How does Kwan use humor to make a serious point here and in other parts of the novel?

4. Discuss the role of gossip in the novel. What kinds of rumors do Nick's friends and family spread about Rachel, and why? How do misunderstandings and misinformation (intentional or not) propel the plot and help define the characters? Consider, for example, the conversations at the Bible study class Eleanor attends (108–109) and the chatter of the guests at Araminta's bachelorette party (262–70).

5. Do you see the events surround Colin's wedding and the ceremony itself as brazen, even crude displays of wealth or are there aspects of the celebrations that are appealing (393–416)? How do they compare to society or celebrity weddings you have read about?

6. What sort of future do you imagine for Nick and Rachel? Is it possible for Rachel to fit into a world "so different from anything [she's] used to" (431)? Does Nick fully understand the reasons for her doubts and unhappiness? What supports your point of view?

7. Why does the author devote different sections of the novel to specific characters? What effect does this have on your impressions of and sympathies for the problems and prejudices that motivate each of them?

DURING THE REIGN OF THE QUEEN OF PERSIA

Joan Chase, Introduction by Meghan O'Rourke

Winner of the PEN/Hemingway Award for Debut Fiction by an American Author
Joan Chase's subtle story of three generations of women negotiating lifetimes of "joy and ruin" deserves its place alongside such achievements as Marilynne Robinson's *Housekeeping* and Alice Munro's *Lives of Girls and Women*. The Queen of Persia is not an exotic figure but a fierce Ohio farmwife who presides over a household of daughters and granddaughters. The novel tells their stories through the eyes of the youngest members of the family, four cousins who spend summers on the farm, for them both a life-giving Eden and the source of terrible discoveries about desire and loss. The girls bicker and scrap, they whisper secrets at bedtime, and above all, they observe the kinds of women their mothers are and wonder what kind of women they will become. But always present is the family's great trauma, the decline and eventual death from cancer of Gram's daughter Grace.

"Moving, unusual and accomplished ... During the Reign of the Queen of Persia is a Norman Rockwell painting gone bad, the underside of the idyllic hometown, main-street, down-on-the-farm dream of Middle America."
—**Margaret Atwood**, *The New York Times*

About the Author: **Joan Chase** was born and raised in Ohio. She graduated from the University of Maryland and later enrolled in the Writing Workshop of the University of Vermont. After being turned down by several publishers, *During the Reign of the Queen of Persia* was released in 1983 and went on to win numerous prizes. Chase is also the author of the novel *The Evening Wolves* (1990) and the story collection *Bonneville Blue* (1991).

Meghan O'Rourke is a poet and former editor at the *The New Yorker*.

April 2014 | Trade Paperback | Fiction | 240 pp | $14.95 | ISBN 9781590177150
NYRB Classics | www.nybooks.com/books

CONVERSATION STARTERS

1. What do you make of the way Chase presents motherhood and mothering in this book? Does daughterhood ever take importance over motherhood?

2. What do you make of the non-chronological sequence of the book? Summers seem to blend together in the narrative and memories zip through the text like starlings. Why might Chase present the story this way?

3. Chase divides the book into five sections, each for a character or couple: Celia, Grandad, Grace and Neil, Elinor, and Gram. Are these characters the most important in the book? If not, what do you think Chase accomplishes in giving them sections? Are the sections telling the story of each character, or is something else at play?

4. During the cheese scene in the Elinor section, the narrators tell us, "Aunt Elinor looked patient, as one who had seen a wider world, one she constantly made visible to the rest of us—accepting the fact that a wider world might mean a weaker place in the old one" (149). In what other ways does the wider world infringe upon the farm?

5. How does Chase treat death in this book? Does death become part of the landscape—simply another facet of the otherwise idyllic life on the farm—or interrupt it violently?

6. How are male characters treated in this book? Are they well-rounded characters with nuanced motivations and conflicts, or are they merely supporting actors, propping up the real work of the female characters? Does this change section to section?

7. The book is filled with hints of sex, but it rarely discusses the act in a straightforward way. When Gram talks about it, she talks about a violent burden, almost another level of daily abuse, but are there any values placed on sex other than the negative ones?

8. What does this book tell you about dependence and independence?

THE END OF INNOCENCE

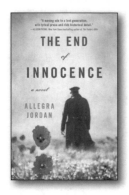

Allegra Jordan

Helen Windship Brooks is struggling to find herself at the world-renowned Harvard-Radcliffe University when brooding German poet Wils bursts into her life. As they fall deeply in love on the brink of WWI, anti-German sentiments mount and Wils' future at Harvard—and in America—is in increasing danger. When Wils is called to fight for the Kaiser, Helen must decide if she is ready to fight her own battle for what she loves most.

"Downton Abbey has found a brilliant successor in this spellbinding tale of love, death, and war. The finest war fiction to be published in many years."
—**Jonathan W. Jordan, bestselling author of *Brothers, Rivals, Victors***

"This is a wonderful story set around prestigious Harvard College prior to America's intervention into the Great War and follows a cast of formidable characters into the early 1930s...More than Harvard's story, it is one of loyalty, love, trust, and betrayal, woven around the war that tore families apart, but eventually drew strength out of long-buried loneliness."
—**Carol Hicks, Bookshelf Stores Inc. (CA)**

"I was moved to tears--three times...Loved the historical detail...I will be recommending it to everyone. This was wonderful!"—**Catherine Coyne, Director, Mansfield Public Library, MA**

ABOUT THE AUTHOR: **Allegra Jordan** was a book reviewer for *USA Today* and head of marketing for usatoday.com for many years. A graduate with honors of Harvard Business School, she blogs in the field of innovation and is a board member of the Harvard Club of the Research Triangle and vice-chair of the Southern Documentary Fund.

August 2014 | Hardcover | Fiction | 320 pp | $24.99 | ISBN 9781492603832
Sourcebooks Landmark | sourcebooks.com | allegrajordan.com

CONVERSATION STARTERS

1. In the beginning of the novel, Professor Copeland states, "There is loss in this world, and we shall feel it, if not today, then tomorrow, or the week after that.... But there is also something equal to loss that you must not forget. There is an irrepressible renewal of life that we can no more stop than blot out the sun. This is a good and encouraging thought." Do you believe Copeland's point of view that this is encouraging? Discuss how this theme emerges throughout the novel.

2. Riley is a handsome British playboy. Many people find this type of young man very charming. Why? What are his redeeming features?

3. What does Helen find so lovely and refreshing in Wils Brandl? What does Wils find so attractive in Helen? What do the two characters have in common? How are they different?

4. Wils, Helen, and Professor Copeland believe in the power of poetry to release energy that can heal the soul. Has this been your experience with poetry? If so, what poets or poems have you found especially healing?

5. As a German who loves America and has British relatives, Wils must decide whether to fight for his country in WWI against classmates and relatives or forgo his homeland and family to be with Helen. What are your thoughts on how he handled his divided loyalties?

6. Have you ever had a relationship with someone others would consider "the enemy"? How did you handle this response from others? What were the challenges and advantages of such a relationship?

7. In the early part of the 20th century, mail in Boston (and America) was routinely searched for obscene materials (like birth control and information about contraception) and its sender punished. How is America different today regarding censorship and privacy?

8. The Christmas hymn "Silent Night" was sung at the Christmas Truce of 1914 in both German and English. Some call that moment the last gasp of innocence in the world—when a war can be called off by a song. Is this true? Where have you seen innocence and beauty interrupt either physical violence (such as a war) or emotional violence?

THE ENGAGEMENTS

J. Courtney Sullivan

Relationships have as many facets as a diamond. There are those who marry in a white heat of passion, those who marry for partnership and comfort, and those who live together, love each other, and have absolutely no intention of ruining it all with a wedding. Evelyn has been married to her husband for forty years—forty years since he slipped off her first wedding ring and put his own in its place. Delphine has seen both sides of love-the ecstatic, glorious highs of seduction and the bitter, spiteful fury that descends when it's over. James, a paramedic who works the night shift, knows his wife's family thinks she could have done better; while Kate, partnered with Dan for a decade, has seen every kind of wedding—beach weddings, backyard weddings, castle weddings-and has vowed never, ever, to have one of her own. As these lives and marriages unfold in surprising ways, we meet Frances Gerety, a young advertising copywriter in 1947. Frances is working on the De Beers campaign and she needs a signature line, so, one night before bed, she scribbles a phrase on a scrap of paper: "A Diamond Is Forever." And that line changes everything.

A rich, layered, exhilarating novel spanning nearly a hundred years, *The Engagements* captures four wholly unique marriages, while tracing the story of diamonds in America and the way—for better or for worse—these glittering stones have come to symbolize our deepest hopes for everlasting love.

*"Sullivan has written an intricate, beautifully timed novel, so delicious in its gradual unfolding that readers will want to reread it immediately to enjoy the fully realized ties." —****Library Journal***

ABOUT THE AUTHOR: **J. Courtney Sullivan** is the *New York Times* bestselling author of the novels *Commencement* and *Maine*.

May 2014 | Trade Paperback | Fiction | 528 pp | $15.95 | ISBN 9780307949226
Vintage | randomhouse.com | jcourtneysullivan.com

CONVERSATION STARTERS

1. *The Engagements'* epigraph refers to diamonds as "nothing more than an empty cage for our dreams-blank surfaces upon which the shifting desires of the heart could be written." What does this tell us about the novel we're about to discuss?

2. Feminism and the role of women is a recurring theme in *The Engagements*. Which character's attitude did you relate to the most?

3. Two of the novel's major characters are anti-marriage, with story lines that are decades apart. How does time change society's attitude toward intentionally unmarried women?

4. On page 27, Evelyn thinks, "Men made mistakes and when they asked forgiveness, women forgave. It happened every day." Does this prove true throughout the novel, with other characters?

5. Did you know that Frances Gerety was a real person? How does that change your feelings about the character?

6. Why do you think Frances is the only character whose story moves through time?

7. On page 100, in a section set in 1972, Evelyn thinks, "Since she and Gerald were young, what it meant to be an American had changed. There was so much emphasis on the self now-self over country, self over family, self over all else. Her son was a shining example of the consequences." How does this play out in more contemporary sections of the novel and with other story lines?

8. While the novel is about marriage, parental relationships also play a role. Discuss the parenting styles of Evelyn, James, and Kate.

9. What did you think about Delphine's reaction to P.J.'s betrayal?

10. On page 175, Meg says to Frances, "Sometimes it just feels like we can't tell what we've given up until it's too late." What other characters could have uttered that line?

11. On page 275, May says to Kate, "It's very rare to find anyone who's absolutely certain that she chose the right ring." What metaphor is at work here?

FALLING FROM HORSES

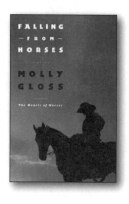

Molly Gloss

In 1938, nineteen-year-old ranch hand Bud Frazer sets out for Hollywood. His little sister has been gone a couple of years now, his parents are finding ranch work and comfort for their loss where they can, but for Bud, Echol Creek, where he grew up and first learned to ride, is a place he can no longer call home. So he sets his sights on becoming a stunt rider in the movies—and rubbing shoulders with the great screen cowboys of his youth. On the long bus ride south, Bud meets a young woman who also harbors dreams of making it in the movies, though not as a starlet but as a writer, a real writer. Lily Shaw is bold and outspoken, confident in ways out of proportion with her small frame and bookish looks. But the two strike up an unlikely kinship that will carry them through their tumultuous days in Hollywood—and, as it happens, for the rest of their lives. Acutely observed, *Falling from Horses* charts what was to be a glittering year in the movie business through the wide eyes and lofty dreams of two people trying to make their mark on the world, or at least make their way in it. Molly Gloss weaves a remarkable tale of humans and horses, hope and heartbreak, narrated by one of the most winning narrators ever to walk off the page.

"I read Falling from Horses *in two gulps. The writing is gorgeous, the setting so beautifully realized, both time and place, the narrative voice unforgettable, and all the characters so real and compelling. Tremendous, page-turning...I could not have loved it more."* **—Karen Joy Fowler, author of We Are All Completely Beside Ourselves and The Jane Austen Book Club**

ABOUT THE AUTHOR: **Molly Gloss** is the best-selling author of *The Hearts of Horses, The Jump-Off Creek, The Dazzle of Day,* and *Wild Life.*

October 2014 | Hardcover | Fiction | 336 pp | $25.00 | ISBN 9780544279292
Houghton Mifflin Harcourt | hmhco.com | mollygloss.com

CONVERSATION STARTERS

1. Bud sets out for Hollywood intending to find work as a movie cowboy. What does he imagine this work will look like? What are his preconceived notions about the Hollywood movie industry?

2. Much of the novel takes place at the cusp of World War Two. Do you see events in the larger world having much impact on the characters' lives? How will the war affect each of them?

3. How is the ranching life of Bud's childhood different from, or the same as, the ranching life he has seen portrayed in western films?

4. Lily came to Hollywood determined to become a screenwriter. What qualities did she possess that might have helped her succeed? What roadblocks stood in her way?

5. Did you think the relationship between Bud and Lily would blossom into romance? What traits in each of them could have led them, instead, toward lifelong friendship?

6. Parts of the novel are set on a ranch in the 1920s and early 1930s, a time of worldwide economic depression, drought, and technological advances. How were these things changing the way of life for ranchers in the West? Can you think of aspects of ranch life that remain the same today as in the 1880s when Elbert Echol and his wife first settled on their ranch?

7. Late in the novel, Bud speaks of ways in which "the cowboy stories went wrong," and he tells us "the humanity has been hollowed out of our movie heroes and villains." What do you think he means by this? Do you agree with his statements?

8. Bud has seen violence and death both in his life on the Echol Creek ranch, and in his work as a stunt rider for the movie industry. Explore the differences between these experiences.

FAMILY LIFE

Akhil Sharma

Hailed as a "supreme storyteller" (*Philadelphia Inquirer*) for his "cunning, dismaying and beautifully conceived" fiction (*The New York Times*), Akhil Sharma is possessed of a narrative voice "as hypnotic as those found in the pages of Dostoyevsky" (*The Nation*). In his highly anticipated second novel, *Family Life*, he delivers a story of astonishing intensity and emotional precision. We meet the Mishra family in Delhi in 1978, where eight-year-old Ajay and his older brother Birju play cricket in the streets, waiting for the day when their plane tickets will arrive and they and their mother can fly across the world and join their father in America. America to the Mishras is, indeed, everything they could have imagined and more: when automatic glass doors open before them, they feel that surely they must have been mistaken for somebody important. Pressing an elevator button and the elevator closing its doors and rising, they have a feeling of power at the fact that the elevator is obeying them. Life is extraordinary until tragedy strikes, leaving one brother severely brain-damaged and the other lost and virtually orphaned in a strange land. Ajay, the family's younger son, prays to a God he envisions as Superman, longing to find his place amid the ruins of his family's new life.

"Riveting... Sharma is compassionate but unflinching."
—**Sonali Deraniyagala, *The New York Times Book Review***

*"A loving portrait, both painful and honest." —**Publishers Weekly*, Starred Review**

About the Author: **Akhil Sharma** is the author of *An Obedient Father*, winner of the PEN/Hemingway Award and was a *New York Times* Notable Book of the Year. A native of Delhi, he lives in New York City.

April 2014 | Hardcover | Fiction | 224 pp | $23.95 | ISBN 9780393060058
February 2015 | Trade Paperback | Fiction | 224 pp | $14.95 | ISBN 9780393350609
W.W. Norton | wwnorton.com

CONVERSATION STARTERS

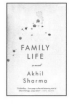

1. The novel opens in the present, when Ajay is forty and his parents are elderly. How does this opening affect your experience of the rest of the novel, which takes place during Ajay's childhood?

2. America is marvelous to the Mishra family at first. If tragedy hadn't struck, do you think that America would have met the Mishras' expectations for it? Or do you think that at least certain elements of their disillusionment were inevitable?

3. How does the Mishras' status as immigrants affect their experience of Birju's accident? How might their lives following the accident have played out differently if they weren't strangers in a strange land?

4. What do you make of Ajay's conversations with God following his brother's accident? Describe the God that Ajay invents for himself. How does his God help him, and how doesn't he? Can you pinpoint the moment in the novel when Ajay stops talking to God?

5. Describe the process by which Ajay becomes a writer. How does writing change the way he experiences his childhood?

6. In the aftermath of Birju's accident, Ajay's mother turns to religion and his father to alcohol. How are these two coping mechanisms similar or different? Do you think that Ajay's own way of coping—academic success—has anything in common with his parents'?

7. Did you find moments in *Family Life* funny, despite its darkness? What kind of humor does the novel possess?

8. Describe the prose style in *Family Life*. What do you think the author achieves through the candor and lack of sentimentality?

9. On the second anniversary of his brother's accident, Ajay thinks, "I couldn't believe that everything had changed because of three minutes" (129). What do you make of this? How does the brevity of the accident itself affect your experience of the passage of time in the novel, which takes place over many years?

10. *Family Life* ends in a moment of ambiguity. What is it about this moment and about Ajay's happiness that tells him he has a problem? Do you think he'll ever escape or solve it?

THE FIRST PHONE CALL FROM HEAVEN

Mitch Albom

From the beloved author of the number-one *New York Times* bestsellers *Tuesdays with Morrie* and *The Five People You Meet in Heaven* comes his most thrilling and magical novel yet—a page-turning mystery and a meditation on the power of human connection. One morning in the small town of Coldwater, Michigan, the phones start ringing. The voices say they are calling from heaven. Is it the greatest miracle ever? Or some cruel hoax? As news of these strange calls spreads, outsiders flock to Coldwater to be a part of it. At the same time, a disgraced pilot named Sully Harding returns to Coldwater from prison to discover his hometown gripped by "miracle fever." Even his young son carries a toy phone, hoping to hear from his mother in heaven. As the calls increase, and proof of an afterlife begins to surface, the town—and the world— transforms. Only Sully, convinced there is nothing beyond this sad life, digs into the phenomenon, determined to disprove it for his child and his own broken heart. *The First Phone Call from Heaven* is Mitch Albom at his best—a virtuosic story of love, history, and belief.

"Beautiful and smart. Perhaps the most stirring and transcendent heaven story since Field of Dreams.*"* —**Matthew Quick, *New York Times* bestselling author of *The Silver Linings Playbook***

"A beautifully rendered tale of faith and redemption that makes us think, feel, and hope--and then doubt and then believe, as only Mitch Albom can make us do." —**Garth Stein, *New York Times* bestselling author of *The Art of Racing in the Rain***

ABOUT THE AUTHOR: **Mitch Albom** is a bestselling novelist, screenwriter, playwright, and award-winning journalist. He is the author of five number one *New York Times* bestsellers.

October 2014 | Trade Paperback | Fiction | 336 pp | $15.99 | ISBN 9780062294401
Harper Paperbacks | harpercollins.com | mitchalbom.com

CONVERSATION STARTERS

1. Are you surprised by the various reactions from the people who receive the phone calls from heaven?

2. How do these phone calls from heaven change the small midwestern town of Coldwater? Do you think it would be different if the same thing happened in a major city?

3. How do the town's different religious leaders handle the news of the calls? What would you do if you were a spiritual guide like Pastor Warren, and one of your parish members broke such news to you?

4. One of the most serious concerns of the religious leaders was the idea that, "if people truly believed they were talking with heaven, how soon before they expected to hear from the Lord?" What are the implications of this question? Do you think this is a legitimate concern?

5. Throughout the novel, Mitch Albom interweaves the story of Alexander Graham Bell and the telephone. Why do you think he includes this? How does it illuminate the novel's message?

6. Is Sully a good man? What emotions motivate him when we first meet him? Is he the same person at the end of the novel? Why is he skeptical from the very beginning? Why drives him to find the truth? Are the answers he finds those he was truly looking for?

7. What advice would you give Sully to help him protect his son, yet help him understand death in the cycle of life?

8. The role of media and technology plays a big part in spreading the news of the phone calls. Is our instant connectedness ultimately a good thing? What about Amy, the journalist who broke the original story? How does she feel about her role? How does her outlook change as the novel progresses? What factors influence her viewpoint?

9. Towns like Coldwater face major social and economic problems today. Do these problems make it more likely that people would cling to a miracle like a phone call from heaven?

10. What propelled Horace to act the way he did? Were his motives pure?

11. What do you think will happen to the characters and this town? What has the impact of the event had on all their lives? Was the event ultimately positive or negative?

THE FRAGILE WORLD

Paula Treick DeBoard

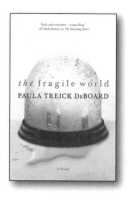

The Kaufmans always considered themselves a normal, happy family. Curtis is a physics teacher at the local high school. His wife, Kathleen, restores furniture for upscale boutiques. Daniel is away at college on a prestigious music scholarship, and twelve year-old Olivia is a happy-go-lucky kid whose biggest concern is passing her next math test. And then comes the middle-of-the-night phone call that changes everything. Daniel has been killed in what the police are calling a "freak" road accident, and the remaining Kaufmans are left to flounder in their grief. The anguish of loss is isolating, and it's not long before this once-perfect family falls apart. As time passes and the wound refuses to heal, Curtis becomes obsessed with the idea of revenge, a growing mania that leads him to pack up his life and his anxious teenage daughter and set out on a collision course to right a wrong.

An emotionally charged novel, *The Fragile World* is a journey through America's heartland and a family's brightest and darkest moments, exploring the devastating pain of losing a child and the beauty of finding healing in unexpected ways.

"Assured storytelling propels Deboard's first novel." —**Publishers Weekly**

"Rich and evocative...compelling." —**RT Book Reviews**

ABOUT THE AUTHOR: **Paula Treick DeBoard** lives with her husband, Will, and their brood of four-legged creatures in Modesto, California. She received a BA in English from Dordt College, and MFA in Creative Writing from the university of Southern Maine and a practical education from countless students in her English classes over the years.

November 2014 | Trade Paperback | Fiction | 432 pp | $14.95 | ISBN 9780778316763
Harlequin MIRA | harlequin.com | paulatreickdeboard.com

CONVERSATION STARTERS

1. Was it surprising that Kathleen was able to move on with her life while Curtis couldn't seem to move past his anger? What causes parents to react differently to tragedies in their family?

2. Would you be able to forgive a person who caused serious injury or death to a loved one—even if that act was unintentional?

3. Robert Saenz, although a fictional character, could be all too real. Curtis believes the judicial system has failed where Robert Saenz is concerned. What might be an appropriate punishment for an action—however unintentional—that has such deadly consequences?

4. Curtis doesn't seem to believe he could ever cause harm to Olivia or Kathleen, although of course his actions could have a devastating effect on their lives, as well. Does this lack of awareness come from a callousness or insensitivity to others, or is he simply blind to everything but his desire for revenge?

5. Consider Olivia's many fears throughout the book. Do these fears seem like a natural reaction to her circumstances, or a sign of a more serious issue? In what ways can fear affect a person?

6. Why does Kathleen take more responsibility than she deserves for what happens at the end of the book? Why doesn't Curtis intervene and publicly take responsibility?

7. When Curtis and Olivia say "Love…Eventually" at the end of the book, do you believe them? Can things work out for the Kaufmans, moving forward?

THE GIRL YOU LEFT BEHIND

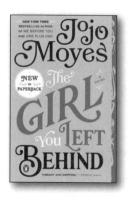

Jojo Moyes

Another *New York Times* bestseller by the author of *Me Before You* and *One Plus One*—a spellbinding story of two women united in their fight for what they love most. Paris, 1916. Sophie Lefèvre must keep her family safe while her adored husband, Édouard, fights at the front. When their town falls to the Germans in the midst of World War I, Sophie is forced to serve them every evening at her hotel. From the moment the new Kommandant sets eyes on Sophie's portrait—painted by her artist husband—a dangerous obsession is born, one that will lead Sophie to make a dark and terrible decision. Almost a century later, Sophie's portrait hangs in the home of Liv Halston, a wedding gift from her young husband before his sudden death. After a chance encounter reveals the portrait's true worth, a battle begins over its troubled history and Liv's world is turned upside all over again.

Moyes (Me Before You) writes with such clarity that one can almost see the eponymous 100-year-old painting at the center of her wonderful new novel . . . an uncommonly good love story." —**Booklist**

"Lovely and wry, Moyes's newest is captivating and bittersweet." —**Publishers Weekly (starred review)**

"Jojo Moyes builds on her strengths in this moving and accomplished new novel. As she did in the best-selling Me Before You, *she asks readers to think in fresh ways about a morally complex issue. . . The Girl You Left Behind is strong, provocative, satisfying fiction."* —**The Washington Post**

ABOUT THE AUTHOR: **Jojo Moyes** is the *New York Times* bestselling–author of *The Girl You Left Behind, Honeymoon in Paris, Me Before You,* and *The Last Letter from Your Lover.* She also writes for a variety of newspapers and magazines. She lives in Essex, England.

June 2014 | Trade Paperback | Fiction | 464 pp | $16.00 | ISBN 9780143125778
Penguin Books | penguin.com | jojomoyes.com

CONVERSATION STARTERS

1. At one point, the Kommandant asks Sophie if they can just "be two people" (72). What did you make of this—did you ever find yourself sympathizing with the Kommandant or any of the German soldiers? Is there room for sympathy on both sides?

2. Does Édouard's portrait of Sophie capture who she already was or who she had the potential to become?

3. Before you knew the truth about Liliane Béthune, how did you feel about the treatment she received at the hands of the other villages?

4. Sophie strikes a deal with the Kommandant in hopes that he, in turn, will reunite her with Édouard. Would you be willing to make a similar trade? Would most men appreciate Sophie's sacrifice?

5. Unlike Hélène, Aurélian angrily condemns Sophie's relationship with the Kommandant. Why do you think Aurelian reacted as he did?

6. Have you ever experienced real hunger? If you were a French village in St. Péronne, how far might you go in order to feed yourself and your loved ones?

7. How did you think Sophie's story would end? Were you surprised by what Liv uncovered?

8. Liv feels that she cannot go on without the portrait of Sophie—it is that important to her. Should a material object hold such significance?

9. Do you think the present-day Lefèvre family's interest in the financial worth of *The Girl You Left Behind*—and their apparent lack of interest in its beauty—mad their claim any less worthy?

10. Why does Liv ultimately choose to try to save the painting rather than her home? What would you have done in her position?

11. Is Paul right to fear that Liv would eventually resent him for the loss of the painting?

12. In general, if a stolen artwork is legally acquired by its current owner, whose claim is more legitimate: the new owner or the original owner and his or her descendants? Should there be a statute of limitations? What if the current owner is a museum?

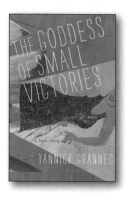

THE GODDESS OF SMALL VICTORIES

Yannick Grannec

Princeton, 1980. Kurt Gödel, the most fascinating, though hermetic, mathematician of the twentieth century, has just died of anorexia. His widow, Adele, a fierce woman shunned by her husband's colleagues because she had been a cabaret dancer, is now consigned to a nursing home. To the great annoyance of the Institute for Advanced Study, she refuses to hand over Gödel's precious records. Anna Roth, the timid daughter of two mathematicians who are part of the Princeton clique, is given the difficult task of befriending Adele and retrieving the documents from her. As Adele begins to notice Anna's own estrangement from her milieu and starts to trust her, she opens the gates of her memory and together they travel back to Vienna during the Nazi era, Princeton right after the war, the pressures of McCarthyism, the end of the positivist ideal, and the advent of nuclear weapons. It is this epic story of a genius who could never quite find his place in the world, and the determination of the woman who loved him, that will eventually give Anna the courage to change her own life.

*"A model of novelistic efficiency which intelligently combines history, theorems, passion, and flamingos." —**Lire***

"Suffice it to say that The Goddess of Small Victories *is an astonishing novel." —**Le Point***

*"A first novel as ambitious as it is accessible." —**Le Soir***

About the Author: **Yannick Grannec** is a graphic designer, freelance art director, professor of fine arts, and enthusiast of mathematics. *The Goddess of Small Victories* is her first novel. She lives in Saint-Paul de Vence, France.

October 2014 | Hardcover | Fiction | 464 pp | $26.95 | ISBN 9781590516362
Other Press | otherpress.com

CONVERSATION STARTERS

1. Why do you think Yannick Grannec chose to write about Kurt Gödel's life from the perspective of his wife? How does this choice change what we see of Gödel? How is it different from what we might have read had this been a biography of the mathematician?

2. Anna often reflects on the sense of purposelessness she feels in her life. (See "The sum of little bits of wasted time and the lateness of others added up to a lost life," (27); "What worries me is that I'm not doing anything with my life," (183)). How does this relate to her professional ambition and her relationships with Adele, her parents, and Leo? How does it compare to Kurt Gödel's passion for his work?

3. How does Adele and Anna's relationship change over the course of the novel? Why does Adele open up to her and not to any of the other people sent to retrieve the *Nachlass*? What light does Adele's story of her life with Kurt shed on Anna's own life?

4. On page 29 Adele says, "Humor is requisite for survival, young lady. Especially here." What purpose does humor serve in the novel?

5. What is the effect of viewing significant historical events and individuals, such as the Anschluss, J. Robert Oppenheimer, and Albert Einstein's death, through the lens of Adele and Kurt's marriage?

6. Adele, Anna, and Kurt all feel marginalized by their communities Why is Adele able to communicate her lonesomeness to Anna but not to Kurt? In what ways do Anna and Adele's outcast status differ from Kurt's?

7. Adele and Kurt both are more concerned with their personal lives than with the political situations around them. How is this reflected in Anna's initial preoccupation with getting Kurt's papers from Adele?

8. What is the difference between the story Adele tells herself and the account Elizabeth Glinka gives about the Gödels' home life? Does it alter Anna's or your understanding of Adele and her life with Kurt?

9. Adele believes she was created "to keep a certain genius from slipping away before his time." In contrast, Anna concludes that "No one has a mission. Adele had loved Kurt; nothing was more important." With whom do you agree and why?

HADES

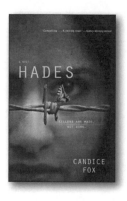

Candice Fox

On a dark night in a junkyard on the outskirts of Sydney, Australia, Hades Archer disposes of things other people either don't want, or cannot face. Old machinery and dead bodies are dismembered with equally cool precision, until two children are delivered for disposal, still alive. Hades nurses them back to health and raises them as his own. They are twins, a boy and a girl, whom he names Eric and Eden.

"Powerful. This is an incredible read! A great murder mystery, Dexter would be proud! This is how a crime thriller should make you feel." —**The Reading Room**

"A frighteningly self-assured debut with a cracker plot, strong characters, and feisty, no-nonsense writing." —***Qantas Magazine***

ABOUT THE AUTHOR: **Candice Fox** served as an officer in the Royal Australian Navy. She currently teaches writing at the University of Notre Dame in Sydney, Australia where she lives. She is completing her Ph.D. in literary censorship and terrorism.

February 2015 | Trade Paperback | Fiction | 320 pp | $15.00 | ISBN 9781617734410
Kensington Books | kensingtonbooks.com | candicefoxauthor.com

CONVERSATION STARTERS

1. A central question in *Hades* is whether Eric and Eden were made killers because of their childhood trauma, or if they naturally were born with a dark instinct within them. Do you think Eric and Eden were always meant to be killers?

2. The organ thief in *Hades* gives those he contacts a difficult choice: in order to save their sick relatives, they have to be willing to sacrifice another human life. Are the people who agree to the plan victims in their own right, or are they just as culpable as the killer?

3. Jason says, "People care for as long as it's socially appropriate . . . they love and they hate and they share and they feel guilt as long as they need to, and not a second longer. You can switch that off whenever you want to. You can make it so that you don't feel anything at all." Do you agree this quote? Why or why not?

4. *Hades* is told from the shifting perspectives of Frank and Hades. How do their perceptions of Eden and Eric differ? How are they the same?

5. Are there any heroes in *Hades*?

6. Hades ultimately makes the decision to raise Eric and Eden as his own children. Can his choice redeem him from his role as Lord of the Underworld?

7. Martina Ducote was able to escape the killer's first attack. How did her fight for survival add to the novel? Was her relationship with Frank a wise decision to make?

8. How do Frank's feelings toward Eden shift during the course of the novel?

9. "I hadn't known then I was dealing with a monster." Frank voices this opinion about Eden. Do you agree with Frank's assessment? How could other characters in the novel relate to the quote: Jason? Eric? Frank himself?

10. *Hades'* author, Candice Fox, is the daughter of a prison parole officer father and a mother who fostered over one hundred children. Her background serves as a foundation to her writing. Are there any elements of your lives that have captured your fascination in novels?

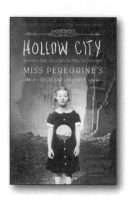

HOLLOW CITY

The Second Novel of Miss Peregrine's Peculiar Children

Ransom Riggs

The extraordinary journey that began in *Miss Peregrine's Home for Peculiar Children* continues as Jacob Portman and his newfound friends journey to London, the peculiar capital of the world. There, they hope to find a cure for their beloved headmistress, Miss Peregrine. But in this war-torn city, hideous surprises lurk around every corner. And before Jacob can deliver the peculiar children to safety, he must make an important decision about his love for Emma Bloom.

Hollow City draws readers in a richly imagined world of telepathy and time loops, of sideshows and shapeshifters—a world populated with adult "peculiars," murderous wights, and a bizarre menagerie of uncanny animals. Like its predecessor, this second novel in the Peculiar Children series blends thrilling fantasy with never-before-published vintage photography for a one-of-a-kind reading experience.

"...a stunning achievement." —Boston Globe

"Ideal for fans of Neil Gaiman and Daniel Kraus, Hollow City blends fantasy and horror into a world that will engross readers and leave them eager for more." —Shelf Awareness

About the Author: **Ransom Riggs** grew up in Florida but now makes his home in the land of peculiar children—Los Angeles. He was raised on a steady diet of ghost stories and British comedy, which probably explains the novels he writes. There's a nonzero chance he's in your house right now, watching you from underneath the bed. (Go ahead and check. We'll wait.) If not, you can always find him on Twitter @ransomriggs. See **ReadingGroupChoices.com for the *Miss Peregrine's Home for Peculiar Children* book profile and conversation starters.**

January 2014 | Hardcover | Fiction | 396 pp | $17.99 | ISBN 9781594746123
Quirk Books | quirkbooks.com | ransomriggs.com

CONVERSATION STARTERS

1. At the end of *Miss Peregrine's Home for Peculiar Children*, the children are starting out on a new, hopeful adventure. Though *Hollow City* begins where the previous book left off, what has changed about the children's outlook? Do they still have hope?

2. Enoch tends to be the antagonist within the group. Do you think Enoch is pessimistic or realistic?

3. Why do you think the hollows and wights chose to pose as Nazi soldiers? How does this element add to their malicious presence in the book?

4. The children spend the entire book running away from hollows while trying to make their way to London. Did you think running was the best plan, or should they have tried to stand and fight, or simply hide?

5. Enoch repeatedly voices the worst-case scenario. Does doing so harm or hurt the group's progress? Is it better to keep spirits high by sugarcoating the truth or to be completely honest about the situation and prepare to face it?

6. The Gypsies live separately from the rest of society, much like the peculiar children. What other similarities do you notice between the Gypsies and the peculiars?

7. The children's stories of their past are mostly sad, especially Emma's. How would you react if your friend or family member suddenly developed peculiar powers?

8. What did you think about Jacob's eventual decision to leave the peculiar children? What decision would you have made in his place?

9. *Hollow City* ends with a spectacular cliffhanger. What do you think will happen in the next book? How will Jacob's newly discovered powers affect the story?

10. If the books in the Peculiar Children series were made into films, whom would you cast to play Jacob?

THE ILLUSION OF SEPARATENESS

Simon Van Booy

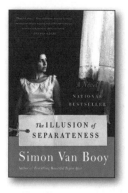

The characters in Simon Van Booy's *The Illusion of Separateness* discover at their darkest moments of fear and isolation that they are not alone, that they were never alone, that every human being is a link in a chain we cannot see. This gripping novel— inspired by true events—tells the interwoven stories of a deformed German infantryman; a lonely British film director; a young, blind museum curator; two Jewish American newlyweds separated by war; and a caretaker at a retirement home for actors in Santa Monica. They move through the same world but fail to perceive their connections until, through seemingly random acts of selflessness, a veil is lifted to reveal the vital parts they have played in one another's lives, and the illusion of their separateness.

"The uncanny beauty of Van Booy's prose, and his ability to knife straight to the depths of a character's heart, fill a reader with wonder.…There are so many wonderful sentences in this book, a reviewer groans for want of room to list them." **—San Francisco Chronicle**

"Masterful prose.…From minimalistic sentences he wrings out maximum impact, stripping away artifice and elaboration in favor of stark, emotional clarity and honesty." **—Boston Globe**

About the Author: **Simon Van Booy** is the author of two novels and two collections of short stories, including *The Secret Lives of People in Love* and *Love Begins in Winter,* which won the Frank O'Connor International Short Story Award. He is the editor of three philosophy books and has written for *The New York Times, The Guardian,* NPR, and the BBC. His work has been translated into fourteen languages. He lives in Brooklyn with his wife and daughter.

July 2014 | Trade Paperback | Fiction | 224 pp | $14.99 | ISBN 9780062248459
Harper Perennial | harpercollins.com | simonvanbooy.com

CONVERSATION STARTERS

1. Define the phrase "illusion of separateness." The author uses it three times—in the epitaph, as the name of a photo exhibit curated by one of the book's characters, and as the book's title. How do all three tie together? What is the author's message to the reader about "separateness"? Is it part of the human condition that we feel isolated? Describe the ways in which all the characters in the novel are connected.

2. In your group, have each member play the game "six degrees of separation." What, if any, links do you share that you had not realized— or consciously recognized—before?

3. Think about the various characters. How did their choices unite the circle of their connection? Focus on one. What might he or she have done that would have broken the link?

4. Does it matter that at the end of the novel, the various characters do not recognize their importance to each other? Is it enough that you, the reader, understand the link between them?

5. At the beginning of the novel, after Martin discovers the truth of his existence, the author writes, "He had been reborn into the nightmare of truth. The history of others had been his all along." What is the author conveying with these words?

6. Amelia describes being blind. Do you think that while sight affords us much, it also closes us off to other aspects of life, and makes us "blind" in another kind of way?

7. Amelia tells us that she believes, "people would be happier if they had admitted things more often. In a sense we are all prisoners of some memory, or fear, or disappointment—we are all defined by something we can't change." Do you agree with her? How are each of the characters defined by something they cannot change? How do they adapt to this defining element?

8. Analyze the structure of the novel. Why do you think the author chose this structure versus straight linear narrative? Would the story have the same emotional impact if it had been told from one or two character's points of view alone? What makes this a novel rather than a collection of short stories?

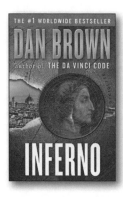

INFERNO

Dan Brown

In *Inferno*, Dan Brown once again offers readers the same heady mix of history, art, symbols, and high-wire tension that catapulted *The Da Vinci Code, Angels & Demons,* and *The Lost Symbol* into international blockbusters. This time the stakes are even higher, as Harvard professor of symbology Robert Langdon must decode the mystery surrounding a virus that has the power to alter the course of human civilization—or possibly end it. Renowned biochemist Bertrand Zobrist has created a virus that will be released in just twenty-four hours and infect the entire human species. Zobrist is a Dante fanatic and he has used references to Dante's great poem as clues to the location and purpose of the virus. Langdon draws upon his own extensive knowledge of Dante's poem and of Florence's splendid art and architecture to decipher Zobrist's riddle. But will he find the virus in time? What makes *Inferno* so compelling is not only Dan Brown's masterful ability to spin a spellbinding tale but his skill at weaving a complex and pressing social issue into the fabric of his narrative.

"A book-length scavenger hunt. . . . Jam-packed with tricks."
—*The New York Times*

*"Fast, clever, well-informed. . . . Dan Brown is the master of the intellectual cliffhanger." —**The Wall Street Journal***

About the Author: **Dan Brown** is the author of numerous #1 bestselling novels, most recently *Inferno*. Previously, *The Lost Symbol* broke the record for the biggest one-week sale in Random House history for a single title. His earlier title, *The Da Vinci Code*, is one of the bestselling novels of all time. Mr. Brown was named one of the World's 100 Most Influential People by *Time* Magazine. He has appeared in the pages of *Newsweek, Forbes, People, GQ, The New Yorker,* and others.

May 2014 | Trade Paperback | Fiction | 576 pp | $16.00 | ISBN 9780804172264
Anchor | randomhouse.com | danbrown.com

CONVERSATION STARTERS

1. What features does *Inferno* share with Dan Brown's other Robert Langdon novels: *The Da Vinci Code, Angels & Demons,* and *The Lost Symbol*? In what ways is it different from those earlier works?

2. Why has Brown used these lines from Dante as an epigraph to *Inferno*: "The darkest places in hell are reserved for those who maintain their neutrality in times of moral crisis"? How does that statement illuminate the novel? What is the particular danger of maintaining moral neutrality in Inferno?

3. What accounts for the frenetic narrative pace of the novel? How does Dan Brown use chapter endings to create suspense? What other devices create a narrative tension that pulls the reader along?

4. What are some of the most surprising twists and turns in Inferno?

5. The brilliant biochemist Bertrand Zobrist asserts some unsettling ideas. He argues that the Black Plague was one of the best things that ever happened to humanity and ushered in the Renaissance. He also believes that the human race won't survive unless we have another mass extinction event. Is Zobrist right about these issues? Is his solution the lesser of two evils or is it too morally repugnant even to consider?

6. How does Langdon use his knowledge of literature, art, and symbology to decipher the clues that lead him to the location of Zobrist's virus? In what ways is Dante's great poem, The Inferno, central to the novel?

7. Sienna Brooks is perhaps the most complex character in the novel. How has her past influenced who she has become? Why does she feel that she has finally found a purpose at the end of the book?

8. In what ways do issues of trust and betrayal play out in Inferno?

9. What does Dan Brown's use of a real-life contemporary movement like Transhumanism add to *Inferno*? Does Transhumanism offer solutions to some of the essential problems that confront the human species?

10. At the end of the novel, Dr. Sinskey invites Sienna to accompany her to a conference to address world leaders about the virus Zobrist released and discuss the issue of population control. Is there a significance to having two women, rather than two men, assume this role?

AN ITALIAN WIFE

Ann Hood

An *Italian Wife* is the extraordinary story of Josephine Rimaldi—her joys, sorrows, and passions, spanning more than seven decades. The novel begins in turn-of-the-century Italy, when fourteen-year-old Josephine, sheltered and naive, is forced into an arranged marriage to a man she doesn't know or love who is about to depart for America, where she later joins him. Bound by tradition, Josephine gives birth to seven children. The last, Valentina, is conceived in passion, born in secret, and given up for adoption. Josephine spends the rest of her life searching for her lost child, keeping her secret even as her other children go off to war, get married, and make their own mistakes. Her son suffers in World War One. One daughter struggles to assimilate in the new world of the 1950s American suburbs, while another, stranded in England, grieves for a lover lost in World War Two. Her granddaughters experiment with sex, drugs, and rock-and-roll in the 1970s. Poignant, sensual, and deeply felt, *An Italian Wife* is a sweeping and evocative portrait of a family bound by love and heartbreak.

"A big, full-hearted grazie to Ann Hood . . . She has given us a feast of a story: impressive in its range, sumptuous in its evocations of love and loss, and deeply satisfying." —**Christopher Castellani, author of *All This Talk of Love***

ABOUT THE AUTHOR: **Ann Hood** is the author of six works of fiction, including the bestseller *The Knitting Circle* and, most recently, *The Obituary Writer,* as well as a memoir, *Comfort.* She is also the editor of *Knitting Yarns: Writers on Knitting.* The winner of two Pushcart prizes as well as Best American Food Writing, Best American Travel Writing, and Best American Spiritual Writing awards, she lives in Providence, Rhode Island.

September 2014 | Hardcover | Fiction | 288 pp | $25.95 | ISBN 9780393241662
W.W. Norton | wwnorton.com | annhood.us

CONVERSATION STARTERS

1. From her marriage to her emigration to America to raising her family, Josephine Rimaldi is not a person with a lot of choices in life. Would you consider her to be an unhappy person? Do you think she would consider herself to be unhappy? Has our definition of what happiness is, what choices a person deserves, and what makes for a meaningful life changed in the generations since Josephine's youth?

2. Describe how the Rimaldi family's relationship to the Catholic Church evolves from generation to generation.

3. Josephine loses a daughter. Martha loses a lover. Elisabetta loses her childhood ambition. Carmine loses his grip on reality. To what extent are Josephine and her children defined by loss? What do they find to live for in the wake of their losses?

4. Compare and contrast Josephine's actual affair with Tommy Petrocelli to her daughter Connie's imaginary affair with Dr. DiMarco. How are the two women's circumstances different, and how are they similar? What are both women trying to escape?

5. We see the Rimaldi family affected by three wars over the course of the novel. Which characters are affected directly, and which indirectly? Can we use this family and these characters as a lens through which to understand how each of these wars changed the country overall?

6. What does it mean to be an "Italian wife"? Does the meaning of that moniker change over the course of the novel for each generation?

7. When and in what circumstances did your family come to America? Do you feel that you are in touch with your heritage? Did you—or did your parents or grandparents—make an effort to assimilate, like some of Josephine's children did?

8. In the novel's final scene, Josephine and her lost daughter are finally in the same place at the same time. Josephine never knows it, although the reader does. What is unique about the reader's vantage point in *An Italian Wife*? How would the novel be different if our perspective was tied to a single character?

THE JAGUAR'S CHILDREN

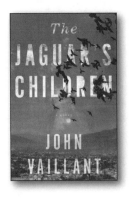

John Vaillant

From the best-selling author of *The Tiger* and *The Golden Spruce*, this debut novel is a gripping survival story of a young man trapped, perhaps fatally, during a border crossing. Hector is trapped. The water truck, sealed to hide its human cargo, has broken down. The coyotes have taken all the passengers' money for a mechanic and have not returned. Those left behind have no choice but to wait. Hector finds a name in his friend Cesar's phone. AnniMac. A name with an American number. He must reach her, both for rescue and to pass along the message Cesar has come so far to deliver. But are his messages going through? Over four days, as water and food run low, Hector tells how he came to this desperate place. His story takes us from Oaxaca—its rich culture, its rapid change—to the dangers of the border. It exposes the tangled ties between Mexico and El Norte — land of promise and opportunity, homewrecker and unreliable friend. And it reminds us of the power of storytelling and the power of hope, as Hector fights to ensure his message makes it out of the truck and into the world. Both an outstanding suspense novel and an arresting window into the relationship between two great cultures, *The Jaguar's Children* shows how deeply interconnected all of us, always, are.

"*The Jaguar's Children is devastating. It's at once a literary mystery, an engrossing tour de force, and a brilliant commentary on humanity's role in the physical world. The voice that echoes out from that abandoned place Vaillant so masterfully creates won't leave me.*" —**Joseph Boyden, author of *Three Day Road* and *The Orenda***

ABOUT THE AUTHOR: **John Vaillant's** work has appeared in T*he New Yorker, the Atlantic, National Geographic, and Outside,* among other magazines. His two previous, award-winning books, *The Tiger* and *The Golden Spruce,* were international bestsellers.

January 2015 | Hardcover | Fiction | 288 pp | $26.00 | ISBN 9780544290082
Houghton Mifflin Harcourt | hmhco.com | thetigerbook.com

CONVERSATION STARTERS

1. What were Hector's motivations for leaving Mexico? What were Cesar's? Did you know much about Oaxaca before you read the novel? If so, how did your perception of the place change over the course of the story? If not, what did you learn and did any of it surprise you?

2. "Who else can grow all their food—sweets and spices, herbs and medicines, corn and beans and squash, even oil for the hair—on one hectare on the side of a mountain?" What secret is Cesar carrying with him? How will it impact the Oaxacans way of life? At the end of the novel, what is your feeling about whether and how their culture can survive?

3. Who are the coyotes? Why do they have that name? What role do they play in the novel and how are they implicated in its outcome?

4. Why is this novel called *The Jaguar's Children*? Where do jaguars make appearances throughout the novel and what is their significance? How does Hector's abuelo's story fit? Hector recalls: "I asked him once, who will dance the jaguar after him. 'Whoever carves the mask,' he said. 'You know where my tools are.'" Does Hector carve a mask?

5. Why do you think the author chose this format for Hector's story—telling it through audio and text files? How did it affect your reading? Discuss the progression of Hector's time in the water tank. How does the author increase the stakes, show the rising tension, and convey the feeling inside the truck?

6. What do you believe happened at the end of the novel? Explore the various scenarios that could have played out for Hector. What impact did the change in perspective have on your reading? Why do you think the author made this choice?

7. The novel explores several periods in the relationship between Mexico and the United States as well as several ways in which these two cultures overlap and influence each other. How has your view on these neighbors changed in the course of the book? Do you see ways in which this relationship might improve?

JEWELWEED

David Rhodes

In *Jewelweed*, David Rhodes—the beloved author of *Driftless*—returns to the small town of Words, Wisconsin, and introduces a cast of characters who all find themselves struggling to find a new sense of belonging in the present moment—sometimes with the help of peach preserves or mashed potato pie. After serving time for a dubious conviction, Blake Bookchester returns home, enthralled by the philosophy of Spinoza and yearning for the woman he loves. Having agitated for his release, Reverend Winifred Helm slowly comes to understand that she is no longer fulfilled by the ministry. Winnie's precocious son, August, and his best friend, Ivan, befriend a hermit and roam the woods in search of the elusive Wild Boy. And Danielle Workhouse, Ivan's single mother and Blake's former lover, struggles to do right by her son. These and other inhabitants of Words—all flawed, deeply human, and ultimately universal—approach the future with a combination of hope and trepidation, increasingly mindful of the importance of community to their individual lives.

"Reminiscent of Steinbeck, with a little touch of Michener."—**Alan Cheuse, National Public Radio's** *All Things Considered*

About the Author: **David Rhodes** worked in fields, hospitals, and factories across Iowa. After receiving an MFA from the Iowa Writers' Workshop, he published three acclaimed novels: *The Last Fair Deal Going Down* (1972), *The Easter House* (1975), and *Rock Island Line* (1977). In 1977, a motorcycle accident left him partially paralyzed. In 2008, Rhodes returned to the literary scene with *Driftless*, a novel that was hailed as "the best work of fiction to come out of the Midwest in many years" (Alan Cheuse). He lives with his wife, Edna, in rural Wisconsin. **See ReadingGroupChoices.com for book profiles and conversation starters of *Rock Island Line* and *Driftless*.**

April 2014 | Trade Paperback | Fiction | 464 pp | $16.00 | ISBN 9781571311061
Milkweed Editions | milkweed.org | davidrhodesauthor.com

CONVERSATION STARTERS

1. Food is a key element in *Jewelweed*. Beginning with the breakfast pie Nate eats in the first chapter, food, taste and smell all seem critical to this story. What are some other instances where food is central to the narrative? How has food played an important role in your life?

2. Early in the novel, Winnie considers "how she might know herself better" (35). In what ways are the other characters trying to know themselves better? Which characters are the most successful?

3. The characters in *Jewelweed* all seem to be yearning for freedom. Freedom looks different for each of the characters, but can the concept be distilled? Do any of the characters find the freedom they seek?

4. Did the justice system fail Blake? Does *Jewelweed* offer a critique of the system?

5. There are glimpses of the fantastic throughout *Jewelweed*—the giant turtle that evades capture, the Wild Boy's ability to be largely unseen, the extraordinarily lifelike statues Lester Mortal creates and then burns as a way of letting go of parts of his past. How does Rhodes make the ordinary seem extraordinary? Does his writing style evoke the fantastic, or does the content?

6. What function does the Wild Boy serve? When the details of the Wild Boy are fleshed out as *Jewelweed* comes to a close, does your opinion of Lester Mortal change?

7. At one point Blake says to Jacob, "Do you ever think maybe there are some things you weren't supposed to get over? Things that would take you the rest of your life to work through?"(209) What hasn't Blake gotten over? What have other characters been unable to let go of?

8. Why do Ivan and August have such a strong bond? How does August's worldview impact his relationship with other characters?

9. Faith is a central theme in *Jewelweed*—religious and otherwise. How does Winnie's faith evolve throughout the course of the book? How does Rhodes create the sacred through language?

10. Blake mentions experiencing "deathless grief" (423). What does he mean by this? Are there other deathless griefs in *Jewelweed*?

THE LAST DAYS OF CALIFORNIA

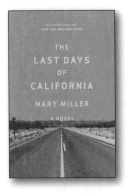

Mary Miller

Fifteen-year-old Jess is on a road trip to the end of the world. Her evangelical father has packed up the family and left their Alabama home behind to drive west in anticipation of the rapture, hoping to save as many souls as possible before the Second Coming. With her long-suffering mother and rebellious older sister, Jess hands out tracts to nonbelievers at every rest stop and gas station along the way. But as doomsday approaches, Jess can't seem to work up any real fear about the apocalypse when her family's troubles loom so much larger.

Sporting a "King Jesus Returns!" t-shirt, Jess's semi-earnest efforts to believe are thwarted by a string of familiar teenage obsessions. From "Will the world end?" to "Will I ever fall in love?" each tender worry is brilliantly rendered with equal emotional weight. With a deadpan humor and savage charm that belies a deep sympathy for her characters, Mary Miller captures the gnawing uneasiness, sexual rivalry, and escalating self-doubt of teenage life in America, where the end always seems nigh.

"[A] terrific first novel. . . . [W]hy worry about labeling a book this good? Just read it." —New York Times Book Review

"[A] beautiful examination of youth and family. . . . Rarely, if ever, have we seen young American womanhood painted in such a raw and honest and heartbreaking way." —Los Angeles Review of Books

ABOUT THE AUTHOR: **Mary Miller** is the author of the short story collection *Big World*. Her work has been published in *Mcsweeney's Quarterly, American Short Fiction, Oxford American,* and other journals. A former Michener Fellow in Fiction at the University of Texas, she currently serves as the John and Renée Grisham Writer in Residence at the University of Mississippi. This is her first novel.

September 2014 | Trade Paperback | Fiction | 256 pp | $14.95 | ISBN 9780871408419
Liveright | wwnorton.com | maryumiller.tumblr.com

CONVERSATION STARTERS

1. Jess spends a lot of time describing the food she and her family eat on the road. What does food mean to Jess—why is it so significant, and do you think the kind of food she eats says something about her?

2. Jess believes that Elise's looks make life easier for her. Do you agree? How would you describe Jess's body image? Why do you think she is so observant of other peoples' appearances?

3. What were your first impressions of each of the Metcalfs? How did your impressions change? Did any characters surprise you?

4. Jess doesn't rebel as openly against religion as Elise does. How would you describe Jess's faith? Do you think her belief in God changes?

5. After Jess's experience with Gabe, Elise tells her, "You're stronger than I am." What makes Elise say that? Why doesn't Jess believe it?

6. Describe each Metcalf's attitude toward the Rapture. Why do they go on the trip? Do they believe the end of the world is only days away?

7. Jess's mother is an enigmatic character. What do you think makes her tick? How would you describe her relationship with Jess? With Elise? Do you think her daughters know her well?

8. Does Jess's experience of being a teenager remind you of your own? Do you relate more to Jess or to Elise, or to another character entirely?

9. What do you think drives Elise's rebellious and reckless attitude? What drives Jess's relative caution? Does the close proximity of the road trip seem to alter their behavior?

10. During the trip, Jess has her first two sexual experiences. What precipitates each encounter? What does Jess get out of them, and how do they affect her?

11. How would you characterize Jess and Elise's relationship? When is it strongest and when most fragile? Is it a typical sibling relationship?

12. Why do you think the novel is called *The Last Days of California*?

13. How does the road trip change each of the Metcalfs? What do you think happens to them after the close of the novel? What kind of future do you see for Jess?

THE LAST POLICEMAN

Ben H. Winters

What's the point in solving murders if we're all going to die soon, anyway? Detective Hank Palace has faced this question ever since asteroid 2011GV1 hovered into view. There's no chance left. No hope. Just six precious months until impact. *The Last Policeman* presents a fascinating portrait of a pre-apocalyptic United States. The economy spirals downward while crops rot in the fields. Churches and synagogues are packed. People all over the world are walking off the job—but not Hank Palace. He's investigating a death by hanging in a city that sees a dozen suicides every week—except this one feels suspicious, and Palace is the only cop who cares. The first in a trilogy, *The Last Policeman* offers a mystery set on the brink of an apocalypse. As Palace's investigation plays out under the shadow of 2011GV1, we're confronted by hard questions way beyond "whodunit." What basis does civilization rest upon? What is life worth? What would any of us do, what would we really do, if our days were numbered?

"...sharp, funny, and deeply wise." —Slate.com

*"A promising kickoff to a planned trilogy. For Winters, the beauty is in the details rather than the plot's grim main thrust." —**Kirkus Reviews,** starred review*

ABOUT THE AUTHOR: **Ben H. Winters** is the author of The Last Policeman trilogy. *The Last Policeman*, the first book in the trilogy, was the recipient of the 2012 Edgar Award from the Mystery Writers of America; it was also named one of the Best Books of 2012 by Amazon.com and *Slate. Countdown City,* the second book, was an NPR Best Book of 2013 and the winner of the Philip K. Dick Award. **See ReadingGroupChoices.com for book profiles and conversation starters for *Countdown City* (Book II) and *World of Trouble* (Book III).**

July 2012 | Trade Paperback | Fiction | 336 pp | $14.95 | ISBN 9781594746741
Quirk Books | quirkbooks.com | benhwinters.com

CONVERSATION STARTERS

1. Do you think Ben H. Winters paints a convincing picture of Concord, New Hampshire, and of the world at large with only six months until the asteroid might collide with the earth?

2. The economy is spiraling downward while crops rot in the fields. Churches and synagogues are packed. People all over the world are walking off the job—but not Hank Palace. What do you think motivates Hank to remain dedicated to his work? And is his character realistic?

3. Hank has finally attained his lifelong goal of becoming a detective but his promotion is due to the fact that all of his colleagues are quitting. Do you think Hank feels the need to prove himself in order to make his dream of being a detective real and fulfilled?

4. When you learned of how the hospital is handling the patients, how did you react?

5. Hank has a complicated relationship with his sister and doesn't like her husband. Were you surprised when Hank took on the risk of looking for Nico's husband?

6. Hank has a brief but intimate relationship with Naomi. Is love at the end of the world possible?

7. Toward the end of the book Hank finds himself alone and seems to be OK with it. Are you surprised that he took in Houdini as a pet?

8. This novel is a mash-up of mystery and science fiction. If you're a fan of mystery and not science fiction, did any of the science fiction aspects of the book appeal to you? (Vice versa for the science fiction fans.)

9. Do you think that Hank, or anyone else, might survive the impact of the asteroid? Or do you believe Hank's days truly are numbered?

10. If you knew there were only six months before the apocalypse, what would your bucket list look like?

LIAR'S BENCH

Kim Michele Richardson

In the summer of 1972, Ella Whitlock is found hanging from the rafters of her own home. Everyone in Peckinpaw, Kentucky assumes that Ella's no-good, junkie of a husband did the deed, or that she just grew tired of enduring his abuse. In the wake of this devastating loss, Ella's 17-year-old daughter Mudas (Muddy for short) discovers strange clues hidden amongst her mama's hair ribbons and recipe cards.

Determined to uncover the truth and clear her mama's name, Muddy enlists the help of her friend Bobby Marshall and follows the clues to Hark Hill Plantation, home of the rich and crooked Roy McGee, the long-rumored leader of a gambling and prostitution ring. Though Bobby passes for white, he has mixed Indian and Black heritage (his great-great grandmother, a slave, was hanged on Hark Hill plantation nearly a hundred years before), a fact which complicates his friendship with Mudas and makes it difficult for them to be seen in public together. In spite of this bigotry, Mudas and Bobby seek comfort in each other's arms. On the trail to find her mama's killer, they uncover corruption so deep that it is rooted to yesterday's sorrows—her mama's death and the hundred-year-old lynching of Bobby's grandmother. If Mudas doesn't piece together the past and present—and fast—she might find herself in a pine box just like her mama.

"One of those rare books I wish I had written. Southern storytelling at its finest. A must read for those who love a nail-biting suspense." —**Ann Hite, author of *Ghost On Black Mountain* and Georgia Author Of The Year 2012**

About the Author: **Kim Michele Richardson** is a volunteer for Habitat for Humanity and an advocate for the prevention of child abuse and domestic violence. She is the author of the memoir *The Unbreakable Child*. *Liar's Bench* is her first novel.

September 2014 | Trade Paperback | Fiction | 256 pp | $14.95 | ISBN 9780871408419
Liveright | wwnorton.com | maryumiller.tumblr.com

CONVERSATION STARTERS

1. The South of 1972 was not far removed from Freedom Riders, police dogs, and water blasts attacking peaceful protesters. How does the Civil Rights Movement influence Mudas? How does it affect her actions, her fears, and her relationship with Bobby?

2. Kentucky straddles the "deep" South and the Midwest's industrial heartland. Mama was torn between those two worlds. Bobby also feels the pull of the big city and dreams of "getting out" of Peckinpaw. Muddy also has high hopes for herself, but she feels a deep connection with her hometown. Do you think she will live out her days in Peckinpaw? Or will her aspirations take her elsewhere?

3. In the large majority of divorces, mothers retain primary custody of the children. In *Liar's Bench*, Muddy remains in her father's care, which would have been particularly unusual in the '70s. Is Adam a good father? Does his gender make him ill-equipped to parent a teenage girl? How might have Mudas' life turned out differently if she had continued to live with her mother?

4. *Liar's Bench* is infused with descriptions of the plants, the sky, the soil, the birds, and their songs. Have we, today, lost the ability to see, feel, and appreciate our natural surroundings? Have we become disconnected from nature?

5. Today we live in the age of information. Everything is accessible, right at our fingertips. Consider how Muddy's story would be different if it happened today. Would it be easier for her to find out the truth about her mama's death? Or would the wealth of information be a smoke screen, making it harder than ever to distinguish fact from fiction?

6. Title IX is a portion of the Education Amendments of 1972 that states (in part) that "No person in the United States shall, on the basis of sex, be excluded from participation in, be denied the benefits of, or be subjected to discrimination under any education program or activity receiving Federal financial assistance. . ." Today, it's hard to imagine there was a time when girls couldn't participate in school sports because of gender. Are there any current policies that we will look back on, fifty years from now, and find unfathomable? Is this how we define progress?

LITTLE MERCIES

Heather Gudenkauf

In her latest ripped-from-the-headlines tour de force, *New York Times* bestselling author Heather Gudenkauf shows how one small mistake can have life-altering consequences.

Veteran social worker Ellen Moore has seen the worst side of humanity—the vilest acts one person can commit against another. She is a fiercely dedicated children's advocate and a devoted mother and wife. But one blistering summer day, a simple moment of distraction will have repercussions that Ellen could never have imagined, threatening to shatter everything she holds dear and trapping her between the gears of the system she works for. Meanwhile, ten-year-old Jenny Briard has been living with her well-meaning but irresponsible father since her mother left them, sleeping on friends' couches and moving in and out of cheap motels. When Jenny suddenly finds herself on her own, she is forced to survive with nothing but a few dollars and her street smarts. The last thing she wants is a social worker, but when Ellen's and Jenny's lives collide, little do they know just how much they can help one another.

"The portrayal of the frenzied speed of a mother's life leading ultimately to tragedy is similar to Lisa Genova's Left Neglected, *but with the additional horror of every parent's worst fear: harming their own child. This novel is full of hope...Recommend to those looking for a quick read with lots to discuss; ideal for book groups." —Library Journal*

ABOUT THE AUTHOR: **Heather Gudenkauf** is the author of the *New York Times* and *USA Today* bestselling novels *One Breath Away, These Things Hidden* and *The Weight of Silence*. She lives in Iowa with her husband, three children and a very spoiled German Shorthaired Pointer named Maxine. She is currently working on her next novel.

July 2014 | Trade Paperback | Fiction | 320 pp | $15.95 | ISBN 9780778316336
Harlequin MIRA | harlequin.com | heathergudenkauf.com

CONVERSATION STARTERS

1. Like many parents, Ellen struggles to balance her personal and professional lives. Discuss how you face maintaining that precarious balance.

2. Ellen's former client Jade steps in to save Avery's life and Ellen finds herself being seen as an unfit mother. Talk about this reversal of roles. How do you think this changed Ellen's view of the parents she works with and how they think of Ellen?

3. Discuss the ways parenthood and adult-child relationships are portrayed in the novel. Think about Jenny's relationships with her father, mother, Maudene, her father's friend, girls, and Ellen's relationship with her own children and the children she works with.

4. Ellen's distractions have catastrophic effects on her daughter's health, her family, and her professional life as a social worker. Talk about a time when you may have had a close call in your life. How did you feel? How did the experience change you?

5. Ellen is charged with a felony and potentially faces a prison sentence. Do you think she should have to serve time behind bars?

6. What scenes or developments in the novel affected you most?

7. Adam quickly forgives Ellen for leaving Avery in the hot car. How would you react in a similar situation? Does Ellen deserve forgiveness? Do you think she will be able to forgive herself?

8. Maudene places herself in a precarious situation by taking a wayward Jenny into her home. Discuss the possible implications of this decision. What would you have done if faced with a similar situation?

9. How do Ellen and Jenny change over the course of the novel? Which character changes the most, which the least?

10. How did your opinion of Jenny's mother change over the course of the novel?

11. In Jenny's young life she has already faced so many obstacles: poverty, abuse, struggles with school, a runaway mother and an unpredictable father. What do you think will become of Jenny?

12. What does the title *Little Mercies* mean to you?

LOCAL SOULS

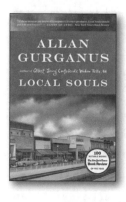

Allan Gurganus

New York Times Book Review Notable Book of 2013

In *Local Souls,* Allan Gurganus offers us three linked novellas, set in legendary Falls, North Carolina—site of his beloved *Oldest Living Confederate Widow Tells All.* We find the small town revolutionized by freer sexuality, loosened family ties, and secular worship. Gurganus celebrates those citizens who stayed home but uncovers certain old habits—adultery, incest, obsession—very much alive in this "Winesburg, Ohio" with high-speed Internet. Writing about erotic hunger and social embarrassment with Twain's knife-edged glee, Gurganus dramatizes the passing of Hawthorne's small-town America. He brings the twisted hilarity of Flannery O'Connor kicking into our new century. Each novella "delivers an ending of true force" (John Irving). Each deepens the luster of Gurganus's well-known empathy and laughter. His dark comedy gives us indelible characters worth loving. Here is a universal work about a village.

"A tour de force in the tradition of Hawthorne. It shows that Gurganus's vast creative and imaginative powers, still rooted in the local, are increasingly universal in scope and effect. The book is an expansive work of love."
—New York Times Book Review

"This book underscores what we have long known—Gurganus stands among the best writers of our time." **—Ann Patchett**

ABOUT THE AUTHOR: **Allan Gurganus**'s books include *White People* and *Oldest Living Confederate Widow Tells All.* Winner of the *Los Angeles Times* Book Prize, Gurganus is a Guggenheim Fellow and a member of the American Academy of Arts and Letters. Adaptations of his fiction have earned four Emmys. A resident of his native North Carolina, he lives in a village of six thousand souls.

May 2014 | Trade Paperback | Fiction | 352 pp | $15.95 | ISBN 9780871407788
Liveright | wwnorton.com | allangurganus.com

CONVERSATION STARTERS

1. "Fear Not" opens and closes at the scene of a high school play. How does this framing device—and the perspective of the first-person narrator—affect your reading of the story? Did you feel closer to, or further from, the action of the story than you would have if there had been no first-person narrator? In what way did the frame lend the story a sense of theater and drama?

2. The character Fearnot is given her nickname before the events of her story unfold. How does your understanding of that name change over the course of the story? How do her actions and experiences reflect and affect the meaning of her name?

3. Fearnot breaks two major sexual taboos over the course of her story. How does the second reflect, answer, or, possibly, redeem the first? What did you make of the revelation at the end, about who the couple at the theater turned out to be? Were you surprised?

4. In "Saints Have Mothers," Jean Mulray's relationship to her daughter, Caitlin, is characterized by jealousy, resentment, and possibly a hint of eroticism, in addition to pride and maternal love. How does this novella—like the previous one—explore what is forbidden and unspoken in family relationships? Did you empathize with Jean's complicated feelings towards her daughter as much or more than you empathized with Fearnot's feelings towards her son?

5. Describe the role that the larger community of Falls plays in "Saints Have Mothers." How are Jean and Caitlin perceived by their peers in town? How does that perception affect them and their relationship, and how does it change over the course of the novella?

6. Shortly after Caitlin returns, Jean says, "Like the rest of Falls, I had turned my child into someone ideal then immortal" (163). What do you make of this? How does the flesh-and-blood Caitlin who returns alter Jean's—and your—perception of the "ideal then immortal" Caitlin that they were imagining in her absence?

7. Describe the effect of the flood in "Decoy." How does it change Doc Roper? How does it change Bill? With regard to Bill's memories of his father, what is the significance of the fact that The River Road has been destroyed?

A LONG TIME GONE

Karen White

When Vivien Walker left her home in the Mississippi Delta, she swore never to go back, as generations of the women in her family had. But in the spring, nine years to the day since she'd left, that's exactly what happens—Vivien returns, fleeing from a broken marriage and her lost dreams for children.

What she hopes to find is solace with "Bootsie," her dear grandmother who raised her, a Walker woman with a knack for making everything all right. But instead she finds that her grandmother has died and that her estranged mother is drifting further away from her memories. Now Vivien is forced into the unexpected role of caretaker, challenging her personal quest to find the girl she herself once was.

But for Vivien things change in ways she cannot imagine when a violent storm reveals the remains of a long-dead woman buried near the Walker home, not far from the cypress swamp that is soon to give up its ghosts. Vivien knows there is now only one way to rediscover herself—by uncovering the secrets of her family and breaking the cycle of loss that has haunted them for generations.

"[A] dedicated artist…Karen White's talent is ripe for the taking."
—The Huffington Post

"White's dizzying carousel of a plot keeps those pages turning, so much so that the book can—and should be—finished in one afternoon, interrupted only by a glass of sweet iced tea." —Oprah.com

ABOUT THE AUTHOR: **Karen White** is the *New York Times* bestselling author of *After the Rain, The Time Between, Folly Beach, Falling Home,* and such Tradd Street novels as *Return to Tradd Street, The Strangers on Montagu Street* and *The Girl on Legare Street.* She grew up in London but now lives with her husband and two children near Atlanta, Georgia.

June 2014 | Hardcover | Fiction | 432 pp | $25.95 | ISBN 9780451240460
New American Library | us.penguingroup.com | karen-white.com

CONVERSATION STARTERS

1. "Home means so many different things . . . It's where your people are." The author creates such a dynamic sense of place for the reader through sensory details and evocative objects such as the heirloom black bed, the watermark from the flood, and the lost diary. What things or memories evoke "home" for you?

2. Does Vivien get the closure she needs with her mother once she returns home? How do Bootsie's death, Carol Lynne's dementia, and Vivien's reliance on prescription drugs complicate things?

3. What is the effect of Carol Lynne's dementia on those around her? What was it like to encounter Carol Lynne only through her diary?

4. In one of her diary entries, Carol Lynne notes, "There's something in the ways of mothers and daughters, I think, that makes us see all the bad parts of ourselves." Do you think this is true? How does this apply to the Walker women? Does each woman grow emotionally from this realization?

5. "Because it was something I'd been born with, a poison in the blood I'd inherited from my mother and she from hers and way on back before anybody alive could still remember." When they left home, what ghosts was each Walker woman chasing? What made each woman return?

6. Carol Lynne's diary also reveals the following sentiment: "[Bootsie] just smiled and told me to wait until I become a mother, and then I will understand that my real destiny will be decided by those not yet born." What does Bootsie mean by this? How do children shape the futures of the Walker women?

7. Did you suspect the identity of the body earlier in the novel? How does this "ghost" affect the lives of the Walker women?

8. How does the author use objects or heirlooms such as the watch and ring to unite the characters' stories across multiple generations? Is there an heirloom you've inherited that is loaded with meaning or inspires curiosity about the past?

9. Did you have any trouble shifting between time lines, which run from the 1920s to the present day? Which era or woman's story was your favorite?

LONGBOURN

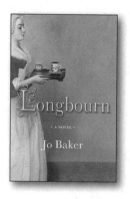

Jo Baker

A *New York Times Book Review* Notable Book, a *Seattle Times* Best Title, *a Christian Science Monitor* Best Fiction Book, a *Miami Herald* Favorite Book, a *Kirkus* Best Book of the Year

In *Pride and Prejudice*, Jane Austen painted an unforgettable portrait of the Bennet family and their adventures in courtship and love, all set against the background of their country estate, Longbourn. Now, in a wonderfully fresh perspective on life at Longbourn, Jo Baker goes behind the scenes and down the stairs to introduce the servants who kept the household running and the Bennets comfortable and blissfully oblivious to everyday toil. The staff at Longbourn is in many ways a family: Mrs. Hill, the motherly housekeeper; her husband, who sees to tasks both inside and outside the mansion; Sarah, the hardworking housemaid; and young Polly, the naïve, often distracted assistant to Mrs. Hill and Sarah. When a new footman named James Smith arrives, things change for all of them-especially for the independent-minded Sarah, whose initial disdain for James gives way to feelings she has never experienced before. As the household frets over the future of the family estate, the Bennet girls navigate the complexities of finding husbands, and Sarah awakens to her own romantic choices. Jo Baker reveals both the vast distance between and intimate connections among the inhabitants of Longbourn. A brilliant reimagining of Austen's beloved novel, *Longbourn* is also a portrait of the disappointments, dreams, struggles, and secrets of the lower classes that stands entirely on its own.

"Rich, engrossing, and filled with fascinating observations. . . . If you are a Jane Austen fan . . . you will devour Jo Baker's ingenious Longbourn."
—O, *The Oprah Magazine*

ABOUT THE AUTHOR: **Jo Baker** was born in Lancashire, England. She is the author of *The Undertow, The Mermaid's Child,* and *The Telling.*

June 2014 | Trade Paperback | Fiction | 352 pp | $15.95 | ISBN 9780345806970
Vintage | randomhouse.com

CONVERSATION STARTERS

1. "He was such a frustrating mixture of helpfulness, courtesy and incivility that she could indeed form no clear notion of him" (39). What lies at the heart of Sarah's confusion about James? Are her feelings based on misapprehensions of James's attitude toward her?

2. Despite the great difference between their stations in life, in what ways are both Sarah and Elizabeth defined by the social strictures of the time? Are their assumptions about what they can and cannot achieve dictated by society or do they reflect their individual personalities?

3. Discuss the significance of the discoveries Sarah makes when she explores James's room (64-65). What does the scene reveal about Sarah's grasp of the emotional complexities behind James's carefully constructed façade? In what respects is this a turning point?

4. What similarities are there between the progression of the courtships of Sarah and James and of Elizabeth and Darcy? What part does pride play in the way Sarah initially responds to James? Is Elizabeth guilty of the same kind of misplaced pride in her initial rejection of Darcy?

5. In addition to the descriptions of the backbreaking work the servants perform, how does Baker illustrate the more subtle yet no less humiliating aspects of being a servant? What interactions between the Bennets and the staff bring out the true nature of the relationship between the classes?

6. Baker continues her story a bit beyond the ending of *Pride and Prejudice*. Do you find her speculations about what happens to Mr. and Mrs. Bennet, their daughter Mary, Mr. and Mrs. Hill, and Polly, satisfying (325-27)?

7. Does a reader's enjoyment of *Longbourn* depend on a familiarity with *Pride and Prejudice*? How does Baker assert an independent voice and vision while using the framework of Austen's novel?

8. Several books inspired by *Pride and Prejudice* have been published. How does *Longbourn* compare to other books you have read about the Bennets and Darcys? Why have reworkings of Austen become so popular?

THE LOVE AFFAIRS OF NATHANIEL P.

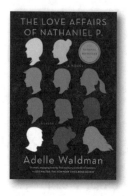

Adelle Waldman

A debut novel by a brilliant young woman about the romantic life of a brilliant young man.

Writer Nate Piven's star is rising. After several lean and striving years, he has his pick of both magazine assignments and women: Juliet, the hotshot business reporter; Elisa, his gorgeous ex-girlfriend, now friend; and Hannah, "almost universally regarded as nice and smart, or smart and nice," who holds her own in conversation with his friends. When one relationship grows more serious, Nate is forced to consider what it is he really wants.

In Nate's 21st-century literary world, wit and conversation are not at all dead. Is romance? Novelist Adelle Waldman plunges into the psyche of a flawed, sometimes infuriating modern man—one who thinks of himself as beyond superficial judgment, yet constantly struggles with his own status anxiety, who is drawn to women, yet has a habit of letting them down in ways that may just make him an emblem of our times. With tough-minded intelligence and wry good humor *The Love Affairs of Nathaniel P.* is an absorbing tale of one young man's search for happiness—and an inside look at how he really thinks about women, sex and love.

"Adelle Waldman just may be this generation's Jane Austen."
—The Boston Globe

ABOUT THE AUTHOR: **Adelle Waldman** is a graduate of Brown University and Columbia University's journalism school. She worked as a reporter at the *New Haven Register* and the *Cleveland Plain Dealer,* and wrote a column for the *Wall Street Journal's* website. Her articles also have appeared in *The New York Times Book Review, The New Republic, Slate,* and *The Wall Street Journal,* among other national publications. She lives in Brooklyn, New York.

May 2014 | Trade Paperback | Fiction | 256 pp | $15.00 | ISBN 9781250050458
Picador | us.macmillan.com | adellewaldman.com

CONVERSATION STARTERS

1. How does Nate see himself, and how does this differ from the way his girlfriends see him? What is your view of Nate? Does he come off as pretentious? As a womanizer? Are you able to sympathize with his thoughts or actions? If you had to summarize what his main character flaw is, what would you say?

2. "Dating is probably the most fraught human interaction there is. You're sizing people up to see if they're worth your time and attention, and they're doing the same to you . . . We submit ourselves to these intimate inspections and simultaneously inflict them on others and try to keep our psyches intact." Do you agree with this summary of the nature of dating? Is it as overwhelming as it is described, or is it really not "that big of a deal" as Nate believes?

3. The book delves into the psyche of a man, yet it is written by a woman. What effect does this have on the overall conversation and tone of the narrative? How would it be different if a man had written the book?

4. Do the male and female characters in the book seem to behave in ways that conform to or differ from our evolving conceptions of gender roles? Does the book present a world in which men and women are equal? If not, what inequalities seem to persist?

5. Despite the fact that Nate initially found Hannah to be different from the other women he dated, his attitude toward her eventually begins to change. Do you think there is a legitimate reason for this change? Or does it reflect a limitation of Nate's? What do you think keeps the relationship going after the initial excitement has died down?

6. Discuss the idea of being seen through others' eyes in the context of the book. Throughout this novel, we see Nate's views on others and also his thoughts on how people view him. Do you feel that it is a natural feeling to be validated through others' opinions? Do we need reassurance from our partners in order to accept ourselves?

7. What do you think Nate takes away from each relationship, if anything? At the end of the novel, is Nate in a relationship that will last?

THE LOWLAND

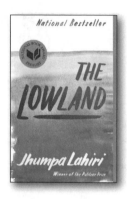

Jhumpa Lahiri

New York Times Book Review Notable Book • Time Top Fiction Book • NPR "Great Read" • Chicago Tribune Best Book • USA Today Best Book • People Top 10 Book • Barnes and Noble Best New Book • Good Reads Best Book • Kirkus Best Fiction Book • Slate Favorite Book • Christian Science Monitor Best Fiction Book • National Book Award Finalist • 2013 Man Booker Prize Shortlist

Subhash and Udayan, brothers born fifteen months apart, come of age in post-World War II Calcutta. The newly won independence from Britain and the partition establishing Pakistan as a separate country has left India struggling with political turmoil; the age-old problems of poverty and class divisions remain a source of social unrest and conflict. The brothers share the adventures and innocent rivalries of childhood, but when Udayan, the younger, more daring brother, joins a radical political group in college, the tie between them begins to unravel. Subhash chooses a different, safer path, leaving India to do postgraduate research in oceanography in Rhode Island. As Subhash slowly adjusts to life in America, Udayan becomes ever more deeply involved with the revolutionary movement at home. In a letter to Subhash, he writes of his marriage to Gauri and his hope that his brother will come home one day to meet her. But it is a shattering tragedy that eventually brings Subhash back to his childhood home and into a strange, life-changing relationship with the young woman who captured his brother's heart.

"[Lahiri's] finest work so far. . . At once unsettling and generous. . . Shattering and satisfying in equal measure." —The New York Review of Books

ABOUT THE AUTHOR: **Jhumpa Lahiri** is the author of three previous works of fiction: *Interpreter of Maladies, The Namesake* and, most recently, *Unaccustomed Earth.*

June 2014 | Trade Paperback | Fiction | 432 pp | $15.95 | ISBN 9780307278265
Vintage | randomhouse.com | jhumpalahiri.net

CONVERSATION STARTERS

1. "Udayan was the one brave enough to ask them for autographs...He was blind to self-constraints, like an animal incapable of perceiving certain colors. But Subhash strove to minimize his existence, as other animals merged with bark or blades of grass" (11). How do the differences between the boys both strengthen and strain the tie between them?

2. Does Subhash's decision to make it "his mission to obey (his parents), given that it wasn't possible to surprise or impress them. That was what Udayan did" (11) follow a pattern common among siblings? What part do their parents play in fostering the roles each boy assumes?

3. What does Udayan's reaction to Subhash's decision to go to America (30) and Subhash's admission that he wanted to leave Calcutta "not only for the sake of his education but also . . . to take a step Udayan never would" (40) convey about the balance between admiration and envy, support and competition, that underlies their relationship? Do you think that Udayan is manipulative, or does Subhash misread him?

4. What aspects of the immigrant experience are captured in Subhash's first impressions of Rhode Island? How do his feelings about school and his roommate bring to light both his pleasure and uncertainties about his new independence? In what ways does Udayan's letter add to his ambivalence about the choice he has made (47)?

5. What does Subhash's affair with Holly convey about his transition to life in America (65-83)? What does it reveal about his emotional ties to his old life and family?

6. The novel presents many kinds of parents—present and absent, supportive and reluctant. What questions does the novel raise about the challenges and real meaning of being a parent?

7. In an interview, Lahiri said, "As Udayan's creator, I don't condone what he does. On the other hand, I understand the frustration he feels, his sense of injustice, and his impulse to change society" (NewYorker.com) Does the novel help you see more clearly the reasons for destruction and deaths revolutionary forces perpetrate to attain their goals? How do you feel about Udayan after reading the novel's last chapter?

MADAME PICASSO

Anne Girard

The mesmerizing and untold story of Eva Gouel, the unforgettable woman who stole the heart of the greatest artist of our time.

When Eva Gouel moves to Paris from the countryside, she is full of ambition and dreams of stardom. Though young and inexperienced, she manages to find work as a costumer at the famous Moulin Rouge, and it is here that she first catches the attention of Pablo Picasso, a rising star in the art world.

A brilliant but eccentric artist, Picasso sets his sights on Eva, and Eva can't help but be drawn into his web. But what starts as a torrid affair soon evolves into what will become the first great love of Picasso's life. With sparkling insight and passion, *Madame Picasso* introduces us to a dazzling heroine, taking us from the salon of Gertrude Stein to the glamorous Moulin Rouge and inside the studio and heart of one of the most enigmatic and iconic artists of the twentieth century.

"[Filled] with colorful accounts of the social scene in turn-of-the-century Paris...[Girard] ably marries history, art, and romance here as Eva remains broadly rendered and famous figures shine." —Booklist

"Early twentieth century Paris and Picasso's lost love come to enchanted, vivid life in Madame Picasso. *With a deft eye for detail and deep understanding for her protagonists, Anne Girard captures the earnest young woman who enthralled the famous artist and became his unsung muse."*
—**C.W. Gortner, bestselling author of** *The Queen's Vow*

ABOUT THE AUTHOR: **Anne Girard** is a writer and historian with degrees in English literature and clinical psychology. She has spent extensive time in Paris and lives in California with her husband and children.

September 2014 | Trade Paperback | Fiction | 432 pp | $14.95 | ISBN 9780778316350
Harlequin MIRA | harlequin.com | annegirardauthor.com

CONVERSATION STARTERS

1. Fernande Olivier and Eva Gouel were both, for a time, the object of Pablo Picasso's obsession. How were the two women different? How were they similar? What do you think were the elements that drew him to them?

2. In the novel, a fair amount of attention is paid to Guillaume Apollinaire's poetry. What do you think Eva found so appealing in it?

3. At one point in the story, Eva finally sleeps with Louis. Did you sympathize with her motivation, or did you feel sorry for Louis, who was being misled? Were her actions out of self-preservation or defiance? Did you find Louis Markus a sympathetic character?

4. A tense conversation takes place in Céret between Picasso, his former mistress Fernande and their friends, who side with her. Did you find yourself sympathizing with Fernande at that point in the story? Did you believe that she truly had learned her lesson and wished to reconcile with him? If so, what made her a sympathetic figure for you?

5. While Eva was immortalized in several of Picasso's Cubist works, there is no known classically painted, or sketched, image of her by Picasso, yet there are many of Fernande and every other prominent woman in his life before and after. What are the possible reasons for this?

6. What did you make of the way some of Picasso's friends, such as the Pichots, refused to betray Fernande for Eva, even knowing that Fernande had been unfaithful, while others, such as Max, Gertrude and Alice, warmed to Eva and even became her devoted friends? Is it impossible to be an impartial friend in that sort of circumstance?

7. Religion is a common theme in the book. What do you make of Picasso's troubled spiritual journey, from his feelings of anger after the death of his sister to his feelings of betrayal over the impending loss of Eva? How do you think his feelings of spite toward God contributed to his actions throughout the novel, particularly during Eva's illness?

8. Prior to reading Madame Picasso, what were your perceptions of Pablo Picasso as a historical figure? Were those perceptions informed by the many biographies of his life, by popular culture (i.e. movies or television documentaries), or his art? How, if at all, were those perceptions changed by reading this novel?

MADDADDAM

Margaret Atwood

A *New York Times* **Notable Book, A** *Washington Post* **Notable Book, A Best Book of the Year:** *The Guardian,* **NPR,** *The Christian Science Monitor, The Globe* **and** *Mail*

Bringing together *Oryx* and *Crake* and *The Year of the Flood*, this thrilling conclusion to Margaret Atwood's speculative fiction trilogy points toward the ultimate endurance of community, and love.

Months after the Waterless Flood pandemic has wiped out most of humanity, Toby and Ren have rescued their friend Amanda from the vicious Painballers. They return to the MaddAddamite cob house, newly fortified against man and giant pigoon alike. Accompanying them are the Crakers, the gentle, quasi-human species engineered by the brilliant but deceased Crake. Their reluctant prophet, Snowman-the-Jimmy, is recovering from a debilitating fever, so it's left to Toby to preach the Craker theology, with Crake as Creator. She must also deal with cultural misunderstandings, terrible coffee, and her jealousy over her lover, Zeb Zeb has been searching for Adam One, founder of the God's Gardeners, the pacifist green religion from which Zeb broke years ago to lead the MaddAddamites in active resistance against the destructive CorpSeCorps. But now, under threat of a Painballer attack, the MaddAddamites must fight back with the aid of their newfound allies, some of whom have four trotters. At the center of *MaddAddam* is the story of Zeb's dark and twisted past, which contains a lost brother, a hidden murder, a bear, and a bizarre act of revenge.

"Lights a fire from the fears of our age. . . . Miraculously balances humor, outrage, and beauty." —*The New York Times Book Review*

ABOUT THE AUTHOR: **Margaret Atwood,** whose work has been published in thirty-five countries, is the author of more than forty books of fiction, poetry, and critical essays.

August 2014 | Trade Paperback | Fiction | 416 pp | $15.95 | ISBN 9780307455482
Anchor | randomhouse.com | margaretatwood.ca

CONVERSATION STARTERS

1. Why are Adam and Zeb so different? Or, are they more similar than they first seem?

2. The MaddAddamites set about building a basic community for themselves, one that meets the need for food, clothing, shelter, and an energy source. If you were in this position, would you do things differently? Should children be taught elementary survival skills?

3. What comment, if any, do you think Margaret Atwood is making about environmentalism in this book, through organizations like Bearlift? Or does Bearlift suffer simply from the human flaws that appear in all organizations, no matter how well-meaning?

4. The Internet has an almost physical presence in *MaddAddam*—the "lilypads," the game Intestinal Parasites. Do you think this is where the Internet is heading? Is it becoming a "real" entity of its own?

5. Is Toby right to trust Zeb? Do you think Zeb's feelings for Toby are genuine?

6. Toby teaches Blackbeard to write. Is that a good thing or a bad thing? What consequences do you think this will have for the Crakers and their new world?

7. Margaret Atwood's trilogy often portrays humans and our future grimly, but it is also both funny and profane. Is Atwood's gallows humor effective?

8. What parallels do you see between the events of *MaddAddam* and recent events in our real world? Are Atwood's three dystopian books exaggerated or could they really be our future?

9. Despite having seemed violent and disposed to eat humans, the Pigoons ultimately display more compassion than many of the humans in *MaddAddam*. Is that because the Pigoons are animals, or is it because of the implanted human tissue in their brains?

10. The Crakers seek stories from Jimmy and Toby to explain the world. What do these stories say about how myths are formed? Is the desire for religion innate within us? What do you think *MaddAddam* is saying about our need for gods and how religions are created?

THE MAGICIAN'S LIE

Greer Macallister

The Amazing Arden is the most notorious female illusionist of her day, renowned for sawing a man in half. One night, with policeman Virgil Holt in the audience, she swaps her saw for a fire ax. A new trick or an all-too-real murder? When a dead body is discovered, the answer seems clear. But under Holt's interrogation, what Arden's story reveals is both unbelievable and spellbinding. Even handcuffed and alone, she is far from powerless. During one eerie night, Holt must decide whether to turn Arden in or set her free… and it will take all he has to see through the smoke and mirrors.

"*A little taste of* The Night Circus, *and little salt of* Water for Elephants, The Magician's Lie *by Greer Macallister is a wonderful combination of magic, vaudeville and the drama of a secret life. Is her story real, or an illusion? Are her magic acts true, or a magician's lie?*" —**Annie Philbrick, Bank Square Books, Mystic CT**

"*The Magician's Lie is a rich tale of heart-stopping plot turns, glittering prose, and a cast of complex, compelling characters. Reader beware: those who enter Macallister's delicious world of magic and mystery won't wish to leave.*" —**Allison Pataki,** *New York Times* **bestselling author of** *The Traitor's Wife*

ABOUT THE AUTHOR: **Greer Macallister** was raised in the Midwest. She is a poet, short story writer, playwright and novelist whose work has appeared in publications such as *The North American Review, The Missouri Review,* and *The Messenger.* Her plays have been performed at American University, where she earned her MFA in Creative Writing. She currently lives with her family in Brooklyn.

January 2015 | Hardcover | Fiction | 320 pp | $23.99 | ISBN 9781402298684
Sourcebooks Landmark | sourcebooks.com | greermacallister.com

CONVERSATION STARTERS

1. The action of *The Magician's Lie* alternates between a single night in 1905, with Arden imprisoned by Officer Holt, and the story of her life that Arden is telling him, which ranges over a number of years. Did you find one storyline more intriguing than the other?

2. As the novel opens, Virgil Holt has just received the bad news that the doctor won't operate on the bullet lodged near his spine. Do you think he would have behaved differently if he were uninjured?

3. "The law is perfect. The men in charge of executing it are not." Officer Holt decides early on that if Arden is innocent, it's his responsibility to free her instead of turning her in, since the courts can't be trusted. Do you think he should have turned her in either way?

4. After Ray breaks Arden's leg, preventing her from dancing for Bonfanti and entering ballet school, she says, "There were so many what-ifs." What do you think would have happened if he hadn't done this?

5. Arden is suspicious of rich people at several points in the book, and feels she can only fit in at Biltmore as a servant. Yet she was raised in wealth by her grandparents. Why do you feel she identifies so strongly with the life she led starting at age 12 instead of her life before that?

6. Adelaide Herrmann isn't close to the people who work for her, except for Arden. Why does Adelaide choose Arden as her protégé?

7. "I let him damage me and try to heal that damage, with his delusions of magic. I talk a good game about risk, but when it all came down to it, I chose something awful and safe." When Ray threatens Clyde, Arden gives up, and allows him to hurt her and essentially keep her captive. Did she have other options? What could she have done instead?

8. As the book ends, Holt has resolved to begin living his life anew, without letting his fear of death get in the way. Do you feel he has been profoundly changed by his experience with Arden? Or do you think these resolutions will fade in the harsh light of day? Where do you think Arden and Clyde's story might go from the ending onward?

9. Whether or not Arden is telling Officer Holt the truth is a key question throughout the book. When did you most believe her? Were there times where you were sure she was lying?

THE MINOR ADJUSTMENT BEAUTY SALON

No. 1 Ladies' Detective Agency (14)

Alexander McCall Smith

Fans around the world adore the bestselling No. 1 Ladies' Detective Agency series and Precious Ramotswe, Botswana's premier lady detective. Ramotswe navigates her cases and personal life with wisdom, humor, and help from her loyal associate, Grace, and the occasional cup of tea. Modern ideas get tangled up with traditional ones in the fourteenth installment in the beloved No. 1 Ladies' Detective Agency series. Precious Ramotswe has taken on two puzzling cases. First she is approached by the lawyer Mma Sheba, who is the executor of a deceased farmer's estate. Mma Sheba has a feeling that the young man who has stepped forward may be falsely impersonating the farmer's nephew in order to claim his inheritance. Then the proprietor of the Minor Adjustment Beauty Salon comes to Mma Ramotswe for advice. The opening of her new salon has been shadowed by misfortune. Not only has she received a bad omen in the mail, but rumors are swirling that the salon is using dangerous products that burn people's skin. Also, associate detective Mma Makutsi, of ninety-seven per cent fame, is pregnant! With genuine warmth, sympathy, and wit, Alexander McCall Smith explores questions about married life, parenthood, grief, and the importance of the traditions that shape and guide our lives.

"The intrepid proprietor of the No. 1 Ladies' Detective Agency in Botswana is determined to remain as steadfast as a constellation in the night sky. But Alexander McCall Smith's beloved sleuth comes to accept the inevitability of change in The Minor Adjustment Beauty Salon." *—The New York Times Book Review*

ABOUT THE AUTHOR: **Alexander McCall Smith** is the author of the beloved, bestselling No. 1 Ladies' Detective Agency series, the Isabel Dalhousie series, the Portuguese Irregular Verbs series, the 44 Scotland Street series, and the Corduroy Mansions series.

June 2014 | Trade Paperback | Fiction | 272 pp | $14.95 | ISBN 9780307473004
Anchor | randomhouse.com | alexandermccallsmith.co.uk

CONVERSATION STARTERS

1. What is the novel saying about friendship, in particular the friendship between Mma Ramotswe and Makutsi?

2. *Kirkus Reviews* has compared Alexander McCall Smith's books to "a warm, understated serving of comfort food." How is this novel like comfort food? And what role does comforting food play in McCall Smith's No. 1 Ladies' Detective Agency novels?

3. Mma Ramotswe believes that "babies—ordinary babies—liked to look at the sky, or watch chickens, or suck on blankets. They did not want to add." What do you think about this view of child rearing? If you've read 44 Scotland Street, compare this view with that of Bertie's mother.

4. Take a closer look at McCall Smith's chapter titles. What do they add to the story? Do you think the author has fun coming up with them?

5. Discuss superstitions in this book and in the No. 1 Ladies' Detective Agency series more generally. There are still many people in Botswana (and throughout the world) with strong local superstitions. What are Mma Ramotswe's and Mma Makutsi's views on them?

6. Though the novel celebrates the birth of Mma Makutsi's baby, it mourns the loss of Mma Ramotswe's and Gwithie's. What is the place of grief in this novel?

7. "It's just that sometimes it all gets too much for women and it would help a great deal if their husbands could be a little bit more modern," says Mma Potokwane to Mr. J.L.B. Matekoni. Discuss this quote. What do you think about the relationship between Mma Ramotswe and Mr. J.L.B. Matekoni? Is it a traditional relationship or a modern one? Compare this quote and the relationships in the novel in light of the cultural conversations around recent books such as Sheryl Sandberg's Lean In and Debora Spar's Wonder Women.

8. Mma Ramotswe holds back and doesn't tell Mma Makutsi how intensely she misses her while she's out on maternity leave, and how much she values their friendship. Why doesn't she say everything she was thinking, and why does the author say that, "our heart is not always able to say what it wants to say and frequently has to content itself with less"? Why is the word not spoken just as important as what is voiced?

MONDAY, MONDAY

Elizabeth Crook

In this gripping, emotionally charged novel, a tragedy in Texas changes the course of three lives. On an oppressively hot Monday in August of 1966, a student and former marine named Charles Whitman hauled a footlocker of guns to the top of the University of Texas tower and began firing on pedestrians below. Before it was over, sixteen people had been killed and thirty-two wounded. It was the first mass shooting of civilians on a campus in American history. Monday, Monday follows three students caught up in the massacre: Shelly, who leaves her math class and walks directly into the path of the bullets, and two cousins, Wyatt and Jack, who heroically rush from their classrooms to help the victims. On this searing day, a relationship begins that will eventually entangle these three young people in a forbidden love affair, an illicit pregnancy, and a vow of secrecy that will span forty years. Reunited decades after the tragedy, they will be forced to confront the event that changed their lives and that has silently and persistently ruled the lives of their children. With electrifying storytelling and the powerful sense of destiny found in Ann Patchett's *Bel Canto*, and with the epic sweep of Jess Walter's *Beautiful Ruins*, Elizabeth Crook's *Monday, Monday* explores the ways in which we sustain ourselves and one another when the unthinkable happens.

"...[E]loquent...Monday, Monday opens with a random, hideous act, but thankfully the novel isn't about that moment or the gunman. The shooting sets in motion an entire lifetime of relationships; from an act of violence springs love, friendship, loss, forgiveness and survival." —San Antonio Express News

ABOUT THE AUTHOR: **Elizabeth Crook** is the author of three previous novels. *The Night Journal* won a Spur Award from Western Writers of America and a WILLA Literary Award from Women Writing the West. She lives in Austin with her family.

April 2014 | Hardcover | Fiction | 352 pp | $26.00 | ISBN 9780374228828
Sarah Crichton Books | us.macmillan.com | elizabethcrookbooks.com

CONVERSATION STARTERS

1. Before reading the book did you know about the incident of the University of Texas sniper in 1966? Do you know anyone who was personally touched by the tragedy?

2. When you see mass shootings on the news today, do you consider how you would react if you were there? Do you believe you would put yourself in harm's way to aid others, as Jack and Wyatt did?

3. Why do you think there was such a long time span between the UT tower shootings in 1966 and the tragedy at Columbine in 1999, and then, after Columbine, such a rapid escalation in school shootings?

4. Shelly and Wyatt both suffer guilt about their love affair. Do you feel that the powerful and unique circumstance in which they first met excuses the affair, or merely explains it?

5. Which characters, if any, might have been happier at the end of the book if Wyatt had initially divorced Elaine, married Shelly, and together they had raised Carlotta?

6. Was Shelly wrong to want to keep Carlotta in her life? Was it a selfish request she made of Jack and Delia during the encounter at Aquarena Springs, given that she could not see how it would turn out? Was it selfish, or generous, toward Carlotta? Would you have made the same request?

7. If you were in Carlotta's place, would you have wanted to search for your biological parents earlier in your life than she chose to? Or perhaps not at all?

8. Of all the scenes in the book, which one, for you, was the most emotional?

9. Extraordinary events in the course of the story cause the characters to evolve dramatically. With which character, by the end, did you most identify?

10. What do you think is the overall theme of the book? What is the commentary on life?

11. Does the final scene, in which Shelly goes up into the tower and looks down at Austin and thinks back on her life and the ways it was changed by what happened from the tower, seem to you sad, or uplifting?

MY ACCIDENTAL JIHAD

Krista Bremer

Fifteen years ago, Krista Bremer was a surfer and an aspiring journalist who dreamed of a comfortable American life of adventure, romance, and opportunity. Then, on a running trail in North Carolina, she met Ismail, sincere, passionate, kind, yet from a very different world. Raised a Muslim—one of eight siblings born in an impoverished fishing village in Libya—his faith informed his life. When she and Ismail made the decision to become a family, Krista embarked on a journey she never could have imagined, an accidental *jihad*: a quest for spiritual and intellectual growth that would open her mind, and more important, her heart.

"A bold piece of writing (and thinking) by an incredibly brave woman." —**Elizabeth Gilbert, author of *The Signature of All Things***

"Lucid, heartfelt and profoundly humane, My Accidental Jihad navigates the boundaries of religion and politics to arrive at the universal experience of love." —**G. Willow Wilson, author of *Alif the Unseen***

"Utterly absorbing . . . A beautiful book." —**Cheryl Strayed, author of *Wild***

ABOUT THE AUTHOR: **Krista Bremer** is the associate publisher of *The Sun* magazine and the recipient of a Rona Jaffe Foundation award. Her essay on which this book is based, "My Accidental Jihad," received a Pushcart Prize. Her essays have been published in *O: The Oprah Magazine, More* magazine, and *The Sun,* and she's been featured on NPR and in the PBS series *Arab American Stories.*

December 2014 | Trade Paperback | Nonfiction | 304 pp | $15.95
ISBN 9781616204495 | Algonquin Books | algonquin.com | kristabremer.com

CONVERSATION STARTERS

1. How does Krista Bremer's definition of *jihad* differ from its common usage in the media—and what does jihad have to do with her love story?

2. How does Bremer's understanding of the hijab (head covering) change when she is in Libya? What benefits and drawbacks does she discover in modest Muslim clothing—and what benefits and drawbacks does she identify from the physical exposure she experienced growing up in Southern California?

3. When she first arrives in Libya, Bremer pities her female Muslim relatives—but she is surprised to discover that they pity her as well. Which aspects of her Western life might they pity, and how does her time in Libya make her rethink notions of freedom and oppression?

4. How does Bremer's understanding of feminism and surrender change over the course of the book? Is surrender at odds with feminism? Is surrender synonymous with defeat?

5. In what ways does Bremer's marriage change her opinions about diversity and tolerance?

6. Bremer encounters a dying grandmother during a family gathering in Libya. How does this woman's experience differ from aging and dying in the United States? What benefits and drawbacks can you identify in her experience?

7. What are specific examples of Islamophobia in the book? What does Bremer's experience convey about intolerance and the perception of otherness in the west?

8. In many ways, this book is about the search for home. What does Bremer convey about home in the final chapter—and do you agree with her definition?

9. Would you call this a strong marriage? Why or why not?

10. Do you agree or disagree with Bremer's assertion that every relationship is bicultural? Which aspects of her struggle are particular to her marriage, and which aspects are universal?

NIGHT IN SHANGHAI

Nicole Mones

Sailing to Shanghai in 1936 to lead a black jazz orchestra, Thomas Greene goes from being flat broke in segregated Baltimore to living in a mansion with servants of his own, and from the classical piano pieces he was trained to play to the toe-tapping swing of the big band era. Song Yuhua is refined, educated, and bonded since age eighteen to Shanghai's most powerful crime boss in payment for her father's gambling debts. Outwardly submissive, she burns with rage, longs for escape, and risks her life spying on her master for the Communist Party. With Shanghai shattered by the Japanese invasion, Thomas and Song find their way to each other and forge a bond from which neither can back down in the turbulent years that follow. Torn between music and survival, freedom and commitment, love and war, they navigate the dangers leading to world war until the moment when they must cast their lots in Night in Shanghai's final, impossible choice.

"With a magician's sleight of hand, Nicole Mones conjures up the jazz-filled, complex, turbulent world of Shanghai just before World War II. A rich and thoroughly captivating read." —**Gail Tsukiyama, author of** *The Samurai's Garden*

"What an incredible thing Mones does in this novel of the compelling, sexy, rich and complicated world of historical Shanghai." —**Marisa Silver, author of** *Mary Coin*

ABOUT THE AUTHOR: **Nicole Mones** is the prize-winning author of three previous novels, *The Last Chinese Chef, Lost in Translation,* and *A Cup of Light,* which have been published in more than twenty-five countries.

March 2014 | Hardcover | Fiction | 288 pp | $25.00 | ISBN 9780547516172
Houghton Mifflin Harcourt | hmhco.com | nicolemones.com

CONVERSATION STARTERS

1. Before the novel begins, Mones offers this Chinese adage: "An inch of time is worth an inch of gold. An inch of gold cannot buy an inch of time." This saying comes from an ancient text that imparted life lessons to children. What lesson do you take from it? What do you think it meant to Thomas, Song, and Lin?

2. Chiang Kai-shek pursued a policy of "first internal pacification, then external resistance" (2), because he thought the Communists posed a greater threat to China than the Japanese invasion. Looking back from today, do you think he was correct? Or do you think Song was right to build her life around opposing this?

3. Song says, "Jazz was the sun around which this paradise revolved" (2). In the 1930s, jazz was very popular around the world, perhaps the defining music of its era. What do you think has been the defining music of your era? How has that music shaped and enriched your life?

4. Musician Charlie Parker said, "Music is your experience, your thoughts, your wisdom. If you don't live it, it won't come out of your horn." What living does Thomas have to accomplish before he can finally throw off his fetters at the piano? What makes it possible for him?

5. "I was reborn first through the movement, and then again, through him. After our time together I knew, no matter where the two of us were, that while he lived, I would never be alone. I knew I would return to him. But just as much, I knew I needed to go north" (180). Many people struggle to find a balance between love and self-actualization. Do you think Thomas and Song made the right decisions? What do you think would have happened to them, and to their feelings for each other, if they had chosen differently?

6. All the major events in *Night in Shanghai* actually happened, and except for Thomas Greene, Song Yuhua, Lin Ming, and David Epstein, almost all the book's characters really lived. The novel ends with a nonfiction-style epilogue. Did the novel's fidelity to true events affect your perception of the story? Do you think there is something different about a story based on true events?

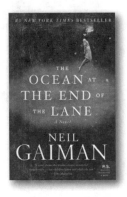

THE OCEAN AT THE END OF THE LANE

Neil Gaiman

A brilliantly imaginative and poignant fairy tale from the modern master of wonder and terror, *The Ocean at the End of the Lane* is Neil Gaiman's first new novel for adults since his #1 New York Times bestseller *Anansi Boys*.

A middle-aged man returns to his childhood home to attend a funeral. Although the house he lived in is long gone, he is drawn to the farm at the end of the road, where, when he was seven, he encountered a most remarkable girl, Lettie Hempstock, and her mother and grandmother. He hasn't thought of Lettie in decades, and yet as he sits by the pond (a pond that she'd claimed was an ocean) behind the ramshackle old farmhouse where she once lived, the unremembered past comes flooding back. And it is a past too strange, too frightening, too dangerous to have happened to anyone, let alone a small boy.

A groundbreaking work as delicate as a butterfly's wing and as menacing as a knife in the dark, *The Ocean at the End of the Lane* is told with a rare understanding of all that makes us human, and shows the power of stories to reveal and shelter us from the darkness inside and out.

"His prose is simple but poetic, his world strange but utterly believable—if he was South American we would call this magic realism rather than fantasy." —*The Times* (**London**)

ABOUT THE AUTHOR: **Neil Gaiman** is the #1 *New York Times* bestselling author of more than twenty books for readers of all ages, and the recipient of numerous literary awards, including the Shirley Jackson Award and the Locus Award for Best Novelette for his story "The Truth Is a Cave in the Black Mountains." Originally from England, he now lives in America.

June 2014 | Trade Paperback | Fiction | 208 pp | $14.90 | ISBN 9780062255662
William Morrow Paperbacks | harpercollins.com | neilgaiman.com

CONVERSATION STARTERS

1. It would be easy to think of the Hempstocks as the "triple goddess" (the Maiden, the Mother, and the Crone) of popular mythology. In what ways do they conform to those roles? In what ways are they different?

2. The narrator has returned to his hometown for a funeral (we never learn whose). Do you think that framing his childhood story with a funeral gives this story a pessimistic rather than optimistic outlook?

3. Because the narrator is male and most of the other characters are female, this story has the potential to become a stereotypical narrative where a man saves the day. How does the story avoid that pitfall?

4. The story juxtaposes the memories of childhood with the present of adulthood. In what ways do children perceive things differently than adults? Do you think there are situations in which a child's perspective can be more "truthful" than an adult's?

5. One of Ursula Monkton's main attributes is that she always tries to give people what they want. Why is this not always a good thing? What does Ursula want? How does Ursula use people's desires against them to get what she wants?

6. One of the many motivators for the characters in this story is loneliness. What characters seem to suffer from loneliness? How do adults and children respond to loneliness in different ways? In the same ways?

7. On page 18, the narrator tells us that his father often burnt their toast and always ate it with apparent relish. He also tells us that later in life, his father admitted that he had never actually liked burnt toast, but ate it to avoid waste, and that his father's confession made the narrator's entire childhood feel like a lie: "it was as if one of the pillars of belief that my world had been built upon had crumbled into dry sand." What other "pillars of belief" from childhood does he discover to be false? How do these discoveries affect him?

8. When the narrative returns to the present, Old Mrs. Hempstock tells our narrator, "You stand two of you lot next to each other, and you could be continents away for all it means anything" (173). What does she mean by this? Why is it "easier" for people, our narrator especially, to forget certain things that are difficult to reconcile?

THE PARIS ARCHITECT

Charles Belfoure

Like most gentiles in Nazi-occupied Paris, architect Lucien Bernard has little empathy for the Jews. So when a wealthy industrialist offers him a large sum of money to devise secret hiding places for Jews, Lucien struggles with the choice of risking his life for a cause he doesn't really believe in. Ultimately he can't resist the challenge and begins designing expertly concealed hiding spaces—behind a painting, within a column, or inside a drainpipe—detecting possibilities invisible to the average eye. But when one of his clever hiding spaces fails horribly and the immense suffering of Jews becomes incredibly personal, he can no longer deny reality. Written by an expert whose knowledge imbues every page, this story becomes more gripping with every life the architect tries to save.

"I read so many books this year that I loved…but my favorite was The Paris Architect. *A beautiful and elegant account of an ordinary man's unexpected and reluctant descent into heroism during the second world war."* —**Malcolm Gladwell,** *New York Times* **bestselling author of** *David and Goliath*

"Architect and debut author Belfoure's portrayal of Vichy France is both disturbing and captivating, and his beautiful tale demonstrates that while human beings are capable of great atrocities, they have a capacity for tremendous acts of courage as well." —*Library Journal*

ABOUT THE AUTHOR: An architect by profession, **Charles Belfoure** has published several architectural histories, one of which won a Graham Foundation Grant for architectural research. He graduated from the Pratt Institute and Columbia University, and he taught at Pratt as well as at Goucher College in Baltimore, Maryland. His area of specialty is historic preservation. He has been a freelance writer for the *Baltimore Sun* and *The New York Times*. He lives in Maryland.

July 2014 | Trade Paperback | Fiction | 384 pp | $14.99 | ISBN 9781402294150
Sourcebooks Landmark | sourcebooks.com | theparisarchitect.com

CONVERSATION STARTERS

1. Why did the majority of people in France refuse to help the Jews during World War II?

2. In the beginning of the novel, Lucien didn't care about what happened to the Jews. Discuss how his character evolved throughout the novel. How did your opinion of him change?

3. Many spouses abandoned each other because one was Jewish. What did you think when Juliette Trenet's husband left her? Is there any defense for what he did?

4. One reason Lucien helped Jews was to get architectural commissions from Manet. Did you agree with the French Resistance? Did Lucien's love of design and the need to prove his talent cross the line into collaboration with the enemy?

5. Discuss the unusual relationship between Lucien and Herzog. Can two men from warring countries be friends?

6. Lucien was already taking an enormous risk by hiding Jews for Manet; why do you think he agreed to take in Pierre?

7. What was your impression of Father Jacques? What kind of role do you think faith plays throughout the novel?

8. Adele had no qualms about sleeping with the enemy. Why would she take such a risk?

9. Bette could have her pick of men but chose Lucien. Discuss what made him special in her eyes. What are the most important qualities you look for in a friend/significant other? Would you be willing to compromise on any of these qualities? For what?

10. If you were under the stairs in the Geibers' place during the Gestapo's search, how would you have reacted?

11. Schlegal was disappointed that the people he tortured always talked. What do you think were the motivations behind someone who talked and someone who didn't? If you were in a situation where someone was trying to get information from you, what would be the final straw to make you talk?

SEA CREATURES

Susanna Daniel

When Georgia Quillian returns to her hometown of Miami, her family in tow, she's hoping for a fresh start. They've left Illinois trailing scandal in their wake, fallout from her husband's severe sleep disorder. For months, their three-year-old son, Frankie, has refused to speak a word.

On a whim, Georgia takes a job as an errand runner for a reclusive artist, and suddenly the future offers new possibilities: time spent with her intense but kind employer might, it seems, help Frankie find the courage to speak—and help Georgia reconcile the woman she was with the woman she has become. But late that summer, as a hurricane bears down on South Florida, she must face the fact that her decisions may have put her only child in danger.

A gorgeous story that "satisfies on every level" (Amazon Best Book of the Month), *Sea Creatures* is a mesmerizing exploration of the high stakes of marriage and parenthood.

"A captivating, haunting novel about the complexities of the human heart and its attachments, terrain as slippery and beautiful and disaster prone as Daniel's South Florida." —**Abraham Verghese, author of *Cutting for Stone***

"There's a charmer at the heart of Sea Creatures*....Almost like an action-filled, emotional memoir....Gripping."* —*Associated Press*

About the Author: **Susanna Daniel** was born and raised in Miami, Florida. Her first novel, *Stiltsville*, was awarded the PEN/Bingham prize for debut fiction. She is a graduate of Columbia University and the Iowa Writers' Workshop, and lives in Madison, Wisconsin.

September 2014 | Trade Paperback | Fiction | 336 pp | $14.99 | ISBN 9780062219619
Harper Perennial | Harpercollins.com | susannadaniel.com

CONVERSATION STARTERS

1. At the book's opening, Georgia remarks, "It seems to me that what worries us most . . . is least likely to happen, while what is most likely is some unimagined event, and how do we prepare for that?" How would you answer this question?

2. Talk about Georgia and Graham's marriage. Are they happy? Could they ever be happy? Was it fair of her to have a child with him? While they are on vacation by themselves, Georgia calls Graham reckless. Is he?

3. Consider the men in Georgia's life: Graham, Charlie, Frankie, and her father. Each has distinctive characteristics and limitations. How do these aspects of their characters influence Georgia and her relationships with them?

4. What draws Georgia to Charlie? Might events have turned out differently if she'd never met him or would her marriage to Graham have changed anyway?

5. How would you cope with a child like Frankie? Is Georgia doing the right thing by using sign language? Compare Frankie's interaction with Charlie and with Graham. Why won't Graham sign with his son?

6. When Georgia meets Dr. Sonia, her new pediatrician, she tells her that she spends every waking minute with Frankie, and the doctor asks her why. Were you surprised at this question? Is a hovering parent necessarily a good parent?

7. What impact does receiving Charlie's mermaid sketch have on Georgia? Were they in love? Could anything have worked out between them?

8. In thinking back over the events involving Graham and Frankie's accident, Georgia asks, "Did I betray my own son?" What do you think? Could Frankie's accident have been prevented? What about Graham—was his fate choice or an accident?

9. Were you satisfied by the ending? Did it all work out the way it should have? Could it have been any different?

10. What is the significance of the title?

THE SIGNATURE OF ALL THINGS

Elizabeth Gilbert

In *The Signature of All Things*, Elizabeth Gilbert returns to fiction, inserting her inimitable voice into an enthralling story of love, adventure and discovery. Spanning much of the eighteenth and nineteenth centuries, the novel follows the fortunes of the extraordinary Whittaker family as led by the enterprising Henry Whittaker—a poor-born Englishman who makes a great fortune in the South American quinine trade, eventually becoming the richest man in Philadelphia. Born in 1800, Henry's brilliant daughter, Alma (who inherits both her father's money and his mind), ultimately becomes a botanist of considerable gifts herself. As Alma's research takes her deeper into the mysteries of evolution, she falls in love with a man named Ambrose Pike who makes incomparable paintings of orchids and who draws her in the exact opposite direction—into the realm of the spiritual, the divine, and the magical. Alma is a clear-minded scientist; Ambrose a utopian artist—but what unites this unlikely couple is a desperate need to understand the workings of this world and the mechanisms behind all life.

"Gilbert's sumptuous third novel, her first in thirteen years, draws openly on nineteenth-century forebears: Dickens, Eliot, and Henry James...Gilbert's prose is by turns flinty, funny, and incandescent." —The New Yorker

ABOUT THE AUTHOR: **Elizabeth Gilbert** grew up on a family Christmas-tree farm and went on to study political science at New York University. Her first book, a short-story collection titled *Pilgrims,* was a finalist for the PEN/Hemingway Award. Her first novel, *Stern Men,* was named a New York Times Notable Book. Her first nonfiction book, *The Last American Man,* was a finalist for both the National Book Award and the National Book Critics Circle Award. Gilbert achieved superstardom with her 2006 memoir *Eat, Pray, Love,* which has sold more than ten million copies. Her follow-up memoir, *Committed,* also topped the *New York Times* bestseller list. Gilbert lives in Frenchtown, New Jersey.

June 2014 | Trade Paperback | Fiction | 512 pp | $17.00 | ISBN 9780143125846
Penguin Books | penguin.com | elizabethgilbert.com

CONVERSATION STARTERS

1. *The Signature of All Things* takes as its first focus not the book's heroine, Alma Whittaker, but her rough-and-tumble father, Henry. Why do you think Elizabeth Gilbert made this choice in her narration, and why are the first fifty pages essential to the rest of the novel?

2. What role is played in the novel by the Whittakers' servant Hanneke de Groot? In what ways is her perspective essential to the story?

3. Alma postulates that there exist a variety of times, ranging from Human Time to Divine Time, with Geological Time and Moss Time as points in between (170-71). How might these different notions of time help to relate the world of science to the world of miracles? Is the miracle of creation just a natural process that took a very long time?

4. Gilbert plays with perspective, not only as it relates to time, but also as it relates to space. During the course of the novel, Alma must adapt to dealing with microscopic space as well as global space. At one point, when she plays the part of a comet in a tableau of the solar system, she even becomes figuratively a part of outer space. How do Gilbert's manipulations of space enrich the experience of reading the novel?

5. Instead of representing Prudence's abolitionist husband, Arthur Dixon, as an unambiguous hero, Gilbert presents him as a somewhat cracked fanatic, who impoverishes and even endangers his family in the name of an idea. What do you think of Gilbert's decision to place the cause of abolitionism, which modern thinkers usually find almost impossible to criticize, in the hands of an asocial, self-denying oddball?

6. Alma's decision to devote her life to studying mosses is compared to a "religious conversion" (163). In *The Signature of All Things*, science and religion often intertwine. Are they ever finally reconciled?

7. As Alma sails toward Tahiti, the whaler that carries her is nearly sunk by a storm. She feels that this brush with violent death was "the happiest experience of her life" (p. 336). Why might she think this, and what does it tell us about her character?

8. Alma claims at the end of the novel, "I have never felt a need to invent a world beyond this world. . . . All I ever wanted to know was this world" (497). How has this limitation to her curiosity helped or harmed her?

SOMEONE

Alice McDermott

An homage to the extraordinary transformations experienced in an ordinary life, *Someone* is the highly anticipated seventh novel from the award-winning author Alice McDermott, beloved for her deft portraits of kinship and memory.

When we first glimpse Marie, who narrates *Someone*, she is a child in glasses waiting for her father on a Brooklyn stoop. In poignant scenes, Marie experiences powerful transitions, though she stays close to home: bittersweet encounters with an awkward young neighbor named Pegeen, who describes herself as a fool; the heartache and hope of adolescence; her brother's brief stint as a Catholic priest; and rediscovered courage when she takes on her mother's role, becoming a wife with a family of her own. Woven through with McDermott's tender, lyrical voice, this masterly work is a crowning achievement by one of America's finest writers.

"A fine-tuned, beautiful book filled with so much universal experience, such haunting imagery, such urgent matters of life and death." —The New York Times

ABOUT THE AUTHOR: **Alice McDermott** is the author of six previous novels, including *After This; Child of My Heart; Charming Billy,* winner of the 1998 National Book Award; and *At Weddings and Wakes,* all published by FSG. *That Night, At Weddings and Wakes,* and *After This* were finalists for the Pulitzer Prize. McDermott lives with her family outside Washington, D.C.

October 2014 | Trade Paperback | Fiction | 240 pp | $15.00 | ISBN 9781250055361
Picador | us.macmillan.com

CONVERSATION STARTERS

1. Why does the memory of Pegeen resonate so profoundly for Marie? Is there a similar story from your youth that has had a lasting effect on your life?

2. What does Marie's mother try to teach her about becoming a fulfilled woman? What exceptional qualities does Marie's father possess? How does their marriage shape Marie's vision of her future?

3. Discuss the novel's Brooklyn neighborhood as if it were a character. What are its most colorful attributes? How is it transformed over the years while Marie grows up? Do its inhabitants support one another, or is their gossip judgmental?

4. Why does Marie resist her mother's attempts to urge her to adulthood, from how to read a recipe to the importance of finding a job?

5. How is Marie able to look past the tragic death of Mrs. Hanson and focus on the loveliness of Gerty and her baby sister, Durna? Throughout her life, what beauty does Marie find in mothering?

6. What did Walter Hartnett ultimately get out of his time with Marie? Was she naïve to fall for him, or was he powerfully persuasive? What made Tom Commeford a good match for her?

7. Discuss the story of Margaret Tuohy. How was Marie affected by the bishop's choice of elegant burial clothes for his sister? What did the experience show Marie about the role of the survivor?

8. As Gabe tells the story of the woman at his first parish who bought mints before attending church each week, what is revealed about the importance of avoiding assumptions? How do perceptions and misperceptions shape the novel's storyline?

9. What is the effect of the novel's first-person narration? As Marie narrates her life, what changes do you notice in her view of the world—literal ones, as she endures eye surgeries, and symbolic ones?

10. Discuss Marie's relationship with her own children. What does she do differently from her parents? What traditions does she carry on? How does McDermott capture the revelations that life and loss bring?

THE STORIED LIFE OF A.J. FIKRY

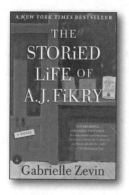

Gabrielle Zevin

A *New York Times* Bestseller, a #1 Indie Next Pick, and a #1 LibraryReads Selection

A. J. Fikry, the irascible owner of Island Books, has recently endured some tough years: his wife has died, his bookstore is experiencing the worst sales in its history, and his prized possession—a rare edition of Poe poems—has been stolen. Over time, he has given up on people, and even the books in his store, instead of offering solace, are yet another reminder of a world that is changing too rapidly. Until a most unexpected occurrence gives him the chance to make his life over and see things anew.

Gabrielle Zevin's enchanting novel is a love letter to the world of books—an irresistible affirmation of why we read, and why we love.

*"Entertaining . . . Engaging and funny." —**The Washington Post***

"This novel has humor, romance, a touch of suspense, but most of all love—love of books and bookish people and, really, all of humanity in its imperfect glory." —**Eowyn Ivey, author of *The Snow Child***

"A wonderful, moving, endearing story of redemption and transformation that will sing in your heart for a very, very long time." —**Garth Stein, author of *The Art of Racing in the Rain***

ABOUT THE AUTHOR: **Gabrielle Zevin** has published eight novels for adults and young adults, including an American Library Association Notable Children's Book, *Elsewhere*. Her novels have been translated into more than twenty languages. She is the screenwriter of *Conversations with Other Women,* for which she received an Independent Spirit Award nomination. She has also written for the *New York Times Book Review* and NPR's *All Things Considered*. She lives in Los Angeles.

January 2015 | Trade Paperback | Fiction | 288 pp | $14.95 | ISBN 9781616204518
Algonquin Books | algonquin.com | gabriellezevin.com

CONVERSATION STARTERS

1. Consider the setting. Why do you think Gabrielle Zevin chooses to set the book on an island? How does the island setting reflect A.J.'s character?

2. Each chapter begins with a description of a short story. Discuss some of the ways the stories relate to the chapters with which they are paired. Is A.J. creating a canon for Maya? How does the book itself function as a kind of canon? If these are A.J.'s favorites, what do they say about A.J. as a reader and as a man?

3. Lambiase moves from an occasional or nonreader, to a reader, to a bookseller. How do you think becoming a reader changes him? Consider the scene where he decides not to confront Ismay about the backpack. Do you think Lambiase's reaction is different than it would have been if he hadn't taken up reading?

4. At one point, Maya speculates that perhaps "your whole life is determined by what store you get left in." Is it the people or the place that makes the difference?

5. When did you become aware that Leon Friedman might be an imposter? What did you make of Leonora's reasons for hiring him?

6. Compare Maya's "fiction" about the last day of her mother's life to Ismay's version. Which do you consider to be more accurate and why?

7. How do you think the arrival of the e-reader is related to the denouement of the story? Is A.J. a man who cannot exist in a world with e-books? What do you think of e-books? Do you prefer reading in e- or on paper?

8. At one point, A.J. asks Maya, "Is a twist less satisfying if you know it's coming? Is a twist that you can't predict symptomatic of bad construction?" What do you think of this statement in view of the plot of *The Storied Life of A. J. Fikry*? Did you guess who Maya's father was? If so, what were the clues?

9. The author chooses to end the novel with a new sales rep coming to an Island Books that is no longer owned by A.J. What do you make of this ending?

10. What do you think the future holds for physical books and bookstores?

THE SUPREME MACARONI COMPANY

Adriana Trigiani

New York Times bestselling author Adriana Trigiani takes us from the cobblestone streets of Greenwich Village to lush New Orleans to Italy and back again, from the tricky dynamics between Old World craftsmanship and New World ambition, all amid a passionate love affair that fuels one woman's determination to have it all.

For more than one hundred years, the Angelini Shoe Company in Greenwich Village has relied on the leather produced by Vechiarelli & Son in Tuscany. This ancient business partnership provides a twist of fate for Valentine Roncalli, the schoolteacher-turned-shoemaker, to fall in love with Gianluca Vechiarelli, a tanner with a complex past . . . and a secret. But after the wedding celebrations are over, Valentine wakes up to the reality of juggling the demands of a new business and the needs of her new family. Confronted with painful choices, Valentine remembers the wise words that inspired her in the early days of her beloved Angelini Shoe Company: "A person who can build a pair of shoes can do just about anything." Now the proud, passionate Valentine is going to fight for everything she wants and savor all she deserves—the bitter and the sweet of life itself.

*"New York ambition clashes with dolce vita ease in Trigiani's delicious latest. . . . Feisty and poignant . . . Readers will root for Valentine and the lessons she learns--which apply equally to designing elegant shoes and to crafting a rewarding life." —**People***

ABOUT THE AUTHOR: **Adriana Trigiani** is an award-winning playwright, television writer, and documentary filmmaker. Her books include the *New York Times* bestseller *The Shoemaker's Wife*, the Big Stone Gap series, and the bestselling memoir *Don't Sing at the Table.*

May 2014 | Trade Paperback | Fiction | 352 pp | $15.99 | ISBN 9780062136596
Harper Paperbacks | harpercollins.com | adrianatrigiani.com

CONVERSATION STARTERS

1. Describe Valentine and Gianluca's relationship. Is he the true love she has waited for?

2. What are the biggest obstacles to their happiness as a couple? What are their greatest strengths? What does Val expect from marriage? How does the reality compare?

3. Is Gianluca a good husband? Is Valentine a good wife? How much can their differences be attributed to age? To gender? To culture? Do you think they found the right balance in their relationship?

4. Is having such a large and close family like the Roncalli clan a blessing? Are there any downsides? How can families impact our romantic relationships?

5. Keeping secrets partially define Val and Gianluca's relationship. What information do they keep from each other and how do they affect the course of their lives? What is the biggest secret?

6. Gianluca wants them to live in Italy. Why doesn't Val want to? Is it possible for them to live part time in both NewYork and Italy while still building the business?

7. Val not only married an older man, she married one who was married before. How do both of these facts shape her marriage? What is it like for her to meet Gianluca's first wife? Why doesn't he like to talk about his first marriage with Val? Why does she need to know about his past?

8. What does building the business mean to Valentine? Is Gianluca right—does she put her ambition ahead of her family?

9. Were you surprised about the turn of events toward the end of the novel? How does Val handle this change? How does her family help her get through it? Should Gianluca have told her about the house? Didn't she have a right to weigh in with her opinion? What do you think the future holds for Val?

10. Discuss the book's title. Do you think it is appropriate for the story? What did Val gain in this novel? What lessons did she learn?

11. What did you take away from reading *The Supreme Macaroni Company*?

THE TRUTH ABOUT THE HARRY QUEBERT AFFAIR

Joel Dicker

The #1 internationally bestselling thriller, and ingenious book within a book, about the disappearance of a 15-year-old New Hampshire girl and, 30 years later, a young American writer's determination to clear his mentor's name—and find the inspiration for his next bestseller

August 30, 1975: the day fifteen-year-old Nola Kellergan is glimpsed fleeing through the woods before she disappears; the day Somerset, New Hampshire, lost its innocence. Thirty-three years later, Marcus Goldman, a successful young novelist, visits Somerset to see his mentor, Harry Quebert, one of America's most respected writers, and to find a cure for his writer's block as his publisher's deadline looms. But Marcus's plans are violently upended when Harry is suddenly and sensationally implicated in the cold-case murder of Nola Kellergan—whom, he admits, he had an affair with. As the national media convicts Harry, Marcus launches his own investigation, following a trail of clues through his mentor's books, the backwoods and isolated beaches of New Hampshire, and the hidden history of Somerset's citizens and the man they hold most dear.

"This sprawling, likable whodunit [is] obvious ballast for the summer's beach totes. . . . Dicker keeps the prose simple and the pace snappy in a plot that winds up with more twists than a Twizzler. . . . [An] entertaining debut thriller." —**Kirkus Reviews**

ABOUT THE AUTHOR: **Joel Dicker** was born in 1985 in Geneva, Switzerland, where he later studied law, and spent childhood summers in New England. *The Truth About the Harry Quebert Affair* won three French literary prizes, including the Grand Prix du Roman from the Académie Française, and was a finalist for the Prix Goncourt.

May 2014 | Trade Paperback | Fiction | 656 pp | $18.00 | ISBN 9780143126683
Penguin | us.penguingroup.com | joeldicker.com

CONVERSATION STARTERS

1. While you were reading the novel, were you conscious of the fact that it was originally written in French?

2. Were Harry and Nola in love? Is true love possible between an adult in his thirties and a fifteen-year-old adolescent?

3. There are no explicit sex scenes between Harry and Nola in the novel. Is it possible that their relationship was unconsummated?

4. How well do you think Dicker captured small-town American life? Are the Quinns a typical American family?

5. Is Marcus a reliable narrator?

6. Do you agree with Marcus's ultimate decision to write a book about "The Harry Quebert Affair"? What would you have done in his position?

[Spoiler warning: Don't read ahead if you don't want to know too much!]

7. Who was Nola Kellergan: a victim, a seductress, or something else?

8. Elijah Stern goes to great lengths to atone for the crime he committed in his youth. Did his actions adequately compensate his victim?

9. Was Harry, in part, to blame for Nola's death because of the way he misled Jenny Quinn?

10. How did the truth about The Origin of Evil affect your opinion of Harry? Should he have publicly admitted that it was really written by someone else?

11. Did you suspect the identity of the true killer?

12. Were you satisfied that justice had been served?

UNBROKEN

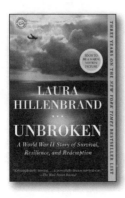

Laura Hillenbrand

#1 *New York Times* Bestseller • Hailed as the top nonfiction book of the year by *Time* magazine

In boyhood, Louis Zamperini was an incorrigible delinquent. As a teenager, he channeled his defiance into running, discovering a prodigious talent that had carried him to the Berlin Olympics. But when World War II began, the athlete became an airman, embarking on a journey that led to a doomed flight on a May afternoon in 1943. When his Army Air Forces bomber crashed into the Pacific Ocean, against all odds, Zamperini survived, adrift on a foundering life raft. Ahead of Zamperini lay thousands of miles of open ocean, leaping sharks, thirst and starvation, enemy aircraft, and, beyond, a trial even greater. Driven to the limits of endurance, Zamperini would answer desperation with ingenuity; suffering with hope, resolve, and humor; brutality with rebellion. His fate, whether triumph or tragedy, would be suspended on the fraying wire of his will.

Appearing in paperback for the first time—with twenty arresting new photos and an extensive Q&A with the author—*Unbroken* is an unforgettable testament to the resilience of the human mind, body, and spirit, brought vividly to life by *Seabiscuit* author Laura Hillenbrand.

"A celebration of gargantuan fortitude . . . full of unforgettable characters, multi-hanky moments and wild turns . . . Hillenbrand is a muscular, dynamic storyteller." —The New York Times

ABOUT THE AUTHOR: **Laura Hillenbrand** is the author of the #1 *New York Times* bestseller *Seabiscuit: An American Legend.* Hillenbrand's *New Yorker* article, "A Sudden Illness," won the 2004 National Magazine Award. She is a co-founder of Operation International Children, a charity that provides school supplies to children through American troops. She lives in Washington, D.C.

July 2014 | Trade Paperback | Nonfiction | 528 pp | $16.00 | ISBN 9780812974492
Random House Trade Paperbacks | randomhouse.com | laurahillenbrandbooks.com

CONVERSATION STARTERS

1. Louie's experiences are singular: It's unlikely that one person will ever again be in a plane crash, strafed by a bomber, attacked by sharks, cast away on a raft, and held as a POW. And yet the word most often used to describe him is "inspiring." What does Louie's experience demonstrate that makes him so inspirational to people who will never endure what he did? What are the lessons that his life offers to all of us?

2. In Louie's boyhood, he was severely bullied, then became a delinquent and hell-raiser. In these experiences, did he already display attributes that would help him survive his wartime ordeal? Did he also show tendencies that foreshadowed the struggles he would face postwar?

3. Louie was especially close to his brother, Pete. If Pete hadn't been there, what do you think would have become of Louie? ?

4. After the war, Louie would say that of all the horrors he experienced in the war, the death of the little duck, Gaga, was the worst. Why was this event especially wrenching for him and the other POWs?

5. Louie, Frank Tinker, and William Harris planned to escape from Ofuna, walk across Japan, steal a boat, and make a run for China. It was a plan that very likely would have ended in their deaths. Was it foolish, or did it offer a psychological benefit that was worth the enormous risk?

6. Louie joined a plot to kill the Bird. Was he justified in doing so? Would it have been a moral act? Do you think Louie could have found peace after the war had he killed the Bird?

7. "Anger is a justifiable and understandable reaction to being wronged, and as the soul's first effort to reassert its worth and power, it may initially be healing," Laura Hillenbrand wrote in an article for *Guideposts* magazine. "But in time, anger becomes corrosive…Louie became so obsessed with vengeance that his life was consumed by the quest for it. In bitterness, he was as much a captive as he'd been when barbed wire had surrounded him." Do you agree?

8. Many of us struggle to forgive those who have wronged us, especially since forgiveness is often so difficult to find. What makes it so hard to let resentment go?

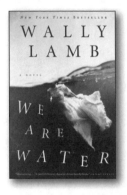

WE ARE WATER

Wally Lamb

With humor and compassion, *New York Times* bestselling author Wally Lamb brilliantly captures human experience through vivid and unforgettable characters struggling to find hope and redemption in the aftermath of trauma and loss.

Annie Oh—wife, mother, and artist—has shaken her family to its core. After twenty-seven years of marriage and three children, Annie has fallen in love with Viveca, the wealthy, cultured, confident Manhattan art dealer who orchestrated her professional success. The two plan to wed in the Oh family's hometown of Three Rivers, Connecticut, where gay marriage has recently been legalized. But this provokes mixed reactions and opens a Pandora's box of toxic secrets—dark and painful truths that have festered below the surface of the Ohs' lives.

Told in the alternating voices of the Ohs—nonconformist Annie; her psychologist ex-husband, Orion; their do-gooder daughter, Ariane, and her rebellious twin, Andrew; and the free-spirited youngest, Marissa—*We Are Water* is vintage Wally Lamb: a compulsively readable and uplifting masterpiece that digs deep into the complexities of the human heart to explore the ways we search for love and meaning in our lives.

*"It's a sign of a good novel when the reader slowly savors the final chapters, both eager to discover the ending and dreading saying goodbye to the characters. We Are Water is a book worth diving into." —USA **Today***

About the Author: **Wally Lamb** is the author of four previous novels, including the *New York Times* and national bestseller *The Hour I First Believed* and *Wishin' and Hopin'*, a bestselling novella. His first two works of fiction, *She's Come Undone* and *I Know This Much Is True*, were both number-one *New York Times* bestsellers and Oprah's Book Club selections.

August 2014 | Trade Paperback | Fiction | 592 pp | $16.99 | ISBN 9780061941030
Harper Perennial | harpercollins.com | wallylamb.net

CONVERSATION STARTERS

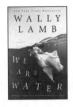

1. Describe Anna and Orion Oh and their relationship. What factors drew them together and what drove them apart? What were your first impressions of each character? Did you see the characters in the same light by the novel's end? Think about their names. Are they fitting for these characters? What other elements like this did you notice throughout the novel?

2. Talk about the Oh children. How do each of them relate to their parents? Were Anna and Orion good parents? What makes a good parent? Are they equally culpable for their impact on their children? How much of our lives are shaped by our families, and how much by our own choices? Choose a character or two from the Oh family and use examples from the book to support your thoughts.

3. Family, tragedy, art, violence, secrets, love, and transformation are the themes at the heart of *We Are Water*. How are Anna's secrets both destructive and productive? What about the other family secrets?

4. As the story unfolds we learn about Anna as a mother and her relationship with Andrew, her only son. Why does she treat him the way that she does? Is she truly aware of her behavior? Why don't the children tell their father the truth about their mother? Were they protecting her?

5. Think about Orion. His profession is helping people, watching for signs, recognizing pain and rescuing his patients. How could he miss Anna's suppressed emotions and those of his children? Was he too busy tending to others to notice his own family's dysfunction? Could he have truly seen it or by being a part of this family was he too close?

6. After Anna shares her terrible secret with Andrew, he makes a crucial choice. What do you think of his actions? Was he morally justified? Is it good that he told his father about what happened?

7. How do each of the Ohs come to terms with who they are? Would you say that they and the novel itself have a happy ending?

8. Orion mentions an article in the *New York Times* about scientists who found that reading fiction stimulates the brain in the same way that real life experiences do. Why do you read fiction? Are novels and stories important? Does this experience match your own?

WHAT I REMEMBER MOST

Cathy Lamb

In a new novel rich in grace, warmth, and courage, acclaimed author Cathy Lamb tells of one woman's journey of reinvention in the wake of deep betrayal. Grenadine Scotch Wild has only vague memories of the parents she last saw when she was six years old. But she's never forgotten their final, panicked words to her, urging Grenadine to run. The mystery of their disappearance is just one more frayed strand in a life that has lately begun to unravel completely. One year into her rocky marriage to Covey, a well known investor, he's arrested for fraud and embezzlement. And Grenadine, now a successful collage artist and painter, is facing jail time despite her innocence.

With Covey refusing to exonerate her unless she comes back to him, Grenadine once again takes the advice given to her so long ago: she runs. Hiding out in a mountain town in central Oregon until the trial, she finds work as a bartender and as assistant to a furniture-maker who is busy rebuilding his own life. But even far from everything she knew, Grenadine is granted a rare chance, as potentially liberating as it is terrifying—to face down her past, her fears, and live a life as beautiful and colorful as one of her paintings.

"The blending of three or more generations and the secrets they harbor keeps this story moving briskly, culminating in a satisfying ending that makes us believe that despite heartache and angst, there can be such a thing as happily ever after." —**New York Journal of Books** on *The First Day Of The Rest Of My Life*

ABOUT THE AUTHOR: **Cathy Lamb**, the author of *Julia's Chocolates, The First Day of the Rest of My Life*, and *Henry's Sisters*, lives in Oregon. She is married with three children, and she writes late at night when it's just her, the moon, and a few shooting stars.

August 2014 | Trade Paperback | Fiction | 498 pp | $15.00 | ISBN 9780758295064
Kensington Books | kensingtonbooks.com | cathylamb.org

CONVERSATION STARTERS

1. What did you think of *What I Remember Most*? What 3 scenes best depict Grenadine Scotch Wild's character?

2. Which character did you most relate to and why? Was there any part of the book that made you laugh or cry? What was your favorite scene?

3. Grenadine says, "I'm a crack shot and can hit damn near anything...I'm a collage artist and painter...I used to have a little green house. I sold it. That was a huge mistake...I can smash beer cans on my forehead...I fight dirty. Someone comes at me, and my instinctive reaction is to smash and pulverize. It has gotten me into trouble...I have a temper, my anger perpetually on low seethe, and I have struggled with self esteem issues and flashbacks for as long as I can remember...I can wear four-inch heels and designer clothes like wealthy women, make social chitchat, and pretend I'm exactly like them. I am not like them at all..." Write down, and then share, how you would describe yourself.

4. Grenadine speaks in the 1st person. However, there are also police and children's services reports; memos, letters from a doctor, a teacher, and Grenadine; a report card; a court transcript; and 3rd person passages from the point of view of Bucky. Did the structure work for you? Why?

5. Marley said, "Women are so picky. If you don't look like Brad Pitt or you're not rich, they don't want you." Grenadine said, "No, they don't want you, Marley, because you look like you have a baby in your stomach, you're unshaven, you drink too much, and all you want to do is talk about yourself and whine in that whiny voice of yours. Would you be attracted to you? No? Then why would a woman be?" Why did the author give Grenadine a job at a bar? If she gave you advice while you were drinking a margarita, what would she say to you?

6. Did you learn anything about living and dying from Rozlyn? Would it have been more realistic, or a better ending for you, if Rozlyn had lived? Why do you think the author chose for her to die?

7. Grenadine said, "I paint what's in my head. I'll twist it up, spin it out, add color, add layers, add collage items, and I keep going until it feels done." If you made a painting or collage that would tell the story of your life, what would it look like? What materials would you use? What would it say about you? Grab the artist in you and sketch it out.

THE WONDER OF ALL THINGS

Jason Mott

On the heels of his critically acclaimed and *New York Times* bestselling debut novel, *The Returned*, Jason Mott delivers a spellbinding tale of love and sacrifice.

On an ordinary day, at an air show like that in any small town across the country, a plane crashes into a crowd of spectators. After the dust clears, a thirteen-year-old girl named Ava is found huddled beneath a pocket of rubble with her best friend, Wash. He is injured and bleeding, and when Ava places her hands over him, his wounds disappear. Ava has an unusual gift: she can heal others of their physical ailments. Until the air show tragedy, her gift was a secret. Now the whole world knows, and suddenly people from all over the globe begin flocking to her small town, looking for healing and eager to catch a glimpse of The Miracle Child. But Ava's unique ability comes at a great cost, and as she grows weaker with each healing, she soon finds herself having to decide just how much she's willing to give up in order to save the ones she loves most.

Elegantly written, deeply intimate and emotionally astute, *The Wonder of All Things* is an unforgettable story and a poignant reminder of life's extraordinary gifts

"Mott allows the magic of his story to unearth a full range of feelings about grief and connection." —**Aimee Bender, *New York Times* bestselling author of *The Particular Sadness of Lemon Cake***

ABOUT THE AUTHOR: **Jason Mott** is the critically acclaimed and *New York Times* bestselling author of *The Returned*, which was adapted for a network television drama series. A Pushcart Prize nominee, Jason was named by *Entertainment Weekly* as a writer poised to break big. He holds a BA in fiction and an MFA in poetry and is the author of two poetry collections. He currently lives in North Carolina.

October 2014 | Hardcover | Fiction | 304 pp | $24.95 | ISBN 9780778316527
Harlequin MIRA | harlequin.com | jasonmottauthor.com

CONVERSATION STARTERS

1. Many characters in the novel feel that Eva has a responsibility to heal others, regardless of the costs to her own well-being. Do you agree or disagree? To what extent do we have a responsibility to help others—both strangers as well as those we love?

2. Did you find Reverend Isaiah Brown to be a sympathetic character or a villain, or a little of both? Why?

3. Heather's motive for committing suicide is ambiguous. Why do you think she took her own life? Do you think she's a bad mother for doing so? Why or why not?

4. Ava and Wash have a special kinship that runs much deeper than the average childhood friendship. Why do you think they have such a powerful connection and how does this bond inform the ending of the novel?

5. Wash's grandmother withholds crucial information from Wash, in the interest of protecting his childhood. Do you feel she is justified in doing so? Why or why not? How would you handle a similar situation in your own life?

6. Discuss the significance of the title, "The Wonder of All Things."

7. Many in the novel feel that Eva has a responsibility to heal others, regardless of the costs to herself. Do you agree or disagree? To what extent do we have a responsibility to help others—both strangers as well as those we love?

8. Did you find Reverend Isaiah Brown to be a sympathetic character or a villain? Why?

9. Heather's motive for committing suicide is ambiguous. Why do you think she took her own life? Do you think she's a bad mother for doing so? Why or why not?

Book Group Favorites

Early in 2014, we asked thousands of book groups to tell us what books they read and discussed during 2013 that they enjoyed most. The top ten titles were:

1. *The Light Between Oceans* by M.L. Stedman (Scribner)

2. *Gone Girl* by Gillian Flynn (Broadway)

3. *Unbroken* by Laura Hillenbrand (Random House)

4. *Me Before You Jacob* by Jojo Moyes (Penguin Books)

5. *The Aviator's Wife* by Melanie Benjamin (Bantam)

6. *State of Wonder* by Ann Patchett (Harper Perennial)

7. *The Book Thief* by Markus Zusak (Alfred A. Knopf)

8. *The Glass Castle: A Memoir* by Jeanette Walls (Scribner)

9. *The Paris Wife* by Paula McLain (Ballantine Books)

10. *Wild: From Lost to Found on the Pacific Crest Trail* by Cheryl Strayed (Vintage Books)

GUIDELINES FOR
Lively Book Discussions

Respect space—Avoid "crosstalk" or talking over others.

Allow space—Some of us are more outgoing and others more reserved. If you've had a chance to talk, allow others time to offer their thoughts as well.

Be open—Keep an open mind, learn from others, and acknowledge there are differences in opinion. That's what makes it interesting!

Offer new thoughts—Try not to repeat what others have said, but offer a new perspective.

Stay on the topic—Contribute to the flow of conversation by holding your comments to the topic of the book.

"[A] haunting, sophisticated mystery."

— The Wall Street Journal

We are Sinclairs.
BEAUTIFUL
PRIVILEGED
DAMAGED
LIARS

"Thrilling, beautiful, and blisteringly smart, *We Were Liars* is utterly unforgettable."
—John Green, #1 New York Times bestselling author of *The Fault in Our Stars*

e. lockhart

we were liars

READ & DISCUSS

- This is an intergenerational story. Is there one generation you feel more empathy for or relate to more closely?

- At times Cady is an unreliable narrator. Which parts of the story do you believe are true?

- A series of fairy tales are woven throughout the story. Which fairy tale do you feel most exemplifies the novel's plot as a counterpoint? Are there other fairy tales you can think of that relate to the story?

Read this. Then LIE.

#wewereliars 🐦 @elockhart Ⓣ WeWereLiars.com

GREAT READS

FOR YOU, FOR YOUR BOOK CLUB

- Novels
- Mysteries
- Historical Fiction
- Narrative Non-fiction
- Classics
- Beloved Authors
- Award Winners

➤ JOIN THE DISCUSSION at ReadingGroupCenter.com, twitter.com/RGCenter or facebook.com/ReadingGroupCenter

➤ SIGN UP for the Reading Group Center e-newsletter on our site and receive exclusive behind-the-scenes publishing news, author updates, and more

➤ PRINT A READING GROUP PLANNER: Download this wonderful 16-page resource and use it to plan your reading

 VINTAGE BOOKS   ANCHOR BOOKS

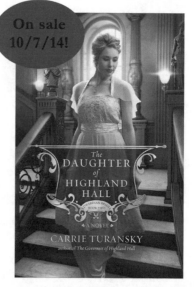

READING GROUP CHOICES' ADVISORY BOARD

Charlie Mead owned and managed Reading Group Choices from 2005 until 2014. He sold the business to Mary Morgan in April 2014. Charlie's business partner and wife, Barbara Drummond Mead, co-owned and managed the business until her passing in 2011. From 1972 to 1999, Charlie served at Digital Equipment Corporation (DEC) and Compaq Computer Corporation, both now part of Hewlett Packard, most recently as vice president of communication accounts worldwide. In 1999, Charlie became vice president of Sales of Interpath Communications Corporation, an Internet infrastructure company, until the company's sale in 2000. From 2000 to 2005, Charlie owned and managed Connxsys LLC, a communications consulting firm.

Donna Paz Kaufman founded Reading Group Choices in 1994 to connect publishers, booksellers, libraries, and readers with great books for group discussion. Today, the bookstore training and consulting group of Paz & Associates is fully dedicated to assisting people around the globe open, manage, and sell their independent bookstores. To learn more about Paz & Associates, visit PazBookBiz.com.

John Mutter is editor-in-chief of *Shelf Awareness*, the daily e-mail newsletter focusing on books, media about books, retailing and related issues to help booksellers, librarians and others do their jobs more effectively. Before he and his business partner, Jenn Risko, founded the company in May 2005, he was executive editor of bookselling at *Publishers Weekly*. He has covered book industry issues for 25 years and written for a variety of publications, including *The Bookseller* in the U.K.; *Australian Bookseller & Publisher*; *Boersenblatt*, the German book trade magazine; and *College Store Magazine* in the U.S. For more information about *Shelf Awareness*, go to its website, shelf-awareness.com.

Mark Nichols was an independent bookseller in various locations from Maine to Connecticut from 1976 through 1993. After seven years in a variety of positions with major publishers in New York and San Francisco, he joined the American Booksellers Association in 2000, and currently serves as Development Officer. He is on the Board of James Patterson's ReadKiddoRead.com, and has edited two volumes with Newmarket Press—*Book Sense Best Books* (2004) and *Book Sense Best Children's Books* (2005).

Nancy Olson owned and operated Quail Ridge Books & Music in Raleigh, NC from 1981 until it was sold in 2013. The shop has grown from 1,200 sq. ft. to 9,000+ sq. ft and sales of $3 million. The bookstore won three major awards in 2001: *Publishers Weekly* Bookseller of the Year, Charles Haslam Award for Excellence in Bookselling; Pannell Award for Excellence in Children's Bookselling. It was voted "Best in the Triangle" in the *Independent Weekly* and *Metro Magazine*.

Jill A. Tardiff is Chair and Event Manager of National Reading Group Month (NRGM), a marketing initiative fostered by the Women's National Book Association (WNBA), a professional development and literacy outreach nonprofit organization. She is WNBA's Main NGO Representative at the United Nations Department of Public Information and its Social Media Manager. Jill was the Association's National President (2004-2006) and the New York City Chapter's President (2000-2006).

Over the past three-and-a-half decades, Jill has held top management positions at Hallmark Cards, Inc., Doubleday BookShops, and Tiffany & Co., as well as principal of Bamboo River Associates, a retail consultancy serving major Japanese publishers and booksellers such as Shueisha Publishing Co. and Kodansha Ltd. Miraiken Group. She has worked as a reporter and columnist at *Shinbunka Weekly*, contributing editor at Shueisha Publishing Co. and *Publishers Weekly*, and advertising manager at *Guernica Magazine*, *Parabola Magazine*, and *Persimmon Asian Literature, Arts & Culture*. Jill is currently involved in the farm-to-table/farm-to-consumer food movement with professional expertise in artisan and farmstead cheeses, and she provides literary cheese-beverage pairing services to book clubs upon request.

INSIDE THERAPY

ILLUMINATING WRITINGS

ABOUT THERAPISTS, PATIENTS,

AND PSYCHOTHERAPY

EDITED BY

ILANA RABINOWITZ

FOREWORD BY

IRVIN D. YALOM, M.D.

ST. MARTIN'S GRIFFIN ❦ NEW YORK

DESIGN BY SONGHEE KIM
Produced by The Reference Works

Library of Congress Cataloging-in-Publication Data

Inside therapy : illuminating writings about therapists,
    patients, and psychotherapy / edited by Ilana
    Rabinowitz ; foreword by Irvin D. Yalom.
        p.   cm.
    Includes bibliographical references and index.
        ISBN 0-312-18671-1 (hc)
        ISBN 0-312-26342-2 (pbk)
        1. Psychotherapy.   I. Rabinowitz, Ilana.
    RC480.I566   1998
    616.89'14—dc21   98-5922
                                               CIP

10 9 8 7 6 5 4 3

Contents

Acknowledgments

I would like to thank my agent, Alex Hoyt, who makes the difficult look easy; Rebecca Koh and Bob Weil at St. Martin's Press for their enthusiasm and work on this collection; Irvin Yalom for helping me see the underlying theme in my selection process and for his brilliant writing about psychotherapy—both fiction and nonfiction; my son, Daniel, for his encouragement and support; and especially my husband, Harold Rabinowitz, who first suggested the idea for such a collection, gave it a name, and helped see it through publication.

Foreword

IRVIN D. YALOM

Many years ago I took a cooking class from an elderly Armenian woman who, during each class, prepared the most delectable dishes of hummus, baba ghanouj, taboulleh, and lahmeh bilajeen. But in my own kitchen, I could never reproduce the full sumptuous flavors of her dishes. What had I missed? I thought I had overlooked nothing: the location of her produce market, the brand names of her ingredients, the precise size of her handfuls and pinches. But still my culinary replications lacked Armenian zest. I began to scrutinize her every step. I noticed that when she finished her preparations she habitually handed the dish to her even more elderly servant to put into the oven. It turned out that the servant was the key to the mystery. Following her on her way to the oven I observed that she leaned over to smell the dish and then, without breaking stride, casually threw in several handfuls of assorted spices and condiments. I knew immediately that these off-the-record throw-ins made all the difference.

Often, when I think about the successful ingredients of psychotherapy, this cooking incident comes to mind. It is not the systematic protocols or the procedural cookbooks that underlie successful therapy, but the extras that experienced therapists throw in when no one is looking. Indeed, in this collection of inquiries into the core of therapy, the reader will find little mention of technique, delineated stages of therapy, or strategic technical interventions.

What *do* the experienced therapists who contribute to *Inside Therapy* consider the "core of therapy"? Although the excerpts differ in form, perspective, and ideological persuasion, each one implicitly or explicitly rests upon (as does every serious inquiry into the process of successful therapy) Carl Rogers's observation that *it is the relationship that heals*. That idea, perhaps psychotherapy's most fundamental axiom—and *axiom* is not too strong a term—posits that the mutative force in the process of personal change is the nature, the texture, of the relationship between patient and therapist. It follows that other considerations (for example, the ideological school, the actual content of the therapy discussion, or the general procedure, be it free association, Gestalt, or psychodrama techniques) are quite secondary.

Nothing the therapist does takes precedence, in my view, over building a trusting relationship with the patient. I have long believed that other activities in therapy—for example, exploration of the past and the search for a unified life narrative—are valuable only insofar as they keep therapist and patient bound together in some mutually valued, interesting, and gratifying endeavor while the real healing force, the therapeutic relationship, is germinating and taking root.

Not only did Carl Rogers demonstrate the centrality of the therapeutic relationship, but his research also identified the specific characteristics of the successful relationship—namely, that the effective therapist relates to the patient in a genuine, unconditionally supportive, and empathic manner.

These findings, central to psychotherapy practice for decades, appear beyond dispute. Not only are they powerfully supported by empirical research evidence but, to the practicing therapist, they seem intuitively correct and self-evident. Yet it is one thing to rate self-administered research scales of support, genuineness, and empathy and quite another thing, as the contributions in *Inside Therapy* demonstrate, to apprehend the actual clinical operation of these characteristics.

Let us focus on the property of genuineness. How is genuineness recognized? Consider, for a moment, the psychotherapy hour. A therapist and patient converse. How can we know if the therapist is being "genuine" with the patient? Does it mean that the therapist shucks the trappings of professional role and becomes a "real person" in the therapy situation? As real *in* the hour as out of the hour? And what about the therapist's feelings and inner experience? Is everything to be expressed to the patient?

For a creative and genuine encounter to occur, the therapist must relinquish a position of certainty. No therapist can predict, with any measure of precision, the future course of therapy. Wobbling and creative improvisation are an integral part of the process, and the genuine therapist must be willing to expose his or her uncertainty and bafflement.

It is not easy for therapists to be transparent. Whenever I lecture to a professional audience on the subject, I immediately sense an autonomic discharge sweeping through the audience: perspiration, enlarged pupils, furtive glances at nearest exits. Therapists fear self-revelation in their practice for many reasons. Some dislike abandoning a role they were taught in their training: the blank screen analytic model, an archaic, mechanistic, and counterproductive model to which even Freud rarely adhered. Other therapists (perhaps those most accustomed to the medical model) are reluctant to relinquish authority and the pretense of omniscience. It is not hard for them to rationalize their choice. They claim that patients demand, and are comforted by, an established expert. They agree with Dostoyevsky's grand inquisitor in *The Brothers Karamazov* who insisted that what man really wants is "magic, mystery, and authority!" And, indeed, throughout many centuries, healers have infantilized supplicants by appealing to blind desire for authority. Consider only the robes and secret rituals of shamanistic and religious healers, or the long medical tradition of writing arcane pharmaceutical prescriptions in Latin.

Other therapists resist the idea of self-revelation for different reasons. They fear that their patients will ask, "How can the blind lead the blind?" They fear that patients will lose faith in healers who acknowledge that they despair for many of the same reasons haunting their patients.

Some of these strong reactions may be assuaged by examining the types of therapist self-revelation. Let us consider three categories: (1) revelation about one's personal life—inner and outer experiences; (2) revelation about one's here-and-now feelings (that is, feelings experienced in the immediate encounter with the patient); and (3) revelation about the mechanism of the psychotherapy process.

Therapists are most threatened by the first category, but I believe that revealing details of the therapist's personal life is far less germane to effective therapy than revelations from the second and third categories.

Revealing *here-and-now* feelings is essential if there is to be a genuine interchange in therapy. Almost always such therapist disclosure deepens the therapeutic relationship. Very frequently in my practice I see patients who have had some prior unsatisfactory therapy. Over and over again I hear the same complaint: The therapist was too impersonal, too uninvolved, too wooden. I have almost never heard a patient complain of a therapist who was too open, too interactive, or too personal.

Revelation about the *mechanism of therapy* is equally important. Psychotherapy is such a powerful process in itself that it has no need to invoke magic, mystery, or authority. "Authenticity, not mystification" is my personal mantra. I advise therapists not only to respond fully to questions about the procedure but also to prepare patients at the beginning of therapy by providing a lucid description of the mechanism of therapy.

There is one other aspect to genuineness that is rarely discussed but that permeates *Inside Therapy*. In many of the chapters we read accounts in which therapists act intuitively, unpredictably—in short *creatively*. In his memoirs, Jung commented that we have to invent a different therapy language for each patient. The subtext to many of the contributions in this volume suggests an even more radical position: that the therapist invent a new *therapy* for each patient.

The idea of inventing a therapy de novo for each patient flies in the face of current trends in therapy. After all, these are the 1990s—

the days of standardized brief therapy protocols, days of managed care administrators who expect therapists to follow a prescribed script for each therapy session, to set treatment goals for each session, and to measure the progress toward that goal. These are the days in which professional task forces devote considerable resources and energy to customizing therapy approaches for each of the standard diagnostic categories.

Inventing a new therapy for each patient? What a fantastical notion, yet a notion that grows less bizarre when we inquire deeper into the idea of genuineness. The genuine therapist is one who has learned to encounter the patient in all the other's uniqueness. Yes, of course, some patient may bring another patient to the therapist's mind. Some incident—a dilemma, life situation, or conflict—may resemble another such incident witnessed before, but the essence of each person entering the therapist's office is unique, and the encounter awaiting both parties will also be unique. I believe that therapy is enriched when the therapist is sufficiently unfettered by ideology to permit a creative therapy to emerge out of the unique encounter. It is the therapist's task to know the other as deeply as possible. Standardized protocols, procedures, and diagnostic formulations merely obstruct the possibility of such knowing.

Creative therapy is shaped by both therapist and patient. In fact, the process of creation of the therapy is an intrinsic part of the work, and therapists must facilitate the patient's creative participation. They may, for example, focus the patient's attention on the nature of the work by posing process questions: "In our meetings thus far, what have we done that has helped you to feel better?" "What brings the two of us closer?" "When are we more real in our sessions?" "In what part of the session do you feel most alive, most engaged?" Such questions help to bring the patient into full partnership in the therapy adventure.

I have considered only a few of the many significant themes that are depicted graphically in *Inside Therapy*. At the present moment, psychotherapy is seriously endangered, and this volume could not be more timely. The managed care movement threatens to undermine the foundations of therapy with its insistence on brevity, on uniformity of procedure, on the adoption of the medical model. The third-party payee vocabulary, in which the psychotherapist is now known as a provider, reveals the depth and seriousness of the conceptual error: The therapist does not provide a technology to one who is in despair but instead builds a human relationship that will ultimately, ipso facto, foment change and growth.

Introduction

ILANA RABINOWITZ

The most intriguing aspect of my experience in therapy—one that I believe has been noticed by many patients—was the subtle yet powerful effect the process had on me almost from the start. Amazingly, after speaking to a total stranger for only a few hours, I felt myself in the throes of powerful emotions about my therapist, about myself, and about people around me. My reaction, it seemed to me, was all out of proportion to the amount of time and the amount of energy expended on the process.

Moreover, unlike any other physician-patient relationship that I had ever experienced (or, come to think of it, any relationship of any kind), the therapist would reveal little about himself or about the process, so I began looking for answers elsewhere.

I am by nature an inquisitive person, but my curiosity was piqued in a way it had never been before, and my mind raced with questions. How does this process work? What makes for a good therapist? What makes for a good therapy session? What is my therapist thinking? How does this person, who is not expressing his feelings, feel about me? What do other people's therapy sessions look like? How do I know if I am working with a capable and competent—or, for that matter, moral and scrupulous—therapist? How is it possible that simply meeting with someone and just talking causes me to have such strong feelings? Finally, I asked myself, What can I do to make sessions more productive?

Many of these questions are addressed in the excerpts collected in this book. That last question, however, is the one that casts its shadow over this entire collection. One might assume that since the patient's involvement is vital to the process, things would progress smoothly and speedily if he or she were accomplished at it. Yet one scours the literature in vain for insight into the mechanics of the procedure at work. As a matter of fact, the situation is something of a paradox. Although the patient's participation is crucial, it is usually counterproductive to prepare for a session, to follow any plan, or to work within any structure, for it is what arises spontaneously in the therapy that really matters.

The situation might be compared to that of a trapeze artist, or rather a duo of trapeze artists: one hurtling through the air and the other a catcher on the second trapeze swing, in which only one member of the team, the catcher, is trained and practiced in his or her art. One hopes that the connections are made and that the performer flying through the air is caught before falling, but hope and chance play very small roles in circus performances; performers in such risky fields rely more heavily on training and practice. Even in traditional medicine, where the patient is often the passive recipient of the physician's ministrations, there are still ways the patient can cooperate with the treatment and "follow doctor's orders." As the level of responsibility assumed by (or granted to) the patient increases in the doctor-patient model, the knowledge and involvement of the patient in the treatment intensify. Nearly no such change can be discerned in psychoanalytic techniques over more than half a century. The patient is still flying unskilled—one might say with the additional handicap of performing blindfolded!

Given the limitations of understanding psychotherapy, what are the important elements of this discipline? Psychotherapy was dubbed "the talking cure" almost at the moment of its inception by Anna

O., its seminal patient. Freud's colleague, Josef Breuer, was treating Anna O. for a variety of symptoms that arose after her father's death. During the course of her therapy (in which Breuer used hypnosis to loosen her memory and her tongue), some of her symptoms were relieved when the memory was dislodged and expressed. As a result of studying Anna O. with Breuer, Freud observed (among a number of other key factors of what would become elements of psychoanalysis) the importance of free association as a means of reaching the unconscious mind. It seems that Anna O. also recognized the importance of expressing her thoughts and referred to the treatment as "chimney sweeping."

Recent attempts to lay a neurophysiological foundation to the process, though well-meaning, fail to recognize the essential character of the process as one that takes place between the patient-talker and the therapist-listener. And just as the talking part of therapy—the patient's part of therapy—is an important part of the process, so is the listening part of the therapy. Freud believed that psychotherapy was first and foremost the art and science of *listening* to patients. It is not the kind of passive, often distracted listening people are accustomed to, but a therapeutic listening that involves the use of a number of techniques. This tool, involving so elemental a part of human experience as to elude the attention of serious science until only recently, is also available to the patient, for it is by hearing one's own voice speak a thought for the first time that the thought is truly observed and validated. It is this special kind of listening that helps the therapist understand the messages that are rattling around in the unconscious mind.

As in any other therapeutic procedure, the quality of the therapist's listening skills makes the difference between successful and unsuccessful therapy. The modern comic may poke fun at the "strict Freudian" who sits dozing as the patient speaks, but anyone who has had the experience of "just *having* to tell someone something" can understand how giving ear to another person might be beneficial and how doing this with skill and understanding can be therapeutic.

What are the qualities of therapeutic listening and in what ways does it differ from everyday listening? In normal listening, one reacts openly to the speaker. One may become defensive or react with delight or horror. A therapist, on the other hand, remains neutral, observing his or her emotional response but not reacting. By being aware of the response, the therapist can better understand how others react to the patient. But by not responding, the therapist does not interfere with the patient's own reactions. In "The Therapist's Personality," George Weinberg describes a therapist's first encounter on the phone with a new patient. The tinge of annoyance that the therapist felt might have revealed something about the patient. He might have realized that his reaction to her unnecessary questions must be similar to the reaction others have to her. Had he been truly listening, he would have realized, Weinberg concludes, that one of the problems that she has in her relationships is that she is insensitive to the boundaries of the people around her. As Weinberg puts it: "The ability to react internally, and at the same time to control outward behavior, is a requisite for the therapist; the good therapist has reason to be proud of his ability to feel and to know what he's feeling."

Leston Havens attempts to delve into the therapist's neutrality in "Freud's Invention" when he characterizes Freud's conception of therapeutic listening as "evenly suspended attention." He writes, "It was not meant to be the listening of a hunter, directed, impatient, intent. That would violate what Freud meant by the even suspension of attention. It is more like the silence of the night, all around yet incomplete. . . ." This type of listening, "Not thinking actively, not trying to explain or predict, makes it easier to hear the successive associations just as they are, still free of imputed meaning or connection, so that something unexpected, even unique, will not pass unheard because a prejudgment has excluded it."

Those easy-to-miss messages are the chief concern of Theodor Reik in "The Third Ear" from his landmark work, *Listening with the Third Ear*. Reik also explains how by being aware of one's own reactions, the therapist can turn the "third ear" inward to hear "how one mind speaks to another. . . . The psychoanalyst who hopes to recognize the secret meaning of this almost imperceptible, imponderable language has to sharpen his sensitiveness to it, to increase his readiness to receive it. When he wants to decode it, he can do so only by listening sharply inside himself, by becoming aware of the subtle impressions it makes upon him and the fleeting thoughts and emotions it arouses in him." This special sense, involving a mythologized new sensory organ, a "third ear," includes a lot of what has come to be referred to as body language in which things are perceived and intuited from what Reik calls the "trifles of observations." Every aspect of the patient's behavior, from the "gesture of a hand" to the "peculiarity of breathing," is noted, "heard" by the analyst. "The psychologist who approaches this valuable field as sober as a judge," Reik warns, "will not capture many data because he will also be as unimaginative as a judge. Only he who is fancy-free and opens all his senses to these impressions will be sensitive to the wealth he will encounter."

Janet Malcolm describes this unusual and paradoxical situation— one that the healer in every therapist must find frustrating—in "Psychoanalysis: The Impossible Profession." A therapist soon discovers the not-so-simple knack of *not* talking. A therapist reports to her that "only after years of terrible and futile struggle did it dawn on me that if I just listened—if I just let her talk, let her blather— things would come out, and that this was what would help her, not my pedantic, didactic interpretations. If I could only have learned to shut up!"

One cannot read these selections without hearing intimations of an Eastern philosophical approach, and this is explored in Mark Epstein's *Thoughts Without a Thinker*, a Buddhist approach to psychotherapy. In a chapter entitled "Bare Attention," Epstein tries to analyze this type of listening (perhaps, one may wonder, contradicting the basic approach of Zen philosophy). Bare attention has four elements: impartiality, openness to both internal and external information, suspension of judgment, and fearlessness to face whatever emerges. Many practicing psychotherapists have, along with Epstein, seen and applied the connection between psychotherapy and Zen philosophy. There is a meditative quality to the attentive stance that Freud described as "evenly suspended attention" and a Zen-like quality to the spontaneous flow of words in free association.

. . .

Not everyone is capable of listening in quite the special way required for effective therapy. Several authors examine these requirements: George Weinberg, in a selection from *The Heart of Psychotherapy*; David Viscott, in a selection from *The Making of a Psychiatrist*; and Erich Fromm, in a selection from his classic *The Art of Listening*. All three describe the personal qualities to be found in a good therapist. The common thread that ties these three views together is the healing motivation of the therapist and the need to focus on the patient. The therapist's own desires and needs are left unsatisfied within the relationship; his or her own agenda is not the issue. It is a generous form of listening that does not often happen in everyday relationships. When therapy goes wrong, it is often because the therapist has an agenda that clouds and obscures the patient's message. Conversely, when the magic moments of therapy happen, it is often because the therapist has succeeded in suspending the rules and abandoning agendas. In Irvin Yalom's "When Nietzsche Wept," the therapeutic relationship turns a corner after both the patient and therapist give up their plan for the therapy and their attempts to manipulate each other and to use therapy as a soap box for their own philosophies.

In three of the case studies, the therapist is particularly spontaneous and creative, leading to a breakthrough and to an important and powerful session. In "I Never Thought It Would Happen to Me," another selection by Irvin Yalom, a patient has been traumatized by the experience of having her purse stolen. At one point, the therapist's attention is drawn to the purse she is carrying, and in a moment of inspiration he asks her to empty it and share its contents with him. The result was, as he writes, "the best hour of therapy I ever gave." In "The Taboo Scarf," the therapist has a sudden impulse to ask his patient to try on a scarf that was left in his office, sensing that she has a strong reaction to it. Again the spontaneous and serendipitous impulse resulted in the turning point of the patient's therapy. The third example of a therapist with exceptional listening skills is found in "A Shining Affliction," in which Annie Rogers carefully details the remarkably perceptive listening process she employs to help a profoundly disturbed child.

During the course of therapy, a patient is bound to feel very badly at times. It is at those times that he or she asks, "Am I being improperly treated, or even abused, by my therapist?" Several excerpts in this book explore situations in which the therapist allows the complex emotions and motives in his own mind to take over the therapy session. The result is a breakdown in the therapeutic value of the treatment. In "Dr. Neruda's Cure for Evil," the therapist assumes that his patient's account of sexual abuse by his mother is a fantasy because the therapist's training tells him that patients typically have sexual fantasies toward a parent of the opposite sex. The fact that he has applied this standard to a patient who had actually been sexually abused by his mother does not help the situation: The patient begins to doubt himself and withdraws further, repressing the experience and spiraling toward another breakdown. In "In a Country of Mothers," the therapist's determination to discover whether her patient is her biological daughter interferes in the therapy and proves disastrous to both patient and therapist.

One result of the fact that a therapist is largely silent and anonymous in the course of therapy—a consequence that addled even Freud—is transference, the association in the patient's mind of qualities and even identities in his or her own life with the therapist. This has been so powerful an idea and so present a principle in the history of psychotherapy that no discussion of the discipline can avoid dealing with it. Several of the excerpts that deal in part with transference show clearly how this phenomenon opens the Pandora's box of emotions, memories, and thoughts that inundate the therapeutic experience.

In "Fine," the therapist humorously describes transference: "What the patient makes the analyst feel (if the analyst is perfectly analyzed, without his own distortions called 'countertransference') is the same as what other people feel from the patient, and is, hence, the neurosis. . . . Freud, who felt unattractive to women and couldn't believe that they wanted to fuck *him*, instead of *acting* took the incredible step of *thinking* about it. He reached the conclusion: 'they're mistaking me for somebody else.' And psychoanalysis—the greatest tool of the century—was born."

A more straightforward description of transference is offered by Gail Albert in "Feelings for the Patient" from *The Other Side of the Couch*: "The patient eventually brings his whole world into my office. It's not what he tells me that's so important—that's the least accurate information I have. It's how he treats me, and how he feels I'm treating him. I know how he acts with his girlfriend because he acts that way with me some of the time. And I know what goes on with his boss or his kids the same way."

The other side of the coin is countertransference, and it is the answer to the question, "Does my therapist have feelings about me?" In "Who Listens?" the therapist is confronted by an attractive, seductive patient with an erotic transference. He overcomes his instincts to respond and helps the patient by examining the negative feelings she causes him to experience and the feelings he remembers from his childhood. In all of the case studies excerpted here, it is clear that the therapist, in spite of his or her apparent neutrality, has feelings about the patient.

In "Final Analysis" from *Tales from a Traveling Couch*, Robert Akeret makes it clear that, much like the patient, the therapist also has questions about the experience. He wonders how helpful he was, what changes he provoked, and how these patients fared years later. What, he wonders, is a basis upon which to determine whether the therapy was successful? What were the goals of therapy in the first place, better self-understanding or simply feeling better? He wonders (along with generations now of therapists and critics of psychotherapy) whether future generations will view the practice as an arcane and pointless mystical activity.

The creative aspect of the process will likely ensure that the "talking cure" will always remain mysterious. It is my intention to unpack some of that mystery with the selections collected here. As long as people talking to people and others listening endures (by no means as certain in our little electronic village as it once was), the healing and salutary effects of giving ear to the deepest hurts and maladies of the mind will still be felt, as will the dangers and scars.

Is it possible for the patient and therapist to collaborate in the healing process without an agenda, without a map? It can be a difficult path with blind alleys, steep uphill climbs, and much stumbling along the way. But when it works—and this collection illustrates that it can and does work—the experience is so powerful and so affecting that one accepts the often unpleasant trip as part of the process.

In recent years, psychoanalysis and psychotherapy in general have been the subject of attack from many quarters. The immeasurability of the results, the fact that people can get worse before or even without getting better, the lengthy process, and problems with some of Freud's theories and with his life have been major reasons that the field has been challenged. These issues are as real and as true as the issues surrounding other areas of medicine, yet psychiatry has been so extensively challenged that health care providers have severely limited its use or ceased to deem it worthy of support.

Psychotherapy is and should be a developing discipline. The fact that some of Freud's theories have been rejected indicates that the science has progressed. Insurance companies rarely refuse to pay for chemotherapy, yet some parallels exist between the two branches of medicine. Some day chemotherapy may well be viewed as a primitive way of dealing with cancer, yet it is part of our limited arsenal in fighting this illness. New treatments, new mixes of the chemotherapy "cocktail," are replaced by more effective, less toxic treatments. Cancer patients often get worse before or even without getting better when given chemotherapy, and the treatment can continue for several years.

The connection between mind and the body, between mental states and physical health, is being understood more with each passing year, revealing a great frontier that points toward the vast amount of research and knowledge yet to be gained. Among the tools with which we foray into that unknown is an appreciation of the role of the unconscious in our total well-being and our appreciation of the power of "evenly suspended attention"—Freud's characterization of listening—as both a research and a therapeutic tool. Wherever that sojourn may lead, this legacy of Freud will, I believe, endure.

And the end of all our exploring
Will be to arrive where we started
And know the place for the first time.

—T. S. ELIOT
Four Quartets, "Little Gidding"

HERBERT S. STREAN

as told to LUCY FREEMAN

In treating a woman who refused to talk for most of the sessions, Herbert Strean describes his frustration and shares his own associations and memories. Although he found it difficult, the doctor remained silent. Sensing that trying to extract words from the patient was the wrong approach and would be forcing the patient to "produce" for him, he simply listened.

I opened the door of my consultation room to face a petite young woman, red hair flowing to her shoulders. She wore a drab October outfit—slacks, sweater, and blouse—all in a sad brown shade. Her pale face held a depressed look that kept her from looking as attractive as she could have, I thought.

"Please come in, Mrs. Winthrop," I said.

She had been referred to me by her brother-in-law, a psychologist. He told me she had severe marital problems, but he didn't elaborate on their nature. I agreed to see her in consultation, to decide if I could treat her and to see if she wanted to work with me. She had called and asked for an appointment in a voice I could hardly hear.

Now she stood at the door of my consultation room, where I spend almost as much time as I do at home. It is a comfortable room, a quiet room; nothing in it is intrusive. Yet it is also a cheerful room, with north-facing windows through which the morning sun streams, unless I draw the beige drapes so the patient can concentrate on his internal world. The drapes at each side, from ceiling to floor, hide five shelves stacked with psychoanalytic journals.

My office is on the fifth floor of a building in New York City near Central Park West in the nineties. Only the First Church of Christ Scientist lies between my office and Central Park. At the moment of Mary Winthrop's appearance, the park held a profusion of reds, oranges, yellows, and fading greens, autumn's colorful palette. The street on which my office is located has been called Libido Lane because a number of pioneer psychoanalysts have lived and worked on it: Dr. Berta Bornstein, Dr. Margaret Mahler, and Dr. Ralph Crowley, a founder of the William Alanson White Institute, which lies farther south on the park.

As Mrs. Winthrop surveyed what she undoubtedly thought of as my lair, she saw, in front of the windows to the right, my desk. On it, hidden from the gaze of patients, are a number of photographs of people important in my life—my wife Marcia; my two sons, Richard and Billy, now postgraduate students; Reuben Fine, founder of the New York Center for Psychoanalytic Training, of which I am now director; my father, Lyon P. Strean, Ph.D., a bacteriologist; and my uncle, George J. Strean, M.D., an obstetrician and gynecologist (I grew up thinking Labor was a town, so often did I hear my uncle say, "There's a woman in labor I have to see").

On the right-hand side of the room are two chairs and a round table that holds a large impressionistic sculpture, *Mother and Child*, appropriate to analytic treatment, I thought when I bought it. The mother, of black marble, and the baby, of white marble, are entwined. Two chairs, one on either side of the table, I use to supervise analytic students or for the occasional patient who prefers to sit up, instead of lying on the couch. Over the table hang three colorful prints of Paris, bought by my wife when we visited that city, which I thought added color to the room in a quiet way.

Against the opposite wall, the patient sees the couch, facing the windows. Beside it stands a small table holding tissues, within easy reach of the patient, to stem the many tears that flow. A second table stands between the back of the couch and my dark brown leather chair and hassock; this table holds my telephone and answering machine.

As I sit in the chair, to my left on the wall hangs a copy of a sensitive and moving portrait of Freud, sketched in 1926 by Professor Ferdinand Schmutzer, a neighbor in Vienna. Freud's eloquent brown eyes seem to show the sorrow within himself and all mankind, a plea for the understanding of the troubled self. At this time of life he was slightly balding, with white hair, white beard, white mustache. Also on the wall are my doctoral degree from Columbia University and an analytic certificate from the Society for Psychoanalytic Training, so patients can know where I have trained—all patients should make sure their analyst is qualified. Nearby is a painting of a farmhouse, given to me by a student I supervised. The scene is somewhat mystical, and it reminds me of Montreal, where I lived as a boy.

Behind my chair is the door through which the patient enters the room. On either side of it are floor-to-ceiling shelves filled with psychoanalytic books. Atop one bookcase stands a photograph of Dr. Theodor Reik, founder of the National Psychological Association for Psychoanalysis, where I received my psychoanalytic training after graduating in 1953 from the School of Social Work of Boston University. Reik sent this photograph to me in 1960, inscribed "To Herb Strean," and I cherish it. Both Freud and Reik, at least in spirit, are my constant companions in this room where I work long hours, often well into the evening.

All this Mary Winthrop could have seen as she first entered the room. But she seemed unaware of her surroundings, as are many patients when they first enter. She made no attempt to walk farther into the room, as though it held the horrors of hell, but stood in silence at the door.

I thought, as I looked at what she wore, that the colors a woman selects tell something about her. If she dresses in red, blue, yellow, orange, green, or purple, she seems cheerful. But if, like Mary Winthrop, she drapes herself in blacks, browns, and beiges, she usually feels depressed, perhaps mourning present or past losses. Mary's monochromatic brown clothing was relieved only by the red of her hair.

She wore no makeup, not even lipstick to give color. She was so slim I wondered if she were anorexic. She could not be called pretty, or even attractive, I thought, because she seemed so depressed. Perhaps after treatment, when she liked herself more and felt happier, she would appear attractive. I remember what Paul Federn, a famous analyst of Freud's day, said to women patients: "I can't promise you too much, but I can promise that you'll be prettier." With more acceptance of herself—her fantasies, her sexuality, her buried anger—Mary would look livelier, more winsome. Men and women seem younger, more appealing, happier, with the dawn of self-acceptance, as the worried, taut, depressed expressions leave their faces.

I gestured toward the two chairs to our right. Mary gingerly sat on one. I took the other, between us the sculpture of *Mother and Child*. I waited for her to speak. She had said not one word.

Still, she said nothing; she just stared at me with almost no expression in the brown eyes, which, when they gained some semblance of emotion, I thought, might be eloquent. I sensed that, for her, talking to me was going to be an arduous task.

I broke the silence. "Perhaps you could tell me what brings you here."

"I'm not very happy." It was all she could get out, her voice barely audible.

Another long silence.

I dared a second question. "Can you tell me some of the things in your life that make you feel unhappy?"

She allowed herself two words: "My marriage."

At least this was a communication, and an important one.

When she called for a consultation, she'd told me she was twenty-two years old, an artist of sorts, and married to a thirty-year-old stockbroker who could afford the seven-room apartment in which they lived on upper Park Avenue.

"How long have you been married, Mrs. Winthrop?"

"Three months." She lowered her brown eyes and looked at the floor, as though she were ashamed of the marriage.

Then, to my surprise, she suddenly offered, "I can't have sex."

"What stops you?"

"I don't know. As soon as my husband comes near me, wants to be intimate, I feel nauseated. Then I break out in hives. Sometimes I run to the bathroom and vomit. Or I have a bowel movement."

I waited for her to go on, pleased she was talking. It seemed to be an effort for her; sometimes I had to lean toward her to catch the words.

She sighed, then said, "We went through a courtship of six months that was only friendly. There was very little touching, holding, or kissing. I felt comfortable with that."

She retreated into another long silence. Heartened by her few words, I said, "Tell me something about your parents." She was a young woman; her mother and father should be alive.

Almost a whisper, "My mother died of cancer when I was six. I was the oldest of three daughters. My father expected me to take over my mother's work. I had to clean the house, shop for food, cook the meals, all the while trying to get high marks in school. I did get some help from Aunt Susan, my mother's sister. She lived down the street."

Mary had obviously been pushed and pressured to become a woman very early in life, I thought, never allowed to enjoy childhood. This meant important stages in her emotional development had been blocked and she would, as an adult, feel unfulfilled, depressed, mourn her lost childhood and adolescence. Her father had forced on her duties that were wifely chores, and she felt exploited, full of rage.

She said, as though in confirmation of my thoughts, "My father drank a lot. He also threw temper tantrums when he was displeased, when I didn't buy food he liked or he found dust on the tables. But he never hit me. Just hurled obscenities. He owned a hardware store and worked hard every day to support us. So I forgave him."

Suddenly, before my startled eyes, she broke out in hives, as her face and hands reddened. She apologized, "I feel nauseated. Like throwing up. This is what happens every time my husband makes sexual advances."

She obviously found it painful to endure intimacy. Her fear and her anger, in psychosomatic fashion, found some release through eruptions on her body rather than in words or actions. This was where Freud first started psychoanalytic theory—what he called the "conversion" of mental agony into physical symptoms—after his friend and mentor, Dr. Josef Breuer, described the success of his treatment of a young woman he called Anna O. This patient had lost drastic physical symptoms such as paralysis of a foot and acute headaches when she began to talk about memories that had terrified her. She referred to her recovery as "the talking cure." Freud credited her for starting him on the road to his monumental discoveries.

I asked Mary Winthrop, "Do you feel nervous with me?"

"Yes." A whisper.

I realized that, for her, talking to me in analysis, recalling painful memories and desires, was like having sex with her husband, in whose presence she also developed hives and felt nauseated. This was not going to be an easy patient, I thought.

As if she had read my mind, she asked nervously, "Will you take me as a patient?"

"Yes," I said. "Can you come three times a week?" This is the minimum for psychoanalysis. Five times a week is preferred but few can afford Freud's ideal schedule.

"That will be fine," she said. "My husband can afford it. He wants me to feel happier."

And probably wants a sexual partner who is not frightened to death of intimacy, I thought. (At this point I had not formulated the notion that a chronic marital complaint is an unconscious wish.)

We set up a three-day-a-week schedule. Then, looking at her watch, she rose like a wraith from the chair, slipped quietly past me, and went out the door, leaving me with my thoughts. I realized her long silences had aroused memories of my youth, when attractive young women did not want to have anything to do with me. As a result of this difficult first session with Mary I recalled the times as an adolescent when, with much trepidation, I would ask a pretty girl to dance, only to be turned down. I felt in Mary's presence, with her brief, sometimes curt responses to my questions, that I was in the company of an angry, silent virgin who warned, "Keep your distance, Buster."

I was trying to cope with my feelings of rejection yet at the same time empathize with Mary's fears. This is one of the major dilemmas of an analyst—he faces his fair share of conflicts as well as challenges. Fundamentally, the analyst responds to these conflicts like any other mortal. When he meets a woman for the first time, sees her become nauseated and break out in hives, he cannot feel pleased with himself nor, despite all the analytic literature to the contrary, can he remain "neutral." He may *behave* neutrally as he tries to empathize with her suffering, but he will experience all the emotions anyone else feels when rejected.

I also thought of what all my mentors in psychoanalysis had told me: ninety percent of my time would be spent listening, not saying a word. But how could I listen to a patient who did not talk? Mary had been silent during most of the first session, responding only briefly to my questions. From most patients would have flowed a stream of words and free associations about spouse or parents or friends or employers. All analysts expect their patients to talk, to say everything that comes to mind.

It takes many years, I would wager, for most analysts to genuinely accept the fact that the patient's talking to an empathic listener constitutes at least fifty percent of the cure. Because young therapists feel they have to earn their keep, they tend to talk too much. This interferes with the patient observing himself, saying what he thinks, feels, and remembers of the past.

I have found that sometimes the most therapeutic session with a patient occurs when I do not utter a single word during the forty-five minutes. For the person who has never been in analysis, it is difficult to believe that as the analyst sits in silence the patient's tensions recede. His thoughts become clearer, and he faces the ways in which he has distorted the important experiences of his life, past and present.

There is another important reason the analyst remains silent. As the patient describes his thoughts and feelings, with limited participation from the analyst, the patient starts to have feelings and fantasies about the analyst. This is what we analysts are talking about when we refer to the "transference." The patient's reactions to the analyst will be similar to his reactions to his spouse, parents, siblings, children, employers, friends, and colleagues. When the patient recognizes this similarity, he will sense how he has written his own script. He has assigned certain roles to the people to whom he feels close, much as he assigned his parents certain roles (among them the role of God, who must grant the child's every wish).

As the analyst listens, what does he think about? The analytic literature provides some answers. For one, he forms "hypotheses"—speculations about possible unconscious meanings of the patient's words and thoughts. He listens for what is *not* said, as well as what is said. He tries to figure out common themes in the patient's thoughts that match themes in his everyday life.

The analytic literature, however, does not describe fully the analyst's feelings, fantasies, and conflicts as he listens to the patient. I have rarely read of an analyst admitting he felt bored in a session, as occasionally happens. Or that he grew sleepy and may even have dozed off for a few seconds, as Dr. Paul Federn once confessed he did. I have fallen asleep three times in my thirty years as an analyst, each time for only five to ten seconds, and each time a dream woke me. The dream was always the same—I was making an interpretation to the patient. The dream tried to compensate for my guilt at falling asleep by carrying out my wish to produce for the patient by giving an interpretation. I found it easy to be empathic to one patient who had a regular early-morning session and would occasionally oversleep, showing up late. He sometimes reported a dream that compensated for his oversleeping; in this dream he imagined he was in my office busily free-associating (carrying out his special task).

Rarely does an analyst talk about his erotic fantasies when an attractive woman on the couch tells him he is the most desirable man in the world. Though a few analysts have married their patients, most will send a patient to another analyst after realizing they have fallen in love. I find it fascinating there are few, if any, statements in the literature relating to one fantasy that many analysts have about attractive women patients—what it would be like to marry them and live with them. (Women analysts readily admit that they think this about male patients.) And, on the other side of the coin, few analysts will talk freely of their retaliatory fantasies—the ones they have when they are being disparaged, demeaned, or cursed by the patient for not being more helpful. At times they must want to say to a provocative patient, "Shut up, you ungrateful son of a bitch."

Analysts feel both pleasure and displeasure while listening to a patient. They may feel temptations of a sexual or aggressive nature, fantasies they must monitor constantly and try to understand. Frequently what an analyst feels in the session—anger, sexual passion, impotency, excitement, indifference—may be what the patient unconsciously wants the analyst to feel, but psychoanalytic relationships are not always this simple. Analysts have written that anything the analyst feels is "induced" by the patient and therefore can be interpreted by blaming the patient: "You want me to feel sexual passion," or hatred or indifference. But it must not be forgotten, and it should be stressed, that the analyst enters the relationship with pre-formed transferences, just as the patient does.

My new patient, Mary Winthrop, was ready to see me as a father who would exploit her and as a mother who had been unavailable since Mary was six. I was all ready to see her as a young date whom I wanted to dance with and seduce. When I discussed this case later with colleagues, instead of talking about my emotional reaction—a wish from adolescence to seduce young women friends—I spoke only of my wish to make Mary "comfortable" in the analytic situation so she would feel "free" to share her memories with me and benefit from the sharing.

At times I have wondered how any male analyst can remain neutral while he is alone in a room with an attractive woman lying on a couch, taking part in what Dr. Reuben Fine calls "the intimate hour." I have sometimes wondered if many analysts have heart attacks and need to take long vacations frequently because they are so busy denying and repressing their own feelings in emotionally charged sessions.

Analysts constantly feel a desire either to oppose or to support the patient. At times they also feel like giving inappropriate advice, such as getting a divorce or leaving a job. Also, all analysts, whether they admit it or not, want their patients to talk. I believe that analysts feel more warmly toward those patients who speak openly about their wishes and fears, make the analysts their most important confidante, relate dreams at almost every session, practically analyze the dreams by themselves in the session, pay their bills on time, and do not offer overwhelming obstacles to treatment. These ideal patients, however, are few in number.

When a patient does not talk freely, the analyst usually asks, "What comes to mind?" or "What are your associations?" Most patients reveal what they have held back, and the analysis moves on. When a patient does not talk—analysts call this a direct form of "resistance"—the analyst will usually ask, "Are you frightened to say what you think?" implying the patient does not have to feel afraid in the analyst's presence; he will not condemn the most violent or vicious of wishes and thoughts. Most patients will soon start to report their thoughts.

Talking to an analyst has different meanings to different patients. To some, it feels like pleasurably making love. To others, it feels like confessing sins to a priest or a parent. Talking may also be a form of exhibitionism, where the patient is onstage and hopes to be applauded. Talking can also make the patient feel like a child being force-fed, or sitting on a "potty" having to "make" for an exacting parent, or having to gratify his mother and father's every request but receiving little or nothing for himself—as in Mary's instance. To some, talking can represent a rape, where the patient must psychologically undress and turn himself over to the rapist/analyst. For many patients, to talk feels demeaning—they must produce for a silent, austere authority who collects a lot of money and does very little while the patient does all the work.

Mary had great difficulty talking freely. She responded to me just as she did to her husband when he pressured her to have sex: she retreated into silence, broke out in hives, and became nauseated; she wanted only to remain passive and silent. Silence meant safety—it was the way she protected herself from her wish to explode in fury and destroy those who had hurt her as a child, and those she now saw, in displaced, distorted fashion, as wanting to hurt her.

After Mary's consultation, the sessions changed into a regular psychoanalysis. In our first meeting, she had confided in succinct form her sexual problem, marital conflict, and a few aspects of her relationship to her mother and father. But for the most part she remained silent—very, very silent—after breaking out in hives and feeling nauseated. It occurred to me that just as she resisted closeness to her husband and felt ill when he wanted intimacy, so, too, did she feel disgusted with the intimacy of the psychoanalytic scene, with the idea of sharing with me her feelings about her past and present. I had asked, toward the middle of the consultation, noticing her pained face, "Are you feeling nauseated?" She had nodded, unable to say a word, fearful she would throw up.

One of the difficult times for an analyst occurs when the patient shows deep distress, as Mary did when she broke out in hives and felt nauseated. At such an overwhelming moment the patient may not be able to talk. It has been axiomatic in psychoanalysis that if the patient can put into words his feelings, thoughts, fantasies, and memories, then bodily symptoms usually vanish. But what can an analyst do when a patient is so terrified of his feelings that he dare not verbalize them?

Here I was with Mary, who would not, could not, talk. I faced a dilemma. On the one hand, I wanted her to speak to me so she would be relieved of her distress. Yet if I pushed her to talk, no matter how gently, it would be as if her husband were pushing her into a sexual act she could not endure because it was so terrifying that to her it would be rape.

How could I show Mary I understood her pain and at the same time try to relieve it?

Sometimes I find it helpful to explain my dilemma to the patient in terms of his experience. So, at the second session, after Mary took her seat and was even more silent than during the first, I said, "I know you're suffering an enormous struggle. You resent being pushed to talk, even though a part of you knows that talking will help you."

She stared at me as if I had not said a word. We spent the rest of the hour in a silence interrupted only by my occasional anxious comments. At one point I said, "It's difficult to talk, I know." Silence. Ten minutes later I tried again: "What comes to mind?" Silence. Then I saw the hives breaking out on her face.

Each time I spoke, trying to persuade her to speak in return, she grew more and more rigid, and I saw the hives spreading. I sighed, gave up, retreated into my silence.

Sudden memories of my mother arose. I thought of how much I had wanted her love and how deprived of it I felt when she punished me by refusing to talk to me. Mary represented in many ways the mother I could never satisfy, no matter what I did. Who kept telling me she wanted nothing to do with me if I did not obey her commands to work hard for her by keeping my room clean and being a very good boy in other ways. The night before this session with Mary I had phoned my mother to ask how she was, only to hear her say nervously, "I can't speak to you now. I'm too concerned because I haven't heard from your sister since yesterday." I felt as unwanted by my mother as I did by Mary, who also did not want to talk to me. I recalled the feeling of childhood and adolescence: "I want the woman—mother—to respond to me but *'segornisht helfun.'* " This was a Yiddish expression my mother often used, meaning, "Nothing helps."

I thought how Mary's husband must have felt when she rejected him, as I now experienced myself as unwanted, impotent, pushed away in loathing. While I knew Mary wanted me to feel some of these emotions, unconsciously telling me how she felt about her husband, like all analysts I had to deal with the rejection in my unique manner, with my habitual ways of coping.

One of my major difficulties in life, on which I spent much time in my personal analysis, was dealing with rejection. Now here in my office, despite all my psychoanalytic sophistication and my awareness

of Mary's conflicts, I was affected emotionally by a woman who silently told me, as my mother sometimes did, "No matter how hard
you try, I will not talk to you."

Most analysts in a similar situation would describe the patient's
behavior as part of Mary's transference and resistance to analysis.
Mary experienced me as she did her husband when he made sexual
advances she could not tolerate, and as she did her father who demanded that she "produce" around the house. In the meantime, I,
like all analysts in such a situation, had to deal with what an unresponsive woman meant to me.

An unresponsive woman means different things to different men
and therefore different things to different analysts. Each analyst, if
he is to help an unresponsive woman patient, must become aware of
his reactions to each such patient. I had to carefully review the many
times I had felt like an impotent, rejected lover to my mother and
to adolescent girl friends. I had to deal with the anger and hurt I
had felt toward them and that I now felt with Mary. I had to keep
these feelings separate from my work with her, as much as possible.
This was to be an ongoing job with Mary and is an ongoing job for
all analysts with every patient. The analyst should ask, "Who does
this patient remind me of? What emotion or wish or fantasy am I
bringing to this analysis that really does not belong but is present
because it is a conflictual part of my life?"

For the next several sessions, Mary found it difficult to say a word.
She broke out in hives, cold sweats, felt nauseated. She told me she
threw up on the street after leaving the building. I continued to feel
weak, frustrated, impotent, but I also felt challenged, and because I
am persistent, I would not give up. I was determined to help Mary
get involved in her treatment so she could live a happier life, free
from the terrifying ghosts of the past.

As I reflected on my need to persuade her to talk and produce, I
realized I was dealing with a second personal problem—my own
strong desire to succeed. I looked at the treatment of Mary as a course
in which I needed to get an A, but which I was flunking. The idea
of failure in any area of life important to me has always been repug-

nant. I realized I was pushing Mary to succeed in treatment and pushing myself to succeed as a therapist, the way I had been pushed as a child.

It was painful but liberating to know that by trying to persuade Mary to talk I was acting out my own ambitions, which she experienced as pressure to produce, something she had resented strongly from early childhood on. I said to myself, "Strean, you jerk, the woman's major resistance is her unwillingness to give you the time of day. She is unable to have anything to do with her husband or anybody else in an intimate sense, and you're trying to force her to do so. No wonder she's so disgusted she wants to vomit when she leaves your office."

After this insight, I could identify with Mary. I recognized the pressures of my past and present to "produce" and all the resentments I, like Mary, had felt. When an analyst can truly see in himself conflicts similar to the ones the patient currently expresses, and when he faces the fact that patient and therapist are similar, this is when we hit therapeutic awareness.

If Mary was to feel better and function better, sexually and otherwise, she needed from me what I had always longed for as a child and adolescent—someone who would convey the message, "I love you whether you produce or not." How could I do this for Mary?

Slowly, it dawned on me that if talking to me was equivalent in her mind to having sex with her husband or producing cleanliness around the house or meals for her alcoholic, demanding father, the best thing I could do was to say in effect, "It's okay if you don't talk. I will still care for you and not abandon you." I realized that Mary's early deprivation of a mother—at the age of six, when she had to become the woman of the house—was a loss she had probably never mourned. Mourning does not come easily to children—nor does it, may I add, to most adults.

This was not an easy decision because, as I have indicated, psychoanalysis gets its results through patients talking, not withholding their thoughts. I knew I was probably going against every psychoanalytic precept I had learned and violating every instruction from my teachers. But I made up my mind to follow through on this (as a golfer, I knew that the follow-through of a swing was vital to a good shot).

The next session, when Mary sat in the chair, I said, with the quiet assurance that follows the facing of a hidden truth, "It's clear to me that my trying to help you talk is making you feel worse. I think it would be best if you do not talk and we see what happens."

I added, "If at some point you want to talk, I will be ready to listen. But it might be helpful now to see how you feel if you do not talk."

Mary's hives, which had appeared when I first started to open my mouth, vanished before I had finished speaking. She looked at me, for the first time, with gratitude in those large brown eyes. She smiled wanly, as though she now felt understood. Her posture changed from a slouch to an erect position. It was clear she felt relieved, as though she'd been granted a pardon from the psychic executioner's sword.

Then, unbelievably, but true to my resolution, for the next four months, three times a week, I would greet Mary with a "Hello" or "Come in," she would nod, sit down beside the paintings of Paris streets, and we would spend forty-five minutes in mutual silence.

At the end of each month she would pay her fee, and I would say, "Thank you for the check." That was it.

Along the way, though I knew that not forcing her to talk was helpful and I could see for myself she felt more relaxed, no longer pressured, I became torn about my approach. I felt somewhat guilty. I was getting paid an ample fee for doing nothing—a violation of the work ethic that was so much a part of my life. During moments of silence, memories arose of my father castigating me for being lazy when I came in second instead of first in my class. And of my mother's constant refrain, "All play and no work makes Herbie a dumb boy." The silence with Mary made me feel as if I were playing hooky from school. I felt like a fraud, violating many ethical imperatives of my own and getting paid for my laziness.

Things got both better and worse. During the third month of this period of silence, Mary's stockbroker husband, Jonathan, phoned. He said in a deep, pleased voice, "I'm calling to express my gratitude, Dr. Strean. I don't know what you're doing with my wife, but she's a new woman. She's lost her depression. And sex is great. You're a genius."

My mouth fell open in amazement. I had not the slightest clue from her that she had changed in any way. To me, she was still the silent, maligned Mary, hiding from herself and me deep, unconscious quarries filled with fear and rage. Could silence have paid off in such high, happy returns? What was I doing that I did not know about?

Her husband followed up his first call by referring several of his friends to me for treatment. He would, from time to time, send notes expressing warm appreciation for the way his wife had changed. I felt mixed emotions. I was pleased Mary and he were enjoying intimacy at long last, and I accepted that my silent approach had somehow helped. Yet I continued to feel like a crook for being paid to sit on my rear, saying not a word.

As I do with all phone calls from patients' relatives, I asked Jonathan, explaining it would be helpful, to tell Mary he had called. I had no way of knowing whether he told her—she still was not speaking to me.

I was tempted to ask if her husband had told her of his call, but recalled the words Freud kept on his desk: "When in doubt, don't."

But then, more out of my own needs than Mary's, at the end of the fourth month, when I could no longer tolerate my guilt and what to me was a fraudulent attitude, I broke the silence.

I asked, "How do you think our work is going these last few months?"

Then she said, "You don't make me put out for you. And it's the first time in my life I've met somebody who doesn't force me to put out."

I felt reassured. She said no more, nor did I. The silence continued for another two months—six in all. She appeared on time, as always, paid at the end of each month for what I still felt was my doing nothing except being there. During the silences I often freeassociated (what else was there to do?) as, over and over, I examined my quandary. On the one hand, I patted myself on the back, thought, "Strean, you're terrific. You figured out a way to help a very difficult person." On the other hand, I felt very uncomfortable doing little except to sit in silence. As I look back on the experience of saying nothing and receiving only silence, minute by minute, it was one of my most difficult hours—hours upon hours, so to speak.

Then after six months of silence, Mary's behavior shifted radically. She started to arrive late for sessions, something she had never done. I knew she was trying to tell me something important through this delinquent act. I felt at long last I had to deal with it verbally.

After she sat down one day, I said to her what I would have said to any patient under similar circumstances: "I've noticed you've been arriving late. I wonder if you feel something you can't tell me that the lateness expresses."

To my utter amazement, words now poured out of the mouth of this previously tongue-tied woman. Not just words but words of vituperative fury. In a loud, clear voice she castigated me: "You lazy bum! You sit on your ass and collect money for doing nothing. I'm thinking of reporting you to your professional organization, exposing you as the fraud you are."

Before I could open my mouth to stand up for myself, she added, "You remind me of my worthless father, who sat on his ass and did nothing while I worked my head and tail off."

I decided to say nothing. Obviously, as I had thought, her lateness was a clue to the buried anger that at long last was starting to reach a conscious level. It now bubbled like lava, from a volcano ready to explode. Up to this moment the anger had been denied because of its intensity at a very early time in her life, when she had been forced to take over her dead mother's duties, and because of her fear of defying her angry, alcoholic father. When she married, it was expressed in her hives and nausea.

Now, after our six months of sharing silences, she felt free enough with me (for the first time in her life free with someone) to dare put into words the hatred she had buried beneath layers of acquiescence. I reminded her of her powerful father and formerly feared husband. At last she could become aware of a rage long denied.

Incidentally, I called Mary "Mrs. Winthrop" for many months because it seemed clear to me that my calling her by her first name would be too frightening to her. It would be a sign of intimacy, a feeling she could not trust or tolerate. But later in treatment, when it was evident she had become involved with me in a human relationship and a psychic journey that embodied a mutual effort, to continue to call her Mrs. Winthrop would be to refer to her in a way I did not experience her. After a year of treatment she was "Mary" and I was "Herb."

I have often been asked by analytic colleagues and students the correct way to address a patient. Actually, there is no correct way, in my opinion. It depends on where analyst and patient are in terms of their relationship. Just as it would be presumptuous of me to call Mrs. Winthrop "Mary" at our first meeting, it would be equally inappropriate, I believed, to call her "Mrs. Winthrop" after I had known her a few years, had been recipient of the most intimate details of her life, and had become the most important person in her life, past and present, at times more important than her mother and father, as I helped her master the traumas of her past.

Many analysts believe that calling a patient by the first name gratifies the patient too much, as if the patient were a child, a lover, a spouse, or perhaps a friend. There is no doubt certain patients use this first-name basis to feel, "Yes, indeed, I am my analyst's child," or "lover" or "spouse." But if a patient wants to be the analyst's child, lover, or spouse, which all patients do at one point or another in treatment, this should be dealt with as an analytic issue.

The longer I have been in practice and the more comfortable I have felt with the patient's wishes and fantasies of intimacy, and the less fearful of my own responses to their wishes for closeness, I have found myself referred to more and more often as "Herb" and less and less often as "Dr. Strean." I have also found myself calling patients by their first names sooner in treatment as I have grown older. I am convinced that when analysts compulsively and rigidly refer to patients as Mr., Mrs., or Miss, unwittingly they show they fear intimate relationships, though perhaps they would be the last ones to acknowledge this fear. Many an analyst avoids calling his patients anything, but this, too, avoids the issue.

When I hear patients refer to me as "Dr." and expect me to use Mr., Mrs., or Miss over a long period of time, I consider this a problem to be explored in the analysis. I will ask the patient what he is frightened of if he calls me by my first name or if I call him by his first name.

As Mary continued her verbal assaults, I felt mixed emotions. On the positive side, just hearing her talk was a pleasure. I knew by expressing her anger she felt safer with me and could learn to know herself better. I also knew the expression of anger would have a curative effect as she realized she did not have to act on it, only face it.

Yet, on the negative side, there was a part of me that took her accusations personally, even though I told myself they were a result of the transference: "Nothing personal in them, Strean. Those verbal blasts are all aimed at her daddy's head for treating her like a beast of burden." Yet I also felt like a fraud when Mary called me a fraud. I felt like a lazy bum when she called me a lazy bum. I felt I was violating the work ethic when she accused me of violating the work ethic.

For the next several sessions she continued her attacks, and I said not a word in my defense. I told her, "I'm glad you feel free to criticize me. This is necessary for our work." But I felt like a bad boy with my mother, not doing my job right. The more I could reflect on how I had often felt with my mother and on how, once again, I was in touch with my wish to be approved by her, the more I could see Mary as someone quite separate from me and my past.

As we said in our book, *Guilt: Letting Go,* when someone feels uncomfortable about attacks by others, he should ask, "What do I feel guilty about that makes me take anyone's criticism so seriously?"

I realized after much thought that I had derived pleasure from Mary's doing nothing and my doing nothing. My silence with Mary was like a dream come true. Not only for Mary was our "non-working alliance" therapeutic, but for me, too. It was a joy of joys I could only vaguely appreciate while experiencing it. How often I would have liked to snarl at my mother and father, my teachers, and later my extended family, "I will *not* work. I will *not* produce for you. I hate you for pushing me."

Mary and I were rebels *with* a cause. I was enjoying going against the psychoanalytic establishment, the parental establishment, and every symbol of authority. When Mary attacked me verbally I realized my discomfort had much to do with my guilt over the pleasure of flouting authority by doing nothing. Even though my approach proved therapeutic, because my fantasies, unconscious most of the time, were ones of rebellion and hostility, I was ready to be attacked because I felt guilty.

As I slowly resolved my need for punishment and no longer had to make Mary into a punitive mother, I could move with her to the next stage of treatment. I showed her I had disappointed her the same way her parents did by seeming unavailable (a small child does not reason that a dead mother is unavailable but can only protest the unavailability). Mary welcomed the fact that I did not have to be a defensive, parental figure. She was visibly touched when I could show understanding of her wish to receive for a change, rather than always have to give—the way she felt as a child and adolescent with her father.

During her eighth month in treatment, by which time she was lying on the couch, she commented, "If you had talked earlier, it would have felt like sour milk. You would have reminded me of my sick mother."

I wondered if perhaps her mother's milk had tasted sour to Mary as a baby, and how this would have affected her feelings about her mother. Perhaps she fantasied, as all children do when a parent dies, she caused her mother's death and was unable to face her guilt. An analyst has to take literally every word a patient utters as a possible clue to the patient's feelings in connection with a long-buried trauma.

The unconscious never forgets a trauma, for part of its function is to keep the trauma repressed so the conscious can deal with everyday life. Mary could not recall the experience of tasting sour milk from her mother's breast or from a bottle her mother held while feeding her. But by recalling the sour milk in connection with her thoughts about me, she told me of a vital fact about her early childhood in relation to her lost mother—a circumstance that caused her fear, anger, and guilt.

From then on, the treatment became similar to the typical psychoanalytic journey. Mary talked freely of dreams and memories. She faced herself slowly without feeling pressured. She was able to mourn her mother's early death and her own cheerless childhood. She became more understanding of her father's alcoholism as a part of his mourning, for he began to drink heavily only after he lost his wife and faced bringing up three daughters.

Mary also had to work through her early-aroused sexual, oedipal passion for her father as she took her mother's place in all respects but the sexual. Her forbidden desire for her father, natural to every little girl so she can later transfer this desire to a more appropriate man, was more intense than that of the average daughter. Mary lacked a mother as the rival who would be a brake on her passions. All feeling for her father would have to be deadened, as it was for her husband, until she entered treatment, faced her hidden fear and fury, and could mourn the devastating loss of her mother at so early an age.

With her new awarenesses, Mary experienced her marriage as more pleasurable. After she left analysis, she went to college, majored in political science, which she had wanted to do but did not dare. Five years later, she wrote to tell me she had given birth to a son and planned to become a professor in political science at a city college within two years.

She ended the letter, "I thank you more than I can put into words for your superb help at a time in my life when I was at the crossroads."

Mary sought help early in my professional career. I was a student analyst, which meant I was supervised in my cases. I was also going through an extensive personal analysis and taking classes in psychoanalytic theory at the National Psychological Association for Psychoanalysis. One supervisor had said, as I told him of the four months of silence with Mary, "You should triple your fee with this woman. You're doing everything that does not come naturally."

This was a time when I felt in doubt about many professional tenets. I have often asked myself if I would act the same way today with Mary. I am not sure. But I believe I helped her by doing what I thought best at that moment in my analytic career.

THE THERAPIST'S PERSONALITY

GEORGE WEINBERG

A practicing therapist reveals what psychotherapy is all about, what it aims to achieve, and what a patient should and can expect from the process. Surprisingly (but then again, not so surprisingly) the chief aim is not the uncovering of the truth; it is rather the healing of the patient, allowing the patient to cope with the facts, regardless of what truth has been constructed by the mind. In this chapter from *The Heart of Psychotherapy*, Weinberg offers keen insights into how the personality of the therapist helps or hinders the therapeutic process. Why do some therapists have thriving practices while others cannot seem to fill their available hours? He outlines the skills and the natural talents that are necessary for anyone to be an effective and successful healer.

The voice of a middle-aged woman came over the phone. She said to the therapist, "I've heard such good things about you. I'd like to schedule an appointment." A few more words of praise and after they agreed on a time, he told her his office address.

"What street is that?"

"Fifty-seventh."

"Which subway do I take to get there?"

"The Eighth Avenue stops nearby."

"Which train, do you know?"

Perhaps feeling mild annoyance, he answered, "The A train, I think." He then returned to the patient sitting across from him. He quickly forgot whatever disturbance he might have felt, and was glad to have another addition to his case load.

This therapist has all the right diplomas—an M.D. degree and psychiatric boards. Still, his practice is faltering, and he doesn't know why. Patients stop treatment with him, for one stated reason or another. Often the alibi is that they can't afford him, their insurance doesn't cover enough. Seldom has there been an outright complaint; he's so prestigious and remote that complaints would seem out of place. He's polite and so are his patients, but he recognizes that something is wrong. Beginners, people who have lesser degrees, and less experience, are doing better. Not just financially—they have a clientele of patients recommending others, a following.

In my office, I ask him about the woman. "What is she like?"

He glances down at his case folder. He has made elaborate notes, as physicians are taught to do so they won't overlook a crucial bit of information. "Has severe headaches," he begins. "She's the third child of four. Her father came here from Poland when he was eleven and owns a dress shop. She works in an accounting office. Was married for two years, and her second husband left her a few months ago. They have a thirteen-year-old child who lives with her. She's depressed, feels that she's not getting what she deserves at the office."

Ten more minutes of facts about her revealed less to me than did the dialogue over the phone, which he was able to recall only after I continually pressed him for details of the way they interacted.

"How did you feel about that phone call?" I asked him.

At first, he couldn't remember having reacted at all; then he recalled a moment of pique at her for asking so many unnecessary questions. He had shrugged off that reaction. He didn't like making value judgments, and it seemed premature to form an opinion about her. Whatever annoyance he felt seemed too unimportant to bother mentioning.

From this incident and how it was handled, we learn about both the patient and the therapist. It would not be wrong to speculate that the woman's obliviousness to boundaries, as shown in that phone call, might have much to do with why her life was going badly. And the therapist's decision not to react, to subdue the feelings he had at the time and forget them, had much to do with why his practice was going badly.

What personal attributes does a therapist need? There are many, and, above all, at the very top of the list and the foundation of his talent is the ability to feel, a readiness to react.

Therapists have often been ridiculed for making too much out of small events, but doing psychotherapy requires seeing essences in particulars and knowing how to use them. This therapist might have spent an hour on demographics without discovering nearly so much about the woman as he would have by choosing three or four particulars and recognizing a trend. His ignoring his own reaction amounted to throwing away precious data. It is far preferable to work with living subject matter, the stuff that happens with the therapist in the session, than with material that the patient merely reports.

In order to utilize moments, to identify and understand them, the therapist needs the ability to feel them. To gloss over such moments, to say, for instance, "Well, this is just a woman who is anxious, and who really can't upset me," is to discard the most vital stuff of which therapy is made. No matter how much craft a therapist learns, he is lost if he suppresses his power to feel ruffled, distressed, helpless, or to feel exhilarated, or even loved by a patient. The ability to react internally, and at the same time to control outward behavior, is a requisite for the therapist; the good therapist has reason to be proud of his ability to feel and to know what he's feeling.

Some people, and this includes certain therapists although not all by any means, see habitually into the grain of human exchanges. They feel it when a bank teller looks at them with ruthless impersonality while he hands them the change. They seem to experience every high and low. Life is an adventure for them, and every moment counts. When someone like this becomes a therapist, the sessions are like big dates in which everything said or done is important.

Others approach life as technicians, and as therapists that's the way they approach their patients. They seem concentrated on the bottom line, the nature of the problem and what must be done to cure the patient, as if any of this were possible without experiencing the patient continually. Included among these therapists are some who don't really sense the presence of other people. They have never trusted their own reactions, if they had them. It has always seemed to them that other people, who responded readily to personal detail, were making "snap judgments." They couldn't stand it when they were asked to remember how a thing was said. In high school, a sister would ask, "Did John say he would call me because you told him to, or did he really mean it?" How should they know? The very question infuriated them.

The therapist who can't recall any reactions to a patient may have had real feelings at the time. He extinguished his responses, or can't remember them because they seemed wrong. For instance, he disliked the patient and is afraid to say so. Supposedly he went into the field because he loves people; here a troubled soul has come to him for help, and he finds he can't stand the patient. It seems too unfair to contemplate, and he doesn't want to admit it, even to himself.

In other cases, the therapist feels incompetent, helpless with the patient. It's important to be aware of having that reaction, and to discern if perhaps the patient has induced this feeling: he makes many people feel futile. It takes courage to recognize and acknowledge to oneself this feeling of helplessness. To the person new in the field or unsure of himself, a reaction like this comes dangerously close to feelings of doubt he often has about whether he belongs in the field at all.

Therapists who are able to react, who have the courage to feel and identify what they are feeling, are almost invariably able to remember the dialogue of their sessions. In this field, passion is the key to memory. Those who react seem vital. True, they encounter difficulties, and they even, at the start of their careers, look more amateur than the deadheads, whose pasty nature may pass as professionalism. Of course, they must learn not to burden patients indiscriminately with their personal reactions. But the ability to react is a first-order requisite, and those who possess it become the more successful therapists by far. Even at the start, although they may bumble and say things they shouldn't, they communicate that life is important.

If you love gossip, you have the chance for greatness as a therapist; if you've always hated it, preferring to concentrate on "bigger things," you will probably be bored in this profession. Not that gossip is desirable; doubtless it does great harm in many cases, and discreetness in life is preferable. But the curiosity about the details of people's lives, implicit in gossip, correlates highly with just what the successful therapist needs.

What else does a therapist need? He must have intelligence. He must have courage—the strength to do what seems right without compromising in order to stay in the patient's good graces. These would be desirable for any parent. One needs the ability to care about another person enough to pursue the beneficial course even if that person is initially displeased. And like a successful parent, the therapist needs flexibility, the ability to switch from one approach to another, and the ability to romanticize another person's life. To see the patient's life as a journey, to appreciate both the shoals and the magic of it, its specialness, is an ideal.

One nominal leader in the field falls asleep repeatedly in his sessions; he is dogmatic, never apologizes. Three or four of his patients have told me about his naps, blaming themselves for being unworthy of this great man. Our patients won't always recognize our faults as such, but will ruminate about their causes, blaming themselves sometimes, which means that we are doubly on our honor, the way parents are. Since there is no higher authority in the room, the harm we do—like much of the good—may never be explicitly cited.

The therapist must have basic humaneness. This means he must be able to admit errors, tolerate frustration, refuse to judge a patient by appearance, age, or social class. A surprising number of therapists become excited when they work with attractive young people, and become almost immobilized if a celebrity chances into their office. They can't wait to tell colleagues that they are treating a movie actor or some other prestigious person. They also are harmed by the inability to see how a materially successful life can be improved.

Many suffer plain and simple envy. And they overdo their emphasis on material success when they work with people who have yet to achieve very much. These therapists do less motivated work with older people and with the handicapped and underprivileged. The good therapist must be aware of the danger of obsession with material things—namely, that one's own sense of worth is not intrinsic but is forever subject to being withdrawn from him. We prefer to think that our therapist would still like himself even after a stock market crash.

Therapists as a group tend to intellectualize too much; they find it hard to acknowledge that much of life is primitive, that love may burst forth in unexpected places, as between homosexuals or people very different in age; they spend years trying to repair relationships where love does not exist, where it never existed, as if fixing up lines of communication, interpreting one person to another can result in anything comparable to the magic that simply appears at times. They try to interpret that magic, whether it is sexuality or sensuality, as if they were frightened of it. Tens of thousands of people have been prevailed on by therapists to try to force relationships to work, only to quit in the end, and thereafter they find the elixir of love's excitement with another person that never appeared even at best in the first relationship. True, there are people who find thrills only in novelty, but therapists must learn to feel the big occasions in people's lives, and to heighten their patients' ability to see them and to rejoice in them. There are irreducibles in life, or if not, they are near irreducibles, and where they are pleasurable, it makes more sense to seize them than to spend decades looking for them where they are not.

Many therapists have never enjoyed the effortless sense of being loved, of belonging; they have not been praised or enjoyed as much when they were children as at least certain of their patients were. One reason some people become therapists is to work out their own problems, to pursue the deep introspective search that begins in childhood, the huge questions about oneself and one's relations with others, the attempt to create for oneself what was not there as a birthright—these are valid reasons for a person to develop a love of psychology. And the desire to help others, often as a way of belonging, of being sure that others will return to them, of reaping appreciation, all have been motives that led people to become marvelous in this field. One difficulty is that they leave the person impaired where *taking* is concerned. It remains hard for the therapist to bask in praise, to enjoy what is given to him without question, to become an effortless recipient of love—in short, to relax when all is well. Tensely, the therapist questions why the patient praises him, thanks him, or gives him a Christmas present, and may join the patient if he expresses skepticism about what someone else has given to the patient. This therapist remains one, as Tennyson put it, "always roaming with a hungry heart"; it seems almost in the nature of his calling. The dangerous consequence is a failure to realize that some things are simply there, and an inclination to keep looking long after they are found.

The ideal therapist, like the ideal parent, should have a sense of extended family. Not just his relatives, but also his friends and his patients are central figures, the worthy. The waiter who brings food for his child is a central figure too. He teaches his child not to mistreat that waiter, not to consider him an inferior creature. Strangers, underprivileged people, passersby, have a respectable status in his life.

Without this sense of extended family, therapists have in subtle ways downgraded their patients. They have been too free in using diagnostic labels, for instance, thinking about their patient as an "alcoholic," or an "addict," or more recently, as "borderline." If someone told them that their mate or their child was an addict or borderline, they would consider it a profound insult. They would find not just the label hard to accept, but the fact that someone they love and into whom they poured so much effort and hope could be summed up by a single word that evokes pity or even contempt. They would feel the callousness of the label that they themselves applied as a matter of course to others. Those therapists with a sense of extended family have always been slower to use labels than others, especially since most diagnostic categories have a very dubious relationship to actual methods of treatment.

Sympathy is an obvious requirement. The therapist needs the ability to sympathize with people without concluding that they are merely victims of mistreatment. Our patients play an active role in creating—or at least, sustaining—their own problems. To exempt them entirely from any sense that they are contributing to their difficulties would be to betray them. The therapist needs the kind of sympathy that does not require perceiving his patients as helpless. Sympathy toward an utter victim is easy; to feel sympathetic toward a person who is acting in ways that harm him takes much more deliberation.

The last trait I want to mention I'd call "insistent egalitarianism." The therapist should always remain aware of the natural ascendancy that the therapeutic relationship offers him. The very nature of the relationship is that of a success talking to a failure. Imagine the contrast when the therapist, socially established and supposedly without problems, talks to a patient about the latter's sexual difficulties or inability to get a job or know what he wants out of life. Humaneness requires taking steps not to let this inherent imbalance undermine the patient.

I think most really good therapists loathe the notion of being a guru, or having disciples. The therapist should avoid strutting or name-dropping, or anything that smacks of contrast between his life and that of the patient. If comparisons obtrude themselves, he does not act diffident or hide them; it's merely that he is aware of the compromised position of the person coming to him for help. He is quick to admire the real strengths of his patients, to underscore them, bring them to the person's attention, and if the patient tends to disparage his own gifts, the therapist addresses himself to that tendency. Too much of psychotherapy in its first hundred years has stressed the problems that patients have, and diagnosis has not focused enough on people's strengths and potential.

These humane attitudes, and the openness the therapist conveys, are at the very core of the service he renders. The quality of his interaction with the patient is determined by these things, and that interaction is of paramount importance in therapy.

Are these essential attributes of the good therapist all natural gifts,

or can they be acquired? Some of them are, to an extent, acquired—
sympathy, a sense of extended family, egalitarianism. Others come
with birth. Observers of newborn infants note differences in the very
first few days of life. One infant is brighter, more social, cheerful,
energetic than the next. Mothers observing differences among their
own grown-up children often add with astonishment that at least
some of these differences were hinted at during the first few weeks
of life. It seems that there are talents, or at least preferences, for
interacting with people, which if not hereditary are in evidence in
very early childhood. Talents like these would naturally tend to go
unobserved, especially if the parent did not share them. Exceptional
sensitivity in a child might even seem like a form of neurosis.

Think for a moment about fields in which talents are commonly
observed, where we expect prodigies. Three somewhat related disciplines stand out: mathematics, music, and chess. The mathematicians
Gauss and Pascal, the composers Mozart and Rossini, were marvels
before the age of ten, and so were many chess players, like Samuel
Reschevsky. Genius can manifest itself to the world at an early age
in those disciplines. Mozart did not need to hear a thousand symphonies to compose one. And there is such a clear-cut ladder of
accomplishment in mathematics that when a prodigy skips five rungs,
he is easily recognized. In chess, the evidence of solving problems
and winning games is indisputable.

Language skills are harder to demonstrate, since, no matter how
great the skill, it takes time to learn the words that serve as tools—in
this regard language suggests the problem of the psychologist prodigy.
Imagine a child of six or seven with a prodigious genius in psychology. He would lack both the language and the authority to convince
anyone of this. I believe that tiny tots differ, for instance, in sensing
when an adult is angry or insincere, or when the adult is boasting
or using them for self-enhancement. The child may refuse to reply
to a compliment, sensing that it is false or manipulative, and his
mother, not aware of this herself, insists that he "behave." There are
children who know while in their mother's arms that she would
prefer to be elsewhere.

The implication is exciting. There are people with extraordinary gifts, who would make exceptional therapists, but who do not themselves recognize that they have these talents. Such gifts must be unblocked and appreciated for them to flourish. With some of the therapists I've trained, we have actually discovered together that they had unrealized gifts to pursue their chosen profession. For instance, one very sensitive woman could recall making very delicate readings of the psychological states of adults when she was a young child, most of which were borne out. Since these inferences were to the effect that she was unwanted by her mother, she preferred to dismiss them. But they continued to gnaw at her. Within a few years of her release from the need to suppress the truth, she became an immensely effective therapist and now has a large following. Growing up, she was incapable of dulling herself to reality, and her reward is that she is able to enjoy life as it is. She brings her entire personality to her work; and though the demands seem great, she has the attributes to meet them.

Psychotherapy demands a great deal from the practitioner. But in these very demands lie the gratifications that it can offer to those who do it well.

THE MAKING OF A PSYCHIATRIST

DAVID S. VISCOTT

David Viscott offers an intimate and personal account of his early training as a psychotherapist. At the same time he openly discusses the type of therapist that is not helpful to his or her patient. People who have experienced what Dr. Viscott refers to as the "omnipotent therapist" will recognize the characteristics: the tendancy to be rigid about the therapeutic rules and to distance oneself emotionally by viewing the patient as sick.

The rule that the therapist must remain anonymous may be the most frustrating for the patient. Dr. Viscott suggests that psychiatrists be flexible with this rule, since it is never an all or nothing rule. He concludes that sharing information about his personal life would be a serious mistake if the patient were a young woman behaving provocatively, but sharing a mutual interest in sports with another patient might be a basis for understanding each other.

There was a lot I had to learn about becoming a psychotherapist.

Therapy is a relationship between two people the purpose of which is to make one of them more human. The goal of therapy is to make the patient more complete, more adaptable, and more feeling. The humaneness of the therapist is an important factor in the therapeutic process. In fact, the success of therapy depends as much upon the

attitudes of the therapist as it does upon his knowledge. Probab.
more, because the best therapists are parents whose kids grew up
without problems.

Patients tend to be lonely and to seek out people who are helpful
or kind to them. Because patients are often aimless, sad, or confused,
it's easy for those treating them to feel powerful and all-knowing by
comparison. This is a potential danger. Unfortunately, some therapists come to believe in their omnipotence; as a result they tend to
devalue any comment their patients make about them or their advice
and to see those remarks simply as the product of the patient's disease
and, therefore, not to be taken seriously, at least not on a par with
the therapist's opinions. If a patient does make a comment about
such a therapist's style or personality which is true and which deserves a response, it is unlikely that the omnipotent therapist will
deal with it as real but will insist upon discussing the comment in
terms of the therapeutic process rather than in human, person-to-
person terms. Such patients' comments can frequently reflect the
healthy side of the patient, and such attitudes of an omnipotent
therapist are dehumanizing and therefore antitherapeutic.

Omnipotent therapists don't regard their patients either as equal
or as human as themselves. They are often threatened by their patients and need to think of them as patients first and as people second. They tend to be rigid about the rules of therapy, unwilling to
get close to their patients, to interact with feelings. They often tend
to see all parts of the patient as sick, even though that is rarely the
case. This puts the patient in a bind, making him feel that he must
not only change what is sick but justify what is not. Patients may
get the feeling they have to prove they are big boys or have minds
of their own to such a therapist. While this struggle commonly appears and varies in most therapy, it will dominate the therapy of a
doctor who, in order to protect himself, needs to believe that his
patients are inferior. They waste much valuable time coming to terms
with the *therapist's* weakness. The real issue is, why does the therapist
make them feel inferior? And usually it's not even discussed.

The omnipotent therapist sees patient after patient appearing to
struggle for independence, and then tends to conclude that the fre-

ıg struggle for independence he sees in his patients
ll therapeutic processes. I believe this is only partly
ly it tends to reflect a special aspect of the omnip-
personality, his attitude, and his defensiveness. In
therapy the patient has got to deal with his therapist's particular
form of defensiveness as well as his own. Hopefully, the therapist is
comfortable discussing his own bias with the patient and thereby can
avoid wasting time. I suspect many therapists will object to this statement and claim that a good therapist will not in any way influence
the issues the patient brings up for discussion. But the only way to
do that is for the therapist not to react at all. And that is being
neither human nor helpful.

It's really not so much the amount of involvement of the therapist's personality that influences what the patient discusses as the
way the therapist handles his involvement. If a therapist is warm and
open, he encourages the patient to deal with his personality as real
and helps him sort out what is not. The patient is then freer to
discuss what he wants than if the therapist stays hidden, except for
an attitude which he would deny was his. The patient then would
tend to test the therapist's hidden attitude and try to force him to
state his belief openly, which he probably wouldn't do. And this
would tend to create issues that are introduced by the therapist even
though he would claim he acted anonymously. Fortunately the omnipotent therapist isn't omnipresent in our ranks, and a good thing
for us and patients that he isn't.

A therapist must develop some special tools. First, he has to learn
the signs and symptoms and classifications of a wide number of emotional diseases. He must understand the basic theories explaining
how each of the various syndromes develops. It's useful to have a
working knowledge of the organization and function of the mind,
although that's only incompletely understood and widely disputed.
A therapist must know how to do a competent mental status examination, understand how defenses work, how typical reactions to
loss and stress manifest themselves, and how thoughts, behavior, and
fantasies are interrelated.

One of the lovely things about becoming a psychiatrist is you learn

THE MAKING OF A PSYCHIATRIST

everybody has all kinds of thoughts, fantasies, and wishes and that having them doesn't mean very much—certainly not nearly as much (or awful) as too many people think. You can have sexual thoughts about people of the opposite sex, of your own sex, animals, and trees. You can have aggressive thoughts about nuns, a baby in its mother's arms, even your own baby, especially your own baby, about your parents, especially your parents. You can have hatred for people you are supposed to love and for people who have just died. You can have perverted, twisted, kinky, obnoxious, selfish, stupid, childish, obsessive, and violent thoughts. The presence of all these thoughts in fantasy is only another proof of the fact that you are human and have feelings.

Feelings that are not dealt with at their source and resolved almost always give rise to other fantasies or forms of behavior whose purpose is to discharge the feeling in some way and "clear" the mental apparatus. In the process of therapy these feelings and thoughts are expressed freely by the patient, with the help of the therapist. The goal is to try to understand them and see where they came from; and to determine what they mean and to learn how to deal with the feelings so they no longer intrude on the patient's life and cause symptoms. Symptoms are created by unsettled feelings in the past intruding upon events in a person's present life. They are the ghosts of unresolved past hurts.

Much of the fear Mrs. Goldman felt when her husband threatened to leave her was the unresolved fear she experienced when her father left her. Mrs. Goldman's feelings of being abandoned in the past became less and less particular about what present event they attached themselves to. They became more generalized, more remotely related to the present. As a result, Mrs. Goldman tended to feel abandoned when *anyone* or *anything* left her. She once, for example, described feeling abandoned when a strange car she had been following on a superhighway for some thirty or forty miles turned off at an exit.

The therapist tries to help the patient find the source of his unresolved feelings and to reattach the feelings to the event that originally caused them. Hopefully, the patient will see the original problem more clearly and will be better able to cope with it than before. If he is able to resolve his original problem once and for all, he will be able to go through life without being burdened by ghosts from his past.

Putting the pieces together and seeing the patient suddenly get better may look good in novels, films, or plays, and sound very simple, but it's not all that common. When it does happen, though, it can really be spectacular!

Andrew Wallace was a college student who was admitted to Bamberg 5 during the fall. He was sleepless and anxious and didn't know why. He took a lot of drugs and overdosed himself with barbiturates. He did not appear suicidal but rather like someone trying to hide from his feelings.

He told me that his father died in his sleep of a heart attack almost four years before. He was the only one at home at the time and discovered his father dead in bed. We talked a good deal about his feelings about the death and funeral, but talking about them didn't seem to make any impact on him. Although he could talk about the events surrounding his father's death, he couldn't feel anything about them. His grief was inhibited and discussing the events that caused his symptoms didn't make him better. He needed to feel his father's death. I decided to plug away again.

"Andrew," I said, "I'd like to go through everything that happened the day your father died."

"But we've done it a dozen times already and it never seems to do any good." Andrew was chewing on a pencil.

"I insist."

"I woke up, went to the bathroom, brushed my teeth, and got dressed. I went by my father's room and called to him to get dressed for work. He didn't answer. I called again and went in the kitchen and started breakfast. Then I went back to his bedroom and be was still lying in bed. I walked in and said 'Are you OK?' He didn't answer. I just knew he was dead."

"What did he look like?" I asked, looking for a way to make him feel something.

"Like he was sleeping." Andrew seemed irritated.

"What did you do?" I pressed.

"I called my brother and sister from the phone on the night table."

"Where was the night table?" I asked, trying to get him to re-create the scene.

"On the other side of the bed, near the wall."

"How did you get to it?"

"I reached over the bed and—"

"You reached over your father?" My chair was squeaking.

"Yes, and I called up my sister and then went to class."

"Did you touch him?" A sudden silence. Andrew's face turned white and his eyes dilated. He gasped for breath.

"Oh, God yes, he was cold! I remember he felt cold and horrible!" Andrew started to cry and shake. He couldn't move from my office for almost two hours. I spent the next two weeks burying the father and resurrecting the son.

Whenever we residents heard about such a key remark that significantly changed a patient's life, we all wanted to intone one just like it. It was an old and powerful wish that is seen throughout the history of man. It is the search for the magic word, like Ali Baba's "Open Sesame," that moves the rock in front of the cave of the forty thieves. It is the magic word to cure the patient. It is also a trap to catch the omnipotence of psychiatrists. Even though right after that session I said "Let there be light" a couple of times to see if I still had the power, I had to flick the wall switch in my office to make the darkness go away—just like any damn mortal.

There is a great temptation to try to interpret patients' problems in such a brilliantly illuminating way that they suddenly understand themselves, are able to face reality and cope with their problems and give up their symptoms. Unfortunately, that's rarely possible. My comment to Andrew was not an interpretation. I merely pointed out a detail which brought back buried feelings. And if I'd told him he used barbiturates to hide his feelings, that remark would have been a clarification.

An interpretation is subtler. Some days later when Andrew was discussing his father again, he got up in the middle of the session and said, "Well, I'll see you. I'm late for class."

"The hour isn't over," I said. "You just now got up to leave the same way you ran out of the bedroom and went to class the day you found your father dead. The feelings are the same." That was an interpretation, tying an event in the therapy situation to an event in the past. A good interpretation, joining past and present, is rare, but when it works it too can be breathtakingly effective. The patient has a concrete example of how he really feels and his therapist gets an enormous sense of power. It can be very heady.

Most of the time you don't make real interpretations, just clarifications. What's more, you shouldn't try because they soon lose their impact. As residents we were all occasionally guilty of trying to summarize a patient's life in one neat sentence, stating how his present activity reflected his past feelings and wishes. I used to call these comments "life sentences," because they summarized a patient's life, and they made an impression that sometimes lasted for years. Statements like "You seem to be the sort of person who seeks out figures in authority to attack and then when you destroy them, feels guilty and unprotected," or, "You seem interested in conquering women as a way of feeling masculine, but when you make it you tend to depreciate the woman for accepting you so that you end up getting no satisfaction, you feel as unsure of your masculinity as ever."

When these statements did make a great difference in patients by allowing them to see themselves in a new light, you felt good about yourself and believed very strongly that there was a great deal in psychiatry—even more than you dreamed of. And you believed that you were pretty damn wonderful for intoning the magic words.

There were other times when you struggled with a patient for months trying to get him to understand what was going on, and when finally you succeeded it didn't help the patient. The patient might have said, "I understand it all now, but I still feel crappy." What you do then is what most of therapy is all about. You help patients to cope with what can't be changed, to accept their own limitations and not to shrink from their own humanness.

This requires that the therapist be in touch with his own humanity and be willing to accept and examine his own feelings when they come up while listening to patients. Sometimes, when talking with

Mrs. Goldman, I would remember times when I was on my own unexpectedly and felt abandoned, my first year at camp or at school. My feelings were sympathetic vibrations touched off by Mrs. Goldman, sort of like harmonics in tune with her emotions. The analysis of these kinds of harmonics sometimes gave me the greatest insights into patients. I sometimes shared these harmonics with my patients with very helpful results. There is a risk in this, of being exposed and of losing your anonymity. I suspect it's often worth taking.

There always was a great deal of discussion among the residents over the question of anonymity. How much should we tell our patients about ourselves? We differed in our opinions about this question. Lovett, predictably, in the style of his psychoanalytic training, believed a psychiatrist should never tell his patient anything about his feelings and not even respond to questions about his personal life. That seemed a little ridiculous to me because Lovett believed this flatly about all patients regardless of their diagnoses. Being anonymous might be a good rule in dealing with some neurotic patients, but it wasn't always valid and it almost surely wasn't the best plan when you were treating psychotic patients or borderline patients who could benefit from some personal feedback. In order to understand this, you may need a little definition of each.

A neurotic is a person whose actions and thoughts in the present symbolically fulfill unresolved conflicts in his past, usually without his being aware of it. Everyone exhibits some neurotic behavior in his life, such as trying to get accepted to the same sorority as your mother even though you may not like it or even approve of sororities. A neurotic symptom can also be the source of a great deal of positive achievement. The need to please one's father has accounted for many successes in this world. God knows my father was a pharmacist who always wanted to be a physician. If the neurotic behavior doesn't interfere with a person's ability to work, love, or be happy, it is probably unnecessary to change it.

A psychotic is someone who often looks and sounds like anyone else except his sense of reality is defective. He is troubled by feelings from the past just like the neurotic, but he perceives the world differently in order to cope with them. He shuts reality out by denying it and holds his feelings in. He is preoccupied with himself and his personal world. He is ambivalent about practically everything. His feelings do not always seem appropriate to his actions, and his thinking is defective. There are large, gaping holes in his logic that everyone else but him can see.

A borderline sees the world like everyone else except he usually brings along his own storehouse of prefabricated feelings and attaches them to everything he sees. He has a preconceived idea of what he will feel and experience. His feelings in the present seem to be derived from events in the past rather than evoked from something in the present. He misses subtleties. He sees things as either black or white and is constantly looking for limits and is often in trouble because he tends to act on his feelings derived from the past.

The present reminds the neurotic of his past, it awakens the *feelings* of the past for the borderline, and it makes the psychotic crawl back into his own world. A neurotic builds castles in the air; a psychotic lives in them; a psychiatrist collects the rent on them; and I guess a borderline is just furious with all of them but doesn't know why.

When a patient has a weak sense of reality the object of therapy is to help strengthen it. When a psychotic asks, "Are you married or single, Doctor?" he is at least in part asking to know something real about his doctor; and showing an interest in anyone outside himself is helpful to the psychotic because it concerns him with reality. It should be encouraged. A neurotic patient might be interested in knowing about his doctor because he likes to fantasize about him and will use anything his doctor tells him as fuel to feed his fantasy production, which is not helpful to him.

There is nothing inherently wrong with fantasy. Fantasy is the mother of thought, the source of creativity, imagination, and wit, and it provides solutions to the great enigmas of this world. In the best sense, fantasy is a possibility which has not yet been thought of, or a reality which has not yet happened. Fantasy is the hundred or so symphonies that Mozart once told a friend he had written in his head for his own pleasure, and it is the dream for a world at peace.

It is only when fantasy supplants reality or is used to escape from reality that it becomes a problem. There's nothing wrong with wanting something or wishing for something, but if you spend all your time wishing you don't get anything.

So it's not useful for some patients to know personal details about their doctor. For them it can be a way of getting the doctor to talk about himself and to avoid the patient's problems. For other patients, it is reassuring to know about their doctor and discover that he's human, that he can get sick, hurt, divorced, or depressed. Discovering that their doctor has feelings like this and still survives is very reassuring to some patients, and makes it possible for them to trust their doctor even more.

Ernie decided he could trust Bert after hearing him urinating in the john while Ernie was sitting in the waiting room in the outpatient department. He apparently figured that any doctor who felt secure enough to piss straight into the middle of the toilet bowl instead of on the side without worrying about who heard the noise must really be sure of himself and able to help him. Mind you, I don't think circulating tape recordings of psychotherapists in the bathroom is going to stamp out mental disease, but this humanizing detail of Bert's life did make Bert more real for Ernie and easier to trust.

As far as my anonymity was concerned, I tried to make common sense my guide. If I was seeing a young woman who doused herself with musk and powdered rhinoceros horn and perfumes, and wore slinky short-short dresses and peekaboo blouses with plunging necklines, and spent the hour crossing and uncrossing her legs trying to get me to look up her dress, and who also had a history of many superficial sexual involvements with men, and on top of this was always looking to the external world to find excuses for her internal emotional difficulties, I would be wrong to tell her anything about myself. To do so would only make her fantasize more about me and make me less effective in helping her. To do so would be encouraging an erotic transference, which means the patient falls in love with the doctor. Unless you're really hard up, I mean *really* hard up, you need this like a hole in the head—most psychiatrists have enough personal problems already and don't need to go out of their way to add on to them.

However, it was not wrong to share my interest in sports with Mr. Parker. It was a real interest and a basis for mutual understanding. In my view it was not unreasonable to tell my psychotic patients a little about myself. It gave them some reality to hang onto.

Dr. Gelb explained to me in supervision, "The best way to get your bearings when patients ask about your personal life is to tell them that you have no reason to conceal anything from them but you'd like to understand why they want to know. Often this opens up into a discussion of their other feelings. Usually you'll discover that they are not interested in you in particular, but in another problem they didn't know how to bring up, and they'll retract the question about your personal life."

Every therapist has to find his own way through this confusion. One needs to walk a line between too cold and too warm. The object is to be human and reasonable and still be a good therapist. I feel being silent as a general rule is a lousy tactic for a therapist and very much out of touch with the loneliness and emptiness that so many people feel in this large, impersonal, cold society of ours. It seems to reinforce the negative side of life.

Why is the question of anonymity so important in therapy and why is there so much concern about how to avoid publicity? The answer, I think, has to do with the issue of transference (any feeling that a patient has about his doctor).

In the classical psychoanalytic tradition, the analyst is very still, almost silent. The patient does all the talking, the doctor listens. In time the patient develops some feelings about his doctor. If the doctor's been playing the game according to plan, he has not revealed himself. He has remained anonymous. All you know about him is that he wants to help and listens to you. You want to know more about him and when your bank sends you his canceled check for the first time, you run like mad to see how his handwriting looks to analyze his character, and you're dismayed to find he endorsed it with a rubber stamp. According to psychoanalytic theory, if he has remained truly anonymous any feelings you have about your doctor are really your feelings about someone else which you have projected onto him. These feelings are called transference. Sorting them out, finding out where they come from, where they belong, and why they are still around is the concern of psychoanalytic therapy.

It looks good on paper. The therapist interprets the patient's feelings about him, which he assumes are the patient's distortions. They may be and then again, they may not. Patients are wholly capable of making some very astute observations about their doctor even if he's silent. If a doctor is open and doesn't believe that everything a patient says about him is a distortion, he can learn a good deal about himself. In reality a doctor cannot be as anonymous as he can in theory. Just because a doctor is silent and doesn't tell his patients about himself doesn't mean that his patients can't learn a great deal about him. They can. They learn almost as much about how he feels as if he told them. Nonverbal signs, like facial expressions, give a great deal away. Even if the patient is not aware that he is picking up clues to his doctor's behavior, he is. The doctor's emotions give him away. The doctor may twitch, may move around a lot or, if he is like me, he may send out little squeaks from his chair (even if the patient is lying down and facing away from the doctor, he can't miss the noises). The doctor may smile, laugh, cough, or do a hundred other things which tell the patient exactly how he feels. The doctor is not anonymous even when he wants to be. You can tell a bastard from a nice guy in a moment if you have any sense at all. It was always funny to me to hear Dr. Gelb tell how he maintained his anonymity with his analytic patients. First, he saw them in an office in his home, which many analysts do. That told them a great deal about their analyst. Second, his waiting room opened onto the main hall and exposed his house with all of its Afro-Jewish art. The aroma of whatever his wife was cooking hit the patient smack in the kisser the minute he walked in. Gelb's patients knew *all about* Gelb.

It is only reasonable to expect patients to conclude a great deal about their therapist that is true, no matter how hard he tries to conceal himself or how much he denies it. His choice of colors, his style of dressing, his choice of the subject of a picture, his magazine subscriptions, the state of care of his house and lawn also give the therapist away. His personality is really very much in evidence. Shhh! Don't say it too loud. He is sometimes the only one who doesn't know it.

Trying to remain anonymous on the ward was not difficult, it was impossible for residents. The patients compared notes about you. They discussed the way you acted with them. When Ernie Stone wasn't playing Ping-Pong and Betsy Lewis wasn't collapsing in the corridor, they would sit together and discuss Bert Feinstein.

"I don't like his beard," Ernie would say.

"He plays with it a lot," said Betsy.

"He does that with me, too. Does he ever say to you, 'We'll talk about it,' when you ask him a very important question and you think he really doesn't know the answer?"

"Does he? All the time, the rat."

"What do you think that means?" asked Ernie.

"I think he's very nervous and doesn't like talking to people," said Betsy, patting her hair. "Do you have a comb?"

"Yuh, I know he's not too experienced because he's so young."

"Young?" said Betsy, fixing her hair in the mirror. "How do I look?" Ernie just shrugged. "How old is he?" she said, making mental bets.

"Twenty-six," said Ernie. "I saw one of the nurses give him a happy-birthday kiss."

Betsy lit up. "No kidding."

"And he's not married either."

"How do you know?"

"I heard one of the nurses, Terry, I think, talking about him."

"Oh, her!" she said, as if she were a rival. "I could fall for Bert."

Ernie winced as he heard Betsy call *his* doctor by his first name as if she had desecrated an altar. He also got angry. "I think you do enough falling around this place already," he said.

Anonymity is maintained not merely to observe patients' distortions more easily (which seems difficult to defend if what I have just pointed out is true) but also to protect the therapist. Many therapists are passive and retiring and don't like to discuss their feelings either—about their patients' problems or about their own lives—in therapy, at home, anywhere. They prefer anonymity because it fits their particular personality as much as their concept of technique. Some therapists who argue that being anonymous with patients is always the best way are really saying that being anonymous is the way for them to be comfortable.

The way one learns to do therapy is to do therapy and to be supervised by other therapists. In the end each therapist must find his own style of interaction and the final judgment of his technique must be how much his patients improve, how much they learn to cope, how much relief they have from their symptoms, and how much their sense of themselves and self-worth increases.

If there were any magic words that would confer on me the ability to help my patients in this way, I swear I'd climb the highest mountain to lie at the feet of the guru who would reveal them to me. But Guru Gelb was fresh out of magical incantations. Anyhow, he preached the word as revealed to Freud in Vienna.

"OK, Dr. Gelb," I said during one of my many supervisory hours, "maybe maintaining anonymity is important with some patients. Let's forget for the moment that I think it's impossible to attain. I admit that sometimes I let my own feelings creep into my therapy sessions. I identify with what the patient has to say. I put myself in their lives. I try to see what it feels like to be them. And I try to give them a little feedback of what I think and feel."

Gelb reamed out his pipe. See, I could tell he was angry by the way he reamed the damn thing. I'm sure his patients could too. He wanted to get every last crusty charred ash out of there. He didn't like what I was saying.

"I think," I went on, "that the empathetic feeling I generate may sometimes get in the way and make it more difficult for me to tell when the patient is distorting his feelings about me. I admit I miss some details but I also think because patients see me as vulnerable and human they're more likely to develop a trust in me. Dr. Gelb, I do think a therapist who stays anonymous may well understand better when his patient distorts what he tells him. . . ." Gelb looked puzzled.

"But I think the patient will tell him much less because he doesn't trust him, and what he does tell him will be more to win over his therapist than to solve his own problems."

"There's an awful lot of theory that goes against that," said Gelb. "The way a patient tries to win over the therapist is often very revealing. You have to keep your distance so you won't get involved, so you'll be able to be objective."

"I think you can be objective and still get involved."

"You're looking for trouble," Gelb warned.

I found it difficult to practice what I preached. It's just so much safer playing silent, especially when the patient corners you. It's easier not answering when you're under pressure. It's easier not giving a human response.

Sometimes I was unable to respond to a patient I didn't particularly like. I couldn't warm up to Mrs. Sacks even though I tried. All I got from her were pounding headaches. I found myself being nasty to her in quiet, subtle ways. When she got angry at me I sometimes pretended she was displacing anger at me that came from somewhere else and not expressing anger I had provoked in her. I found that when I hid behind the mask of psychiatrist I became a counterfeit therapist, and to the same degree a counterfeit human being. I hated doing that, but when I felt unsure of myself I sometimes found myself acting silent and passive. There were times when being silent and giving the patient the time and space to move freely was indicated, such as when I needed more material to find my direction. I don't object to silence at times like that. I object to the times when one of my patients needed a human response from me and I was too overwhelmed to respond. Perhaps I held back because I needed someone to respond to me in the same way and I couldn't admit it or was afraid of losing control of my feelings. So what if I did? Oh, I can say that easily enough now, but at the time it frightened the hell out of me.

"The way you can tell which one is the therapist," Bert once said, "is that the therapist sits on *that* side of the desk and the patient sits in *this* chair."

"What do you do in an office where there is no desk?" I had asked.

"Oh, my God," said Bert. "I don't know, and I've spent weeks trying to figure out who's who."

All year long Gelb and I discussed what a therapist should do in the best of all possible worlds. Gelb made a lot of valuable comments. "The goal of the therapist is to understand the patient. Everything the therapist says and does should be directed toward that end. If you're ever in doubt about what you're doing, reconsider your questions and try to make them reveal as much as possible about the patient's feelings. And relate their feelings in the present to their feelings in the past.

"Always interpret the style of the patients' behavior before you interpret what they tell you. If someone is acting angry and hostile and telling you about a flower show they went to, point out that they are angry. Don't get tricked into talking about the flower show. When a patient tells you something painful and does it in a way that doesn't show he is feeling pain, point out the discrepancy to him and ask him if he understands it.

"Get the patient to want to understand himself, to spend time thinking about why he does what he does, even when he isn't with you. Always ask patients how they feel about things, but be careful not to lead them into feeling what you think. Let them discover it for themselves, they'll accept it more. It's their job to feel. It's your job to help them.

"One of the most useful statements to make to a patient who tells you a painful story is, 'It must have been very difficult for you.' It makes you the patient's ally. The object of all of this is to open the patient up to himself.

"If you do have an insight about the patient, keep your mouth shut. Let the patient discover it for himself. There's no need to tell patients everything you see and discover about them. It will just overwhelm them and they won't be able to accept it. They have to move at their own pace. If only one person sitting in the room with the therapist has insight into the patient's problems, it should be the therapist. In time, both may. If it's the patient who has the insight and you don't, *you've* got a problem."

Unless things have changed by the time this book gets to print, this is still not the best of all possible worlds and it is not always possible to do and say the exact right thing at the right time with every patient. I used to think it was when I first watched Dr. Gavin, but in the past few months I'd seen him pull a few blunders. And I've seen Gelb and Karlsson make stupid errors, too. Everyone's human.

You learn a lot doing therapy both about the patient and about yourself. You get to meet a lot of the women you're glad you never married, and you learn that no matter how bad your problems get there's still someone worse off than you. You also learn how to wing it, how to improvise with a patient and still come out smelling like a rose. In fact, some of your best therapeutic moments happen in a flash of insight, just at the point when you think you're hopelessly cornered.

Mr. Hall was a young man I evaluated on the medical service one night when I was on call. He was easily the most boring and pedantic person I'd ever listened to, and I went to an Ivy League school where my professors routinely sent their shirts out to be stuffed. I fell asleep in the chair at his bedside. I just zonked off to sleep.

Mr. Hall said, "Are you asleep?"

I woke with a start, flushing away an image of a trip to the Grand Canyon when I was eight, and a fleeting glimpse of the face of Carla Bellingham, the first girl who ever let me unbutton her blouse. I stared at this man, sitting bolt upright buttoning his hospital Johnny and demanding to know why I had fallen asleep on him.

"The nerve," he began.

"Yes, I did fall asleep," I said, sounding as if I'd planned it this way, "and do you know something, Mr. Hall, that was the first time I ever fell asleep listening to a patient. I must say you have been absolutely the most boring person I have ever listened to." Mr. Hall's mouth fell open. "Mr. Hall"—I took the chance—"I think you wanted me to become bored with what you were talking about so I would get off the track and not ask you revealing questions. Mr. Hall, you've told me absolutely nothing about what is really bothering you or what you really feel. Now please cut the crap with me and start being honest."

Mr. Hall finished buttoning up his hospital gown, looking for something to say. In a while he admitted he was afraid to talk and was using words to push me away. He told me about the problems he'd been having with his wife and acknowledged he was having an affair. He felt relieved to get it all off his chest and thought I was terrific! I got a complete history in half the usual time and wrote one of my clearest, most succinct notes in his chart. I looked at the note and thought about the entire incident.

I also wondered whatever happened to old Carla Bellingham.

I enjoyed improvising with patients. I once saw a deaf mute in therapy on Bamberg 5, a man who became depressed following the loss of his job. I tried to learn sign language, but mostly I would type out my comments. He would talk with his hands and his voice, but he was difficult for me to understand. Although I learned only a few words in sign language, I once noticed when he was talking about taking care of his wife and trying hard that he mistakenly made the sign which meant pushing her away. It was a slip, just like a slip of the tongue, when a person says something he doesn't mean to say but which reveals how he really feels.

When I told Gelb about it he really ate it up, thought it was fascinating. That's the sort of person Gelb was. I found him to be gentle, bright, if a trifle academic and a bit hesitant about taking bold steps with patients, even if such moves seemed clearly indicated. I really liked Gelb. He was warm, appreciative, and totally without malice. When he was doubtful about one of my tactics he was totally fairhanded about it. He wasn't interested in putting me down, only in understanding. The world could be in flames, but if he understood why he was happy.

I suppose I really did want to go into therapy or analysis with him during the early months of my training, something specifically forbidden by Dr. M. Austin Noyes, the chairman of the department. No resident could be in treatment with his supervisor. For good reason, I supposed, but that didn't stop me from wanting.

I threw my back out shoveling snow, which came early that year. I was flat on my back for two days. I could do anything but sit in a chair. A nice injury for a psychiatrist! I stood up, talking to my patients. One little gray-haired psychotic man thought I was crazy and refused to stay in the office with me, even after I explained why I was standing. I tried standing during supervision with Gelb but got tired. When I sat down I felt great for the first five minutes and then I started to ache in the small of my back. By the time I stood up I was ready to play the hunchback of Notre Dame. I got sympathy from my patients trying to score points, but the reactions of my fellow residents were mixed. Marty just made fun of me. Bert offered to bring me lunch. Lovett wanted to know what feelings I was secretly repressing. D. J. wanted to know if I had slipped a disc at the fifth lumbosacral intervertebral space. Terry, God bless her hysterical character, wanted to rub my back.

I couldn't sit down in supervision, so without asking Gelb I lay flat down on Gelb's analytic couch. Gelb, of course, was sitting in his usual seat behind the couch, reaming out his pipe. He stopped reaming the pipe when I lay down. He stopped the sentence he had begun. I think he stopped breathing.

"Relax, Jerry," I said. "I threw my back out and it just hurts like hell to sit."

I could tell he didn't believe me. He said so.

"I don't believe you," he said. "You want to talk about it?"

"It's true," I said, staring up at that horrible tribal mask on his door. "That's a horrible mask, Jerry," I said.

"That's what all my patients say the first time they lie down on the couch," he said, and then added in typical psychoanalytic style, "So's your mask—now do you want to tell me what's going on?"

I started to laugh and suppressed it, because I got these shooting pains down my legs whenever I laughed or coughed.

The more therapy I did, the more inventive I like to think I became. I liked trying to find ways to put the patients' problems in clearer perspective for them. During the first few months of residency I found myself drawing diagrams that outlined what a patient was feeling, where the feeling came from, where it went, what symptoms it caused and why.

"You see, you, the circle with the X in it, are angry with your husband. That's him in the circle with the H in it. But you can't express it." I drew an arrow going from the circle with an X to the one with the H. "Instead you take it out on yourself." I made the arrow miss the H and turn back to the X.

It was pretty stupid and I feel silly even telling you about it. I did that for about two months. Not all the time. Just when I felt insecure. I never was honest enough to tell Jerry Gelb about it. I was sure he would tell me I was being childish and was afraid he would think I didn't know anything. And I still had these visions of being drummed out of the corps.

About this time I was developing a very ornate system of taking notes while listening to my patients. My notes were terrific. Except there was one thing wrong. I was paying so much attention to taking notes that I sometimes missed valuable clues from my patients. Why was I taking notes? Probably to be sure I had all the answers to the questions Gelb used to ask afterward. I hated not knowing all the answers. Supervisors had a way of asking, "And how did he feel about his sister when he was young?" You probably would never in a million years think to ask some of the questions supervisors asked, so you took notes and said, "We haven't gone into that yet" which freely translated meant, "I forgot to ask." And you did forget to ask about a lot of things. Taking notes was sometimes helpful in organizing your thinking when you were listening to a patient, but it could be a crutch and a way of keeping aloof.

I came to see taking notes as a hindrance and figured that if the patient said something really important I would remember it—that is, if I was tuned into the patient and the sort of person he was. If I wasn't, taking notes wouldn't nearly make up for it. When a patient is suffering from a severe loss, every loss he mentions shows like a bloody wound anyway. You don't need notes to be on the lookout for what concerns him. Sometimes I wrote brief notes after the sessions to record the gist, the direction of the hour. I gave up taking notes when I saw patients, except for writing down statistics such as addresses and the like. In time, I needed less to hide behind than when I began, and came to see notes as a mask.

"So what do you think therapy is all about?" I asked Marty DiAngelo over lunch.

Marty looked very serious and thoughtful and sipped his coffee. Could you believe this, for once I was going to get a serious answer. D. J. smiled her accepting warm smile at him. Marty said, "Therapy is an arrangement in which a patient pays a doctor some money which obligates the doctor to listen and keeps him from going away no matter how badly he is treated or what the patient says to him. After a while the patient gets to feel guilty over the way he's been acting toward this doctor. After all, even if the doctor is paid to listen and takes all the abuse, he still is a person. So the patient begins to look at how he acts and tries to be nicer to the doctor. And then after a while the patient starts being nicer even to people he isn't paying to listen to him. And that's what therapy is."

"You're probably right," D. J. said.

In learning about therapy, I learned a great deal more about myself and about doctors. I was not called by divine inspiration to the practice of medicine. I became a physician because I thought it would be an interesting career and because I thought I would enjoy doing what physicians did. I elected to become a physician by taking the courses required to get into medical school and by doing well enough to get accepted, and finally by working hard enough to get through.

There was no mystery, no great sense of personal sacrifice, no overwhelming self-denial other than having to study on weekends because I had to get a good grade in organic chemistry when my college roommates were off to Skidmore to sample the lovelies in the freshman class. I had to give up a few years to the study of some meaningless details which I would have to know exceedingly well just to get my degree and never have the opportunity or need to use ever again. But that too was no big sacrifice. People who tell you medical school is a struggle are putting you on. It's mostly a bore.

Doctors are only people. They're not saints whose word is the final and absolute end. Their knowledge is often tentative, their understanding empiric and imperfect, and their motivations frequently mixed. The doctors who hid behind the mask of privileged sainthood, who refused to come down from their high horses, were always irritating as hell to me. Doctors who didn't understand they were only human were less likely to admit they made mistakes or that their patients could sometimes be right and they could sometimes be wrong.

When a doctor feels he's been called to the profession, and many really do even though they will strongly deny it, he demands respect for his authority just because he is a doctor and because he feels he has struggled to become what he is. Doctors become doctors for reasons of their own, and patients owe them no reverence.

As I learned to be a therapist, I decided I would much rather a patient felt kindly toward me because I'd helped him than feel in awe of me because I was a physician. Whatever struggle I confronted in becoming a physician was a personal one. I wasn't trying to solve the problems of mankind, I only wanted to fulfill myself and be happy in my work. If mankind were the better for it I would be pleased, but my joy would first have to come from my work itself, from being me, from myself.

As I became more confident, I felt less need to hide behind the mask of being a physician and more willing to give of myself.

The process of becoming a psychiatrist, whatever it was, had apparently begun.

FREUD'S INVENTION

LESTON HAVENS

In this chapter, Lestor Havens provides insight into two important questions about psychotherapy: What is the therapist doing behind all of that silence? How does one tell when a patient is better?

The invention of Freud's that Havens refers to is evenly suspended attention, where the therapist remains neutral, anonymous, and quiet. This device, which could also be called therapeutic listening, requires the therapist to be creative and open. This is part of creating a safe place where the patient can feel accepted and free enough to uncover the painful recesses of the psyche. The patient is allowed the space to function independently and freely, while allowing the analyst, from a detached position, to hear more clearly what the patient has to say.

Freud invented, in the silences of psychoanalysis, a method of correcting a particular human problem so specific and effective as to defy any substitution or even alteration. A great invention is like a piece of great wit: it seems in retrospect the only answer. Recall G. K. Chesterton's reply to the question, What book would you most like with you on a desert island? "Huntington's Guide to Practical Shipbuilding." Freud's invention is like that.

Imagine a young person very attractive and a little uncertain.

Imagine further a mother of this only child a little hovering, a little too eager to be helpful and advisory. This not uncommon situation puts the young person at risk of what we can term "imagined incapacity": the half-conviction of being unable to do all sorts of things that in fact she probably can do. Of course the imagined incapacity has to be explained, justified to its possessor, and to this end the various bodily sensations and mental preoccupations that everyone has, of anxiety and uncertainty, signals that any close listener to the body's vicissitudes will be able to hear—these "explain" the hesitancy. The sensations and preoccupations provide reasons for worry and doubt that no student of life and the body need be without.

Beneath this little drama of hesitation lies another. Freud also noted that people at the edge of independence, on the cusp of leaving family and launching out into life, often retain as the other side of this independence a family closeness that is both more and less than family affection. It has some of the earlier coloring of the ties to parents, with its physical demands, deep-running libidinal currents, and heightened sensations. And it retains some of the egocentricity that marks childhood relationships: "they" exist for me. The individual has not yet reached that insecurely held feature of later life in which others are both separate from us and as important as we are to ourselves. There occur too such features of independence as arrogance and wildness that are easy to confuse with an earlier time of life. Thus the young person at the Oedipal cusp has a foot in both worlds, and so subtle and intermixed is the relationship between them that it is not easy to determine whether a symptom is a symptom or, instead, a sign of health and movement. Is anxiety really that, or simply excitement?

Just as hysterics—as the most vehemently articulate of the above patients were called—to a significant extent invented psychotherapy, so psychotherapy continues to discover itself in the encounters with hysterics. This is so for a paradoxical and disconcerting reason: hysterical patients are often more adventurous and mature than their helpers. Standing at the edge of new life, sometimes constrained by timid elders who are frightened to appreciate this new creature they have borne, the hysterics invite a rethinking of the conventional, a recasting of the old into the still hesitant vision they have of the new. It therefore behooves their helpers, once again, to respect what the patients have to say. Psychoanalysis easily loses this respect in its sometimes complacent sense of grasping everything. We often forget that the arrogance of youth is a necessary part of young confronting old, whether in life or science. Freud set here, as in so much else, a splendid example. Remember what he did. The chief obligation of elders remains to make what has been learned interesting enough so it is not neglected by the next generation.

My young patient was very pretty. It was easy to imagine why so many hurried to counsel and guide her. Further, she presented herself dramatically, sometimes sensationally, with a full, literal disclosure of her varied sensations, so that any therapist had much to contemplate and analyze. She could even seem a little mad. The sober psychopathologist might suspect megalomania, exhibitionism, volatility, much else. Yet it all seemed to me mostly the high spirits of youth, combined with a wonderful, often teasing imagination. I had to remind myself of the perils of psychological judgment.

She came to see me because her mother, herself a psychiatrist, thought she needed to. The beautiful daughter was in college in a nearby city, had experienced one turbulent relationship after another, and was encouraged to "share" the resulting emotions with the mother. I suspected that each amplified the other's feelings because this sharing, far from calming the patient down, exacerbated her agitation and led to threats of flight, even suicide. I noted, however, that all through these whirlwinds, the patient went on her very successful academic way.

I also noted that, even at her most volatile, there was an important corrective tendency in her associations. "I can't go on," she would cry out, and then a little later, "There is a paper I must finish on Monday." "I can't imagine a future without Carl," and five minutes later came the description of a new interest. The corrections were often immediate and trenchant; she never left the earth for long. I took this to mean that her self-reflective capacity was strong, that even the most intense feelings or extravagant fantasies did not overwhelm her capacity to apply reason, sustain a judgment, even calm herself down, unless (and this is a critical "unless") someone she trusted did not collude in her excitement. I quickly saw that my job was in part to maintain an emotional neutrality that could not be set afire.

There was one more significant feature of her associations: she "triangulated," over and over again. If she mentioned a boyfriend, one of his past loves soon appeared. Discussion of mother led to father. The pattern of her mental reflections was three-part, seldom the patient and only one other person. I have come to trust this as a sign of a basically stabilized inner life. It has often been claimed that triangulation means the patient's development has incorporated a secure family experience that anchors mental life. It may also explain the self-correcting tendency I have just remarked on: no one voice speaks alone. As is true of lucky families, each spouse brings a note of sanity and correction to the utterances of the other. Perhaps this was now a firm part of her selfhood.

So I felt free to settle down and listen. I used Freud's invention, which seemed just right for this patient. I became removed, largely anonymous and silent, spoke only to elicit associations, and practiced an evenly suspended attention. In order to grow, she needed to be left alone. But her compelling attractiveness, complaints, dependence, and uncertainty combined to make this almost impossible. What she needed was a device that at the same time captured her expectation of being helped and did not exploit it. Of course this is a "being alone" with someone, but that someone must leave her alone. We will see that Freud's invention is as precise as penicillin, and very similar in its mode of action.

This neutrality is not entirely what it seems. It is the emotional facet of a certain kind of leaving alone. The therapist is not neutral about the patient's making it on his or her own; quite the contrary, the neutrality of silence can also conceal a prayer. The secret prayer has been wonderfully rendered in a poem of Richard Wilbur's, "The Writer":

In her room at the prow of the house
Where light breaks, and the windows are tossed with linden,
My daughter is writing a story.

I pause in the stairwell, hearing
From her shut door a commotion of typewriter-keys
Like a chain hauled over a gunwale.

Young as she is, the stuff
Of her life is a great cargo, and some of it heavy:
I wish her a lucky passage.

But now it is she who pauses,
As if to reject my thought and its easy figure.
A stillness greatens in which

The whole house seems to be thinking,
And then she is at it again with a bunched clamor
Of strokes, and again is silent.

I remember the dazed starling
Which was trapped in that very room, two years ago;
How we stole in, lifted a sash

And retreated, not to affright it;
And how for a helpless hour, through the crack of the door,
We watched the sleek, wild, dark

And iridescent creature
Batter against the brilliance, drop like a glove
To the hard floor, or the desk-top,

And wait then, humped and bloody,
For the wits to try it again; and how our spirits
Rose when, suddenly sure,

It lifted off from a chair-back,
Beating a smooth course for the right window
And clearing the sill of the world.

It is always a matter, my darling,
Of life or death, as I had forgotten. I wish
What I wished you before, but harder.

In its turn, anonymity involves reducing oneself to a presence. The purpose is not to conceal or hide. I answer whatever I am asked if the question does not seem a distraction. The point is not to intrude: the patient is to be left alone. The failure to answer a nondistracting question is, in fact, an intrusion, of one's absence. This justifies what is otherwise contradictory in the theory of psychoanalytic work: the analyst is told to be anonymous, but in fact he is known to the patient by his appearance, his office, his very name.

It was, of course, the silence, this extraordinary listening, that set analytic work off most dramatically from what had preceded it. We will see in a moment that this listening has often been misunderstood. It was not meant to be the listening of a hunter, directed, patient, intent. That would violate what Freud meant by the even suspension of attention. It is more like the silence of the night, all around yet incomplete, because wind, trees, and insects sound out; so the therapist's chair creaks, or the therapist himself, again presence not absence. Moreover, this silence draws from the patient, also expectant and waiting, the very excitement and hopes that have impeded the patient's independent functioning. The stage is set.

The evenly hovering or suspended attention (as it has been differently translated) represents the most subtle and crucial aspect of Freud's technique. It included not only the avoidance of formulating, reaching for meaning, or even thinking about any aspect of the patient's associations in particular, but a whole state of mind difficult to describe. Any description is your own; this concept lies at the frontier of psychological work. Thus directing attention means interpretation and intrusion when the goal is to allow the fullest, freest development of the person's own thoughts; again, the patient is to be let alone. But it is most difficult to describe what substitutes for directing attention. Perhaps the phrase "pure presence" will do—an accompanying that does not stay too close, an interest that does not itself attempt to be interesting. Freud emphasized one result of evenly suspended attention that illuminates the attention itself. The analyst should be surprised, that is, pure presence opens the way to surprise. Not thinking actively, not trying to explain or predict makes it easier to hear the successive associations just as they are, still free of imputed meaning or connection, so that something unexpected, even unique, will not pass unheard because a prejudgment has excluded it. Now this is a paradox. Why should surprise be an experience of the drifting mind when formulation itself invites surprise by laying down expectations that can be violated? Indeed, can there be any surprise at all unless there is some prejudgment to run aground?

Students of creativity have suggested that the creative moment must bear contradiction. Einstein grasping that the freely falling body is also at rest, Picasso seeing at once before and behind, Freud suggesting that a passive stance might penetrate most deeply and sharply—it is the capacity to hold two apparently irreconcilable positions at once that makes these examples of creativity what they are, creative, surprising. This is not a far cry from those insights that give psychotherapeutic work its own moments of glory: it is a hearing freely.

One day my patient said she was feeling terrible. She had eaten everything in sight, been outraged at her mother, thought she might end it all. I felt some inward panic of my own, and struggled against the wish to do something that would quiet the storm. Most of all I found myself furiously thinking, figuring, wondering why. In very many situations it is hard not to think, and the well-trained professional person has very many thoughts. I believe it was Aristotle who said that anger is the emotion closest to logic. Certainly those angriest of patients, the paranoids, have a great penchant for thought; they too explain, and in that explaining put us down. So the generation of thought in my own case might be a function of anger. I didn't feel like evenly suspending my attention.

Gradually I quieted myself down. Here thinking was useful: I remembered how many of these tropical storms had come and gone. Thinking this way I was also not paying close attention to her and perhaps caught less of her excitement. When I came back from my solitary trip, I was surprised to hear her say, "As soon as I went back to the dorm and worked on that paper, I felt better." She had found the same solution that I had.

An evenly suspended attention permits opposites to coexist in the mind; the suspension of logical insistence permits even the most disparate elements to come together. I believe it is this unforced mingling that allows fresh combinations to appear and shed their light. Note that the process of discovery is not occurring to the therapist's mind—I was not thinking about the patient. The free passage of thoughts in the patient's speech and the therapist's mind occupies a space between the two; discoveries are not made by separate minds, but spring up in the common space. This is a microcosm of a greater cultural fact, that new ideas occur to the culture at large, often in several places at once.

Surprise is a result of random mingling, of the failure to impose a familiar or conventional grid of meaning, and of these two factors together: the real shows itself when convention is somewhat suspended. It is not that well-established ideas or hard-won truths will be abandoned, because they take good care of themselves, from force of habit and the attraction of the revered. The need is to prevent them from altogether overwhelming fresh perceptions.

What was she to do, stay close to her beloved mother, venture forth on her own, or wander between the two, as she was doing? Here again there was a temptation to discuss and decide, and here again the genius of Freud's invention shows itself. My interest, silence, and waiting invited her expectation that we would indeed discuss and decide. What other reason was there to be here? Furthermore, her natural, healthy reaching out into my anonymity, the fact that she was paying me quite a lot, my obvious concern for her, all these concentrated her hopes of a new and more successful parenting in the treatment.

Earlier I compared Freud's invention to the action of penicillin, another material that enters into a relationship in order to block a pathological result. In the case of penicillin, the relationship is between the penicillin molecule and the wall of the invasive bacterium. Penicillin first attaches itself to the cell wall and then prevents the cell-wall metabolism from operating in its usual way. So it was to be for my patient. The very psychotherapeutic elements that concentrated her expectations, the silence, neutrality, anonymity, and evenly suspended attention, also frustrated the pathological acting out of these expectations. She was accustomed to others' reinforcing her calls for help, her dependence, the conviction that she did not have resources enough to succeed on her own. Treatment required a method that could support her hopes while they were one by one replaced with successes of her own. I could not tell her she was now on her own and would make it, for she could only learn that by doing. If she acted at my command, it would be only one more dependence. Nevertheless, we wonder, why does any sensible person—and my patient was sensible—talk to a silent listener? One reason I have mentioned: patients like this one are self-centered, deeply interested in themselves; and they allow themselves this pleasure without the conventional hesitation affecting the rest of us. In addition, it's true that I was responsive: I listened alertly, and my face conveyed much. But there is a still more sensible reason for her continued talking. One of my patients, another bright college student, said it clearly. He had been puzzled for a while, then remarked, "Maybe you think I can make it on my own."

The treatment also required that she concentrate her expectations on me. Otherwise she would once again look to someone else to continue her dependence. The dependence had to be held in suspense, that is, half believed in, or she would not stay with me long enough to know what she could do. She had to be held in suspense because the victory must be achieved in each of the great territories in which we live: the body, our life with others, and our work.

She began to advance on all three fronts very soon. In the beginning she told of the puzzling relationship she had with her body. She loved it, often studied it, loved others' pleased responses to it, but could not control it. Or, better, she could not control her relationship to it: one day she would feed it next to nothing, the next gorge it. And the body's image in her eyes alternated just as sharply: most often she enjoyed and even treasured it; then one part, her nose or legs, would seem grotesque. She was especially prone to experience fatness, although her weight did not fluctuate much and her fear of fat never reached the extremes of a full-blown anorexia. She sometimes looked into a funhouse mirror of herself, the changing image of which reflected her desires, partial images of envied others, often an imposed glimpse of her mother, even her gift for caricaturing popular conventional images and distancing herself from them. But the relationship with her body was more than mirrored. The body was also an object she both inhabited and could stand apart from. As a child, she said, she had not noticed her body as a separate object: then she was her body. Pubescence had typically created the new relationship, when her body had independently flowered. For one thing, she could not keep up with it, and it always surprised her. What would it do next, could she tame it, satisfy it, make it her own? Sometimes the starving and gorging seemed the wild gestures of a genuinely puzzled master desperate to manage the beast.

Sexuality both heightened her alienation from the body and retrieved part of her identification with it. More quickly than most adolescents I have known, she saw that others identified her with her body more than she did, that she could use it at once to bring others close and to keep them at a distance. She even discovered the extraordinary extent to which many men identify women with their bodies and hope to use the body's responsiveness to control the person inside. Early on she discovered that lovemaking is not only the occasion of alienation from one's body—when the body is manipulated for the control of a soul—but also of new identification. When love joins lust, there is an ecstatic harmony that is as much a harmony between self and body as it is between the partners.

It is characteristic of these wonderful young people who can truly leave home that the discoveries of alienation and renewed identification are made both at home and abroad. She gradually gained distance from her mother, but she also discovered and valued those things in herself that she knew were also her mother's. The mother too had a volatile spirit and felt deeply. Once this had been a bond between them, later the patient resented it, still later it became a memory and something lovable, almost a foible each could recognize and begin to control. It was not as if the renewed identification distanced the quality itself. It was more as if it brought it home, like a familiar piece of furniture good for some things and not so good for others.

I could say she "matured," if I knew what that meant. Often I know what it is supposed to mean: settling for the conventions and expectations of some group, or mastering a set of tasks, such as intimacy or autonomy. But how do we test for such results, when they are so easy to simulate and, more important, are sometimes set aside when a life has different or conflicting purposes? Just as conventions and expectations can fix a lethal straitjacket on individual differences, so standards of health on the basis of admirable traits ignore the way human situations can call up the need for the most bizarre qualities.

Instead I judge the success of psychotherapy in two ways. Does the patient's appearance change? Does he get new friends? What people may say to you about their treatment can often be misleading. Some must justify an expensive psychotherapy, or others want to please the doctor or themselves. Many cling to treatments that years later are viewed as tortures. My father once described a fellow lawyer in New York whose majestic name and eagle-like appearance kept his clients in thrall. Young lawyers learned he was easy game for any suit on contracts or wills he had made. But his clients, bleeding and bankrupt, swore by him.

But a change of appearance is significant. It may be seen first in a new gesture, the way a patient looks at you or holds her head. In someone known well, these unfamiliar things are startling. Some patients look better, less mousy or withdrawn. But there are patients like my college student, who lose their shine. Perhaps they have been too beautiful, too stunning to be real, and the extraordinary attractiveness is tempered. I like to think they no longer have to please so much. Friends too must change when a person changes. Most often what seem to me predatory or conventional types are left behind. Much of what passes for friendship, acquaintanceship among men, and what seems so common among women, one person using the other to invade or manipulate, these are replaced. The daunting requirements of friendship, so defiant of our evolutionary heritage, that a friend should be both close and open, are now and then met. The psychotherapist has also provided safe enough conditions for simultaneous closeness and openness. The job passes to friends.

I said that Freud's invention was like a piece of great wit. I could also have compared it to a detective story: a suspicion turning into a solution that is sometimes a salvation. This is what happened here. I suspected she could make it on her own, that her complaints of dizziness, purposelessness, a kind of intellectual vertigo before any large piece of work, were efforts at recruitment or, better, casting for a play that if repetitious was always interesting. She was dramatic in the precise sense that she re-created her family drama everywhere she went.

The solution could not be simply an unmasking. I could not rise up from the audience shouting that the characters were only Mr. Actor, Mrs. Actress, and little Mary Actress, not the more gripping father, mother, and child portrayed. No doubt she would have found some way to make my denunciation part of the drama, the work of a jealous sister, perhaps, or a betrayed uncle. Or, had I persisted, she might have done what George Bernard Shaw did with his balcony denouncer, modestly joining the critic midst all the applause: "I quite agree with you, but who are we two against so many?"

No, the solution had to be an integral part of the play itself, a different and surprising ending, like the ending of a detective story. What makes the difference in a mystery is the detective: he makes it come out right. But the detective cannot rewrite the story, much as he likes to explain it afterward. He must use his suspicions to solve the problem, in this case much as Agatha Christie solved one riddle by having her detecting person almost become the riddler's victim. The drama there was heightened by the nearness of the miss, which every psychotherapist can testify to.

A patient very like mine once asked a wise therapist what in God's name he was doing through all those long silences. He replied, "I am just trying to keep out of your way." That is not so easy. I described one panic of my own, and there were others. My patient had patterns of symptoms that could have driven a neurologist wild, or made the neurologist wonder how any largely descriptive psychiatry, any psychiatry resting on symptoms and signs, can survive hysteria. The greatest difficulty was that I had myself to deal with as well. I have had patients I loved too much or maybe did not love rightly enough. I kept wanting to do more, prove my helpfulness, probably beneath it all win their love. Somewhat angry, prickly types, in my experience, are most likely to turn the therapists into real victims because therapists may feel they need to prove their devotion. In Richard Wilbur's image, it is better just to wish.

The solution is a salvation for a reason that I think is little appreciated. I believe psychological health is little better today than physical health was two hundred years ago, when people died young or of a dozen diseases, as the very poor still do. We do not know the measurements of psychological longevity, but surely to be moribund psychologically is to lack imaginative freedom, to lose a living connectedness, to see the future as apart from present and past. Such seems to me the fate of many of our people even in their twenties and thirties. This is not to say that they are permanently dead. Perhaps the greatest privilege and joy of doing psychotherapy is bringing the psychologically moribund back to life. This is what I mean by salvation.

I am not surprised. If the thrust of Freud's invention is right on a large scale, then a person's reaching a free and relatively independent state must be exceptional. A suitable degree of holding back from the lives of our children must be rare. And rarer still is its accompaniment by prayer and hope. If this is so, growing into one's own remains exceptional, our people are poorly prepared for life, and psychotherapy remains the thriving business it is.

I did not tell her when to come, how often, whether to sit up or lie down. I set no termination date. I had confidence in her and wished her freedom. She did not abuse my trust, and when she was ready to go, she left. She did not need me any more, nor me to tell her so.

THE THIRD EAR

THEODOR REIK

Here is a lucid explanation of the primary tool of psychoanalysis by one of its most renowned practitioners. Theodor Reik was adept at explaining how the analyst uses his or her own emotions and reactions to communicate with and understand the patient. In this chapter from *Listening with the Third Ear*, Reik eloquently describes the special listening process that a therapist practices, a process that invokes all the senses and many recesses of the conscious mind. It is only by using this heightened form of attention, Reik argues, that the therapist may decipher the meaning—true meaning—of the patient's words and actions. More than any other psychoanalyst, Reik imbued the therapeutic process with a kind of mystical awareness that had the unintended result of turning the heads of many professional and would-be analysts.

The psychoanalyst has to learn how one mind speaks to another beyond words and in silence. He must learn to listen "with the third ear." It is not true that you have to shout to make yourself understood. When you wish to be heard, you whisper.

What can an analyst teach his younger colleagues in this direction? Very little. He can speak of his own experiences. He can report instances, which have the value of illustrations only. And he can—

above all else—encourage the younger generation of analysts to un-learn all routine. We speak of routine only in the gathering of unconscious material through observation, not of the use which the analytic technique makes of it. We have to insist that in the area of observation he keep fancy-free and follow his instincts. The "instincts," which indicate, point out, hint at and allude, warn and convey, are sometimes more intelligent than our conscious "intelligence." We know so many things that "aren't so" but, we must admit, we guess many things that seem to be impossible but "are so." Young analysts should be encouraged to rely on a series of most delicate communications when they collect their impressions; to extend their feelers, to seize the secret messages that go from one unconscious to another.

To trust these messages, to be ready to participate in all flights and flings of one's imagination, not to be afraid of one's own sensitivities, is necessary not only in the beginnings of analysis: it remains necessary and important throughout. The task of the analyst is to observe and to record in his memory thousands of little signs and to remain aware of their delicate effects upon him. At the present stage of our science it is not so necessary, it seems to me, to caution the student against overvaluation of the little signs or to warn him not to take them as evidence. These unconscious feelers are not there to master a problem, but to search for it. They are not there to grasp, but to touch. We need not fear that this approach will lead to hasty judgments. The greater danger (and the one favored by our present way of training students) is that these seemingly insignificant signs will be missed, neglected, brushed aside. The student is often taught to observe sharply and accurately what is presented to his conscious perception, but conscious perception is much too restricted and narrow. The student often analyzes the material without considering that it is so much richer, subtler, finer than what can be caught in the net of conscious observation. The small fish that escapes through the mesh is often the most precious.

Receiving, recording, and decoding these "asides," which are whispered between sentences and without sentences, is, in reality, not teachable. It is, however, to a certain degree demonstrable. It can be demonstrated that the analyst, like his patient, knows things without knowing that he knows them. The voice that speaks in him, speaks low, but he who listens with a third ear hears also what is expressed almost noiselessly, what is said *pianissimo*. There are instances in which things a person has said in psychoanalysis are consciously not even heard by the analyst, but none the less understood or interpreted. There are others about which one can say: in one ear, out the other, and in the third. The psychoanalyst who must look at all things immediately, scrutinize them, and subject them to logical examination has often lost the psychological moment for seizing the fleeting, elusive material. Here—and only here—you must leap before you look; otherwise you will be looking at a void where a second before a valuable impression flew past.

In psychoanalysis we learn to collect this material, which is not conscious but which has to become conscious if we want to use it in our search and research. That the psychoanalyst immediately recognizes the importance and significance of the data brought to his attention is a stale superstition. He can be content with himself when he is able to receive and record them immediately. He can be content if he becomes aware of them. I know from conversations with many psychoanalysts that they approach this unconscious material with the tools of reason, clinical observation, meditation, and reflection. They approach it, but that does not mean that they even come close to it. The attempt to confine unconscious processes to a formula like chemical or mathematical processes remains a waste of intellectual energy. One doubts if there is any use in discussing the difference between the two types of processes with such superior minds. The Austrian poet, Grillparzer, and the German playwright, Hebbel, lived at the same time (about one hundred years ago) in Vienna, without meeting each other. Grillparzer was reluctant to speak with Hebbel, who was inclined to reflection and brooded over many metaphysical problems. Grillparzer admitted he was too shy to converse with the prominent, meditative playwright. "You know," he said, "Mr. Hebbel knows exactly what God thinks and what He looks like, and I just don't know."

It seems to me that the best way to guess something about the significance of "insignificant" data, the way to catch the fleeting impression, is not to meditate, but to be intensely aware of them. They reveal their secrets like doors that open themselves, but cannot be forced. One can with conviction say: you will understand them after you have ceased to reflect about them.

No doubt, the third ear of which we often speak will appear to many not only as an anatomical, but also as a psychological, abnormality—even to psychologists. But do we not speak of hearing with the "inner ear"? What Nietzsche meant is not identical with this figure of speech, but it is akin to it. The third ear to which the great psychologists referred is the same that Freud meant when he said the capacity of the unconscious for fine hearing was one of the requisites for the psychoanalyst.

One of the peculiarities of this third ear is that it works two ways. It can catch what other people do not say, but only feel and think; and it can also be turned inward. It can hear voices from within the self that are otherwise not audible because they are drowned out by the noise of our conscious thought-processes. The student of psychoanalysis is advised to listen to those inner voices with more attention than to what "reason" tells about the unconscious; to be very aware of what is said inside himself, *écouter aux voix intérieures*, and to shut his ear to the noises of adult wisdom, well-considered opinion, conscious judgment. The night reveals to the wanderer things that are hidden by day.

In other words, the psychoanalyst who hopes to recognize the secret meaning of this almost imperceptible, imponderable language has to sharpen his sensitiveness to it, to increase his readiness to receive it. When he wants to decode it, he can do so only by listening sharply inside himself, by becoming aware of the subtle impressions it makes upon him and the fleeting thoughts and emotions it arouses in him. It is most important that he observe with great attention what this language means to him, what its psychological effects upon him are. From these he can arrive at its unconscious motives and meanings, and this conclusion again will not be a conscious thought-process or a logical operation, but an unconscious— I might almost say, instinctive—reaction that takes place within him. The meaning is conveyed to him by a message that might surprise him much like a physical sensation for which he is unprepared and which presents itself suddenly from within his organism. Again, the only way of penetrating into the secret of this language is by looking into oneself, understanding one's own reactions to it.

The reader is asked to think this over. A little known and concealed organ in the analyst receives and transmits the secret messages of others before he consciously understands them himself. And yet the literature of psychoanalysis neglects it. There is one word that may make claim to being a rarity in psychoanalytic literature (with the exception of Freud): the word "I." With what fear and avoidance does the analyst write about his own method of coming to conclusions, about his own thoughts and impressions! The devil himself could not frighten many analysts more than the use of the word "I" does in reporting cases. It is this fear of the little pronoun of the first person singular, nominative case, that accounts for the fact that reports of self-analysis are such a rarity in our literature. The worship of the bitch-goddess objectivity, of pseudo precision, of facts and figures, explains why this is the only book that deals with this subject matter, or which insists that the subject matters. In our science only the psychical reality has validity. It is remarkable that the unconscious station which does almost all the work is left out of analytic discussions. Imagine discussing the science of sound, acoustics, without mentioning the ear, or optics without speaking of the eye.

Nothing can, of course, be said about the nature of those unconscious impressions we receive as long as they remain unconscious. Here are a few representative instances of some that became conscious. They concern the manner, not the manners, of persons who were in the process of psychoanalysis, little peculiarities, scarcely noticed movements, intonations, and glances that might otherwise have escaped conscious observation because they were inconspicuous parts of the person's behavior. People generally tend to brush aside observations of this sort as immaterial and inconsequential little things not worthy of our attention.

In the hall that leads from my office to the apartment door, is a big mirror beside a clothes tree. Why did I not observe that a young, pretty woman patient of mine never looked into the mirror when she put on her coat? I must have seen it before, but it came to my attention only after the fifth psychoanalytic session. I was aware that she spoke without any emotions about her marriage or her family, and I became suspicious that her remoteness and coolness were expressions of a schizophrenic disease. Walking behind her to the door I observed that she did not even glance at herself in the mirror, but I did not recall perceiving this trait before. I must have perceived it before without noticing it and, when I paid attention to it now, I did so because I saw it as an additional symptom. I had seen the patient walk to the door in front of me five times, and I know now that, unlike other women, she never looked into the mirror. Now I also became aware of how carelessly she treated her hat, that she threw it on rather than put it on. It gained significance now—why not before? Why did I recall only then what I had often said before, namely, that men who treat their hats with great care are usually not very masculine and women who do not pay any attention to their hats are, in general, not very feminine?

I am choosing this instance as representative of many others in which we become aware of a slight divergence because we miss a certain detail of behavior. Experience in psychoanalysis teaches us that we are inclined to overlook the absence of a usual bit of behavior, although it is often a valuable clue and can become a part of the psychological circumstantial evidence we need. That something is not present where we expect it, or that something is not in its usual place or order, is less conspicuous than the presence of something unusual. Only when the trait appears important or when it is missed immediately will it become conspicuous by its absence. Otherwise, we generally ignore what is not there. Sometimes, just the observation of the absence of such little features leads to understanding. The other day I read a mystery story in which a murder is committed during a theater performance. The audience is searched and the fact that one man has no tie yields a precious clue.

In contrast to the case mentioned above, I observed very soon after the beginning of an analysis that a patient, a middle-aged man, spent a long time before the mirror in the hall, smoothing his hair before he put on his hat, and so forth. This trait came to mind when the patient reported that almost every night through the window of his darkened bathroom he spied on women undressing and that the sight often made him masturbate. My peeping patient was also potentially an exhibitionist. Later on it became obvious that he identified himself in his unconscious fantasies with the women he watched.

Perceptions of such a vague character, impressions that almost elude us, support us in reaching certain stations on our road to insight. We appreciate their value when we have learned to control our impatience and when we do not expect immediate, but rather intermediary, results from these trifles of observations. The smell of a perfume, a gesture of a hand, a peculiarity of breathing, as well as articulate confessions and long reports, give away secrets. Sometimes an observation of this kind scarcely deserves the name of observation but proves important none the less. Sometimes a transient impression remains unnoted until it occurs often. Only its repetition makes us realize its presence. Peculiarities of voice, of glancing, often reveal something that was hidden behind the words and the sentences we hear. They convey a meaning we would never have guessed, if we had not absorbed the little asides on the fringes of the stage that accompany the main action. Men speak to us and we speak to them not only with words but also with the little signs and expressions we unconsciously send and receive. Observation of these signs begins with our isolating them from the total pattern of the behavior. When we succeed in doing this, we can make the impression clearer and stronger by repetition. Their psychological evaluation and interpretation occur sometimes to the psychoanalyst immediately, sometimes later on as we follow the trail. In the process of "catching" these elusive signs we must trust to our senses and not follow the voice of "reason" which will try to brush them aside. The psychologist who approaches this valuable field as sober as a judge will not capture many data because he will also be as unimaginative as a judge. Only he who is fancy-free and opens all his senses to these impressions will be sensitive to the wealth he will encounter.

The trail uncovered by first impressions sometimes leads to insights that could otherwise be obtained only after a long time and by dint of hard psychological digging. A young graduate student at Harvard started his analysis in a very low voice. His manner of speech appeared deliberate and considered. I asked him to speak louder. He made an effort to do so, but after two minutes dropped back to a low tone that became almost inaudible. At first I had the impression that he was shy or timid and that it was difficult for him to speak of the serious conflicts that had disturbed his childhood. This impression could not explain his manner of speaking because his voice was not only low but also exceptionally deep, and it was as if he chose his words very deliberately. Whatever his reasons, whether shyness, disturbance, or emotions that had to be controlled, you cannot analyze someone without hearing what he has to say.

After trying my best to catch what he mumbled, I decided to interrupt what seemed to be a monologue that excluded an audience. My first impression had given way to another. His manner of speaking was much more significant for his personality than what he had to say to me in this first session. Neglecting everything else, I entered into a discussion of his low-voiced and controlled way of speaking and insisted that he tell me all that he knew about it, at the same time asking him again to make himself heard. We soon arrived at the insight that his low voice and dignified manner were a late acquisition that had developed as an expression of his opposition to the shrieking, high, excited voices of his parents, especially of his mother. There was a story in that, a story we meet frequently in American-born children of East-European immigrants. In this case it was further complicated by the neurotic conflicts of the young man. His parents had retained the behavior and manners of the old country when they came to the United States. They spoke loudly and with vivid gestures. They were highly temperamental and made no effort to control the expression of their emotions. Entirely Americanized, the boy began to feel ashamed of his parents and developed this characteristic manner of low speaking and overcontrolled dignity as a counteraction to the temptation to speak and act like the members of his family. He acquired, so to speak, a second personality superimposed on his originally passionate and excitable nature. Early conflict, especially with his mother, intensified and deepened this reaction-formation whose external signs were his way of speaking and similar traits. Analyzing these features, we soon arrived at the core of his neurotic conflicts.

In this case a practical necessity of the analytic situation forced the analyst to turn his attention to a special trait of personal behavior, which, if it had been less clearly developed, might have remained unobserved. The first analytic session thus started with the discussion of this special characteristic, an exception that proved justified as well as useful.

The analyst can achieve some psychological insight into a patient even before the beginning of treatment if he will only trust his impressions as soon as he becomes aware of them. A young woman made an appointment to consult about the possibility of continuing her psychoanalysis with me. She told me she had broken off her analysis with Dr. A. some months ago. I listened to the story of the conflict that was making it impossible for her to return to her first psychoanalyst. She rapidly sketched the difficulties in her marriage, her social relations, and her professional life. There was nothing, it seemed to me, unusual in what she told me; nothing an analyst does not meet with in many patients. She seemed to be intelligent enough, sincere, and friendly. Why did I feel a slight annoyance with the patient after she left? There was nothing in our conversation that could explain such a feeling. As my attention turned to other patients, I brushed aside the vague impression.

When the patient telephoned two days later, I did not recognize her name and did not remember that she had promised to call me. Now I was forced to follow the rule: analyst, analyze yourself!

I remembered feeling slightly annoyed, but I had not become aware of any reason for this feeling. It was certain that I had not disliked the patient, and certainly she had not done or said anything during the consultation that could have annoyed me. Well, there was the conflict with Dr. A. I had the impression that the analyst had lost patience with his patient at the end—perhaps after she had provoked him many times—and that she could not take what he had told her about herself. She had definitely rejected my suggestion that she return to Dr. A. and try to continue the analysis with him.

But that could not possibly have annoyed me. She was entitled to decide that herself, and I scarcely knew Dr. A.

What was it then that made me displeased with her? Now it slowly came back to me. There were two things she had said the unconscious significance of which I had not realized but had nevertheless sensed. At the end of our conversation she had asked me if I would continue her analysis. Before I had time to answer she had wondered whether I would advise her to go to Dr. N., another psychoanalyst, whom she did not know. The question was asked rather casually, but it had left some trace in me of which I now became aware. It seemed strange. The young lady had consulted me about her neurotic troubles, had asked me whether I would bring her analysis to its end, and then whether she had not better go to Dr. N. instead. I had advised her, of course, to go to Dr. N. Now, over the telephone she said that Dr. N. had no time for her and that she wanted to continue with me. Her question concerning Dr. N. during the consultation appeared at first quite natural and not in the least conspicuous, a question just like any other. Looking back at it, however, it took on another character. I remembered that she had looked at me with a leer, and I understood now, much later, what her sidelong glance and her question meant. It was a provocation of a teasing or malicious kind.

I want to make this element clear. Compare this situation with similar ones. What would we think of a patient who asks to be treated by one physician and then during the consultation asks whether he ought not to go to another physician? It did not make sense and yet I had to assume that there was some concealed sense in it. When you go to a shoemaker to have your shoes repaired, you do not ask him whether you should take the same shoes to another shoemaker. You do not ask a girl to dance and then wonder aloud whether you should not rather dance with another girl.

When I suggested that she go to Dr. N., I must have been reacting unconsciously to the unconscious meaning of her question. I was not surprised or annoyed, as might be expected. On the contrary, I re-acted as if her question were the most normal thing. Only later did I realize that it was extraordinary. I reacted not only to the question but also to the look with which she asked it, as if to say: "If you doubt whether to come to me or to Dr. N., please go to Dr. N. I do not want you as a patient." I reacted as if I had understood the meaning of the glance while I did not even notice it consciously. I had been aware of a slight annoyance after her visit, but not of what had annoyed me. My unconscious reaction then (in my answer) and later (not remembering her name and our agreement) showed that I had somewhere, hidden even from myself, understood well enough that her question was really a provocation.

After that I remembered that the sidelong glance had appeared again at the end of the consultation. The patient had casually mentioned reading a rather unfavorable review of one of my books in the *Psychoanalytic Quarterly*. As far as my conscious thoughts went the review did not affect me. But that is not the point here. Why did she mention it? Where was the need to say it? It seems that I felt annoyed, not at being reminded of the criticism, but by her intention in reminding me of it, which I sensed. Well-bred and well-educated, she would certainly not say to a stranger she had just met at a dinner or cocktail party, "Oh, I read an unfavorable review of your last book just two days ago." Why did she do it just before leaving my room and why this sidelong, expectant glance? Considering her otherwise excellent manners, there must have been an unconscious hostile or aggressive tendency in her remark.

What was gained by my insight, what was the advantage in catching these imponderable expressions that had appeared incognito? There was more than one advantage—besides the satisfaction of the psychological interest. That side glance was revealing. It not only observed; it was observed; and for a fleeting moment I caught the real face behind the mask. The situation was like that of a masquerade at which a person has the advantage of seeing a lady who believes herself unobserved, without her mask. Later, when he meets her again in disguise, he will know her identity. This early insight proved very useful later on. It was a promising beginning and it helped me in the difficult situations that emerged in the later phases of analysis. It was much easier to understand the masochistic provocation to which the patient resorted again and again. And it was easier to convince her finally that some unconscious tendency in her forced her to make herself disliked. I had, of course, overcome my initial annoyance quickly after I understood its reasons and, forewarned and forearmed by my early insight, I could tolerate the provocations much better than my colleague, who had yielded to the temptation to become angry with her.

The discussion of this case and the many others that follow seems to present a good opportunity to inject a few remarks about the psychoanalyst himself. What kind of psychoanalyst, some readers will ask, can feel annoyed or impatient? Is this the much-praised calm and the correct scientific attitude of the therapist? Is this the pure mirror that reflects the image of the patient who comes to psychoanalysis with his troubles, symptoms, and complaints? Is this the proper couch-side manner? The question is easily answered. The psychoanalyst is a human being like any other and not a god. There is nothing superhuman about him. In fact, he has to be human. How else could he understand other human beings? If he were a block of wood or a marble statue, he could never hope to grasp the strange passions and thoughts he will meet with in his patients. If he were cold and unfeeling, a "stuffed shirt," as some plays portray him, he would be an analytic robot or a pompous, dignified ass who could not gain entry to the secrets of the human soul. It seems to me that the demand that the analyst should be sensitive and human does not contradict the expectation that he should maintain an objective view of his cases and perform his difficult task with as much therapeutic and scientific skill as is given him. Objectivity and inhumanness are two things that are frequently confused, even by many psychoanalysts. The sensitiveness and the subjectivity of the analyst concern his impressionability to the slightest stimuli, to the minute, almost imperceptible indices of unconscious processes. It is desirable that he be as susceptible, as responsive and alive, to those signs as a mimosa is to the touch. He should, of course, possess the same sensitiveness to, and the same faculty for fine hearing of, the voices within himself. His objectivity, his cool and calm judgment, his power of logical and psychological penetration as well as his emotional control, should be reserved for the analytic treatment. He will not feel the temptation to express his own emotions when his psychological interest outweighs his temperament. He will be able to check and control impulses that he has in common with his patients when he remembers that his task is to understand and to help them. It is ridiculous to demand that an analyst, to whom nothing human should be alien, should not be human himself. Goethe has expressed it beautifully: If the eye were not something sunlike itself, it could never see the sun.

The instances reported above contrast with others—alas, so many others—in which I remained unaware of those trifles, of those little revealing signs, or in which I observed them much later, sometimes even too late. It does not matter how much or how little too late. It makes no difference whether you missed your plane by only a few minutes or by a few hours. In every one of those cases my lack of sensitiveness was punished by additional work, an increased intellectual and emotional effort that would have been unnecessary if I had been more impressionable or observant. In almost all of them there was also a hindrance in myself that blocked me or dulled the sharpness of my observation. Here is such a case, one of many:

A young man had come for psychoanalysis because he wanted to rid himself of many nervous symptoms and some serious difficulties he was encountering in his private and professional life. I succeeded in a relatively short time in freeing him of his most oppressive symptoms, but the other difficulties remained. They seemed to be stationary and did not improve. I often told myself that something in me hindered my deeper penetration into that secret. But I could not find the road that led to it. The young man had obliging, open manners and showed brilliant intelligence, wit, and humor. What a pity that all these gifts remained sterile and displayed themselves only when he talked! His intellectual endowment and his emotional alertness made everything he said interesting whether he talked about his own symptoms, about his complicated relations with relatives and friends, his past emotions and experiences, or of the present, of a sexual adventure, or money matters. He knew how to tell a tale about himself or others. He was stimulating as well as stimulated. Nothing changed, however, in his inner situation after he had lost his most serious symptoms.

One day he told me that his sweetheart, who had listened to his stories for a long time, had smilingly asked, "But, John, why do you make such an effort? I am not a girl whom you met yesterday." My eyes were suddenly opened wide by this remark of a third person. I had really overlooked the fact that the young man had not talked to me, but had entertained me in the last weeks. The girl was right, so absolutely right. He dazzled people. He bribed them with his reports, which were always very alive and vivid, vibrant and interesting. In speaking of himself, however, he did not give of himself. He spent himself, but he did not surrender. He figured in his reports like the story-teller in a modern novel narrated in the first person—a story by Somerset Maugham. In talking about himself, ostensibly quite freely, he was hiding himself. Listening to him with sharper ears, I now received a new impression of his inadequacy-feelings, which made it necessary for him to conquer all people anew whenever he met them, to use his endowments to win them over and thus overcome his deep sense of insecurity. I had let myself be bribed like so many others by these great, ever recurrent efforts. Then along came a young girl whose psychological knowledge did not surpass that of other students of Vassar or Smith and gave me a lesson I would not forget. She hit the target easily and casually, reminding the young man that he need not exert himself. She had said, "I am not a girl whom you met yesterday," and with these nine words she had shown the path for which I had searched in vain. I took my hat off to this unknown Vassar girl and felt thoroughly ashamed of myself. Who had taught her the fine art of psychological observation and discernment? You do not learn such things in the psychology department at Smith or Vassar. I was ready to believe that the girl was smart enough, but it was not her intelligence that had spoken like that. It was her heart that had told her.

Experiences of this kind (I could tell many more) make us psychoanalysts modest about our psychological endowment—or should make us more modest. There was I, who thought myself a trained observer, and I did not recognize what was so obvious. "What is a trained observer?" I asked myself. He is a man who is trained to pay attention to certain things and to neglect others. He is a man who overpays attention to features he expects to see and remains in debt to others that escape his notice.

BARE ATTENTION

MARK EPSTEIN

Thoughts Without a Thinker, the book from which this excerpt was taken, looks at psychotherapy from a Buddhist perspective. The connection between meditation and psychotherapy is most apparent in what Mark Epstein calls "bare attention." This is a technique similar to Freud's "evenly suspended attention." During the activity of meditation referred to as "mindfulness," one attempts to observe his or her thoughts without judgment, letting those thoughts flow freely. As a matter of fact, the requirements of bare attention—neutrality, openness, and the ability to be "astonished"—are near paraphrases of Leston Havens's description of evenly suspended attention in "Freud's Invention."

The key to the transformational potential of bare attention lies in the deceptively simple injunction to separate out one's reactions from the core events themselves. Much of the time, it turns out, our everyday minds are in a state of reactivity. We take this for granted, we do not question our automatic identifications with our reactions, and we experience ourselves at the mercy of an often hostile or frustrating outer world or an overwhelming or frightening inner one. With bare attention, we move from this automatic identification with our fear or frustration to a vantage point from which the fear or frustration is attended to with the same dispassionate interest as anything else. There is enormous freedom to be gained from such a shift. Instead of running from difficult emotions (or hanging on to enticing ones), the practitioner of bare attention becomes able to *contain* any reaction: making space for it, but not completely identifying with it because of the concomitant presence of nonjudgmental awareness.

A patient of mine illustrates this point directly. Temporarily abandoned by his mother at the age of six because of her nervous breakdown, Sid developed one obsessive love after another in his adult years, all with women with whom he had only brief affairs. He would pursue them relentlessly, calling them on the phone, writing them long, painful letters that spelled out how he had been misunderstood, and talking to them endlessly in his mind to explain his good intentions and to detail how he had been wronged. Each obsession lasted the better part of a year, and he rejected as unhelpful any interpretations I made about the feelings for these women being related to unexamined reactions from the time of his mother's unavailability. Our sessions would usually get no further than Sid repeating over and over again, "It hurts, it hurts." After many sessions such as this, I finally began to encourage Sid to go more deeply into his pain, to feel the hurt *and* all of his reactions to it without necessarily acting on it. There was no immediate breakthrough, but several months later, Sid appeared for his weekly session in an obviously less agitated state of mind.

"You know, something that you've been saying actually helped," he began. " 'Just feel the pain,' you said. Well, the other night, instead of dialing Rachel's number, I decided to give it a try. And I decided, even if it kills me, that I would just lay there and feel the pain. And I did."

At that point, Sid looked at me in silence with a look that managed to convey both deep pain and triumph. He had begun to use bare attention to tame his mind. No longer driven to act out his pain by obsessively calling the women who he dreamed would assuage it, Sid managed to interrupt the behavior that was only perpetuating his isolation. In so doing, he began the process of accepting his own most difficult feelings. The paradox of bare attention, however, is that in this acceptance is a simultaneous letting go. The horror, or fear, at the pain that had made Sid run to these women for protection had only made the pain more intractable. Only by being with the emotions directly could Sid see them for what they were: old feelings, never fully experienced, that had conditioned his entire emotional life. By finding a way to be with those feelings without endlessly reacting to them, Sid was able to experience himself as something other than just a wrongfully rejected lover. He was making the shift from emotional reactivity to nonjudgmental awareness, not in the service of denial, repression, or suppression, but of growth and flexibility.

One famous Japanese haiku illustrates the state that Sid managed to discover in himself. It is one that Joseph Goldstein has long used to describe the unique attentional posture of bare attention:

> *The old pond.*
> *A frog jumps in.*
> *Plop!*

Like so much else in Japanese art, the poem expresses the Buddhist emphasis on naked attention to the often overlooked details of everyday life. Yet, there is another level at which the poem may be read. Just as in the parable of the raft, the waters of the pond can represent the mind and the emotions. The frog jumping in becomes a thought or feeling arising in the mind or body, while "Plop!" represents the reverberations of that thought or feeling, unelaborated by the forces of reactivity. The entire poem comes to evoke the state of bare attention in its utter simplicity.

THE ART OF PSYCHOANALYSIS

Freud counseled a very similar state during the practice of psychoanalysis. He appears to have stumbled on it while analyzing his own dreams, making some use of a previous interest in the art of hypnosis. Freud makes reference to this particular deployment of attention throughout his writings, when he discusses the interpretation of dreams, free association, and "evenly suspended attention," the attentional stance that he recommends for practicing psychoanalysts. There is no evidence that Freud was influenced directly by Buddhist practices, but the resemblance of his attentional recommendations to those of the Buddha cannot be denied.

Freud's major breakthrough, which he refers to over and over again in his writings, was his discovery that it was actually possible to suspend what he called the "critical faculty." This suspension of the critical faculty was, in fact, what made the practice of psychoanalysis possible for Freud. It is a feat that he accomplished with no outside help, one that he apparently taught himself without knowing that this was precisely the attentional stance that Buddhist meditators had been invoking for millennia.

Freud's writings on the subject reveal the first essential quality of bare attention—its impartiality. Repeatedly admonishing psychoanalysts to "suspend . . . judgment and give . . . impartial attention to everything there is to observe," Freud insisted that in this state it was possible to understand psychic phenomena in a unique fashion. While remaining interested in psychic *content*, he was nevertheless encouraging his followers to practice evenly suspended attention, a kind of beginning meditation. His instructions have all the clarity of those from the best Buddhist teachers. In his definitive article on the subject, Freud can be appreciated in his best Zenlike form:

> The rule for the doctor may be expressed: "He should withhold all conscious influences from his capacity to attend, and give himself over completely to his 'unconscious memory.'" Or, to put it purely in terms of technique: "He should simply listen, and not bother about whether he is keeping anything in mind."

This state of simply listening, of impartiality, is at once completely natural and enormously difficult. It is a challenge for therapists to put aside their desires for a patient's cure, their immediate conclusions about the patient's communications, and their "insights" into the causes of the patient's suffering so that they may continue to hear from the patient what they do not yet understand. It is all the more challenging to turn this kind of attention on oneself, as is required in meditation practice, to separate oneself from one's own reactions, to move from an identity based on likes and dislikes to one based on impartial, nonjudgmental awareness. Bare attention requires the meditator to not try to screen out the unpleasant, to take whatever is given.

OPENNESS

The next important quality of bare attention—openness—grows out of this ability to take whatever is given. Requiring the meditator to scan with a wide lens, not a narrow one, this openness establishes a receptive intrapsychic environment for exploration of the personal and private. It is the openness of a mother who can, as D. W. Winnicott pointed out in his famous paper "The Capacity to Be Alone," allow a child to play uninterruptedly in her presence. This type of openness, which is not interfering, is a quality that meditation reliably induces.

The late composer John Cage, heavily influenced as he was by Buddhist philosophy, illustrates just this openness in his discussions of sound and music:

> If you develop an ear for sounds that are musical it is like developing an ego. You begin to refuse sounds that are not musical and that way cut yourself off from a good deal of experience. . . . The most recent change in my attitude toward sound has been in relation to loud sustained sounds such as car alarms or burglar alarms, which used to annoy me, but which I now accept and even enjoy. I think the transformation came through a statement of Marcel Duchamp who said that sounds which stay in one location and don't change can produce a sonorous sculpture, a sound sculpture that lasts in time. Isn't that beautiful?

When we can develop this attitude toward our own internal car alarms, we can begin to feel the relevance of the Buddha's approach.

A patient who recently consulted with me had just this task facing him, because of his own version of the screeching alarms that made him want to shut down. Paul was the only child of an extraordinarily agitated and complaining mother whose husband had abandoned her when Paul was six. He had spent the better part of his preadolescent years alone in his house with his mother, sleeping in her bed and comforting her when she was down. He had remarkably few childhood memories, but he did recall his father having broken his favorite record because he would listen to it over and over again and cry to himself. As an adult, Paul was anxious and depressed much of the time and complained of not feeling real. He described himself as a "bundle of nerves" who was great at coping but felt no underlying excitement or confidence in what he was doing. He had a hard time saying what he felt anxious about, however, and a surprisingly difficult time exploring his discomfort in his first sessions with me. He was afraid to look at his anxieties, he revealed: they reminded him of his mother's and made him feel as if he was as disturbed as she had seemed.

Paul's work in therapy was to learn to apply bare attention to his own anxiety, about which he knew very little. His first reaction was to be afraid and to clamp down on the anxiety. When he learned to isolate that initial reaction, to be with his fear, he was then able to distinguish *his* anxieties from those of his mother, and to realize that his parents had been unable to meet, or hold, those very feelings when they arose in him. Both psychotherapy and meditation had something basic to offer Paul: each in its own way could teach him how to be with his feelings without judging them the way his parents had. Only out of being with those actual feelings could Paul begin to gain some confidence in himself as a real person.

Bare attention requires an *openness* to both internal and sensory experience that does not often survive our childhoods. The child who is forced, as Paul was, to cope reactively with a parent's moods, loses touch with his or her own internal processes. Compelled to respond to the parent's needs, such a child relinquishes the ability to stay open to what necessarily seems less urgent, even if that is his or her own self. Thus, the false self is constructed and the narcissistic character, who does not really remember how to feel, is born.

By separating out the reactive self from the core experience, the practice of bare attention eventually returns the meditator to a state of unconditioned openness that bears an important resemblance to the feeling engendered by an optimally attentive parent. It does this by relentlessly uncovering the reactive self and returning the meditator, again and again, to the raw material of experience. According to Winnicott, only in this "state of not having to react" can the self "begin to be."

ASTONISHMENT

As noted before, bare attention is impartial, nonjudgmental, and open. It is also deeply interested, like a child with a new toy. The key phrase from the Buddhist literature is that it requires "not clinging and not condemning," an attitude that Cage demonstrated with regard to the car alarms, that Winnicott described in his "good enough mothering" notion, that Freud counseled for the psychoanalyst at work, and that meditation practitioners must develop toward their own psychic, emotional, and physical sufferings. The most revealing thing about a first meditation retreat (after seeing how out of control our minds are) is how the experience of pain gives way to one of peacefulness if it is consistently and dispassionately attended to for a sufficient time. Once the reactions to the pain—the horror, outrage, fear, tension, and so on—are separated out from the pure sensation, the sensation at some point will stop hurting.

The psychoanalyst Michael Eigen, in a paper entitled "Stones in a Stream," describes his own first mystical experience in just these characteristic terms:

> I remember once being in emotional agony on a bus in my 20's. I doubled over into my pain and focused on it with blind intensity. As I sat there in this wretched state, I was amazed when the pain turned to redness, then blackness (a kind of blanking out), then light, as if a vagina in my soul opened, and there was radiant light. The pain did not vanish, but my attention was held by the light. I felt amazed, uplifted, stunned into awareness of wider existence. Of course

I did not want the light to go away, and was a bit fearful
that it would, but above all was reverence, respect: it could
last as long as it liked, and come and go as it pleased. It was
an unforgettable moment. Life can never be quite the same
after such experiences.

This kind of experience can truly come as a revelation. When we
see that staying with a pain from which we habitually recoil can lead
to such a transformation, it makes us question one of our basic assumptions: that we must reject that which does not feel good. Instead, we discover, even pain can be interesting.

OUR OWN MINDS

A further quality of bare attention, its unafraid nature, grows out of
this interest. The psychiatrist R. D. Laing, at one of the first confer-
ences on Buddhism and psychotherapy that I attended, declared that
we are all afraid of three things: other people, our own minds, and
death. His statement was all the more powerful because it came
shortly before his own death. If bare attention is to be of any real
use, it must be applied in exactly these spheres. Physical illness usually provides us with such an opportunity,

When my father-in-law, an observant Jew with little overt interest
in Eastern philosophy, was facing radical surgery not so long ago, he
sought my counsel because he knew of some work I was engaged in
about stress reduction. He wanted to know how he could manage
his thoughts while going into the surgery, and what he could do
while lying awake at night. I taught him bare attention to a simple
Jewish prayer; he was gradually able to expand the mental state that
developed around the prayer to encompass his thoughts, anxieties,
and fears. Even in the intensive care unit after surgery, when he
could not tell day from night, move, swallow, or talk, he was able to
use bare attention to rest in the moment, dissolving his fears in the
meditative space of his own mind. Several years later, after attending
Yom Kippur services, he showed me a particular passage in the prayer
book that reminded him of what he had learned through his ordeal.
A more Buddhist verse he could not have uncovered:

A man's origin is from dust and his destiny is back to dust, at risk of his life he earns his bread; he is likened to a broken shard, withering grass, a fading flower, a passing shade, a dissipating cloud, a blowing wind, flying dust, and a fleeting dream.

The fearlessness of bare attention is necessary in the psychological venue as well, where the practice of psychotherapy has revealed just how ingenious and intransigent the ego's defenses can be. Even when they are in therapy, people are afraid of discovering things about themselves that they do not wish to know.

An accomplished artist named Maddie demonstrated this in a recent therapy session with me. "I don't want to be here," she declared. "I don't want to be your patient. I find it humiliating. I'd rather just be your friend." Maddie did not want to talk about the only topic she had to discuss with me therapeutically, namely, the way she made herself unapproachable with her lover. "It's the same with you as it is with her—it's too much work," she would say.

Somehow I was able to get Maddie to pay attention to her reluctance to being my patient. In turning it from an obstacle to a self-generated feeling, Maddie began to cry. This she found terribly embarrassing and curiously satisfying. Her impulse to cry, it seemed, was something that she was living in fear of. She had all kinds of voices in her head about it: crying was weak, unacceptable, inappropriate, humiliating, and not allowed, and any impulse to approach her lover was automatically stifled out of a fear of a similar breakdown with her. She had retreated to an angry, petulant, and defensive position; any attempt to reach out from this place evoked feelings of fear.

This fear is what, in psychoanalytic circles, is often called resistance. The fearlessness of bare attention must take this very fear as object: in contacting it, the patient can then become more real. In bare attention, the courage or fearlessness that can look at any manifestation of this insecurity is always combined with an equally strong patience or tolerance for that very feeling. Some psychoanalytic schools have made the mistake of relentlessly attacking the resistance, with the idea of releasing the underlying true self. This approach lacks the quality of tolerance that allows people to actually own their resistance, thereby evoking some grudging respect for their own involvement in creating it.

From a Buddhist perspective, there is really *nothing but* resistance to be analyzed; there is no true self waiting in the wings to be released. Only by revealing the insecurity can a measure of freedom be gained. When we can know our fear as fear and surround it with the patience of the Buddha, we can begin to rest in our own minds *and* approach those to whom we would like to feel close.

My use of bare attention with Maddie was applied with this in mind. It was necessary first to explore her defensive and angry posture and then her underlying fear and sadness. Maddie *was* her resistance: as she embodied it by becoming the angry, spiteful, frightened person who did not want to be my patient, she began to cry and experienced a *real* moment with me, about which she was deeply ashamed. At each level, the correct understanding of bare attention permitted her, in the words of the Buddha, not to tarry and not to struggle. As Maddie learned to be with her own feelings with the combination of courage and patience that bare attention requires, she became both more humble and more forthcoming, more capable of the intimacy that she both feared and craved.

PSYCHOANALYSIS
The Impossible Profession

JANET MALCOLM

Freud's observation that making the unconscious conscious reduces symptoms is the basis of psychoanalysis and of many forms of psychotherapy. The tool that a psychoanalyst uses, according to the therapist in this excerpt, is to make the patient aware of the behavior he or she uses to avoid thinking and feeling undesirable things. The "scalpel" that the therapist uses is to say, "Look there," when significant material is presented. When the patient eventually does look, progress is made.

At the beginning of his second year of training at the New York Psychoanalytic, Aaron Green received his first case—a twenty-two-year-old woman—from the Treatment Center. It was a case he now regards with a mixture of horror, pleasure, amusement, puzzlement, self-criticism, and self-satisfaction. "For the first two years of this analysis, I was in agony over it," he recalled. "I cursed the people at the Treatment Center for giving me such a case. I felt totally incompetent and impotent. I dreaded the time of day when her hour came. The analysis lasted seven years, and today I'm rather proud of it. The patient came into analysis a very unhappy young girl with some very troublesome hysterical symptoms, and she left with all the symptoms gone and married to a dentist. But it took me a long time to realize that I wasn't failing with her.

"I remember when she first came into my office—a short, plump, self-conscious girl, who giggled and gave vapid, inconsequential answers to the questions I asked her. We had a few sessions sitting up, and then one day I said, 'Why don't you lie down on the couch?' She giggled and walked over to the couch and arranged herself on it gingerly, with a lot of tugging at her skirt, and went on talking in her inane, girlish, monosyllabic way. This kept up for three or four sessions. Then one day she walked in and didn't *get* on the couch, she *threw* herself on it. She bounced up and down and began to *rail* at me. 'You don't *do* anything for me,' she said. 'You just sit there and don't *do* anything. You don't tell me anything. What kind of business is this? Why don't you *do* something for me? Why do you just sit there?' She went on and on, berating me for my coldness and passivity and indifference to her sufferings—and that was the true beginning of the analysis. But I didn't know it. I sat there cowering under her anger and irked with her for not knowing that what I was doing as I 'just sat there' was classical Freudian analysis. I found her in every way disappointing. I had expected a patient who would free-associate, and here they had sent me this banal girl who just blathered. I didn't understand—I was so naïve then—that her blathering *was* free association, that blathering is just what free association is. Worse than that, I thought I had to instruct her on the nature of her unconscious. I would laboriously point out to her the unconscious meaning of what she said and did. Only after years of terrible and futile struggle did it dawn on me that if I just listened—if I just let her talk, let her blather—things would come out, and that this was what would help her, not my pedantic, didactic interpretations. If I could only have learned to shut up! When I finally did learn, I began to see things that Freud had described—to actually see for myself symptoms disappearing as the unconscious became conscious. That was an incredible thing. It was like looking through a telescope and realizing that you are seeing what Galileo saw.

"But for the first two years that case seemed like a personal misfortune. I wanted to throw her back at the Institute and say, 'What?

You gave me *this* for a first case?' She was so nasty and unpleasant. She was so uncoöperative and unappreciative. If I heard her say it once, I heard her say it a thousand times: 'So *what?*'—in a nasty, sneering voice. 'So *what?*' I felt demeaned, put down, furious, frustrated, impotent. My fury often caused me to act in unanalytic ways toward her. I'm ashamed of that. I would do many things differently now. But the interesting thing—the incredible thing—is that what I did didn't matter. She sneered and scoffed at everything I said, but she came faithfully five times a week, month after month, year after year, and the analysis bubbled along, in spite of her belligerence and mistrust and my innocence and ignorance."

"You say that just 'letting things come out' helped her," I said. "That sounds like the old cathartic method."

"Yes, yes," Aaron said. "That old stuff that Freud and Josef Breuer wrote about in *Studies on Hysteria* hasn't really changed. Analysis is still cathartic. We're still trying to 'transform neurotic misery into common unhappiness' by setting in motion a process whereby motivation gets expressed directly, rather than going off sideways into symptoms. Freud and Breuer called this 'abreaction.' We no longer use that term, and we have a more refined knowledge of the kinds of obstruction that the mind puts up against the threat of change, but the process is essentially the same. In the case of this girl, when I finally learned to shut up, stuff began to spew out of her—stuff that was barely on the fringes of her consciousness but that caused her to change just by being brought out. In the popular imagination, the analyst is an authoritarian, dominating figure who has rigid control over a malleable, vulnerable patient. What this case forcibly impressed upon me is that the reverse is true—it is the patient who controls what is happening, and the analyst who is a puny, weak figure. Patients go where the hell they please. All the analyst can do is say, 'If you'll deign to listen to me for a moment—if you could just divert your attention to this particular place instead of that one—you may see that . . . et cetera, et cetera.' That's all he can do. In this case, all I could do was every now and then direct the patient's attention to what she was doing in her attempts to keep that stuff from spewing out—something she preferred not to watch. That's called 'the analysis of the resistance,' which doesn't mean that you shake your finger at the patient and say, *'You're resisting!'* That's the worst thing you can do, and I'm afraid I sometimes did do it in the first years of that case. The right way is just to point out to the patient how he keeps himself from thinking certain things and feeling certain things, so that he becomes self-conscious and the evasion doesn't work so automatically. That's all. That's the analyst's scalpel. He can't open up his patient's mind and reach in and start tinkering. The only thing he can do is tell the patient, 'Look there,' and most of the time the patient doesn't look. But sometimes he does, and then his automatic behavior becomes less automatic."

I had read a writeup of the young woman's case which Aaron had prepared for the American Psychoanalytic Association as a prerequisite for certification and membership, and had found it baffling, irritating, boring, insulting to women, and self-damning. In its unrelenting pursuit of sexual matter and meaning, it brought to mind the Dora case, in which Freud often conducted himself more like a police inspector interrogating a suspect than like a doctor helping a patient. "Aha!" Freud would say to poor Dora, an attractive and intelligent eighteen-year-old girl suffering from a nervous cough, migraine, and a kind of general youthful malaise. "Aha! I know about you. I know your dirty little secrets. Admit that you were secretly attracted to Herr K. Admit that you masturbated when you were five. Look at what you're doing now as you lie there playing with your reticule—opening it, putting a finger into it, shutting it again!" I sensed some of the same badgering and needling quality in Aaron's case history. I asked him whether his own behavior might not have provoked some of the girl's belligerence and antagonism.

"My analytic behavior was not everything it should have been," he agreed. "I was very unschooled and very intent on getting analytic procedure down pat. I come out of that writeup looking pedantic and constricted, and there is some truth to that impression. There is some truth to Leo Stone's characterization of the beginning analyst as a rather ludicrously rigid and unyielding person. I take full responsibility for the excruciating and ill-advised things I did in that analysis. She was often 'right,' and I was often 'wrong.' And for all that, for all my oafishness and pompousness, her basic attitude toward me—the transference—was quite unaffected by what I said and did, had its own rhyme and reason, went its own way. My unanalytic behavior muddied the water, made the transference harder to discern and point out convincingly to the patient, but it didn't *create* the transference. If I had been St. Francis of Assisi, she would have said 'So *what?*' no less frequently and sneeringly."

I mentioned a paper I had read by Ralph Greenson on "the non-transference relationship," in which the author relates a number of horrendous stories about rigid beginning analysts. In one of these cautionary tales, a beginning analyst comes to his supervisor and tells him about an oddly unsatisfying session he has had with a patient who came in with his head swathed in an enormous bandage. Following strict analytic technique, the young analyst made no comment on the bandage, and silently waited for the patient to start free-associating. No associations came: the patient was struck absolutely speechless by the analyst's unbelievable insensitivity and inhumanity. In another example (this one appears in Greenson's book *The Technique and Practice of Psychoanalysis*), an anxious young mother tells her candidate analyst how desperately worried she is about her ailing baby. The analyst says nothing. His silence and lack of compassion cause the patient to lapse into a miserable, tearful silence of her own. Finally, the analyst says, "You're resisting." The patient quits the analysis, saying to the analyst, "You're sicker than I am." Greenson, concurring with this opinion, advises the candidate to seek further analysis.

"Yeah," Aaron said. "I know those stories of Greenson's. They are very heartrending and affecting, and completely off the mark. If you look at them closely, they just don't hold up. In the case of the mother with the sick baby, it wasn't the analyst's lack of 'compassion' that caused the patient to break off treatment—it was his poor analytic technique. There are a hundred things he could have said to her other than 'You're resisting' which would have been helpful, which would have led somewhere, but which would have been neutral. The job of the analyst isn't to offer the patient sympathy; it's to lead him to insight. It was the same thing with my first case. The trouble wasn't my lack of compassion for the patient but my lapses from analytic neutrality. It isn't that I should have accepted the presents she brought me—though maybe I could have refused them less priggishly—but that I should have analyzed the motive that lay behind the gift giving in a more rigorous and thoroughgoing manner."

"But what *about* that priggishness?" I asked. "Can you leave it out of account? Greenson says that it's important for the patient to distinguish between his transference reactions to the analyst and his realistic perceptions of him. He says of the woman with the baby that her reactions to the analyst were 'realistic.'"

Aaron shook his head. "That's taking such a crude and simplistic view of analysis—and of life," he said. "It perpetuates the myth that what goes on in the analysis is different from what goes on in real life. It gives analysis an 'as if' quality. It says the transference isn't real. But the transference *is* real—as real as anything out there. And, conversely, 'the real relationship'—whatever that is—is not exempt from analytic scrutiny. If the analyst comes into the session and insults the patient, and the patient says 'So it's true! You really hate me!' and the analyst says 'Yes! I really hate you!' does this mean that all the patient's irrational and fantastic ideas about the angry parent of childhood are now *negated*? Are now not to be investigated? Now fall outside the pale of analytic scrutiny?

"I remember a seminar I once attended that was led by a brilliant and flamboyant Hungarian analyst named Robert Bak. The issue under debate was the nature of transference, and I raised my hand and asked rhetorically, 'What would you call an interpersonal relationship where infantile wishes, and defenses against those wishes, get expressed in such a way that the persons within that relationship don't see each other for what they objectively are but, rather, view each other in terms of their infantile needs and their infantile conflicts? What would you call that?' And Bak looked over at me ironically and said, 'I'd call that life.'

"In both analysis and life, we perceive reality through a veil of unconscious infantile fantasy. Nothing we say or do or think is ever purely 'rational' or 'irrational,' purely 'real' or 'transferential.' It is always a mixture. The difference between analysis and life is that in analysis—in this highly artificial, extreme, bizarre, stressful, in some ways awful situation—these infantile fantasies come into higher relief than they do in life, become accessible to study, as they do not in life. The purpose of analysis isn't to instruct the patient on the nature of reality but to acquaint him with himself, with the child within him, in all its infantility and its impossible and unrepudiated and unrepudiatable longings and wishes. Terms like 'the real relationship' and 'therapeutic alliance' and 'working alliance' simply obscure and dilute and trivialize the radical nature of this task."

"So you share Charles Brenner's dislike of those terms, and his uncompromising view of analytic technique."

"I do. I think that Brenner's uncompromising—you might even say fanatically pure—way of doing analysis permits you to find things out that you would not find out under a less rigorous procedure. It also, paradoxically, gives the patient more freedom than he has under the more relaxed analytic techniques. Ruthless and authoritarian though it seems, strict analytic neutrality is the more libertarian alternative. When you temper the rigors of analysis with judicious doses of kindliness and friendliness, you are taking away some of the patient's freedom, because *you* are deciding what is best for him. But doing analysis in Brenner's pure and undeviating way is very hard. It demands a great deal of the analyst, and puts him under a tremendous strain. No one likes to hurt people—to cause them pain, to stand silently by as they suffer, to withhold help from them when they plead for it. That's where the real wear and tear of analysis lies—in this chronic struggle to keep oneself from doing the things that decent people naturally and spontaneously do. One hears a lot about the abstinence that the analytic patient has to endure, but the abstinence of the analyst is more ruthless and corrosive. The 'working alliance' and the 'therapeutic alliance' and the 'non-transference relationship' are all what Brenner calls resistive myths—myths that analysts who are unable to tolerate analytic abstinence have invented to justify their lapses from neutrality. They say, 'Oh, I don't have to act analytically now. This is the therapeutic alliance, this is non-transference'—as if they were stepping into some no-man's-land where all bets were off and the analyst and the patient could assume a relationship different from the one of analysis proper. But there is no such neutral zone, there is no 'other' relationship, there is no honest way of escaping the pain and stress of doing analysis.

"Let me illustrate with an incident from my practice. I once arrived fifteen minutes late for an appointment with a patient. I was appalled by my oversight and apologized profusely to the patient. Now, the analysts of the lenient sort would say, 'You did the right thing. It's good to admit it when you've made a mistake; it's good to show the patient you're only human. It's an empathetic response. It strengthens the therapeutic alliance. It makes him feel you're on his side.' And so on. But I knew I should not have apologized. I knew I should have waited to learn what the patient's response to my lateness was, instead of rushing in with my apology. In my self-analysis of the lapse, a rather vicious analyst joke came to mind, which goes like this: A new woman patient comes to a male analyst's office, and he says, 'Take off your clothes and get on the couch.' The woman gets undressed and lies down on the couch, and the analyst gets on top of her. Then he says, 'You can get dressed now and sit in that chair.' She does so, and the analyst says, 'O.K. We've taken care of my problem. What's yours?' It's a silly joke, and a vicious one, but it gets at something fundamental. In that situation of being late, I acted like the analyst in the joke. I put my own interests before those of the patient. I felt guilty about my lateness, and by apologizing I was seeking forgiveness from the patient. I was saying to him, 'Let's take care of my problem—never mind about yours.' "

FEELINGS FOR THE PATIENT

GAIL ALBERT

It is unrealistic to expect a therapist to remain completely neutral to a patient, yet neutrality is required as a technique. The therapist has feelings, both positive and negative, both mild and strong about his or her patients. The term for these feelings is *countertransference*. In this view from *The Other Side of the Couch*, several therapists share their personal experiences and reactions to patients and offer their thoughts on how to keep their own reactions and emotions out of the way of treatment.

Freud wrote that analysts could never be truly neutral, for they wish the patient to get well. Still, he believed the analyst should strive to work for the patient's recovery without any personal stake or emotional involvement. Emotional responses, of whatever kind, were shameful, to be analyzed and eradicated as quickly as possible.

Later writers modified Freud's position. They recognized that even an exhaustive psychoanalysis couldn't erase all the therapist's emotional responses. The issue is that her responses and desires, no matter how "normal" or expectable, ought not to be allowed to interfere with the treatment.

Gary said, "Where I run into trouble is in liking a patient so much that I don't push hard enough for material that's going to get them feeling angry at me. The transference is always ambivalent and they always have mixed feelings toward me, but there are times when it's just so nice meeting with someone that it's very easy to let pass clues to their having more negative feelings. I'm human, too, and I like having a patient smile at me, or say thank-you at the end of an hour. Most of the time I get so little thanks it's an enormous temptation to sit back and bask in the warmth when it's offered."

"I treat a number of models," Steve said, "and there's no way in the world I couldn't have a sexual reaction occasionally." His voice sharp, he added, "But it helps to remember that their seductiveness toward me has nothing to do with me. It's transference. They might find me attractive if they met me at a party, but first of all, many of them wouldn't, and secondly, they wouldn't find me that attractive." He was quiet for several seconds, looking out the window. "Actually, I felt most tempted with a patient who wasn't beautiful, someone I genuinely would have gone out with if she weren't in treatment with me. We had a lot of interests in common, and a lot of shared feelings about things. But I had to accept that my interest and desire couldn't be acted on. The taboo is absolute: you don't have sex with a patient."

He paused again. "Everyone in the business knows of a famous analyst who told a patient she was too attractive for him to treat her, sent her to someone else, and eventually married her." Steve's voice was earnest. "I've had two women patients ask me why I couldn't do the same with them. After all, it was quite a precedent. But I think that story has scared a lot of people. The idea that it's ever possible to break the taboo, even after sending the person to someone else, is very frightening. The therapist is supposed to be absolutely above temptation—just as with the incest taboo. The taboo may be broken in reality by some people, but the idea of breaking it is, *and should be,* revolting."

He hesitated. "With the woman I liked so much, I thought for a while that I might have to send her to someone else, but I didn't want to tell her even that I was having that kind of problem with her. I thought it would be too damaging, so I paid for supervision of her case for several months, and while this was happening I met Barbara, my second wife. Once I met her, the problem receded, and ultimately it vanished. I had someone I was happy with. The fact that I found my patient attractive, that we would have been lovers if I'd met her under other circumstances, became just a fact, not an intrusion on the therapy. In fact, at that point my finding her attractive could be more clearly communicated to her, and it added immensely to her self-esteem."

Steve added, "The truth is that I have to be careful whenever the patient and I have something important in common. I treat someone who has a passion for cars. Well, I spent half my teen years under the hood of a Mustang convertible, and sometimes I just want to ask him to say more. I'd enjoy the conversation. Or last year, when I was buying a new car, I really wanted to ask him his opinion . . . because he undoubtedly knows more than me. I'll be able to do that when we're nearing termination. I'll want to introduce more reality into our relationship then. I'll want him to get me off the pedestal he has me on right now. I'll want to equalize our positions. And even before we reach termination, there will be times when asking him about cars will increase his self-esteem enormously. But in a general way, I don't see anything like that as part of the therapy hour, because that hour is basically his to use in whatever way is important to him at that time. My intrusion of my own needs is just that, an intrusion, and one for which he's paying. And it's even a kind of extortion, because there's no way he'd feel in a position to tell me not to waste his time.

Gary said, "It comes up whenever the patient is a person you'd really like to have as a friend. Because you can't. Whatever the legitimacy of your feelings, the patient is caught up in a mix of transference and reality in which the transference dominates. The two of you can't be friends, because they'd be going out with a fantasy, and you'd never untangle the mess you'd made of treatment." He paused. "This is entirely different from the rare times you offer a patient something to drink or even eat, because those are clear therapeutic interventions where it's important to actually fill in a deprivation. These aren't moves you make because you want to—and you don't make them lightly either."

In an ideal treatment, neither therapist nor patient oversteps the boundaries of the therapeutic relationship: the therapist always acts in accordance with the patient's needs, and the patient doesn't make demands the psychiatrist finds unacceptable. But many patients do go beyond the acceptable limits of behavior. Some break the rules by phoning the psychiatrist at all hours of the day and night, or by paying late or not at all. Some break agreements about not drinking or taking drugs or cutting their arms. Others lie about taking essential medication that they've agreed to take. Occasionally, a patient follows the psychiatrist home or threatens her or her family.

The more unacceptable the behavior, the more it complicates the therapeutic relationship. In these cases, the psychiatrist has emotional responses that must be acknowledged. She must allow herself to become aware of her anger, resentment, or fear. She also has to tell the patient how she feels, and discuss the behavior in sessions. If the psychiatrist doesn't acknowledge the problem, she is all too likely to treat the patient with covert resentment or even to terminate the treatment in anger.

Michael said, "It's necessary to tell someone when they're doing something you find unacceptable. And you don't have to hide your anger either. It's a piece of reality the patient can incorporate and make use of to understand what goes on between normal people.

"The other night a patient left a message with my service that he had to speak with me urgently. This is a depressed man, not someone I normally think of as a suicide risk. But I could always be wrong. So I spent several hours trying to reach him." He pursed his lips. "The kicker was that his line was busy. I called the operator because I thought he might be talking to friends, but it turned out he'd taken his phone off the hook. When I spoke with him the next morning, he said he had gone to sleep, and I told him I was furious, that he had no right to leave an emergency message and then make it impossible for me to get through. I said he'd taken up my whole night,

I was worried, he had a responsibility to me to be available once he said it was an emergency.

"Some psychiatrists wouldn't have felt comfortable showing they were angry, but I see no reason not to. It's appropriate, and appropriateness is part of what the patient has to learn from me. And far better I tell him what he's done than risk having my resentment spill over in the treatment. And once I told him I was angry, we could talk about how he mistreated me, acting helpless and vulnerable while exerting tremendous control over me—manipulating me. But I want to be clear. I didn't yell at this man, and I didn't go on for ten minutes about what he had done to me. I just told him openly and with feeling that I was angry and that I felt he had no right to treat me as he had. And then we could examine his behavior in treatment." He eyed me narrowly, his tone blunt. "I don't want you to hear me saying it's all right at times to express anger as a license to abuse the patient. He's still the patient, you're still the doctor, and your obligation always remains to behave responsibly and with restraint."

Ideally the therapist is like a sponge, soaking up the patient's very essence and responding empathically to his needs, hearing his inner voice and saying precisely what will be most useful to his growth. Obviously, psychotherapy can never be continuously at this level. This is a fantasy even the most dedicated therapist can't live up to. However empathic she may be, the therapist is only human. As one psychiatrist said, "Empathy is exquisitely sensitive to any disturbing influence. Fatigue, a cold, a new love affair—any of them can interfere with the ability to let go of your own concerns and put yourself in the patient's shoes." The psychiatrist also comes to the session with her own quirks and style, inclined to irritability or withdrawal under stress, or to be too ready to jump to the rescue. No one can always respond with the patient's best interests in mind.

In the early years of the psychoanalytic movement, therapists were expected somehow to be free of any interference from their own wishes and needs. Once the impossibility of this was acknowledged, however, their feelings became viewed as one more tool of treatment.

Whatever the kind of psychotherapy being provided, sophisticated therapists nowadays are marked by the ability to decode their own responses as well as patients, treating their feelings during the hour as neither meaningless nor irrelevant, but as signals that point to something the patient is calling forth. Some of these feelings are expectable human responses that are largely independent of a given therapist's specific life experiences; and they are sometimes referred to as "counterreactions."

Even more important to the treatment, however, are those feelings that are rooted in the therapist's own particular life experience and childhood. In this sense, her own transference feelings (from her past onto the patient) are an inevitable part of treatment, for even the thoroughly psychoanalyzed psychotherapist continues throughout life to respond in part to other people—including patients—as if they were significant persons of childhood, feeling herself cared for or rejected, approved of or criticized, understood or misunderstood, and responding to those feelings in characteristic ways.

In treatment, "countertransference" refers to an upswelling from the psychiatrist's own unconscious of such feelings, coming from her own past and transferred now onto the patient. The more thoroughly she knows herself, the more realistically in the present her reactions are likely to be in the treatment hour, the milder are those countertransference responses that do occur, and the easier they are to spot. But the truth is that the attempt to keep reality and illusion in entirely separate boxes is impossible, and in practice the boundaries between realistic perceptions and unconscious distortions blur for therapist as well as patient. The critical issue is that countertransference can be useful if it is monitored by the therapist and an interference in the treatment if it is not.

"When I was in psychotherapy," Gary said, "the psychiatrist I was seeing had a nasty, sarcastic sense of humor. My father used sarcasm as a weapon, so I'm very sensitive to it—and I don't think it's legitimate with any patient. You have to be careful using humor at all, because patients are so vulnerable, they easily see themselves as the butt when you don't intend it. And in retrospect, I'd say that his sarcasm during the session was a countertransference response when

I was particularly depressed or in turmoil. I still remember one time, I was really upset, I was crying, and I said, "You're just sitting there. You don't do anything." Now there are lots of ways you can answer that. I know that now, but what he said is branded on my brain: 'Somebody in this room has to keep his head.' As if I had no right to feel frightened about the way I felt. It wasn't reassurance; it was rejection. And I'd say in retrospect that he felt over his head, and he was particularly anxious because I was a psychiatric resident."

Each therapist is likely to have a particular array of countertransference responses (for example, anger, sarcasm, attempts at control, overprotectiveness) that are likely to be triggered when the right buttons are pushed, and even the best therapists may be unaware of countertransference while it is happening.

Looking back on events, Steve talked about the countertransference issues that surrounded his divorce. "No matter how 'amicable' the divorce, it triggers whatever feelings you have about being rejected and unloved," he said. "You feel an immense sense of loss, of grief, of abandonment, of failure, and of anger at the other person for doing this to you . . . and it's all muddled with your other experiences in life, particularly those as a child. Given my mother's chronic depression, and my feeling that I was the least-loved child in my family anyway, I had to overcome enormous feelings of worthlessness and fury.

"And afterward I realized that throughout this time I was not only too impatient with patients' demands on me, but much less supportive to most of my women patients than I normally am, and much more inclined to look for ways in which they were at fault, like my mother. And part of my defensive reaction also involved a kind of hardness, a 'What the hell do you need anybody for anyway?' that left me very insensitive to people's needs for love. I really pushed patients toward independence that year in a way that often disregarded other issues." He stopped for a minute. "I was seeing one man who had three young kids, and rather than try to assess more clearly what was happening between him and his wife, and whether they could be reconciled, I encouraged him—I see that in retrospect—to leave the marriage." He spoke slowly and reflectively. "The issue with countertransference is precisely that it's out of consciousness. You learn to look for cues to its existence, particularly for anything unusual you do with a particular patient or at a particular time, any change in routine, or how you act, but it's all too easy not to look, particularly when your own life is in turmoil."

Laura, too, talked about how insidious countertransference could be. "Anytime you find yourself thinking about a patient more than you normally do, you have to ask yourself about it. As soon as they become special, worth more of your energy and commitment than someone else, it's either that they're really in serious trouble and you'd better figure out what's gone sour in the treatment, or it's countertransference."

Laura then told me a story that illustrated not so much countertransference as what seemed more like an enormous need to feel powerful, in control, and even invulnerable, what has been described previously as the omnipotence fantasy. She said, "A patient walked into my office, sat down, and said, 'You're working too hard.' Without even thinking, I said, 'No, I'm not. Why do you think so?' And he said it was something about my bodily posture when I stepped into the waiting room to greet him. Then at the end of the hour I told him I'd already given him his bill, he denied it, and I suddenly realized I hadn't. I'd only billed the patient before him. So I told him he was right, I was working too hard."

When Laura told me this story, I burst out laughing, because she was still leaving out the most relevant fact. She saw this patient just before she went on vacation, and she had already told me that she was so tired she wasn't sure she could make it through her last day of work. Yet she couldn't admit her fatigue when he called her on it. She could only use an error of billing as a signal after the fact that he was right. Here the patient responded to an aspect of their real relationship, only to be met by her denial of vulnerability.

In fact, I was shocked by the number of psychiatrists I spoke with who seemed unwilling to admit vulnerability or other unpleasant realities of their work. One man is known particularly for his ability to treat unusually difficult adolescents, yet he told me with a straight face that most of his patients weren't particularly "sick," that they had merely "made messes of their lives." I called him on it, and he ended up getting out his appointment book to show me. Then he was shocked: "manic," he read, for one patient, "schizophrenic" for another, "attempted suicide" for a third, and so on down the page.

Several psychiatrists, not just this man, swore that they saw few difficult patients, although they have reputations for working with people most therapists find untreatable; one told me she never tolerated abusiveness when the very voice of the patient coming into her office after our interview was so filled with contempt it made my skin crawl. Others said they'd limited their schedules, although I know they often saw patients back-to-back for hours, or before seven in the morning, or after dinner, or on weekends. But the most appalling denial has to do with the potential for violence.

"I know of only one psychiatrist who sees dangerous patients as a regular part of his practice," Steve said with disarming reasonableness, "and I've been told he keeps a gun under his chair. But anyone can get threatened occasionally. It's an inevitable aspect of the work. And no one hears a threat to themselves or their family with complete neutrality, particularly if the possibility of danger is real." He looked relaxed and sure of himself. "But patients seldom pose a serious threat in a personal way. I know that so-and-so is going to make me the target of his rage and hate at some stage of treatment, but I count on the affection that's developed between us, and on his knowing that hurting me will cost him his treatment. And because we have a relationship of trust, he's likely to tell me his dangerous impulses well before he acts on them. So that I have a genuine opportunity to resolve the issues peacefully . . . and to protect myself if I need to."

"I'm much more troubled by threats to my family than to myself," another psychiatrist said wryly, "although I'm aware that some of that is a neurotic feeling of my own omnipotence and invulnerability, and some of it has to do with my training."

Then he added: "One of my friends had a patient tell him she was going to kill him so that the two of them could go to heaven together. He warned her to forget that idea and keep in mind that he'd never speak to her again if she killed him. And he wasn't too worried until she called to say she was leaving town to buy a revolver. At that point he called the police, but it took a week to trace her, and he moved his family to a motel to wait it out. The cops eventually picked her up at the airport, with a revolver, and she was jailed prior to a commitment hearing." He explained that a number of his friend's colleagues convinced him that he owed her a final visit at the jail. "When they met, she pulled a knife from her bra and stabbed him. And his colleagues still felt he was right to see her."

The story fascinated me. For however one analyzes this as masochism, grandiosity, omnipotence fantasy, and—perhaps—terrible judgment in the name of physicianly responsibility, it was not just one psychiatrist's error but a comunally agreed upon value within this psychiatrist's peer group.

Harold Searles, the brilliant psychotherapist of chronic schizophrenia, wrote an essay that seems relevant, entitled " 'The Dedicated Physician' in the Field of Psychotherapy and Psychoanalysis." He says:

> Typically, to the extent that one feels bound by the traditional physician's role, one feels wholly responsible for the course of the patient's illness, and feels it impermissible to experience any feelings toward the patient except for kindly, attentive, long-suffering, and helpful dedication. The psychiatric resident, in particular, relatively fresh from the dedicated-physician atmosphere of the medical school and general internship, is often genuinely unaware of feeling any hatred or even anger toward the patient who is daily ignoring or intimidating or castigating him, and unaware of how his very dedication, above all, makes him the prey of the patient's sadism. It has been many years since a young schizophrenic man revealed to me how much sadistic pleasure he derived from seeing a succession of dedicated therapists battering their heads bloody against the wall of his indifference, and I have never forgotten that.

Few patients are as obnoxious as those we encounter in some of Searles's writing. (I always have to remember that Searles is legen-

dary for his specialized treatment of intractable—and usually un-
medicated—schizophrenic patients.) Still, the young (or not so
young) therapist may have a need to save the patient that over-
powers all other concerns. Some of this need is sanctified in the
physicianly role, and some of the need has its roots in the omnipotence fantasy. The need to save the patient is also one of the most
ubiquitous of countertransference phenomena, rooted in the psychiatrist's past. This rescue fantasy stems in large part from the therapist's own unconscious drive to save someone close to her in her own
childhood, usually a parent and sometimes a sibling.

"There are a few patients you feel you have a special relationship
with," Laura said, "patients you feel especially connected to and
whom you feel you can help when even the most experienced therapists have failed over and over again." She frowned in concentra-
tion. "And the truth is that sometimes the patient evokes that
response in you precisely because there *is* a match between them and
someone very important in your past, so that you really do understand them in a special way. *And* because you also put out a superhuman effort, you sometimes work a miracle."

Almost everyone I interviewed had one patient, maybe two, almost always at the beginning of his or her career, who called forth
the most extraordinary efforts, efforts no one could manage more
than a few times over the course of professional life. In looking back,
all of these psychiatrists said the motivating force was the rescue
fantasy.

The effort they had put in is unimaginable to an outsider. When
the treatment worked, it was also in part because these psychiatrists
communicated an unshakable conviction that they could help. Their
patients mobilized their own efforts, too, because they knew that this
was probably their last chance: if they couldn't do it with that psychiatrist, they were really lost. On the other hand, no therapist can
allow the rescue fantasy to propel her too many times without risking
total burnout.

Laura continued. "On the whole, the feeling that you can do what
no one else has been able to manage should be taken as a cue to
reconsider, to realize that you're in the midst of countertransference,

and that you can't trust what you feel. What it means is that this person reminds you of your mother, or your father, or whoever's craziness got you into this field in the first place, and emotionally you're back in the past trying to hold them up or put the pieces back together."

Steve said, "Beginners sometimes do so extraordinarily well when experienced therapists have failed . . . not only because they have a special connection with a particular patient, but because they're motivated to put out everything they have. . . . As you undergo your own analysis, you're likely to become suspicious of these cases and much less likely to act on the feeling." He shifted his weight in his chair. "In fact, you become completely drained if you respond to many patients so uncontrolledly. . . . And these are often disastrous treatments anyway. Because they're based on countertransference and not on a realistic assessment of the patient. To the extent you really do understand them, that's fine, but often you're wrong. You just think you do. And you're also putting an enormous burden on them to get well for your sake."

When I asked John about the rescue fantasy, I expected a disclaimer. Instead he agreed on its ubiquity. "Most psychiatrists I know have the impression that we come from families with considerable pathology, like mine," he said. "That we're drawn to the field by an unconscious wish to save the parent or sibling or whoever it was who was so important and in need of rescue." He looked tired. "Why else would I be willing to spend my working day listening to craziness?"

But Gary was the one who spoke most clearly about his personal experience. The pain was still evident in his voice. "I've never lost the response completely. It's one reason I treat such difficult patients, but Maureen called it fourth full-blown. Partly because I hadn't been analyzed yet, so I didn't even know what was going on. I had no idea why I was so totally obsessed with her.

"I was my parents' only surviving child," Gary continued. "But my mother had a stillborn daughter a year before I was born. When I was in analysis, we explored my guilt about surviving my sister— at replacing her—and I discovered how much of my enormous commitment to patients came from my continued need to save her for my mother's sake. In the course of seeing Maureen I began dreaming about bringing my sister back to life, breathing her mouth-to-mouth, and offering her to my mother alive and well. And sometimes I dreamed the baby was Maureen. And that was the drive, my identification of Maureen with my sister, and my unconscious craving to finally make right what I'd never been able to do in my real life.

"By the time she taunted me about my mother's death, I'd resolved most of the rescue fantasy. But I didn't fully disentangle Maureen from the identification with my sister until that moment." He paused. "I'd never known that baby. I only wanted to save her so my mother wouldn't be depressed anymore. Once my mother died, what residual fantasy I still carried became even less powerful—it was simply too late. And when Maureen screeched that she was glad my mother was dead, it wasn't just her inhumanity to me that I resented; I finally saw Maureen as herself. The cord was cut. My sister was gone."

Countertransference can be a problem in any treatment that's going badly, even in the absence of the rescue fantasy. Gary said, "I still find that the most difficult patient for me is the one who isn't doing well. If they've been in treatment with me for a year, and nothing I've tried has done them significant good, I feel guilty even now, after twenty years in the profession. For a while I'm likely to redouble my efforts, but if I still feel I'm failing, this is the patient I'm likely to be late for, or whose appointment I'm likely to forget." He looked at me sharply. "Unless you've been in treatment yourself, you have no idea how wounding it is when a therapist doesn't show up to see you or books someone else into your time.

"And that's what I really have to watch out for: how I can turn on a patient who's disappointed me, not even just in screwing up a meeting but in really hating them, in catching myself thinking about deliberately not returning a phone call, in hearing myself make nasty jokes about them to colleagues, or even stopping treatment without thinking it through. I know, in retrospect, that I didn't stop with Maureen just because I no longer identified her with my sister. I was furious with her, and I acted on my fury by refusing to treat her anymore. In reality, I couldn't continue to see her. She'd really used up all my ability to work with her . . . but at that moment, I also couldn't stand the sight of her. It wasn't *dis*interest; it was hatred.

"Anytime you screw up an appointment, or overbill a patient, or find your attention wandering, you have to use that as a cue to examine what's happening. Particularly if the treatment isn't going well." Gary was quiet for a moment. "And if you can't disentangle yourself and see what to do differently, you have to ask for a consultation and see what the consultant recommends."

The beginner and the unanalyzed therapist are particularly vulnerable when treatment goes poorly—or with a patient who is particularly demanding or abusive. Feeling helpless, guilty, and unable to set appropriate limits, these therapists often come to hate the patient.

Michael said, "The hardest thing to teach residents is to keep from being stepped on all the time. Not only that they don't have to rescue everyone no matter what, but also to set limits . . . to say, 'You don't call my house, and you can't sit here for an entire hour and insult me endlessly.' " He spread his hands. "It's not that patients can't say what pops into their heads, that's a necessity, but it can't stay at the level the patient often begins at [without destroying the treatment]. . . . I see this as a sleight of hand. The patients will say something, and I'll say, 'Now, I don't agree with that at all,' and they'll look very interested and say, 'But I thought I was supposed to say whatever popped into my head.' And I say, 'You are, but I'm equally free to disagree totally with what you say. I didn't say you shouldn't say it, but on the other hand, this is our life here, and I'm giving you my thoughts.' "

Michael's voice was dry. "I'll tolerate an enormous amount of abuse from a patient, where I feel they're too ill to incorporate anything I say. But if a healthier patient says, 'You have the ugliest office. It sucks. You have no taste, no sense,' I answer, 'Lets take a look at it. You're not so deeply into aesthetics [that] it can keep you going a whole hour. It's obviously something else.' "

Gary said, "When I was starting out, I'd be much more thrown for a loop by patients insulting me, but now I'm fairly disentangled from this kind of thing. The issue is that they're doing to me what they always do. My job is to reframe it so that we can get at the real underlying feelings. Not to take it personally." He paused, looking at one of his photographs on the wall, dunes and a winding trail through high grass. "On the other hand . . . when the patient who's doing well goes on and on about how they're not making any progress, I feel quite able to cut in: 'Wait a minute, last month you got a new job. You're going out with a woman now. What the hell do you mean you're not better?' Because I owe it to myself—and my patient—not to walk out of here at the end of the day wanting to slit my throat. If the work gets too burdensome, and I really feel like shit, it's going to reflect in poor treatment. Better I call the patient on it immediately, with full awareness of what I'm doing."

He swiveled his chair and put his feet on the desk, speaking more slowly now. "Sometimes when I call in a consultant, they'll tell me that I'm screwing up the treatment, that I've missed something important. And for me, that usually means I've allowed the patient to abuse me: I'm not setting limits on telephone calls or on how much they insult me, or on the fact that they don't pay their bills unless I beg them. And that in doing this, I've gotten hooked in, and I'm engaged in some behavior that matches something in their own past, rather than standing back and interpreting it to them dispassionately.

"I treat a young woman who never pays me on time," he went on. "Although she comes from a very rich family, I have to nag her for each payment, and she is always late by several weeks or a month. Of course she is a very difficult patient. She's insulting and contemptuous and very demanding, with a lot of emotional storms and phone calls. But I realize periodically that I fall into a countertransference bind with her again and again. Yes, she's difficult, but it's my choice to treat her. I could tell her I won't work with her if she doesn't pay on time. The real issue is that I'm willing to put up with her abuse to the point of getting furious at her. Once I disentangle her behavior from my own willingness to be victimized, I can point out the contempt behind her stringing me along, and connect it to the way she treats men in general. Even my fury is relevant because this is a woman who—before her treatment with me—would pick men up in bars and get beaten up."

The more sophisticated the therapist, the more likely she is to catch countertransference reactions and the less likely they are to interfere with the treatment. If she feels that her reaction needs a comment (as part of the "real relationship") but is essentially irrelevant to the patient's own problems, she can simply say that she was tired or distracted or just made a mistake. But sometimes deciphering her response may be critical to understanding the patient.

Laura gave an example. "I've been seeing someone for five years, three times a week. The second session after my vacation she was silent, and finally when I got it out of her, she said I'd ended the prior session a few minutes early. I was really angry, because I've put in years of work with her, and also because for a moment I felt the way I used to when my mother would accuse me of rushing out the door to get away from her. And I don't even think I let her go early; we compared watches and hers was a few minutes slow. But I was able to use how I felt, and tell her how she focused on these few minutes, one hundred and twenty seconds, rather than the five years of our work together. And we also talked about her other feelings, of my not being there, like her parents, because of my vacation. And so although she came in not seeing me at all, within twenty minutes the whole transference was right there, out on the table for us to look at." She smiled. "It ended up as one of the most rewarding sessions we've had, and it wouldn't have happened if I hadn't been aware of how angry I became, and able then to relate it to what she was doing to me."

In talking about countertransference, Steve returned to his experience with Carole, the mute teenager he saw at the beginning of his training. "I got to the point where I'd anticipate that glassy look of hers when I'd wake up in the morning. My heart would pound walking into her room, and I'd feel queasy, and I used to think about whether she'd answer me if I hit her over the head with a hammer. I'd say the stupidest things, trying to encourage her, things like, 'I guess you find it hard to talk to me'—really stupid statements. And sometimes I'd talk about the weather, or a book I'd read, until I ran down, and once I yelled I was going to read the newspaper if she wasn't going to talk to me.

"Searles writes that our humanity is validated by the people around us. If it's not validated, we experience ourselves as things. And sitting with Carole, I shared her experience of being a thing. And then I had that dream, in which I was a piece of furniture, a table, and my supervisor put his feet on me and said, 'At least he's good for something.' And I finally brought it all into supervision and understood that my feelings toward her had meaning for the therapy. That's what they meant by 'using the countertransference.' And I stopped being so angry at her. In fact, I came into our meeting—I remember it was a rainy March day—and I told her my dream, and she looked up at me, and she *spoke*. And she said very sympathetically, 'It feels awful, doesn't it?'"

Essential clues to the important themes of treatment, countertransference reactions are often intertangled, hard to unravel, and largely out of consciousness. It is particularly frightening to beginners to have feelings toward patients that are so strong, so unphysicianly, and so irrational. These feelings are the most disturbing a therapist experiences. It takes a while to learn that even the most lunatic responses may be valuable countertransference cues for treatment.

As Gary added, "The worst is sitting with a patient and feeling that you're going to suffocate if they don't stop talking, or finding yourself thinking about murdering them, or starting to yawn uncontrollably, or getting a hard-on. Those are messages from your unconscious, direct responses to the patient, cues you need to respect and use. But those kinds of reactions can really make you feel you're losing your mind.

"When I worked with Maureen," he went on, "I'd sometimes get very embarrassing erections and find myself thinking about what she'd be like in bed. That still happens to me sometimes with very ill people, but it took me years to realize it was a cue to me that I was denying how ill my patient was, and in particular that I was feeling hopeless about her at that moment. I finally learned that my response means the patient has gotten worse and I'm trying not to know it. I still don't feel entirely comfortable with it, but I accept it as part of the way my mind works."

SOMETIMES I FEEL LIKE A DIRTY OLD MAN
The Woman Who Tried to Seduce Me

HERBERT S. STREAN
as told to LUCY FREEMAN

Patients often experience erotic feelings toward a therapist. Freud found it so common that he theorized that these feelings were actually the memory of feelings toward a parent of the opposite sex being transferred to the therapist. Therapists must deal with these feelings, but as this excerpt shows, it is not always easy to distance oneself when the expressions are from an attractive and stimulating patient.

Herbert Strean exposes the hazards and rewards of dealing with an erotic transference while explaining the dangerous results of becoming personally involved with a patient.

A beautiful—and I do not use the word lightly—twenty-nine-year-old woman, slim, with dark brown hair that fell in soft curls to her shoulders, stood at the door. She wore an expensive tailored dress of blue and green print that fell in soft folds to her knees. A wide-brimmed straw hat of deeper green suited the spring season. The heels on her black patent leather pumps were three inches high.

She had informed me during a phone conversation that she had been married for eight years and was the mother of a four-year-old boy. She also said she had been in treatment with another therapist.

I knew this, for he had called me and confessed that for the first time he had allowed himself to be sexually seduced by a patient. He gave me her name, Susan Brown, and said she lived in a fashionable community in New Jersey.

He explained that he could no longer treat her and asked if I could. He was an M.D. and did not want his colleagues to know of the affair. He had suggested she see me, a nonmedical psychoanalyst with a doctorate in social work. He knew I had treated several therapists, both M.D.'s and non-M.D.'s, who had had affairs with patients. I had helped them understand why they engaged in these forbidden alliances, an absolute no-no for any therapist.

"I'm so glad you could see me, Dr. Strean." Susan Brown's voice was soft, seductive, her blue eyes ablaze with friendliness.

I gestured toward a chair; she glided over on those highest of heels and lowered herself into it like a dancer.

Without a moment's delay she dove right into the sexual waters. "Dr. Strean, I know that Greg"—the pseudonymous analyst—"has told you of our affair. I'm thoroughly enjoying it, but my relationship with my husband and son is suffering, and Greg feels I should break off with him and continue analysis with you."

She added wistfully, "I have never had much sexual satisfaction with my husband. He seemed loving before our marriage, but soon after the wedding he started to treat me coldly. Now he doesn't appeal to me, at least not the way Greg does. Greg is giving and warm. He gets inside my soul."

I thought, if she feels he gets inside her soul, she certainly would be receptive to his getting inside her body.

She then asserted, "I know patients are not supposed to have sex with their analysts, but I don't feel my affair has caused any conflict. I'm upset because I want to leave my husband and son. That's the reason I came for help. Not to get out of the affair with Greg."

For a patient, to have an affair with an analyst is exciting; I could see in Susan's first interview that this was a triumph she relished. I also knew that though she felt loved she also felt guilty at having turned the treatment into an affair so important she wanted to leave her family.

I had other thoughts, too. I could understand why my colleague had broken a sacrosanct rule: Susan was beautiful and seductive and engaging; she radiated an unusually attractive warmth. She reminded me of the first girl I ever had a crush on, a girl whose face and body had sexually aroused me when I was fourteen. She had also frightened me, though, because my erotic feelings were so overwhelming. I never acted on my feelings for Florence; the best I could do was tutor her in Latin. As I talked with Susan Brown, I recalled that when I first saw Florence, my family had just moved from Canada to the United States. Suddenly flooded with memories of Florence, I felt stimulated by the very thought of her. I was also stimulated by my new patient, but I kept the "hands off" policy firmly in mind.

Several times as Susan talked I fantasied making love to her. I not only empathized with my unfortunate colleague but envied him as well. Florence, in my adolescence, had been romantically involved with a boy named Marvin, and I had envied him. Now, thirty years later, in the first interview with Susan Brown, my oedipal drama was revived. Treatment would be in essence another Latin lesson, while Greg, like Marvin, enjoyed all the fun.

As I listened to Susan, I thought of what had happened in her therapy sessions with Greg—what analysts call "the erotic transference." The analyst uses this technical term to gain emotional distance when a patient falls passionately in love with him, as many patients do—women with male analysts, men with female analysts, and some with analysts of the same sex.

Freud was well aware of the discomfort, anxiety, and stimulation an analyst could feel when a woman patient fell in love with him. My own feeling is that Freud wrote in detail about the erotic transference because he was tempted to accede to it on one or more occasions. He refrained because he understood his own countertransference and knew that an affair would only harm the patient. He knew that such a sexual liaison was comparable to incest. He also knew it could be even more damaging in that the patient who came to him for relief from her suffering would be victimized even more if she became sexually involved with the analyst.

Yet I have often felt it is ridiculous to dismiss a woman patient's show of love with the interpretation that she really desires her father. Analysts, myself included, can defend themselves with such inter-pretations, or they can change the subject, or they can sink into profound silence. But the helpful analyst, in the spirit of Freud, aids the patient by asking her to verbalize her fantasies. Only then can she face unresolved childhood conflicts.

Why, if the patient is eager to have sex with the analyst, does the analyst not gratify her wish? There are several valid reasons. First, such gratification turns analysis into a love affair. This interferes with, and sometimes destroys, all chances of the patient's psycholog-ical growth. A love affair, while perhaps temporarily gratifying to both patient and analyst, never leads to inner change for the patient. Furthermore, as patients who have had sexual liaisons with therapists point out, analysts do not have any particular expertise as lovers. They are probers of the mind, not the body. An analyst is trained to do psychoanalysis; he holds no diploma in lovemaking.

Another serious consequence of such a liaison is that sooner or later the patient may want more than an affair. Most analysts are not prepared to marry their patients, so the affair usually makes the patient feel rejected and exploited. Virtually every patient perceives the analyst as a parental figure. As a result, most of these sexual liaisons are mutually unsatisfactory because both parties are uncon-sciously involved in an incestuous relationship and the resultant guilt usually prevents pleasurable sex. Incidentally, I made a study of ther-apists who came to me for help because they were involved sexually with patients. Most of them reported that when they embarked on the affair they felt deeply depressed, unhappy with their marriages, or disillusioned with themselves or with life in general.

As I thought of my future work with Susan, I recalled clinical experiences with women who had strong erotic transferences. Many times an analyst is so overwhelmed by a patient's falling in love with him that he forgets to delve psychologically with the patient into what this behavior means to her. It can hold many meanings for the patient; it can be a bid for reassurance, a cover-up for hostility, an attempt to demean the analyst by taking him out of his professional role, a wish to be nurtured (turning the sexual experience into the earliest childhood wish to be fed at the breast), a defense against homosexuality, or all of these at different times in the analysis.

It was not possible with Susan, as it is not possible with any patient, to tell in advance the meaning her erotic feelings had at the moment. Very early in training, I learned that each patient has to be understood in terms of her unique past, her unique experiences throughout life, and her unique ways of coping.

An erotic transference is hard to handle, for me and for most analysts, I believe, because many patients, if their sexual demands are not gratified pronto, become vindictive and make threats, including suicide. But no matter how stimulated and excited the analyst may feel, no matter how badly he wants to avoid hurting the patient's feelings, he must say no to anyone insisting on immediate sexual gratification.

While the wish to express erotic feeling is always present, in this instance the patient is not saying, "I have a wish I want to understand," but "I must have you sexually or I might kill you or kill myself or ruin you or ruin myself because I will be so furious if you refuse me."

It is always difficult to say no to someone who insists on yes, and at the same time the analyst wants to prevent the patient from feeling guilty about her sexuality, but he has to say, in essence, "You cannot gratify your sexual wishes with me." The danger here is that the patient may unconsciously assume this means her sexual desire for anyone else is also forbidden.

I add parenthetically that most, if not all, of the sexually demanding patients I have treated feel very guilty about their sexual desires, and many of them lack a fulfilling sexual life. Thus the analyst has to say no to a wish he wants the patient to feel is natural— accepting the fulfillment of her erotic drive. One of the major tasks in any analysis is to liberate the sexual instinct, but like the good parent with the growing child, the analyst tries to help the patient accept sexual impulses without the need always to gratify them at once.

This is one lesson of all analyses: that we cannot always immediately have what we want. There is no doubt that intense erotic transferences make heavy demands on the therapist, but for an analyst to accede to a patient's sexual demands, as Greg did, is destructive to the patient and to the analyst as well. As I pointed out above, however, to ignore the sexual demand is almost equally destructive, for the analyst is thereby saying to the patient, "You are not a sexual person to me." This is a painful rejection and often an untrue statement, but it is a far more practical way of handling the situation.

The truth often is, as it was in Susan's case, that the analyst finds the patient sexually appealing but knows that for her good as well as his own there can be no sex between them. The patient over time must slowly accept this. The therapist cannot just say it once, she may have to hear it many times before she finally accepts it.

Susan, who came to therapy three times a week, seemed troubled at first about telling her husband she wanted to leave him. She also expressed guilt about taking Greg away from his wife. She alluded to other problems, such as being unable to enjoy sex with her husband. She told me she'd had two affairs prior to her marriage. Her relationships with men always started with her falling "madly in love," but she would lose interest in the man after several sexual "encounters," as she called them, eventually would come to loathe him, and finally would leave him. She felt this way with her husband, and I wondered if she would soon feel the same way toward Greg.

This pattern of "falling in love," then becoming tired of and angry at the previously loved one, was true of Susan's relations to both men and women. She would build a close, warm relationship with a woman, wind up arguing, then feel indifferent. As I listened to her describe her major *modus vivendi*, I wondered when she would fall in love with me and how and when she would reject me. She seemed to follow this pattern with everyone in her life.

Knowing Susan was a woman who eventually ran away from a man induced in me some interesting countertransference problems. As an adolescent I was always challenged by the woman who held herself back, and Susan reminded me of Florence, not only because she was beautiful and filled with energy but also because she withheld herself from me. Just as I had been challenged at fourteen and on other occasions, I was now challenged by a patient. I told myself that

Susan would eventually leave me. How, I wondered, could I keep her?

The interest in a woman who is hard to get and hard to keep is an old story for psychoanalysts. Such a woman is really the "mother" no child ever fully gets to keep for himself but who always seems enticing. Like Mona Lisa's smile, she is both seductive and rejecting. Susan was my Mona Lisa of the moment. She stimulated me, excited me, but I knew she was prepared to get rid of me if I allowed her to become the temporary oedipal victor.

I was challenged, but I was also aware of traps into which I could fall with this enticing woman. She revealed such a trap to me one morning when she confessed, "I was seduced not only by Greg but by two other therapists as well. I really try to be a good patient, but something happens when these men want me sexually. I know it's no help to me to screw my analysts, but they get to me."

She tried to present herself as a victim of circumstance, and concomitantly I realized she possessed a very limited amount of insight into her wish to turn the therapeutic relationship into a fleeting love affair—a coup on the couch.

For her first six sessions, however, she seemed to take therapy seriously. She produced many thoughts, and she free-associated to her dreams, fantasies, and past history like a well-trained patient. As she talked, she reflected, again like a well-trained patient, on her relationship with her father. "He was a very cold, unavailable, and distant man," she said. "My mother was critical and demanding but endlessly seductive toward him, and I think most of the time this turned him off."

Her dreams and fantasies centered on the theme of searching everywhere for a man—a father who would love only her—but finding each man unresponsive. I had the impression during these first sessions she was trying to please me, to cooperate with me. To give me what I wanted to hear—dreams, fantasies, childhood memories, the stuff of which an analyst's dreams are made.

I also had the feeling she was working hard to impress me instead of facing her own conflicts. I even felt mild irritation because I sensed she was trying to manipulate me, giving an apple to the teacher rather than free associations to an analyst.

Then, in her seventh session, Susan suddenly changed her approach. She threw herself on the couch, said accusingly, "You're really a very cold man. Just like my father." Then plaintively, tears starting to flow: "Couldn't you be a little warmer? Couldn't you show some love?"

Her plea for love induced a variety of feelings in me. On one level I felt sorry for her, as I always feel sorry for anyone in tears. I felt the impulse to gratify this seemingly deprived child who appeared in distress and craved love. Had I seen her earlier in my career, before I'd had so much personal analysis, I actually might have tried to be warmer and more giving. But now I knew better. Any woman who had successfully seduced three therapists couldn't be that deprived. On the contrary, Susan was acting like a clever child, trying to make me feel sorry for her so she could more easily seduce me.

The best approach at this time was to explore the conflicts causing her over-intense wish for love. I asked, "What are you feeling that makes you want warmth and love from me?"

She burst into a rage. "That's a stupid question!" she snapped. "It's like asking somebody who is thirsty why he wants water. You're really a cold potato." Then she propelled herself off the couch and without another word walked out of my office.

At that moment I felt many emotions. On the one hand I felt the impulse to shout after her, "You spoiled brat, sit down and behave yourself. You want what you want when you want it and if you don't get it you throw a temper tantrum." But I also felt some doubts about myself. Was I too rejecting, too limiting? Maybe Susan was right— I was a cold potato. (I had been compared to many things but never to a potato.)

Like all analysts, I am often the butt of patients' intense anger. Though I know no analysis can be successful without such displays of anger, I always feel a certain tension—a normal reaction—in the face of hostility or disapproval.

I studied my reaction to Susan after she walked out of the office. I thought of the time I had felt dismissed and unloved by my mother or by other women in my life. Susan triggered my greatest vulnerability as a human being and my greatest limitation as an analyst: when I feel rejected, I respond in one of two ways. Sometimes I ask, What's wrong with me? What does that person disapprove of? Like a child whose parents do not love him. At other times I want to attack the person for not loving me—how dare he? I felt both feelings with Susan. On the one hand I wondered, How have I misbehaved? On the other hand, I thought, that bitch. She doesn't love me the way she should.

My feelings toward Susan were those of a guilty, rejected little boy and, at the same time, those of a boy who wanted to kick his mother in the teeth for not loving him. These reactions are triggered in all of us when we feel unwanted. Only after many years of personal analysis was I able to acknowledge the child in me, to be aware of my little boy reactions. Then, much later in life, I learned to withstand the verbal abuse of my patients as they transferred their outrage to me.

I have rarely heard analysts acknowledge their discomfort in the face of massive hostility and rejection by patients, but I believe analysts would suffer fewer heart attacks if they could admit that, even though they know the abuse is just a transference, it can still hurt. No matter how mature an analyst or anyone else becomes, the child within is always alive and susceptible to anger and pain.

At Susan's next session she apologized for her "performance" and said, "I know you want to help me." For the following several sessions she talked of how she had lacked approval and emotional warmth from her father, who was always away on business trips or out playing poker "with the boys."

A few sessions later she spoke again of her yearning for a warm, loving father, then suddenly asked, "Will you hold me close for just a little while?" She added hastily, "For reassurance."

She was presenting herself once more as a deprived little girl neglected by a cold father. My subjective reaction was similar to the one I had felt earlier in her treatment: I felt sorry for her, wanted to gratify her wish, but had to refuse her request. Then I wondered, as I have before and since, if I was in the right profession.

In response to her plea to hold her, I asked, "What are you feeling and thinking that makes you want physical assurance at this moment?"

She raised her slim body, clad in black silk, from the couch, and announced defiantly, "I'm leaving forever." She walked out the door.

Susan did not appear for her next three sessions. She did call to leave messages on my answering machine, however: "You no-good son of a bitch. You have an icy personality. You sure are a cold potato," and so forth. I was to hear that description of myself throughout her analysis.

During her absence I felt a vast array of emotions. I wanted to lash out at her for making me feel so impotent and ineffective, so deserted, so abandoned. Though the conscious, rational part of my ego told me Susan was behaving like an angry, impulsive child who wanted to hurt me when she did not get her way, I faced the fact that a part of me was raging because I was not getting *my* way.

Analysts have to be ready for all eventualities, including desertion by patients, yet during Susan's absences I found myself reliving a very painful part of my childhood. This explained my intense anger and mild to moderate depression at her failure to appear.

When I was between five and eight, my mother sometimes punished me by saying, "If you don't behave, I'll send you to a reformatory." She occasionally went so far as to pack my suitcase for such a journey. I knew a reformatory was a school for bad boys, a place where dreadful things went on, and I tried my best to behave. As a child I never knew whether my mother was serious, but these threats made me feel depressed and furious at her. This is precisely how I felt with Susan. I was not sure whether she was just threatening to leave—throwing her weight around to scare me, as my mother did— or really meant she was through.

I got in touch with the little boy in me, the child who saw Susan as a mother, the child who was begging, "Please don't leave me, I need you," but who was also raging, "Mother, I want to kill you for not loving me." Thereafter I could see Susan more realistically.

During one of her message calls I picked up the phone, said, "This is Dr. Strean."

After a silence she asked, "Will you still see me?"

"I've been keeping your hour open because I wasn't sure of your plans," I said quietly.

I felt great relief when she said, "I'll be there next Monday."

I was no longer defeated; I could once again work with my challenging patient (un-really my challenging mother and challenging girlfriend). When I found myself elated about Susan's return, I realized it was as though my mother were saying, "I'm not sending you away. Let's make up." But I knew if I conveyed any sign of pleasure to Susan she would torment me with more threats. I was in another classic analytic dilemma: I felt happy she was behaving the way I wanted her to, but I knew that to show much joy would only reinforce her infantile behavior, gratify her childish fantasies.

For me, it has never been easy to accept a patient's threat to quit treatment, and I doubt it is easy for any analyst. Not only is there potential loss of income but inevitably the analyst asks himself, Did I do something wrong? Could I have done something more effectively? The anxiety and self-questioning I experienced in the early years of my practice still linger on when a patient threatens to walk out. I have frequently likened psychoanalysis to playing golf: you can always better your score; there is always room for improvement.

Having a patient threaten to abandon treatment is a bit like having a spouse threaten to leave a marriage. Being an analyst is quite different from being a spouse, of course, but there are similarities between an analytic relationship and a marriage. In both, two human beings form a partnership and try to live with each other. Each must make certain accommodations to the other, and the potential for conflict is strong. Just as most husbands and wives at one time or another are convinced they deserve a better partnership, so are most patients certain they deserve a "better" therapist. As a result, the threat to quit treatment maybe is not uncommon.

Although I'm sure many analysts have difficulty with this issue, I feel my own anxiety at the threat of separation is stronger than that of most of my colleagues. As with any psychological difficulty the reasons are, as we say in psychoanalysis, "overdetermined," meaning there are many reasons for the same act or the same symptom. One of those reasons comes immediately to mind and has to do with my father.

During the first twenty-one years of my life, my family moved eighteen times. Saying good-bye to friends, relatives, and neighbors was always a sad occasion for me, and I always felt angry that the permanent and familiar had suddenly been taken away from me. My father, when he felt frustrated, simply abandoned a situation. One time, for example, we moved to a new house because he did not like the sound of the dog barking next door. Another time we moved because a neighbor played the piano too loudly. My father was too afraid of his anger to confront those who frustrated him. He preferred instead to pack up all his possessions and move. My mother always complied, and I tended to identify with her and submit to my father's edicts, as did my sister.

Before my father became a bacteriologist, he practiced dentistry at an office in our home. I saw his dental chair lifted into a moving van seven or eight times, and each time wished it would break in two. This was obviously a revengeful fantasy toward my father for what I felt he was doing to me—breaking me in two emotionally. I also wanted the dental chair destroyed because my father was *my* dentist, and I hated his drilling and at times pulling my teeth. I reasoned if there were no dental chair I would be protected from such pain. In hindsight, I think he was probably as upset and fearful as I was, but I experienced him as a cruel sadist who was out to tear me apart.

Through my experience in warding off feelings of helplessness, weakness, desperation, and anger when a patient threatens to leave, I have become an expert in dealing with such patients and I have helped other analysts salvage untreatable cases. I am particularly sensitive to those conflicts that provoke patients to want to leave treatment.

Susan threatened to leave because I was not gratifying her desire to be loved continually and intensely. I was upset by her leaving me temporarily, but I felt that if I chased her, she would so enjoy the chase that she would constantly threaten to leave. I thought she would return if I did not beg her. Therefore, I did not call her when she skipped those three sessions. In other situations, however, I have phoned patients, because I was convinced they needed more than anything else a sign I wanted them to return. The reasons for termination and termination threats are many, and each person who threatens has to be responded to differently.

A few sessions after her return, Susan showed up with a proposal. She entered the room, walked to the chair, not the couch, and announced, "I want to stop this kind of treatment because I feel I'm not ripe for psychoanalysis. I think it would be a good idea to go into group therapy with another analyst. Instead of being in analysis with you, I'll be your friend."

She was once again trying to remove me from my role as analyst, turn me into a lover.

"What bothers you about being in analysis with me? You say you'd rather be my friend than my patient. Why?"

She replied, "I feel so beneath you as a patient. I can't stand your power over me. You seem like a big prick. I feel like a nothing, wiped out. The only way I can feel like a somebody is to get you to fall in love with me and go to bed with me."

Her statement was honest and I felt empathy toward her. She was admitting she could feel human only when she could get a man to fall in love with her. To show her that I understood, I said, "I realize it is hard for you to like yourself as my patient, that only if you seduce me will you feel like somebody."

She responded with a smile. "You are the most wonderful man I've ever known. You're kind. You're understanding. You're brilliant. And you have such sex appeal. I'm glad you're so dedicated to your profession and I respect you for what you're doing—trying to help me rather than screw me."

At first I was taken in by her turnabout. She seemed to say she loved me as an analyst, not a sex object, and I felt grateful. I was no longer a cold potato. She now believed I felt warmly toward her. I also felt proud of myself for having turned a promiscuous woman who seduced therapists into a cooperative patient.

Without another word she resumed her sessions on the couch. Between sessions I thought of her at times, realized there were moments I felt more like her boyfriend than her analyst. I finally realized she was one of the cleverest women I had ever met. She knew the way to my heart was to tell me what a fine analyst I was. All else having failed, she hoped this would make me love her.

I became more and more convinced that beneath Susan's compliments lay a powerful manipulative attitude. She sensed what each man wanted to hear and used this knowledge to try to get him in her grasp. Even her dreams had a manipulative quality.

One night she dreamed she was applauding me as I received accolades at an analytic convention. The next night she dreamed my books were reviewed in the *New York Times* with the highest of praise. In her third dream I was elected president of the American Psychoanalytic Association. She figured out just those situations that would enhance my narcissism.

Had I been less experienced at the time, less aware of the fact that being preoccupied with a patient between sessions was a sign of unresolved countertransference, I might have succumbed to Susan's clever advances. I should also add that I had a few erotic dreams about her, but used those dreams to her therapeutic advantage, not to gratify my own feelings.

Eventually it became clear to me that Susan was not trying to understand herself through analysis. Instead, she was figuring out how to defeat me as an analyst. Having recognized this, I told her one day, "You are still working very hard to seduce me by telling me all the things you think I want to hear, rather than trying to understand your own conflicts."

She became infuriated. "You are a cold, hostile, arrogant man," she said. "You're very insensitive to a patient's needs. I want to rip you into twenty pieces. I would enjoy attending your funeral!" As she vented her anger session after session, I kept recalling Congreve's lines in the play *The Mourning Bride:* "Heaven has no rage like love to hatred turned, / Nor hell a fury like a woman scorned." Written in 1697, the words have never lost one iota of truth.

When she realized I was not going to retaliate with anger, Susan tried another ploy. She accused me of being a "weak, fragile man," of being intimidated by her. She said she would find an analyst who was "more potent." At the same time, however, I felt irritated by her attempt to make me jealous. I felt actually jealous and I pictured her leaving me, finding another analyst, rejecting me as a lover.

I decided to tell her this. I said, "You're trying to make me jealous."

She took this to mean I felt jealous and changed her attitude. "I didn't know you were capable of human emotion," she said. "I'm glad to know I can finally make you jealous."

She then told me that with all my dedication to psychoanalysis, I was "an understanding human being," for I could acknowledge human emotions in myself. Then she described her strong erotic fantasies about me. She talked about how much she would enjoy having my penis inside her, how much gratification my caressing her breasts would bring. She concocted some of the most seductive situations, fantasies, and wishes I have ever heard from a patient.

Though I knew her defenses well, I was moved by her soft voice and now more caring attitude toward me. Again I found myself feeling like quite a man. I felt I must be something of a Romeo if a woman as beautiful as Susan wanted me sexually. But as stimulated as I felt, I constantly reminded myself of how she used sexuality as a means of manipulation, a way of buttressing her shaky self-image and precarious self-esteem.

Once again I pointed this out to her and once again she became furious. But this time she did not walk out. She remained, and she started to face her own feelings, though it was a full year before she could accept the fact I was available to her only to help her understand herself.

The more I did not gratify her wishes, the more she could understand the childhood dramas and dreams she was trying to act out with me. She finally realized they focused on her "stimulating but withdrawing" father, who had left her feeling, in her words, "high and dry sexually." This was what she had wanted to do with me and other men—leave them "high and dry" as revenge against her frustrating father. She acted out with them what she saw as the tragedy of her sexual life. At the same time she unconsciously got even with her father, since each man represented him.

Susan finally realized she was more at war with men than in love with them, as she had thought. Her wish for vengeance against her father for not making her his true love had dominated much of her emotional life as well as her behavior toward men. She also realized she had mimicked her very seductive mother, who occasionally managed to win her husband's erotic attention.

As Susan began to focus more on her internal conflicts and became less concerned about seducing me, her marriage improved and her relationship with her son became more loving. She ended the affair with Greg (I had known this would occur as each became more fully analyzed).

Through my work with Susan I became more empathic toward those therapists who abdicate their therapeutic role to become lovers of patients. Had I been less experienced and less thoroughly analyzed, however, I wonder whether Susan might not have succeeded in adding me to her list of lovers, thus helping me fail as a psychoanalyst.

DR. NERUDA'S CURE FOR EVIL

RAFAEL YGLESIAS

In this novel, Rafael has come to a psychiatrist, Dr. Halston, at the suggestion of his uncle, the boy's guardian. Rafael does indeed have a troubled past that haunts him. When he was a young boy, the family was attacked during an outing by men who raped his mother while Rafael watched helplessly. His father then fled to Cuba because his life was threatened by the attackers. After the father left, Rafael was sexually molested by his mother, as she spiraled into an increasingly consuming madness.

Dr. Halston makes many mistakes that are apparent in this session. First, having treated Rafael's mother creates a great deal of confusion, as Rafael assumes that the doctor has heard much of his story before and has already formed an opinion about him. Second, the doctor's narrow understanding of emotional problems does not allow him to listen to the truths that his patient is disclosing. During this session, Rafael senses that something in wrong with this "treatment."

By Monday I was desperate. Waiting for my session, the day passed slowly. Losing my virginity hadn't chased away the cosmic terror always at my elbow, ready to suffocate me with panic. I composed a sentence that I repeated to myself when I felt it came too close—I am alone, a stranger on a rock spinning in a meaningless universe. Using those inadequate words to describe the awful sensation helped a little, but only as a stopgap until I could turn in all the secrets to my doctor.

"So," Halston said. "What's new?"

"I want to tell you the big one." There were all sorts of odd reactions throughout my body: ears ringing, stomach flopping, throat so tight the words had to be squeezed out.

Halston raised his brows, a vivid expression thanks to his bald head. "Why?"

"Why?" I was astonished.

"What's happened that makes you want to tell me?"

"I don't know." I was annoyed. "I just want to tell you."

"Okay."

"Don't you *want* me to tell you?"

"This is your time to talk about whatever you want."

I shut my eyes to dismiss the anger I felt at his game playing. When I opened them, Halston had propped his head on his chin and leaned sideways in his chair, an attitude that seemed to indicate only the mildest curiosity. "So. What's the big one?"

"I . . ." The speaking of it was harder than I expected. I mean physically hard. There were all sorts of explosions inside. I could have sworn I heard my heart pop and that my chest filled with blood. "I lied about my father."

"You lied about your father to whom?"

"To the judge, to the police. I didn't want to live with him anymore so I told lies." Now the discomfort left me, perspired away, although there was no sweat. I felt that kind of relief: cooling down to a pleasant exhaustion. "I said he was a Communist, that he treated me badly. Whatever Uncle's lawyers wanted."

"And they were all lies?"

"Well . . . Not the part about the passport."

"The passport?"

"He used a different kid's picture to make a passport to get me out of the country. It was against the law, but it wasn't . . ."

"Wasn't what?"

"Well, it wasn't really a crime. He didn't have time to get one for me and I knew all about it. I didn't mind."

"But he did do it?"

"Yes."

"And it is illegal?"

"Yeah."

"So, what did you lie about?"

"Well, I said he was a Communist and . . ."

"He wasn't a Communist?"

"No, not really. He *had* been, but . . ."

"He had been. How recently? I mean, from the time you said he was a Communist?"

"I don't know. A few years."

"I see."

Silence. Halston kept his casual pose.

"So you're saying I didn't lie?" I asked.

"I wasn't saying anything. I just asked."

"Oh come on!"

"Oh come on, what?"

"You're playing word games. I said those things to hurt him, to get away from him. I didn't really mean them. I said he was mean to me. He wasn't mean to me."

"I see. Then why did you say those things about him?"

"Because I was angry at him."

"About what?"

"About leaving my mother and me."

"Leaving your mother and you?"

"Yeah, after the attack. You know, he went to Cuba. And that's when she got sick. You know all about that."

"You keep saying I know all about that."

"That's the first time I've said it."

"You've said it before. Why do you think I know all about it?"

"Because my mother must have told you."

"Why don't we forget what I know from your mother? You said she got sick after he left?"

"Yeah, that's when she stopped talking, writing things down on paper—"

"She stopped talking?"

"Yeah."

"Why?"

"She said everything had to be kept—" I stopped before I said the next word—secret. The revelation felt like a slap. I looked at Halston.

He was still sideways in his chair, only mildly interested. "Yes . . . ?"

"I see. I was imitating what she did. But she didn't—I mean, when she started bothering me, she didn't stop moving." I laughed. "She kept painting the apartment."

"Bothering you?"

"Yeah, when she would, you know, in bed . . ." I gestured, inviting him to supply the proper term. I had no word for it. Incest was wrong, since that implied intercourse and activity on my part.

Halston frowned. He lifted his chin off his hand and straightened. "When she would do *what* in bed?"

"You know." I was ashamed. Besides, I thought, he knows; why did I have to spell it out?

"I don't think you should assume I know anything. Why don't you tell me? If I know already, so what? I can stand hearing things twice."

My irritation at his playacting was strong. I looked away and talked to the floor, both to spare myself embarrassment and to hide my annoyance. "She didn't talk. She wrote things on paper, tore them up and flushed them down the toilet. And she kept painting—"

Halston interrupted, a very rare occurrence. Also, impatience crept into his usually neutral tone, "Yes, you said that before. But what did you mean, she *bothered* you?"

"I was getting to that!" I snapped at him. "She kept painting my room so I had to sleep with her."

"You *had* to sleep with her?"

"Well, I couldn't sleep in my room."

"So you had to share her bed?"

"Yeah."

Silence. Halston stared at me. He adjusted his glasses and nodded for me to continue.

"Well, I didn't understand what was going on, but, you know, she rubbed up against me and you know . . ." I trailed off.

"I don't," he said and continued to gaze at me with an intense, cold expression.

"Didn't she tell you?"

"Forget that I knew your mother."

I smirked. "That's a little hard."

"For the purpose of giving me information about her. I'm sure that's not too difficult. You said she rubbed up against you and . . ." He gestured for me to continue.

I looked away. "You know . . . She came."

"She came?"

"I don't know what to say!" I was infuriated by his coyness. What was the point of embarrassing me?

"You're saying that she rubbed up against you until she had an orgasm?"

"Right." I continued to avert my eyes. I was sad for her and angry that he had needlessly forced me to repeat her sin. "I mean, when I had sex with Sandy—"

"Pardon me?" Halston interrupted. His tone was full of feeling. He sounded outraged.

"I forgot to tell you. I mean, we didn't get to it." I looked at him boldly, proud of myself. "I lost my virginity on Saturday."

"Rafael," Halston leaned over his desk toward me. He usually called me Rafe. "What kind of game is this?"

"Game?" Now I felt I was in trouble. I hadn't been quick enough before, but my senses came alive to the fact that something was wrong.

"You come in here and say you're going to tell me your big secret and that turns out to be something everybody knows."

"What? What do you mean, everyone?"

"Anyone who knows your story. Your uncle has custody of you. Isn't it true that your entire family knows this story? Everyone you know is aware that you testified in court about the passport and your father's politics."

I was confused. For a moment, I couldn't see how he was wrong, although I was sure he was, and also I didn't understand why he was angry. "I guess."

"And then you casually drop these bombs. That your mother bothered you in bed and that you lost your virginity to your cousin. You say those things as if they aren't secrets."

"I didn't lose my virginity to Julie. I did it with Sandy. Her friend."

Halston waved his hand, dismissing the fact. "When did your mother bother you?"

"After my father left, before she—you know, before she went crazy and got arrested at the U.N." I understood now, understood the misunderstanding, and I was frightened. "She never told you?" I asked plaintively. Another blocked memory was unstuck for me: Ruth pretending to be catatonic and whispering to me that Halston was a fool. I was in danger. All my senses told me so: I wanted to run. But where?

"Forget about what you think your mother told me. Let's pretend I never met her. Tell me what you think she did in the bed with you?"

Think. He used the skeptical word think. "It was nothing."

"Nothing? You said before she had an orgasm."

"I don't know for sure. I was a kid."

"Why did you say she had an orgasm if you weren't sure?"

I was exposed. Part of me, the chess player in me, cursed my brain for having left myself so undefended. I couldn't contest him. We had come too far; and I thought we had made the journey together, abandoning the usual lies and tactics. I appealed to him to stop trying to defeat me. "Look, don't you understand why what I did to my father is a big secret? I've been living with my uncle because he thinks I hate my dad and that I hate my mother, but I don't, I just wanted his money. I wanted to live well and I was angry at my dad. He never did anything bad to me. It's secret, a real secret. You can't tell anyone."

"Why? What would happen if everyone knew?"

"A son who lies about his father? Who lies to his uncle?"

"What lies?"

"That I want him to be my father. That I love him."

"You've told him that?"

I nodded. Surely he must see, he had to understand. How could he have listened to the story of my life and not comprehend what I had done?

"Did you tell your uncle what your mother did with you in bed?"

"No!" I was appalled.

"No? Not even that night when your mother was arrested and you wanted him to take you with him?"

"No."

"Wouldn't it have been another reason for him to pity you and rescue you?"

"It isn't a lie."

"I didn't say it was a lie."

"But you think I'm lying?"

"Why do you think I don't believe you?"

"I don't. I don't think anything. Look, all she did was hug me close and rock back and forth and she . . . I didn't really understand until I was with Sandy and I realized what Mom was doing."

"I see. So you realized only this Saturday what happened years before?"

"No. I just understood it better."

"If you didn't think what your mother did was so wrong, why didn't you tell me about it sooner?"

I held my head in both hands, rubbing my forehead, trying to reason it out. I wasn't used to talking about the past. Its pictures were clear in my mind. Without words, without their labels and their judgments, what had happened was simple. Only the words changed what they meant, that's the way it seemed to me: "There is nothing either good or bad, but thinking makes it so."

"I thought maybe my uncle found out, maybe he knew from you." That wasn't true. The instant I said it, I realized I never had such a thought. I simply didn't think much about whether anyone else knew. I didn't want to remember it had happened, and with my mother dead, to speak of it was merely cruel. Cruel and shameful.

"I see." Halston glanced at the clock, pulled his thick glasses off with his left hand and rubbed his eyes with the right. "Your father had left. Your mother wasn't talking, writing things on paper and she painted your room."

He was believing me. I nodded eagerly and helped. "She never finished painting it. That's why I had to stay in her bed every night."

Halston put his glasses back on. "How many nights?"

"I don't know. A month. Two months. I can't remember."

"And every night she rubbed against you?"

"No, no. A few times." I remembered the first time, the gentle passage of air through my room. "Actually the first time was in my bed."

"She came into your bed. Your father was away—"

"It was the night he sent his letter. I think it was that night."

"What letter?"

"The letter explaining why he wasn't coming back to live with us."

"You slept in your mother's bed for a month or maybe two and a few times she rubbed up against you and made sounds?"

"She moaned. And moved around. You know, like she was excited."

"And you understood that she was having an orgasm?"

"I didn't know what an orgasm was. How could I understand?"

"Then how did you know she wasn't crying?"

"What are you saying!"

"Calm down. I'm only asking questions. Sit in your chair."

I hadn't realized I was out of it. I wasn't standing, actually. I was perched on the chair's edge. I sat back, stiff with anger. "What are you trying to tell me? That it didn't happen?"

"I'm not trying to tell you anything. I don't know what happened. Only you know. But you don't seem to be sure. You seem to have made up your mind on Saturday when you had sex with this other girl. I just want to help you to be sure. I think it's important for you to know what you feel and what you think happened."

I looked at the edge of his desk, at the carved mahogany lip and tried to project the past. What was there? A dark room, waking from sleep, her legs capturing me, rocking, low moans, her trembling. Were they sobs? Had I misunderstood?

"Let's go back to before your father wrote the letter. You saw your parents being attacked in Tampa. You saw something happen to your mother. What did you see?"

"I saw her naked. I saw a man—" I stopped. A man peed on my mother, that's what I remembered.

"You saw what? What was the man doing to her?"

"He was peeing."

"You saw pee come out onto your mother?"

I said nothing. The *Gusano* had an erection. He pointed his erection at my mother's face. No. On a city street? Out in the open? How could that be? I gave up, uneasy and angry. "What was he doing? You tell me."

"I don't know. You do. You were there."

"Of course you know. Mom must have told you."

"Your mother was ill. Very ill. You're not. It's possible, even probable, that you can remember better than she could. I know there's part of you that wants to be ill, but you're not. You can remember clearly and understand what you remember, especially if you don't think about how you wished things were, or what your uncle wishes happened, but what actually did happen."

"But I don't remember clearly. I was scared. He was doing something, maybe planning to rape her, maybe peeing, I don't know."

"I understand. But yet you're so sure your mother had an orgasm with you in bed?"

"I'm not sure."

"You're not sure?"

I wasn't. I looked down at my lap and wished I could see into myself and know the simple truth, no matter how ugly. "Why would I make it up?" I asked aloud.

"That's an interesting question," Halston said, his voice friendly again. He glanced at the clock. "Our time's almost up. Maybe you should think about that. Did you want your mother to have sex with you?"

I could hardly breathe. Had everything in my head been a lie? Were the secrets not secrets, the lies not lies, the truth a fantasy? Had I been hiding nothing?

"But if it isn't true, I'm crazy," I blurted out, not really talking to Halston.

"That's interesting. Why do you say that?"

"I'd have to be."

"Does it shock you to know that at one time or another, all boys fantasize about being their mother's lover?"

I shook my head no. Actually, it did. It shocked me, in this context, down to the bottom of my soul. I had vague knowledge, the conversational and literary awareness of Oedipus and of Freud using it to make a famous theory, but that went no further than a shadowy notion that sleeping with your mother leads to madness and that merely having the desire somehow caused emotional distress. What Halston was really referring to, infantile sexuality, was unknown to me.

"It doesn't shock you?" Halston repeated.

"You mean, they dream about it?"

"No. There's a period of time when all children wish to be their parent's lover."

I nodded wisely, although again I didn't really understand.

[I'm not a fan of ignorance and I don't approve of the general direction of modern education, toward specialized knowledge, and I dislike the silly love of professional jargon in psychology and psychiatry—indeed, writing this in laymen's language is an attempt to counteract that. However, all that said, I sometimes wish educated people knew a lot less about psychology and psychiatry, rather than the partial and distorted information they do possess. Too often, in our time, an educated person discussing human psychology resembles a five-year-old operating a Mack truck.]

"What I mean to say," Halston glanced again at his clock, "is that having sexual wishes and fantasies toward a parent is a universal experience during a certain time in childhood. But, of course, they aren't acceptable to us. Even as children, they are taboo. So people sometimes distort, or become confused, about events or feelings or even just wishes toward their parent. Our time is up," he said. He smiled awkwardly. "We'll talk about this tomorrow."

By now, of course, professionals can foresee the course of my therapy with Dr. Halston. He took me through the rape, my father's desertion, and my mother's incestuous behavior, and—without making any direct assertions, so that I felt the insights were mine—convinced me of several important conclusions about my past. First, that whatever the anti-Castro Cuban may or may not have been doing to my mother while my father was being beaten and humiliated, I saw it as a sexual attack because, out of terror, that was how my unconscious translated the reality, using my own taboo wishes as source material for worldly evil. I knocked down the Cuban with the gun, horrified by the sight of my id on top of my mother, castrating my father in the process (the image of his "decapitated head" in the hands of his attacker), and substituting for him as my mother's protector (with dangerous psychic consequences to myself). Hence, I felt that I had driven my father away from us (murdered him) and that I was obliged to take his place as my mother's lover, "forced," as it were, to fulfill the taboo Oedipal fantasy for which my mother, instead of me, was punished by madness and suicide. Of course, if Dr. Halston were presenting this interpretation, he would do so in much more learned—and coded—language, and without the details you have read of the actual events, many of them uncomfortably inconvenient to his analysis. Since Halston was in theory, if not in practice (he never put me on the couch and was only casually interested in my dreams), an unreformed Freudian, educated and trained in the 1930s and 40s, he is an easy target for criticism by a psychiatrist of my generation, but it is important to remember that, however misguided, he was applying his skill as he had been taught, and that he expected this understanding would help me. Even a great surgeon, holding a rusty penknife, can't perform a successful heart transplant.

FINE

SAMUEL SHEM

The darkly comic tale of Dr. Fine, analyst in training, gives the pseudonymous author an opportunity to present his at times poignant and at times hilarious view of his profession, his patients' lives, and his own less-than-perfect personal life—all while someone is killing off the analysts of Boston.

In this chapter, Fine tries to recall what he has been taught about helping his patients, though he cannot seem to distill out his own perceptions of his patients—or are they perceptions of himself? Over the course of a long therapy, it is difficult to believe that there are never any sessions where the therapist's own turmoil does not take over the hour.

Although her name was Duffy Adams, Fine had nicknamed her "Dora, the Hysteric," after Freud's famous case (*Dora, an Analysis of a Case of Hysteria*, 1905). This, common practice at the Boston Institute, helped Fine keep in mind the rules for the analysis of a hysteric. She was one of his two control cases, part of his training to become an analyst. The other was his Five o'clock (P.M.): Maurice Slotnick, alias "Ratman, the Obsessive." Fine had to report each session to his supervisor at TBI, Vergessen, and so he was always wary of making analytic "mistakes." If Fine failed his hysteric, he'd have to repeat with another, adding five more years to his training; a failed obsessive meant another five-year bid. His palms were sweaty—such was the pressure to do a "perfect" session. Vergessen was said to have done seven, one in front of the two-way mirror at the Institute. V.'s mentor, the legendary Semrad, had done dozens; and the mysterious Frau Metz was rumored to do them every time out! (Though Metz was said to have said: "The truly *gemütlich* session—total silence, no analyst, no analysand—is impossible." Like the Heisenberg "uncertainty principle," Fine thought.) Fine knew that his competitiveness was his Oedipal rivalry with "The Man Behind the Cleaver," his pop, and he accepted this. ("In the Oedipal fight there are no winners; it's how you lose that counts"—Vergessen.)

Fine opened the door and saw his hysteric: twenty-six, rich WASP, only child, many love affairs, inappropriate marriage, no children, frigidity, appropriate divorce, remarriage, divorce, many more love affairs, worse frigidity, genital-phase arrest, meteoric rise to top job at Federal Reserve Bank of Boston, paralyzing frigidity, analysis, presently in midst of erotic transference to her analyst, Fine. He thought:

An example of the most profound aspect of human nature: unanalyzed, we continually do things that wreck our lives.

As soon as she saw him, she jumped to her feet. From the harmonic recoil of her breasts, Fine saw that once again she was braless. Honeydews. His years of training had shown him that any detail of body and/or dress was a holograph of the psyche, and with Sherlock Holmsian precision he noted her freshly shampooed flax-blond hair, and her green eye shadow and hot-pink lipstick (Stephanie had pointed out that women who wear such makeup spend lavishly on sexy underwear). And why is "Dora," today, dressed all in black?

Without realizing it, Fine did not meet her gaze. He made no real contact with her. He hardly saw her at all.

She seemed on the verge of tears, and waved a newspaper at him, snuffling. Hysterical, from *hysterikos* (Greek), womb; the seventeenth-century theory that such symptoms were caused by a womb that casts off and wanders through the body, filling the mind with toxic vapors. She did not say hello because she knew Fine would

not respond. As he followed her into the office, staring at the un-
dulating lace edge of her panties, Fine wondered how this sniffling
"loose" blond sex bomb could be the highest-ranking woman at the
Federal Reserve? A jiggle, the yen plummets? A wiggle, a million
Germans get nostalgic about Auschwitz? Her scent? Sex. Her flaunt-
ing her body like this, knowing I cannot respond, is sadistic! Scary!
Testosterone, the only hormone that peaks in the morning, is critical
at puberty in the development of spatial awareness. What good is
that, Fine?! He sat, took up his pen and pad, ready to work through
the frigidity hidden under all this heat. ("Hysterics suffer from rem-
iniscences"—Freud.) Undress her mind, Fine. Listen, but not too
carefully, for "selective inattention"—"listening with the third ear"—
is key. What a job: you get paid to daydream! *Rule:* the affective, or
emotional, content of the first thing a patient says is what the whole
session will be about. *Feeling* never lies. On edge, he honed in on
doing an A+ session. Wouldn't it be great today if I could say nothing at all!

"Did you see this morning's paper? Oh God I'm so scared for you,
Dr. Fine, did you see it, huh?"

Affective word: "scared." Follow it. She waited for a response, and
in deference to the Monday-morning crust, Fine decided to give her
a gift, a psychoanalytic grunt: "Umphgh?"

"Someone killed another psychiatrist—right across the bay in Boston! Shot him! Dr. Timothy Myer—did you know him? The second
one murdered in two months! I'm terrified for you! If you were to
die I don't know what I'd do!" She gathered herself up and, voice
trembling, barely in control, said: "I'd *kill* myself! I really really
would! I had the pills in my hand not an hour ago!"

What a great beginning! Beneath this silly chatter about murder
(Fine *did* vaguely know the victim—an arrogant, C+ practitioner)
lies that gold nugget of analysis, a "transference neurosis"! She's distorting her "real" relationship to me, her analyst, in a way consistent
with the hidden neurotic conflicts of her infancy! Her fear that I be
killed is the same as her wish that I be killed. ("There are no neg-
atives in the unconscious"—Vergessen.) The task: to find out who
these feelings she is putting onto me belong to.

"Imagine—sitting here in your office, vulnerable, anybody can walk in, you're so innocent and trusting, they pull a gun—"

Fine watched, incredulous, as she did something she hadn't done since the initial session: she turned on the couch, propped herself up on her hands, and stared at him. He found himself sighting straight down her half-unbuttoned blouse at her breasts! Oh, that uncanny knack of hysterics to sense my sensual obsession and use it to put me on the spot. Her breasts hung down, swinging, seeming to swell out against their curved topology before being pinched in by the rosy nipples. Cranshaws! Fine felt a stirring in his pants—the classic Führersitzer sign for diagnosis of hysteria! He marveled, anew, at being a tool: what the patient makes the analyst feel (if the analyst is perfectly analyzed, without his own distortions called "countertransference") is the same as what other people feel from the patient, and is, hence, the neurosis. To make these unconscious distortions conscious is analysis, cure. Hysterics cause erections; obsessives cause somnolence; schizophrenics cause the hair on the back of your neck to stand on end; depressives get you down; psychopaths get you to cash bad checks. She's using her eroticism to attack.

"Oh, Dr. Fine, it made me realize how much I love you!"

Fine looked from her breasts to her eyes, felt her hunger, and was filled with the wish to fuck the living daylights out of her. A hundred years ago Breuer had been confronted with this same situation, when Dora turned on his couch and embraced him. Scared, Breuer told Freud, who'd been through similar stuff. Breuer returned the embraces. Freud, who felt unattractive to women and couldn't believe that they wanted to fuck him, instead of *acting* took the incredible step of *thinking* about it. He reached the conclusion: they're mistaking me for somebody else. And psychoanalysis—the greatest tool of the century—was born. Fine was staggered that here he faced the same choices as those brave pioneers of the mind: return the embrace, repel the embrace, or make himself *meta* to the embrace and, with the patient, work it through, explore the feelings and thoughts that *are* it, and by bending the bars of the neurosis, free this poor sex-riddled female from yet another fruitless pacing around her cage.

"I really do love you!"

Eye to eye, Fine felt flummoxed, and glanced at her boobs.

"Don't you have any feeling at all when I say that?! All you can do is look down at my breasts? Answer me!"

Fine knew she had him, and, feeling guilty, riffled his head for the "correct" response. Still in the opening ten minutes, too early to interpret. Intense feeling here. ("When they talk thought, you talk feeling; when they talk feeling, you talk thought"—Reuben, expert in anal aggression, Fine's rival at TBI.) Play it safe—address the defense—the resistance—use the "what keeps you from" line: "Yes and *what keeps you from* lying back down on the couch?"

"Come off it! You're leching after me and we both know it— AHH!—what's *that*?" Fine, perfect analyst, never moved, as she pointed at his heart. "Something's in your pocket, something's moving around in your pocket! Icky! What is it?"

"You have the fantasy that something's moving in my pocket?"

"It really is—look! Ucky!"

"And tell me about this fantasy, hmm?"

"It's no fantasy, it's real. It actually *is*!"

"Yes, and what are your thoughts about this 'is,' hmm?"

"Oh God! You make me so mad—I could kill!"

Fantastic! This tawdry murder, even if real—it might be her fantasy or joke—is providing terrific material for the session.

"Look—I don't mind that you're weird and inhuman—I don't even mind that you stare at my boobs—but I can't stand your staring in secret like a Peeping Tom. At least have the decency to admit it!"

Inwardly wincing, Fine tried hard to keep his face a blank screen for her projections. How do they do it! How do these hysterics intuit their analyst's weaknesses, every damn time! She's right. I should admit it. She's making me feel like a rapist, like I'm totally incompetent to deal with her, either as an analyst or as a man. She's as demanding as my wife! Fine had an urge to tell her all this, and with the urge, felt strangely closer to her, more *with* her. Tell her. But no. My feelings have no place in the analysis. Trapped by her intense gaze, Fine shifted his own to the photo of Freud. Rumor had it Freud couldn't stand eye contact with patients (in a Ferenczi letter he'd called patients *gesindel:* "rabble"), and had sought out couch-and-chair. Fine glanced next at the photo of Vergessen, and, desperately merging two famous techniques—the "counterprojective" and the "empathic"—mimicked the earnest tone of the great V.: "Yes, and *how hard it must be* for you to have these strong feelings for me. These erotic feelings—these *sexual* feelings, hmm?"

"What!!" she said, startled. "Yes, perhaps it is . . ."

Fine knew from her silence that he'd hit home. This was the story of her life. She did this with everybody. Under control again, he mimicked V.: "*Tell* me about these feelings, hmm?"

"OK, Dr. Fine, Ok. . . ." and she rolled back on her back and said "Breasts—I have the fantasy of your touching my breasts. Drives me crazy. I see you reaching from where you're sitting and putting your long thin fingers on my shoulder, my neck . . ."

What a great case! Long thin fingers?! Mine are short and fat! Fine, relieved, now knew he could let her go on associating until about the twenty-five-minute mark, at which time he would enquire as to *who*—mom, pop, this Uncle Savage we'd heard so much about who'd often locked her up with him in the maid's closet—these long thin fingers belonged to, on the little girl's buds, the hairless musky pudendum. And she thought that this *murder* was the issue, imagine that?! How cleverly V. had first introduced me to transference:

"You have a date with Marilyn Monroe. What comes to mind!"

"I better wear my gabardine coat."

Smiling, the sly albino: "Why your *gabardine* coat?"

Sheepishly, Fine: "My *mom* wears gabardine coats!"

"*That's* transference."

The implications, Fine thought, are staggering. We distort all relationships, we are always treating the other like mom, pop, or Uncle Savage. We paint every person with the colors of our childhood. A great gap exists between self and other, and all closeness is a mere shouting across that gap. One never is "as I really am." Stephanie does not believe this, but thinks that we can get closer, and demands this from me. Her resistance to getting analyzed is itself a neurotic defense, in need of analysis. If patients only knew: therapy is not the telling of the story, but the analysis of the *resistance* to the telling and the *transference* distortion by the teller of the told. Not past but present—analysis is in the here and now.

For Fine, transference was a double distortion, for he had the extraordinary fate of being a man often mistaken for other men.

"—your penis. With the tip of my tongue I'm licking the soft skin underneath, then I run my tongue up to the top—it's like a cap on a mushroom, or a hot-pink rosebud—"

Helluva profession: seventy-five an hour to listen to a gorgeous blonde talk about sucking your Weimar—oops!—weiner? Most powerful tool of the century. Why can't my wife do that! Our oral sex has stopped. How lucky I am to have found psychiatry!

Yet it had not been easy. Fine's first year with Fumbles had been an unhappy, stressful time. His whole world had come tumbling down around his ears. It had also been the first year of his psychiatry residency, when he'd done six months of internal medicine in a hospital—frightening and disgusting. In his psychiatry training, he'd felt totally incompetent. While everyone regresses in analysis, Fine, as usual, had done it more and deeper, and after a few months had turned into a bawling infant on Fumbles's couch. He was unsure of everything! Totally lost, he missed Stephanie terribly. She'd gone to Paris, and Fine couldn't stand it. He wrote voluminous passionate letters, made long sobbing calls across time zones waking her in the middle of the night. His paranoia, inflamed by his analysis, raged— he was sure she was having an affair. He begged her to come back. After all she was his wife! She, enjoying her freedom, resisted. Fine said to Fumbles: "I've got to fly over to see her!"

"If you got to fly, so fly," said Fumbles.

So Fine flew.

She'd never seen him so vulnerable. He, crying out for help, touched her soul. He stirred up old, caring, almost maternal juices in her. He needed her, desperately. He would kill himself! He wimpered and pleaded with her for a whole weekend, and then, so as not to miss his Monday morning session with Fumbles, left.

She came. She gave up her job in her father's business, came back to Boston, moved in with Fine, and, through contacts she'd made through John in Southie, got a job in politics, working for the senator, first in "cultural affairs," and then, in fitness. And Fine, comforted, continued his analysis and his residency. With her support, he righted himself, and soon began to enjoy the challenge of learning to become a psychiatrist. He came to think that in his neurosis lay a real gift: an acute sensitivity to the mental state of others. With Fumbles he conceptualized his hyperacute attention as a healthy side of his lifelong paranoia—he thought himself one of a whole generation of Jews propelled into psychiatry by bigotry. Having been on guard against people, he now was rooted in people. When he joined the Institute, he felt *at home*. And he discovered, too, the power of therapy: contrary to public impression, as a psychiatrist you really could cure. Most diseases of the body—lung, heart, liver, kidney—have no cure; doctors palliate. But as a psychiatrist he found he could lock into a person's life at a crucial moment, and tip the balance in a life-saving way. Out on a ledge? We bring you back! Through therapy armed with insight, you may never go out on the ledge again! Most patients are so psychologically unaware, even a simple insight can bring enormous change—like saying: "*Think* about what you feel." The greatest. And the greatest of the greatest? Analysis. In-depth five times a week for years, bringing about true change of personality. Fine felt exuberant, full of that zest for life that had been his salvation. The only real problem he'd encountered was not to *show* his "zest." As Vergessen asked: "Zest? What place does "zest" have in the work?" It was years before Fine analyzed out his "zest" as his own neurotic need, and stifled it. It came from his—

   "—*mother?*"

Silence. Uh oh. Trouble. Fine knew that this was the end of a question, and, wondering if it demanded a response, checked the clock. The twenty-eight-minute mark? Perfect time for an interpretation, but his attention had floated too far off! Damn—the session is going so well—I've said almost *nothing*! One of my best sessions ever! He tried another grunt—"Rghmphgph"—but the silence continued, and the tension mounted. He felt himself *blocking*! What to say?! ("When you don't know what to say, say '*Tell* me about it'— 'it' being the last word heard"—Vergessen.)

   "Mm, yes, and *tell* me about . . . your mother?"

"OK," said Six o'clock, relieved. "Her long thin fingers, with their perfectly manicured nails . . ."

The fingertips on the breasts are Mom's?! She is treating *me* as if I were her mother? And all the others—lovers, enemies, pop, Uncle Savage, even her own mom—as if they were her mom! In *The Fine Theory: Biology and Psychology: Resynthesis*, Fine was trying to join body and mind in a general theory of being. Now he keyed on *Part II: Psychology:* Freud had been expert in genital-Oedipal struggles (father); since his death, others had looked earlier in development, at pre-genital-Oedipal (mother). Freud saw men and women as two sides of the same coin. The thinking was symmetric, linear. Fine saw himself making the twentieth-century leap that Einstein had made in physics: he was bringing nonlinear, relative thinking to the study of human development. Rather than men and women being two sides of the same coin, they were two different currencies. Fine had written in *Anal. J.*: "Relationships are relative. All fetuses start off female. In the womb, in a great military rush of testosterone, half split off as male. Thus, the first asymmetry: men *separate from*, warring; women *stay with*, relating." The key, Fine realized, was "empathy": the ability to put yourself in another person's shoes, feelingly. Fine had data that the capacity for empathy is qualitatively different in women and men (female newborns respond more than males to other babies' cries of distress). After all, who ever heard of *"men's* intuition"? Of a *"matriot"*? Yes, when testosterone kicks in, empathy gets kicked out.

Thus Freud's most famous question, stuck in the side of the century: *"Was will das Weib?"* ("What do women want?"). Fine saw this as Freud's admission that, given his limited empathic skills, the female was beyond him. Hadn't he called women's psychology "the dark continent"? Yet that question is easy, far easier than asking *"Was will der Mann?"* What *do* men want, anyway? Hard to say. Women are so different from men that a qualitatively new theory, centered on empathy, is needed. The empathy-schism lay at the heart of the failure of male-female relationships, of the human sacrifice called "marriage." Women want "intimacy"; men see this as "demand"; men want, say, "expression"; women see this as

"distance." All of this in the name of love. Yet with two such disparate feeling-concepts of "love," what chance do "relationships"
have? One needed to find the missing link between biology and psy-
cho—

"—so why in the world can't I make it with men? Every time I
get involved, I get terrified! Because of my body, my sexiness, I'm
pursued everywhere, these men try to meet me—the way they do it
is so comical!—I meet someone, they seem fine—oops—"

"Umph."

"—we talk, we get to know one another, I warn them that I'm a
handful, that I have to feel *related* in order to go down—to go further
in the relationship I mean, and they say okay, and we relate—I only
choose nice warm men, inept warm men, actually, like Woody Allen
and you—I mean like you only warmer—"

Fine, impaled, grunted louder: "Umph!"

"—and then, finally, we get into a room, a room with a bed, into
a bed, they start to put their hands on my breasts, and there I go—
Miss Eskimo of the Back Bay! It happened again over the weekend!
I can't stand it! I don't want to be frigid, I want to really make love!
No matter how hot I get at the tenderness, I get ice cold at the
touch! I hate myself for it! And I hate my mother! Hate hate
hate!—" She burst into tears, sobbing.

What a great case! Fine thought. ("WASPs are God's Frozen People"—Dr. Pelvin, chief of Stow-on-Wold.) As with an Eskimo and
snow, so with an analyst and tears—twenty different kinds. These?
"Self-hate." We love to see tears, for it means we've ripped through
the defenses and have gotten a straight shot at the affect. Dr. Leon
Bergeneiss, the ranking Jungian-Freudian at TBI, often claimed, with
pride: "I have never failed to make a female patient cry." Fine, feeling happy, let her cry on. Her tears are proof, he thought: she can't
hate mom without hating herself. Women are connected/men are
separate. She is opened up—zap her now! A glance at the clock—
exactly the "correct" time! Here comes the cruncher—the single
Fine interpretation.

"Umghrgch!" Fine cleared his throat. She stopped crying.

In an empathic tone: "You are searching for a good mother in me, in men. But when they touch your breasts, you feel your own bad mother's fingers, and your 'relational-self' is transformed. You relate to all of us as your own bad mother. And how could you help, then, but freeze, hmmm?" Not bad. Wordy, even prolix, not surgical like Vergessen, not colloquial like Semrad, and certainly not the mythical "golden bullets" of Frau Metz. Yet without the sadism of Bergeneiss or "Crusher" Gold, the TBI giant whose hobby was pro wrestling. The "correct interpretation," yes. Let's see what she does.

The clock moved. Six o'clock did not. She lay there, weeping softly, shoulders shaking, not bothering to search her purse for a hankie. Fine, in the notorious debate at the Institute on "whether or not it is the responsibility of the analyst to provide Kleenex," had come down firmly on the side of orthodoxy, and there were to be found no Kleenex in his office. Keenly, Fine analyzed these tears: "grief, mourning." He saw clearly that in the session her tears had gone from (A) hysterical-manipulative through (B) infantile-regressed to (C) mature-adult. Just as they were supposed to! He watched her shoulders shaking, heard her sobs, saw her wet cheeks and reddening nose and congratulated himself: a virtually perfect session! Fine said: "It's time for us to stop."

Good analysand that she was, she got up, went to the door. He arose and walked halfway across the room behind her, once again admiring her valentine of buns, slightly a-swish, but, somehow, now, less provocative and sadistic. She opened the inner door, turned to him, and said: "Thank you."

"You're welcome good night."

"*What?!*" she said, shocked to have gotten a response after the session was technically "over." This had never happened before, and she looked at him, amazement in her eyes.

Oh no! Fine thought. Me and my courtesy! After a session like this, to ruin it with a "doorknob" comment?! One of the dumbest mistakes in the book! How could I do this? She's looking straight at me, like she expects something. What now! Panic! ("In panics, cough"—Vergessen.) Fine coughed.

"Why Dr. Fine, you're blushing!"

Fine, in a total curfuffle, coughed harder.

"Maybe they were wrong to laugh at you! You're human, after all, honey—ciao!"

Fine watched her instantly transform herself back into her hysterical mode—the jiggle, the wiggle, the "honey," the "ciao"!—and wondered again who the "they" are who "laugh" at him. As if she were in cahoots with my wife. Six o'clock finally left.

Shattered, Fine slumped down onto the couch. Associate. I can't take endings: as a boy saying nighty-night to my dear mother, I felt such heights of love for her that as she left, my fear spiraled terribly, down the steep slope of sleep. Oh! This'll set us back months! How can I face Vergessen in supervision? In an effort to firm himself up, Fine decided to suck the first Finestone of the day. He went to his desk, opened the small inlaid-cedar box he'd bought in Marrakech. Within were several chalky-white stones the size of prunes, similar to the stones sold in flower shops to put around potted plants. Finestones. He and his research assistant, the sinewy Ms. Ando, had perfected the process of polishing the rough stones to a milky-smooth surface. Finestones were the practical application of *Fine Theory, Part 1: Biology.* They were high in calcium. Calcium, with two positive charges, attracts negative-charged things, neutralizing negativity, forming links, binding, firming up. He had high hopes for marketing them, to reach vast segments of America. Fine put one into his mouth.

Plop. Suck.

Soon he felt firmer. He went downstairs, bracing for his wife, homing to breakfast. On the stoop lay the folded *Boston Globe:*

PSYCHIATRIST SLAIN IN OF
SECOND IN PAST TWO MO

Fine was shocked, feeling that same sick, "it can't be so!" revulsion he'd gone through with awful regularity over the last twenty years, from John Kennedy through John Lennon. So Six o'clock was accurate after all. Why would anyone want to kill a psychiatrist? He sighed, resigned. The world is going to hell. Statistics show that modern-day America is shifting, diagnostically, toward more severe psychopathology. While the percentage of psychotics stays the same (across culture and throughout history, 1 percent of the population is always schizophrenic), in the past decades in the USA the percentage of character disorders (borderlines, narcissists, psychopathic killers, drug addicts, etc.) has increased, neurotics declining proportionately. The diagnostic spectrum, like a child's toy of steel-balls-in-clown's-eyeballs, has tilted, and tilted back, bunching the sickies in the middle. There's a shortage of healthy neurotics for analysis. Desperate for cases, some analysts are advertising—even hooking neurotics in Harvard Square. I'm lucky. Happiness is having two healthy neurotics.

Fine thought the headline, somehow, too lurid. To cheer himself, he began whistling his father's favorite tune, "Some Enchanted Evening." He went into the kitchen and put the paper, like a joint of *trayf* meat, on the table for his wife. His headache abated, a bit, and he remembered that he'd forgotten something, but for the life of him could not recall, now, what.

IN A COUNTRY OF MOTHERS

A. M. HOMES

Out of some of the most prosaic reasons for therapy come the most startling discoveries. Yet A. M. Holmes forces the reader to wonder if some bizarre cause and effect is not at work here: If the patient is not interesting enough, then the therapist has the tools to make matters more engaging. In this novel, Jody Goodman enters psychotherapy in hopes of getting what amounts to career counseling, but the therapist, Dr. Claire Roth, comes to believe that Jody is the daughter she gave up for adoption as an infant years ago. In a decidedly unorthodox session, during which the therapist's lack of neutrality becomes painfully clear to the patient, Dr. Roth uses her guile and talents to direct the conversation in a way that serves her needs, and her needs alone.

"Do you think about your brother a lot?" Claire asked. Five minutes into the session, Jody was starting to space out. It was pouring rain outside. She looked past Claire and out the window. Somehow it was easier to look over Claire's shoulder than to deal with things inside.

"Would it be better if I closed the blind?" Claire asked.

"No. Sorry," Jody said.

"How would you describe your relationship to your brother?"

"My relationship? He died before I was born."

"Do you think of him as your friend? Your enemy?"

"My ghost," Jody said. "I am him, he is me."

"What does that mean?" Claire asked, eyebrows raised.

Jody shrugged. This was getting a little too close for comfort.

"Did your parents want a boy, or did they purposely adopt you because you were a girl?"

"They adopted me before I was born," Jody said, annoyed. "The deal was, whatever the baby was, it was theirs. The guy who was in on it called my parents when I was born and said, 'Your package is here and it's wrapped up in pink ribbons.' Isn't that incredibly queer? 'Your package.' What did they do, mail-order me?"

"People didn't talk about adoption very openly twenty-five years ago."

"Tell me about it," Jody said.

"Why don't you tell me," Claire said.

They were silent. Rain splattered down onto the air conditioner outside, and Jody forgot where she was for a minute, slipping back and forth in time and geography.

"The whole year I was nine," she said, "I thought I was going to die. Every day I waited. I didn't know how it would happen—if it would be a sudden, quick snapping thing or something that would creep across me for days or weeks. After that, regardless of what happened, I always felt like one of those miracle cancer patients who lives despite the odds."

"What made you think you were going to die?"

"He was nine when he died and somehow in my head I figured all children died. That was just the way it went."

"Depressing," Claire said.

"Very," Jody said.

"Did you ever have fun?"

"Yeah," Jody said, laughing. "I played funeral home with the kid who lived next door. I made her lie down flat and then I covered her face with baby powder." Jody paused. "You're looking at me funny."

"You say the most upsetting things and somehow they sound funny. I'm not sure whether you're kidding."

"The funnier it gets, the less I'm kidding," Jody said dryly. "Can we change the subject?"

"Do you find it difficult to talk about your family?"

"No, it's like eating a York Peppermint Patty, uplifting, refreshing, get the sensation."

"You're very angry."

"Annoyed, not angry. When I get angry, little flames start coming out of my ears, it's a whole different thing."

What do you want from me? Jody was tempted to ask.

"I'm curious why you're having such a hard time today," Claire said. "The trip to L.A. went well, so there should be some acknowledgment of success, but you don't seem willing to discuss that, either. Maybe you want me to know that despite your ability to succeed, there's still something you need me for."

Jody shrugged. She was nailed. She tried to play it cool.

"I'm here," Claire said. "You can tell me the most horrible thing in the world or the most wonderful thing. Either way I'm still here."

"My life, my brother, my family has made me into a very different person from the one I was born as," Jody said. "When I think about it, I have the sensation of being separated from myself. I'm not into this adoption thing, okay? I love my parents, I really do. But there's something, some strange something. Maybe it's from being adopted, maybe it's just me, but I don't get too attached to anyone. To anything. I don't want to. I'm convinced that if do, I'll get fucked over. Call it fear of rejection, whatever.

"When you're a baby you look at your mother's face and it's your face. She smiles at you and at that moment she is you. When you're a little older, you smile back at her and somehow the smile on your face is her smile, it's you becoming her."

Jody paused and looked at Claire, who was nodding intensely. Though she didn't usually wear makeup, Claire had lipstick on, and one side of it went up above the lip line, making her look a little demented. Jody forgot what she was thinking for a second.

"But when you're adopted, you look up at your mother and she's trying to look at you, to understand you, and in my case there was also this ghost of a child between us. What I saw was not a mirror;

it was neither myself nor my mother, but something confusing and much less clear. The root it plants is a strange kind of detachment, an insecurity." Jody stopped and fixed on Claire.

"Do you still feel the insecurity?" Claire asked.

Jody sighed. She wondered if shrinks made their families stay up late at night and talk about everything in microscopic detail. So fucking obsessed, no surprise that they worked in offices by themselves. No one could stand to be around them.

"There is something, some lack of something."

"What?"

Jody flashed Claire a hard look. Even if she knew, she wouldn't tell anyone, ever.

Claire didn't react except to glance at the clock and then pick up her appointment book and start flipping through the pages. Were they out of time? Jody wondered. It was as if they'd been under water and suddenly had raced back to the surface for air.

"There's a lot to talk about," Claire said.

Jody nodded.

"Would you like to keep going?"

Jody didn't know exactly what Claire meant.

"We could have a double session," Claire said. "I'm not seeing anyone until five. What do you think?"

Jody shrugged. She still wasn't clear about what was going on. She'd never heard of anyone going overtime. Didn't Claire have better things to do? Didn't Jody have a job? A life?

"Do you want to stay?" Claire asked.

Of course Jody wanted to stay, didn't everyone? But at the same time, she'd had enough. She'd said the things she'd said knowing that within the hour Claire would throw her out. There were no major consequences. You didn't have to live with your words for more than fifty minutes. That was the beauty of therapy, you always ran out of time. You could always say something incredibly important in the last five minutes and there was nothing the shrink could do except say, We'll have to talk about that next week, or, It's so interesting how you save the very best things for last. No matter what, you left when the hour was up. That was one of the rules.

"Well?" Claire asked.

Jody shrugged.

"Are you leaving it up to me?"

She nodded.

"Then let's keep going—but first I have to go to the bathroom. I'll be right back."

Claire walked out, leaving the door open. Jody never had a shrink who went to the bathroom before. She'd always thought they were like teachers: they just didn't go.

Claire's purse was on her desk along with a huge stack of notes, a pile of yellow legal pads. Jody could have gone through everything. She could have stolen Claire's wallet and then played dumb. She could have flipped through her appointment book, making a list of the names and numbers of all her other patients. Later that night she'd be able to sit down with a bowl of popcorn and make crank calls.

Hi, I'm calling for Claire Roth. She asked me to let you know that you're so incredibly neurotic that it's driven her crazy and she had to be admitted to the hospital. Hi, this is Claire Roth's secretary. She asked me to leave you a message: get a new shrink.

The phone rang just as Claire was coming out of the bathroom. "Don't answer it," she yelled, running back into her office, picking up just as the tape clicked on. "Hello," she said, breathless.

From her side of the room, Jody could hear a woman's voice squeaking through the receiver.

"I'm with someone now," Claire said curtly. "Can I call you later?"

"So," Claire said, hanging up and sitting back down in her chair. "Tell me how your parents adopted you."

The mood had completely changed. They'd come back to the surface and now, with barely a breath of air, Claire wanted to go under again. Jody wasn't sure she could do it. If she'd been the person she wished she was, the great pillar of strength and wisdom, she would have explained that while she was grateful for the offer, she'd had enough for one day and really had to get back to work.

"Do you know the details about where you came from?" Claire asked.

"Yeah," Jody said. "The sperm bashed its head against the egg and here I am."

"How romantic," Claire said. "But did you come from an agency or an orphanage?"

"You really want to hear all this?"

Claire nodded.

"My parents told me I came from an agency."

"How old were you when they told you?"

"Just born," Jody said. "I came home from the hospital and they said, 'Hi, how are you? This is the house, this is the kitchen, this is the front hall, we'll take you to your room. Oh, and by the way, you're adopted, but don't think twice about it.' "

"Do you remember them telling you?"

"They always told me. They had this book, not something in general circulation, but like something an adoption company would sell you. A two-volume boxed set, *The Adopted Family*. One book was a picture book for the kid, and the other was the more serious stuff for the adoptive parents, things like what problems you might have, how to love the stranger's child, blah, blah, blah."

"Was finding out you were adopted traumatic? Do you wish they hadn't told you?"

"It's like learning your name. You don't remember learning it, it's just there, it belongs to you. I'm adopted. A-D-O-P-T-E-D. It's the first word I learned to spell."

Claire grimaced.

"Kidding," Jody said. Every time she said something, Claire's face flashed a reaction. At first Jody had really liked that—it was proof that a human being was sitting across from her—but sometimes she wished everything wasn't so damn interesting, didn't mean so much to Claire.

"Everything is not a natural disaster," Jody said. " 'Adopted' . . . I know the word, but what does it mean? I have no idea."

"Do you *feel* adopted? Earlier you were talking about your mother and not mirroring her."

"Yeah, but I don't know if that comes from being adopted or having a dead brother."

"How long before you were born did he die?"

"Six months."

"It is kind of close," Claire said.

"I know." Jody was tempted to tell Claire to take a tranquilizer or to point out that therapeutically speaking, all Claire's expressions might not be a good thing. If Jody were not Jody, if she were a seriously disturbed maniac, someone who couldn't take a little criticism, all Claire's heaving and hoing might throw her right over the edge. Fortunately, what Jody was saying was old hat. There were no shocking new revelations about her past. She was telling the story of her life, and the facts came easily.

"Barbara used to hound me about didn't I think it was strange that an agency would give an infant to a family whose child had just died. She kept pestering me, like maybe she knew something I didn't, but she never came out and said it. Anyway, I used to bug my mom for information, I always had the feeling that there were things nobody was telling me. I'd hit her up for a recount whenever I knew she'd be weak, like the kid's birthday or the anniversary of his death."

"How did you know when his birthday was, or when he died?"

Fucking detective, Jody thought. "My mother would say, 'Today's Blank's birthday. Today it's ten years since Blank died.' I never heard her tell anyone else, but she'd always tell me in a kind of conspiratorial whisper."

"That wasn't very fair, was it?" Claire said, then quickly added in a soft voice, "I wish you'd tell me his name."

Jody shrugged, her stomach turning in on itself; it was as if Claire was asking Jody to share her brother. Jody was aware of the betrayal, the obviousness of leaving her brother's name out, but she had to keep something for herself. Claire couldn't have everything.

"Anyway, I'd hit her for info, and then when I was about twenty, it came out that they didn't get me from some agency, but on the black market, and the lady who lived next door went to the hospital to pick me up because my mom was too chicken to meet my real mom. They traded me in the back of a cab for an envelope of money."

Jody glanced at Claire, who looked as if she were having an allergic reaction. Her nose and eyes were all red. "The thing that kills me— well, among the things that kill me—is no one will tell me how much they paid for me. I mean, I'd like to know. I asked and my mom said, 'Whatever it was, it wasn't worth it.' "

Claire looked surprised.

"She was kidding," Jody said. "The other thing that kills me is that it's still not clear to me if Barbara knew something or not, and if she did, how come she played along and didn't tell me?"

"I don't know," Claire said. "You'd have to ask Barbara."

"No one ever tells me shit."

"Do you feel like people are purposely deceiving you?"

A fucking obvious test question. Did Jody also think people were out to get her? That everyone was working together in a plot to ruin her life? She looked at Claire as if to say, Don't you think I see what you're getting at? Don't fucking condescend to me. Fuckwad.

"Is there some reason why people would keep the truth from you?" Claire asked.

Jody shrugged.

"What else do you know?"

"Why are we talking about this?" Jody asked.

"Why?" Claire said.

"Yeah, what does being adopted have to do with going to UCLA?"

"You tell me."

"No, you tell *me*."

Claire looked at the clock. "Well, neither of us can say much more today. Let's talk for a minute about your schedule. Do you work every day?"

Jody nodded.

"Are you going to keep working until you leave for California?"

"That's a big subject if we're out of time," Jody said.

"So let's talk about it more later," Claire said. "What's tomorrow like for you?"

"Fine," Jody said, wondering how the hell she'd pay for all this. All of a sudden she needed to see Claire all the time. Not once a week but every day. She had the urge to tell Claire everything, even the things she really didn't want her to know. It was as if Jody needed to unload herself, her whole self, to empty everything onto Claire and then, scrubbed clean, leave for California. And Jody also had the strangest gut feeling that Claire somehow needed her as well; she reprimanded herself for it. That was truly sick, a sure sign of major neurosis. Of course Claire didn't need her, she had a life of her own: a husband, probably kids, and a million other patients, including the one who'd just buzzed into the waiting room.

"We really have to stop," Claire said. "Is nine-thirty all right?"

"In the morning?"

Claire laughed. "Too early?"

"It's all right," Jody said. Didn't Claire know that America worked from nine to five, that structure was good for people? Nine-thirty in the goddamn morning was way too soon. Nothing was going to happen between now and then. Jody would eat dinner, watch TV, sleep, then be back here with Claire. Why was Jody throwing herself at Claire? Moreover, why was Claire letting her do it? Shouldn't Claire set some limits, say something like, I know you'd really like to see me again soon, but it's not healthy, not productive. You must learn to solve your own problems, be independent, otherwise how are you going to get to California and make a name for yourself?

The rain had stopped, and a veil of late-afternoon sun was poking through dark clouds. Somewhere—maybe in Vermont, where Claire probably had a weekend house—there was a beautiful rainbow. The air was warm from the rain. Jody crossed Houston and walked up to Washington Square, which was empty, the junkies temporarily chased out by the weather. A couple of street people pushing grocery carts were circling each other, staking out the best bench. She walked east toward Broadway, not at all sure where she was going. It was twenty past five. She'd been in the shrink's office for the whole fucking afternoon.

The phone rang at ten-thirty and Jody knew a stranger was calling. She'd already said goodnight to her mother, Michael was out of town and wouldn't have bothered to take her number, Ellen was on a date, and Harry was at an opening at the Museum of Modern Art.

"Hello," Jody said, prepared to hang up without saying another word. She held the phone in one hand and, with the other, pulled back the window shade enough so she could peek outside, as though the caller would be standing at the pay phone on the corner.

"I don't think you know me," a man's voice said.

Jody was tempted to slam the phone down, but there was something kind of nervous and pathetic about the voice. Jody let go of the shade.

"This is Peter Sears. Ann gave me your number."

Ann who? Jody wondered.

"She told me you were living in the city and suggested I call you."

Peter Sears had gone to Wesleyan along with Jody and about fifty people named Ann. His father was a famous record producer, and she'd considered trying to be friends with him, but she realized this impulse was based more on his father's success than on any qualities Peter himself might have had, so she ignored him. Plus, he was good-looking, really good-looking, so good-looking, in fact, that Jody couldn't figure why he was calling her in the first place.

"So, how is Ann?" she asked, still not sure who they were talking about.

"Fine," Peter said. "She said that since graduation you've been doing some film work."

"A little. I'm helping Harry Birenbaum on a project," Jody said, figuring that Peter would recognize Harry's name. Harry and Mr. Sears probably played whatever it was that men played together. "But in the fall I'll be going to UCLA."

"Wow, great."

Yeah, wow, great, Jody thought. Every time she said "UCLA" a wave of anxiety washed over her. At least it sounded good to other people.

"What have you been doing?" Jody asked.

"Some writing," Peter said.

He probably didn't have to work. Jody imagined Peter living a life of extreme luxury in the brownstone his father owned but never lived in for more than three days in a row. Peter probably woke up at ten A.M., watched cartoons until eleven, drank fresh-squeezed juice in bed, and finally got up around noon, giving the maid a chance to straighten up before doing the shopping.

"I have tickets to a screening of *Tin Beard* tomorrow night and was wondering if you might want to go."

"I saw it already, last week," Jody said. "It's not great."

"There's a party at the Ark afterwards—would you want to go to that?"

"All right," Jody said, as if she'd been talked into something.

"Pick you up at ten-thirty."

Jody hung up, curious how come Peter Sears had to dig up strangers from college in order to get a date. She tried to remember which Anns he'd been friends with. There were four of them—interchangeable as far as Jody was concerned—Ann Weinstein, Ann Salzman and Anns Bankowsky and Willers.

The phone rang again. It was either Peter Sears calling to say he'd come to his senses and there was no way he was going anywhere with Jody, or the guy at the phone booth on the corner had finally found her number. She peeled back the shade and looked outside again. The phone booth was empty.

"Hello," Jody snapped, turning on the answering machine even though it was after the fact.

"Is everything all right?"

Jody was silent, terrified.

"Jody, are you there? It's Claire Roth."

"Yeah, I'm here," Jody said.

"Sorry to call you at home. I was looking at my book and realized I made a mistake. I have to change our appointment time for tomorrow. Would four-forty-five be all right?"

"Yeah, sure, fine."

"Are you sure you're all right?"

"Positive," Jody said, banging her knee against the filing cabinet nervously, again and again. Tomorrow it would be black and blue and she'd look at it and wonder if it meant something, leukemia or hemophilia.

"Good. Then I'll see you tomorrow," Claire said. "Night."

Her voice was as soft as they pretended Kleenex was on television. It floated down over Jody and she breathed it in like a kiss.

SOLITAIRE

ROBERT LINDNER

Robert Lindner's *The Fifty-Minute Hour*, first published in 1954, revealed to the public for the first time inner workings of therapy sessions. It was a pathbreaking and shocking book that heightened interest in the subject at a time when psychotherapy was more widely being considered as a treatment for emotional ailments. The book stayed in print for an astonishing thirty-two years.

In "Solitaire," a patient with a severe eating disorder, the then rarely diagnosed bulimia, unearths her past, getting worse before she gets better. Finally, the unconscious desire that led to her problem is brought to the surface and is relieved by a compassionate, talented therapist.

LAURA

Sooner murder an infant in its cradle
than nurse unacted desires.
—WILLIAM BLAKE, *Marriage of Heaven and Hell.*

Laura had two faces. The one I saw that morning was hideous. Swollen like a balloon at the point of bursting, it was a caricature of a face, the eyes lost in pockets of sallow flesh and shining feverishly with a sick glow, the nose buried between bulging cheeks splattered with blemishes, the chin an oily shadow mocking human contour; and somewhere in this mass of fat a crazy-angled carmined hole was her mouth.

Her appearance astonished and disgusted me. The revulsion I felt could not be hidden. Observing it, she screamed her agonized self-loathing.

"Look at me you son-of-a-bitch!" she cried. "Look at me and vomit! Yes—it's me—Laura. Don't you recognize me? Now you see, don't you? Now you see what I've been talking about all these weeks—while you've been sitting back there doing nothing, saying nothing. Not even listening when I've begged and begged you for help. Look at me!"

"Lie down, please," I said, "and tell me about it."

A cracked laugh, short and rasping, came from her hidden mouth. The piglike eyes raised to some unseen auditor above, while clenched fists went up in a gesture of wrath.

"Tell him about it! Tell him about it! What the hell do you think I've been telling you about all this time!"

"Laura," I said more firmly, "stop yelling and lie down"—and I turned away from her toward the chair behind the couch. But before I could move she grabbed my arms and swung me around to face her. I felt her nails bite through my coat and dig into the skin beneath. Her grip was like a vise.

She thrust her face toward mine. Close up, it was a huge, rotting wart. Her breath was foul as she expelled it in a hoarse, passionate whisper.

"No," she said. "I'm not going to lie down. I'm going to stand here in front of you and make you look at me—make you look at me as I have to look at myself. You want me to lie down so you won't have to see me. Well, I won't do it. I'm going to stand here forever!" She shook me. "Well," she said. "Say something! Go on, tell me what you're thinking. I'm loathsome, aren't I? Disgusting. Say it! Say it!" Then suddenly her grasp loosened. Collapsing, she fell to

the floor. "O, God," she whimpered, "please help me. Please . . .
please . . ."

I had never met anyone like Laura before, nor had I encountered
the strange symptoms she presented. In the literature of morbidity
occasional reference was made to a disorder called bulimia, or pathological craving for food; and I had of course met with numerous
instances of related oral disturbances, such as perverted appetite or
addiction to a specific food. As a matter of fact, one of the most
amusing incidents of my career concerned a case in this category. It
happened at the Federal Penitentiary in Atlanta, where I had been
sent on a special assignment during the first years of the war. One
day I received a note from an inmate requesting an answer to the
engaging question, "Do you think I will get ptomaine poisoning from
eating tomatoes on top of razor blades?" I showed this provocative
communication to my colleagues in the Clinic who thought, as I did,
that someone was pulling my leg. In reply, therefore, I wrote the
questioner that the outcome of such a meal depended on whether
the razor blades were used or new. Much to my chagrin, a few days
later the X-ray technician called me into his office and exhibited
two pictures on the stereoscopic viewer, inviting me to look at the
"damndest thing you ever saw." I looked. In the area of the stomach
I saw a number of clearly defined, oblong shadows. "What the heck
are those?" I asked. "What do they look like to you?" he responded.
I looked again. "To me," I said, "they look like—well, I'll be
damned! Razor blades!"

We called the inmate from the hall where he had been sitting
hunched over on a bench, moaning with pain. When he saw me, he
complained, "I did what you said. I only ate new blades like you told
me. . . . Now look what's happened!"

"Musta been the tomatoes, then," was the technician's dry comment.

When the surgeons went to work on this man they discovered him
to be a veritable walking hardware store. I was present in the operating room when they opened him up, and my eyes bulged with
amazement as they carefully removed piece after piece of the junk

he later told us he had been swallowing for many years. Somewhere in my private collection of psychological curiosa, I have a photograph of the debris collected from this man's interior. It shows not only numerous fragments of razor blades, but also two spoons, a coil of wire, some bottle caps, a small screw driver, a few bolts, about five screws, some nails, many bits of colored glass and a couple of twisted metallic objects no one can identify.

Laura's difficulty, however, did not involve the perversion of appetite but something far more distressing psychologically. She was subject to episodes of depression during which she would be seized by an overwhelming compulsion to gorge herself, to eat almost continuously. A victim of forces beyond her ken or control, when this strange urge came upon her she was ravenous—insatiable. Until she reached a stage of utter exhaustion, until her muscles no longer responded, until her distended insides protested with violent pain, until her strained senses succumbed to total intoxication, she would cram herself with every available kind of food and drink.

The torment Laura suffered before, during and after these fits (as she called them) is really beyond description, if not beyond belief. Articulate as she was, I could not appreciate the absolute horror, the degradation, the insensate passion of these wild episodes until, with my own eyes, I saw her in the midst of one. Her own report of the onset and course of these experiences, a report I heard many times, is as follows:

"It seems to come out of nowhere. I've tried to discover what touches it off, what leads up to it, but I can't. Suddenly, it hits me. . . . It seems I can be doing anything at the time—painting, working at the Gallery, cleaning the apartment, reading, or talking to someone. It doesn't matter where I am or what's going on. One minute I'm fine, feeling gay, busy, loving life and people. The next minute I'm on an express highway to hell.

"I think it begins with a feeling of emptiness inside. Something, I don't know what to call it, starts to ache; something right in the center of me feels as if it's opening up, spreading apart maybe. It's like a hole in my vitals appears. Then the emptiness starts to throb—at first softly like a fluttering pulse. For a little while, that's all that happens. But then the pulsing turns into a regular beat; and the beat gets stronger and stronger. The hole gets bigger. Soon I feel as if there's nothing to me but a vast, yawning space surrounded by skin that grabs convulsively at nothingness. The beating gets louder. The sensation changes from an ache to a hurt, a pounding hurt. The feeling of emptiness becomes agony. In a short while there's nothing of me, of Laura, but an immense, drumming vacuum."

I remember asking her, when she reached this point in her description, where the hunger started, at what place in the course of this weird, crescendoing compound of emptiness and pain the compulsion to eat entered.

"It's there from the first," she would say. "The moment I become aware of the hole opening inside I'm terrified. I want to fill it. I have to. So I start to eat. I eat and eat—everything, anything I can find to put in my mouth. It doesn't matter what it is, so long as it's food and can be swallowed. It's as if I'm in a race with emptiness. As it grows, so does my hunger. But it's not really hunger, you see. It's a frenzy, a fit, something automatic and uncontrollable. I want to stop it, but I can't. If I try to, the hole gets bigger, I become idiot with terror, I feel as if I'm going to *become* nothing, become the emptiness—get swallowed up by it. So I've got to eat."

I tried to find out, in the early days of her analysis, if there was any pattern to her eating, any design, any specificity.

"No," Laura told me. "It's just a crazy, formless thing. There's nothing I *want* to eat, nothing in the world that will satisfy me—because, you see, it's the emptiness that has to be filled. So it doesn't matter what I swallow. The main thing, the only thing, is to get it inside of me. So I stuff anything I can find into my mouth, loathing myself while I do it, and swallowing without tasting. I eat. I eat until my jaws get numb with chewing. I eat until my body swells. I swill like an animal—a pig. I get sick with eating and still I eat—fighting the sickness with swallowing, retching, vomiting—but always eating more and more. And if my supply of food runs out, I send for more. Before it comes I go mad with the growing emptiness, I shiver with fear. And when it arrives I fall on it like someone who's been starved for weeks."

I would ask her how the frenzy ended.

"Most of the time I eat myself into unconsciousness. I think I reach a state of drunkenness, or something very like it. Anyhow, I pass out. This is what usually happens. Once or twice I've been stopped by exhaustion. I couldn't open my mouth any more, couldn't lift my arms. And there've been times, too, when my body just revolted, refused to take in any more food.

"But the very worst is the aftermath. No matter how the fit ends, it's followed by a long sleep, sometimes for as much as two whole days and nights. A sleep of sick dreams that go on and on, terrible dreams I can hardly recall on awakening—thank goodness. And when I awaken I have to face myself, the mess I've made of Laura. That's even more horrible than what's gone before. I look at myself and can hardly believe the loathsome thing I see in the mirror is human, let alone me. I'm all swollen, everywhere. My body is out of shape. My face is a nightmare. I have no features. I've become a creature from hell with rottenness oozing from every pore. And I want to destroy this disgusting thing I've become."

Three months of intensive analytic work had passed before the morning Laura confronted me with her tragically distorted body and insisted I look at it. They had been stormy months for both of us, each analytic hour tearful and dramatic as Laura recited the story of her life. In the recounting she could find no relief, as many other patients do, since it was a tale of almost endless sorrow in which one dismal incident was piled upon another. Used as I am to hearing the woeful stories of abuse, neglect and unhappiness that people bring to an analyst, I was nevertheless moved by Laura's narrative and could hardly help expressing my sympathy. By this I do not mean that I verbalized the feelings she aroused in me, for the discipline of these long years of practice and the experience gained through the many errors I have made safeguard against such a gross tactical blunder; but in small ways of which I was largely unaware I communicated my compassion to her. With Laura, this turned out to be a serious mistake. Typically misreading my attitude for one of pity, hardly had the analysis begun than she set out to exploit more and more of it.

Paradoxically, just because I somehow betrayed sympathy for her, she charged me increasingly with a total lack of warmth, and upbraided me almost daily for my "coldness," my "stonelike impassivity," my "heartless indifference" to her suffering. Our meetings, therefore, followed a curious pattern after the first few weeks. They would begin with one of her moving chronicles, to the telling of which she brought a remarkable histrionic talent; then she would wait for some response from me: when this was not forthcoming in the manner she desired, she would attack me viciously.

I recall one such hour quite clearly, not only because of its content but also, perhaps, because it preceded by a few days the episode I described earlier; and the contrast between the way Laura looked on the day I have in mind and her appearance only a short while thereafter remains vivid in my memory. For Laura between seizures was nothing like the piteous wreck she made of herself at those times. Although poor, she always dressed becomingly, with a quiet good taste that never failed to emphasize her best features. The ascetic regime she imposed on herself between bouts of abnormal eating kept her fashionably thin. Her face, set off in a frame of hair so black that it reflected deep, purple lights, was not pretty in the ordinary sense, but striking, compelling attention because of its exotic cast. It conveyed an almost Oriental flavor by the juxtaposition of exceptionally high cheekbones, heavy-lidded brown eyes, a moderately small, thin nose with widely flaring nostrils, and an ovoid mouth. On the day I wish to tell about, one could hardly imagine the ruin that was even then creeping up on her.

She began the hour with her usual complaint of fantastic nightmares populated by grotesque forms whose exact description and activities always eluded her. These dreams occurred every night, she said, and interfered with her rest. She would awaken in terror from one, often aroused by her own frightened screams, only to have another of the same kind as soon as she fell asleep again. They were weird dreams, she claimed, and left her with only vague memories in the morning of surrealistic scenes, faceless figures and nameless obscenities just beyond the perimeters of recall. Water—endless, slow-moving stretches of it, or torrential cascades that beat upon her with the fury of whips; footsteps—the haunting, inexorable beat of a disembodied pair of shoes mercilessly following her through empty corridors, or the mad staccato of an angry mob of pursuers; and laughter—the echoing hysteria of a lone madwoman's howl of mockery, or the shrieking, derisive chorus of countless lunatics: these three elements were never absent from her nighttime gallery of horrors.

"But you can't remember anything more?" I asked.

"Nothing definite—only water again, and being chased and the sound of laughter."

"Yet you speak of odd shapes, rooms, landscapes, action of some sort, scenes. . . . Describe them."

"I can't," she said, covering her eyes with her hands. "Please don't keep after me so. I'm telling you everything I remember. Maybe they're so terrible I have to forget them—my dreams, I mean."

"What else could you mean?" I entered quickly.

She shrugged. "I don't know. My memories, I guess."

"Any particular memory?"

"They're all terrible. . . ."

I waited for her to continue, observing meanwhile that her hands were no longer over her eyes but interlocked tightly over her forehead, the knuckles slowly whitening and the fingers flushing as she increased their pressure against each other.

"I'm thinking," she began, "about the night my father left. Have I ever told you about it?"

. . . It was raining outside. The supper dishes had just been cleared away; Laura and her brother were sitting at the dining-room table doing their homework. In the kitchen Freda, the oldest child, was washing up. Their mother had moved her wheel chair into the front bedroom, where she was listening to the radio. The apartment, a railroad flat on the edge of the factory district, was cold and damp. A chill wind from the river penetrated the windows, whistling through newspapers that had been stuffed into cracks around the frames. Laura's hands were stiff with cold. From time to time she would put her pencil down and blow on her fingers or cross her arms, inserting her hands beneath the two sweaters she wore and pressing them into her armpits. Sometimes, just for fun and out of boredom with her sixth-grade geography lesson, she would expel her breath toward the lamp in the middle of the table, pretending the cloud it made was smoke from an invisible cigarette. Across from her Little Mike, intent on forming fat letters according to the copybook models before him, seemed unaware of the cold as he labored. Laura could tell which letter of the alphabet he was practicing from watching his mouth as lips and tongue traced familiar patterns.

When the door opened, Little Mike glanced up at her. Their eyes met in a secret communication of recognition and fear as heavy footsteps came down the hall. Bending again to their lessons, they now only pretended to work. In the kitchen Freda closed the tap so that she, too, could listen.

In a moment, they heard their father's grunting hello and a mumbled reply in kind from their mother. Then there was a creak of the springs as he sat heavily on the bed, followed by the sharp noise of his big shoes falling to the floor when he kicked them off. The bedsprings groaned again as he stood up.

"Peasant," they heard their mother say over the music from the radio, "if you're not going to bed, wear your shoes. It's cold in here."

"Let me alone," he replied. "I'm not cold."

" 'I'm not cold,' " their mother mimicked. "Of course you're not cold. Why should you be? If I had a bellyful of whisky I wouldn't be cold either."

"Don't start that again, Anna," he said. "I'm tired."

"Tired," she mocked. "And from what are you tired?—Not from working, that's for sure."

"Oh, shut up, Anna," he said wearily over his shoulder as he walked through the doorway. Behind him there was the click of the dial as their mother shut off the radio, then the rasping sound of her wheel chair following him into the dining room.

Laura looked up at her father and smiled. He bent to brush his lips against the cheek she offered. The stiff hairs of his thick mustache scraped her skin and the smell of whisky made her slightly dizzy. Straightening, he ruffled Little Mike's hair with one huge hand, while with the other he pulled a chair away from the table.

"Freda!" he called as he sat down.

The older girl came to the door, smoothing her hair with both hands. "Yes, Papa," she answered.

"Get the old man something to eat, huh?" he asked.

Anna wheeled herself into the space between the table and the open kitchen door where Freda stood. "There's nothing here for you," she said. "You want to eat, come home when supper's ready. This ain't a restaurant."

Ignoring her, he spoke over her head to Freda. "Do like I said, get me some supper."

As Freda turned to obey, Anna shouted at her. "Wait! Don't listen to him!" She glared balefully at her husband, her thin face twisted with hate. When she spoke, the veins in her long neck stood out and her whole shrunken body trembled. "Bum! You come home to eat when you've spent all the money on those tramps. You think I don't know. Where've you been since yesterday? Don't you know you've got a family?"

"Anna," he said, "I told you to shut up."

"I'm not shutting up. . . . You don't care what happens to us. You don't care if we're cold or starving or what. All you think about is the lousy whores you give your money to. Your wife and children can rot for it matters to you."

"Anna," he started to say, "the kids . . ."

"The kids," she screamed. "You think they don't know what kind of a rotten father they've got? You think they don't know where you go when you don't come home?"

He slammed his palm down on the table and stood up.

"Enough!" he yelled. "I don't have to listen to that. Now keep quiet!"

He started for the kitchen. Anticipating him, Anna whirled her chair across the entrance. "Where're you going?" she asked.

"If you won't get me something to eat I'll get it myself."

"No you won't" she said. "There's nothing in there for you."

"Get out of my way, Anna," he said menacingly, "I want to go in the kitchen."

"When you bring home money for food you can go in the kitchen," she said.

His face darkened and his hands clenched into fists.

"Cripple!" he spat. "Move away or I'll—"

Her laugh was short and bitter. "You'll what? Hit me? Go ahead—hit the cripple! What're you waiting for?"

Framed in the doorway they faced each other, frozen in a tableau of mutual hatred. Behind the father Laura and Little Mike sat stiffly, eyes wide and bodies rigid. In the silence that followed Anna's challenge they heard the rain slap against the windows.

Their father's hands relaxed slowly. "If you don't move out of the way," he said evenly, "I'm getting out of this house and I'm never coming back."

"So go," Anna said, leering up at him. "Who wants you here anyway?"

Like a statue, he stood still for a long minute; then he turned and walked swiftly toward the bedroom, followed by their eyes. Now the tense quiet was broken by the noises he made as he moved around the next room, and shadows, cast by his tall figure, crossed and recrossed the threshold.

On Anna's face, when she became aware of what he was doing, the look of triumph gave place to alarm. Her bony fingers clutched the wheel of her chair. Hastily, she propelled herself around the table. In the doorway, she stopped.

"Mike," she said, "what're you doing?"

There was no answer—only the sound of the bedsprings twice, and the firm stamp of his shoes against the naked floorboards.

"Mike"—her voice was louder this time and tremulous with fright—"where're you going?—Wait!"

The wheel chair raced into the bedroom, beyond sight of the children. They listened, their chests aching with terror.

She clutched at his coat "Mike. Wait, Mike," she cried. "Please don't go. I didn't mean it. Please.... Come back. Come into the kitchen. I was only fooling, Mike. Don't go."

He pulled away from her, lifting her body from the chair. Her hands broke the fall as useless legs collapsed. The outer door slammed. Then there was the slapping sound of rain again between her heavy sobs. . . .

"—He meant it," Laura said. "I guess she went too far that time. He never did come back. Once in a while he'd send a few dollars in a plain white envelope. On my next birthday I got a box of salt-water taffy from Atlantic City.... But we never saw him again."

She fumbled with the catch on her purse and groped inside for a handkerchief. Tears were streaming from the corners of her eyes. Some caught on the lobes of her ears and hung there like brilliant pendants. Idly, I wondered if they tickled.

She dabbed at her eyes, then blew her nose noisily. Her bosom rose and fell unevenly. The room was quiet. I glanced at my watch.

"Well?" she said.

"Well, what?" I asked.

"Why don't you say something?"

"What should I say?"

"You might at least express some sympathy."

"For whom?"

"For me, of course!"

"Why only you?" I asked. "What about Freda, or Little Mike or your mother? Or even your father?"

"But I'm the one who's been hurt most by it," she said petulantly. "You know that. You should feel sorry for me."

"Is that why you told me this story ... so that I'd feel sorry for you?"

She turned on the couch and looked at me, her face drawn in a grimace of absolute malice.

"You don't give an inch, do you?" she said.

"You don't want an inch, Laura," I responded quietly. "You want it all ... from me, from everybody."

"What d'you mean?" she asked.

"Well, for example, the story you just told. Of course it's a dreadful one, and anyone hearing it would be moved, but—"

"—But you're not," she almost spat. "Not you. Because you're not human. You're a stone—a cold stone. You give nothing. You just sit there like a goddam block of wood while I tear my guts out!" Her voice, loaded with odium, rose to a trembling scream. "Look at you!" she cried. "I wish you could see yourself like I see you. You and your

lousy objectivity! Objectivity, my eye! Are you a man or a machine?
Don't you ever *feel* anything? Do you have blood or ice water in your
veins? Answer me! Goddam you, answer me!"

I remained silent.

"You see?" she shouted. "You say nothing. Must I die to get a
word out of you? What d'you want from me?"

She stood up. "All right," she said. "Don't say anything. . . . Don't
give anything. I'm going. I can see you don't want me here. I'm
going—and I'm not coming back." With a swirl of her skirt she
rushed from the room.

Curious, I reflected, how well she enacted the story she had just
told. I wondered if she knew it too?

Laura came back, of course—four times each week for the next two
years. During the first year she made only few—and those very minor—advances so far as her symptoms were concerned, particularly
the symptoms of depression and sporadic overeating. These persisted:
indeed, for several months following the "honeymoon" period of
analysis—when, as usual, there was a total remission of all symptoms
and Laura, like so many patients during this pleasant time, believed
herself "cured"—her distress increased. The seizures of abnormal appetite became more frequent, and the acute depressions not only
occurred closer to each other in time but were of greater intensity.
So, on the surface, it seemed that treatment was not helping my
patient very much, even that it might be making her worse. But I
knew—and so did Laura—that subtle processes had been initiated
by her therapy, and that these were slowly, but secretly, advancing
against her neurosis.

This is a commonplace of treatment, known only to those who
have undergone the experience of psychoanalysis and those who
practice the art. Externally, all appears to be the same as it was before
therapy, often rather worse; but in the mental underground, unseen
by any observer and inaccessible to the most probing investigation,
the substructure of the personality is being affected. Insensibly but
deliberately the foundation of neurosis is being weakened while, at

the same time, there are being erected new and more durable supports on which, eventually, the altered personality can rest. Were
this understood by the critics of psychoanalysis (or better still, by
friends and relatives of analysands who understandably complain of
the lack of evident progress), many current confusions about the
process would disappear, and a more rational discussion of its merits
as a form of therapy would be made possible.

For a year, then, Laura seemed to be standing still or losing ground.
Chiefly, as in the episode I have already related, she reviewed her
past and, in her sessions with me, either immediately or soon after,
acted out their crucial or formative aspects. My consulting room
became a stage on which she dramatized her life: my person became
the target against which she directed the sad effects of her experience. In this manner she sought compensation for past frustrations,
utilizing the permissive climate of therapy, to obtain benefits she had
missed, satisfactions that bad been denied, and comforts she had
lacked. Since the total effect of this pattern of emotional damming
had been to cut her off from the many real satisfactions life offered,
and to force her energies and talents into unproductive and even
self-destructive channels, I allowed her, for that first year, almost
endless opportunity for the "drainage" she required. The idea behind
this attitude of complete permissiveness in therapy was to hold up
to her a mirror of her behavior and to let her see not only the
extravagance of the methods she used to obtain neurotic gratification, but also the essential hollowness, the futility and the infantilism
of the desires she had been pursuing by such outlandish methods all
of her life. Finally, the procedure was designed to illustrate, in sharp-
est perspective, the impossibility of securing basic, long-lasting and
solid satisfactions from her accustomed modes of behavior. The latter
aim, of course, set definite limits on my responsiveness to her conduct: I had to be careful to measure out to her, at the proper time
and in correct amounts, the rewards she deserved when these were
due her as a consequence of mature behavior toward mature goals.

Yes, this first year with Laura was a trying one, not only for her
but for her analyst. I often wished she had chosen someone else to

take her troubles to, and could hardly help hoping, on those many occasions when she threatened to break off treatment, that I would never see her again.

One episode from this time haunts me. I set it down here to show the strain she placed me under as much as to illustrate my technique with her and the weird dynamics of her neurosis that were uncovered by this technique.

According to my notes, what I am about to tell took place in the eleventh month of psychoanalysis. By that time the pattern of treatment had stabilized, I was in possession of most of the accessible facts of Laura's life, and the more obvious psychodynamics of her personality disorder were known to us. She, meanwhile, was in a period of relative quiet and contentment. It had been a month or more since her last attack, her job at the Gallery was going well, and she had recently formed a promising relationship with an eligible young man. It was on the theme of this affair that the first of these two crucial hours began, for Laura was deeply concerned about it and wished ardently that it might develop into something more rewarding and more lasting than her many previous romances.

"I don't want to foul this one up," she said, "but I'm afraid I'm going to. I need your help desperately."

"In what way d'you think you might foul it up?" I asked.

"Oh," she replied airily, "by being my usual bitchy self. You know—you ought to since you pointed it out; you know how possessive I get, how demanding I become. But I'd like, just for a change, not to be that way. For once I'd like to have a love affair work out well for me."

"You mean you're thinking of matrimony?" I asked.

She laughed brightly. "Well," she said, "if you must know, I've had a few choice daydreams—fantasies you'd probably call them—about marrying Ben. But that's not what I've got my heart set on now. What I want is love—I want to give it and I want to get it."

"If that attitude is genuine," I said, "you don't need my help in your affair."

She ground out the cigarette she was smoking against the bottom of the ash tray with short, angry jabs.

"You're horrible," she complained, "just horrible. Here I tell you something that I think shows real progress, and right away you throw cold water on it."

"What d'you think shows progress?"

"Why my recognition of giving, of course. I hope you noticed that I put it first."

"I did."

"And doesn't that mean something to you? Doesn't that show how far I've come?"

"It does," I said, "if it's genuine."

"Goddammit!" she flared. "You call *me* insatiable; *you're* the one who's never satisfied. But I'll show you yet."

She lit another cigarette and for the next few moments smoked in silence. Quite naturally my skepticism had shaken her confidence somewhat, as I had meant it to do, since I knew from experience how much she was given to these pat, semianalytical formulations that were consciously designed to impress as well as mislead me. I was just considering the wisdom of pursuing the topic she had opened and getting her somehow to explore her real goals in this new relationship when she began talking again.

"Any how," she said, "that's not what I wanted to talk about today. I had a dream. . . . Shall I tell you about it?"

I have found that when a patient uses this way of presenting a dream—announcing it first, then withholding until the analyst asks for it; actually dangling it like some tantalizing fruit before the analyst's eyes but insisting he reach out for it—the analyst had better listen closely. For this particular mode of dream presentation signifies the special importance of the dream, and it can be anticipated that it holds some extraordinarily meaningful clue to the patient's neurosis. Unconsciously, the patient, too, "knows" this, and by the use of the peculiar formula communicates his inarticulate but nonetheless high estimate of the dream's value. More than this, he is offering the dream, when he invites attention to it this way, as a gift to the analyst, a gift that has implications extending far beyond the dream itself and including the possibility of surrendering an entire area of neurotic functioning. His reservations about giving up a piece of his neurosis and the gratifications he has been receiving from it are betrayed by his use of "shall I tell you about it?": he wants assurance, in advance, that the sacrifice will be worth while, that the analyst will appreciate (and love him for) it, and that he (the patient) will experience an equal amount of gratification from the newer, healthier processes which will henceforth replace the old. For this reason the analyst must be wary of reaching for the tempting fruit being offered him: to grasp at it would be to rob his patient of the painful but necessary first steps toward responsible selfhood, and to commit himself to bargains and promises he has no right to make.

Therefore, when Laura held out the gift of her dream, although I was most eager to hear it, I responded with the evasive but always handy reminder of the "basic rule": "Your instructions have always been to say what comes to you during your hours here. If you're thinking of a dream, tell it."

"Well," she said, "this is what I dreamed. . . . I was in what appeared to be a ballroom or a dance hall, but I knew it was really a hospital. A man came up to me and told me to undress, take all my clothes off. He was going to give me a gynecological examination. I did as I was told but I was very frightened. While I was undressing, I noticed that he was doing something to a woman at the other end of the room. She was sitting or lying in a funny kind of contraption with all kinds of levers and gears and pulleys attached to it. I knew that I was supposed to be next, that I would have to sit in that thing while he examined me. Suddenly he called my name and I found myself running to him. The chair or table—whatever it was—was now empty, and he told me to get on it. I refused and began to cry. It started to rain—great big drops of rain. He pushed me to the floor and spread my legs for the examination. I turned over on my stomach and began to scream. I woke myself up screaming."

Following the recital Laura lay quietly on the couch, her eyes closed, her arms crossed over her bosom.

"Well," she said after a brief, expectant silence, "what does it mean?"

"Laura," I admonished, "you know better than that. Associate, and we'll find out."

"The first thing I think of is Ben," she began. "He's an intern at University, you know. I guess that's the doctor in the dream—or maybe it was you. Anyhow, whoever it was, I wouldn't let him examine me."

"Why not?"

"I've always been afraid of doctors . . . afraid they might hurt me."

"How will they hurt you?"

"I don't know. By jabbing me with a needle, I guess. That's funny. I never thought of it before. When I go to the dentist I don't mind getting a needle; but with a doctor it's different. . . ." Here I noticed how the fingers of both hands clutched her arms at the elbows while her thumbs nervously smoothed the inner surfaces of the joints. "I shudder when I think of having my veins punctured. I'm always afraid that's what a doctor will do to me."

"Has it ever been done?"

She nodded. "Once, in college, for a blood test. I passed out cold."

"What about gynecological examinations?"

"I've never had one. I can't even bear to think of someone poking around inside me." Again silence; then, "Oh," she said, "I see it now. It's sex I'm afraid of. The doctor in the dream *is* Ben. He wants me to have intercourse, but it scares me and I turn away from him. That's true. . . . The other night after the concert he came to my apartment. I made coffee for us and we sat there talking. It was wonderful—so peaceful, just the two of us. Then he started to make love to me. I loved it—until it came to having intercourse. I stopped him there: I had to, I became terrified. He probably thinks I'm a virgin—or that I don't care for him enough. But it isn't that! I—do and I want him to love me. Oh, Dr. Lindner, that's why I need your help so much now. . . ."

"But other men have made love to you," I reminded her.

"Yes," she said, sobbing now, "but I only let them as a last resort, as a way of holding on to them a little longer. And if you'll remember, I've only had the real thing a few times. Mostly I've made love to the man—satisfied him somehow. I'd do anything to keep them from getting inside me—poking into me . . . like the needle, I guess."

"But why, Laura?"

"I don't know," she cried, "I don't know. Tell me."

"I think the dream tells you," I said.

"The dream I just told you?"

"Yes. . . . There's a part of it you haven't considered. What comes to your mind when you think of the other woman in the dream, the woman the doctor was examining before you?"

"The contraption she was sitting in," Laura exclaimed. "It was like a—like a wheel chair—my mother's wheel chair! Is that right?"

"Very likely," I said.

"But why would he be examining *her*? What would that mean?"

"Well, think of what that kind of examination signifies for you."

"Sex," she said. "Intercourse—that's what it means. So that's what it is—that's what it means! Intercourse put my mother in the wheel chair. It paralyzed her. And I'm afraid that's what it will do to me. So I avoid it—because I'm scared it will do the same thing to me. . . . Where did I ever get such a crazy idea?"

—Like so many such "ideas" all of us have, this one was born in Laura long before the age when she could think for herself. It arose out of sensations of terror when she would awaken during the night, shocked from sleep by the mysterious noises her parents made in their passion, and incapable yet of assembling these sounds into a design purporting the tender uses of love. The heavy climate of hate, the living antagonism between her parents, made this impossible; so the sounds in the night—the "Mike, you're hurting me," the moans and cries, the protestations, even the laughter—impressed upon her the darker side of their sex, the brutish animality of it and the pain. And when the disease struck her mother a natural bridge of associations was formed between the secret drama that played itself out while Laura slept—or sometimes awakened her to fright—and the final horror of the body imprisoned on the chair.

I explained this to Laura, documenting my explanation with material the analysis had already brought out. For her, the interpretation worked a wonder of insight. Obvious as it may seem to us, to Laura, from whom it had been withheld by many resistances and defenses, it came as a complete surprise. Almost immediately, even before she quit the couch at the end of that hour, she felt a vast relief from the pressure of many feelings that had tormented her until that very day. The idea that sexual love was impossible for her, the idea that she was so constructed physically that the joys of love would forever be denied her, feelings of self-dissatisfaction and numerous other thoughts and emotions collected around the central theme of sex— these vanished as if suddenly atomized.

"I feel free," Laura said as she rose from the couch when time was called. "I think this has been the most important hour of my analysis." At the door she paused and turned to me with moist, shining eyes. "I knew I could count on you," she said. "And I'm very grateful—believe me."

When she left, in the ten-minute interval between patients during which I ordinarily make notes, attend to messages or read, I reviewed the hour just ended. I, too, had a feeling of satisfaction and relief from it. And while I did not consider it to have been her most important hour—for the analyst's standards are markedly different from the patient's—nevertheless I did not underestimate its potential for the eventual solution of Laura's difficulties. I therefore looked forward to her next hour with pleasurable anticipation, thinking that the mood in which she had departed would continue and hoping she would employ it to stabilize her gains.

The session I have just described took place on a Saturday. On Monday, Laura appeared at the appointed time. The moment I saw her in the anteroom I knew something had gone wrong. She sat dejectedly, chin cupped in her hands, a light coat carelessly draped about her shoulders. When I greeted her, she raised her eyes listlessly.

"Ready for me?" she asked in a toneless voice.

I nodded and motioned her into the next room. She stood up wearily, dropping the coat on the chair, and preceded me slowly. As I closed the door behind us, she flopped on the couch sideways, her feet remaining on the floor. In the same moment she raised one arm to her head and covered her brow with the back of her hand. The other arm dangled over the side of the couch.

"I don't know why we bother," she said in the same flat voice.

I lit a cigarette and settled back in my chair to listen.

She sighed. "Aren't you going to ask me what's wrong?"

"There's no need to ask," I said. "You'll tell me in due time."

"I guess I will," she said, sighing again.

She lifted her feet from the floor, then squirmed to find a more comfortable position. Her skirt wrinkled under her and for some moments she was busy with the tugging and pulling women usually go through in their first minutes of each session. Under her breath she muttered impatient curses. At last she was settled.

"I don't have to tell you I went to bed with Ben, do I?" she asked.

"If that's what you're thinking of," I said.

"I think you must be a voyeur," she commented acidly after another pause. "That's probably the way you get your kicks."

I said nothing.

"Probably why you're an analyst, too," she continued. "Sublimating . . . isn't that the word? Playing Peeping Tom with your ears. . . ."

"Laura," I asked, "why are you being so aggressive?"

"Because I hate you," she said. "I hate your guts."

"Go on."

She shrugged. "That's all. I've got nothing more to say. I only came here today to tell you how much I despise you. I've said it and I'm finished. . . . Can I go now?" She sat up and reached for her purse.

"If that's what you want to do," I said.

"You don't care?" she asked.

"Care isn't the right word," I said. "Of course I'll be sorry to see you leave. But, as I said, if that's what you want to do . . ."

"More double talk," she sighed. "All right. The hell with it. I'm here and I may as well finish out the hour—after all, I'm paying for it," She fell back on the couch and lapsed into silence again.

"Laura," I said, "you seem very anxious to get me to reject you today. Why?"

"I told you—because I hate you."

"I understand that. But why are you trying to make *me* reject *you*?"

"Do we have to go through that again?" she asked. "Because that's my pattern—according to you. I try to push people to the point where they reject me, then I feel worthless and sorry for myself, and find a good excuse to punish myself. Isn't that it?"

"Approximately. But why are you doing it here today?"

"You must be a glutton for punishment, too," she said. "How many times must I say it?—I hate you, I loathe you, I despise you. Isn't that sufficient?"

"But why?"

"Because of what you made me do over the week end."

"With Ben?"

"Ben!" she said contemptuously. "Of course not. What's that got to do with it? All that happened was that I went to bed with him. We slept together. It was good . . . wonderful. For the first time in my life I felt like a woman."

"Then what . . . ?" I started to say.

"—Keep quiet!" she interrupted. "You wanted to know why I hate you and I'm telling you. It's got nothing to do with Ben or what happened Saturday night. It's about my mother. What we talked about last time . . . That's why I hate you so. She's haunted me all week end. Since Saturday I can't get her out of my mind. I keep thinking about her—the awful life she had. And the way I treated her. Because you forced me to, I remembered things, terrible things I did to her . . . That's why I hate you—for making me remember." She turned on her side and looked at me over her shoulder. "And you," she continued, "you bastard . . . you did it purposely. You fixed it so I'd remember how rotten I was to her. I've spent half my life trying to forget her and that goddam wheel chair. But no; you won't let me. You brought her back from the grave to haunt me. That's why I hate you so!"

This outburst exhausted Laura. Averting her head once more, she lay quietly for some minutes. Then she reached an arm behind her.

"Give me the Kleenex," she commanded.

I gave her the box of tissues from the table by my chair. Removing one, she dabbed at her eyes.

"Let me have a cigarette," she said, reaching behind her again.

I put my cigarettes and a box of matches in her hand. She lit up and smoked.

"It's funny," she said. "Funny how I've clung to everything I could find to keep on hating her. You see, I always blamed her for what happened. I always thought it was her fault my father left us. I made it out that she drove him away with her nagging and complaining. I've tried to hide from myself the fact that he was just no good—a lazy, chicken-chasing, selfish son-of-a-bitch. I excused him for his drinking and his neglect of us all those years. I thought, 'Why not? Why shouldn't he run around, stay out all night, have other women? After all, what good was she to him with those useless legs and dried-up body?' I pushed out of my head the way he was before . . . before she got sick. The truth is he was never any different, always a bum. Even when I was small he was no good, no good to her and no good to us. But I loved him—God! how I loved that man. I could hardly wait for him to come home. Drunk, sober—it didn't matter to me. He made a fuss over me and that's why I loved him. She said I was his favorite: I guess I was. At least he made more over me than the others.

"When I'd hear them fighting, I always blamed her. 'What's she picking on him for?' I'd think. 'Why doesn't she let him alone?' And when he went away, I thought it was her fault. Ever since then, until Saturday, I thought it was her fault. And I made her suffer for it. I did mean things to her, things I never told you about, things I tried to forget—did forget—until this week end. I did them to punish her for kicking him out, for depriving me of his love. His love!

"Would you like to hear one of the things I did? I've thought this one over for two days. . . . Maybe if I tell you I can get rid of it."

. . . Everyday on the way home from school she played the same game with herself. That was the reason she preferred to walk home alone. Because what if it happened when the other kids were around? How would she explain it to them? As far as they were concerned she didn't have a father. Even on the high-school admission blank, where it said: "Father—living or dead—check one," she had marked a big X over "dead." So what would she say if, suddenly, he stepped out of a doorway, or came around a corner, or ran over from across the street—and grabbed her and kissed her like he used to? Could she say, "Girls, this is my father?" Of course not! It was better to walk home alone, like this, pretending he was in that alley near the bottom of the hill, or standing behind the coal truck, or hiding be-

hind the newsstand by the subway entrance . . . or that the footsteps
behind her—the ones she kept hearing but there was no one there
when she turned around—were his footsteps.

The game was over. It ended in the hallway of the tenement
house, the same house they had lived in all of her life. If he wasn't
here, in the smelly vestibule, on the sagging stairs, or standing ex-
pectantly on the first-floor landing in front of their door, the game
had to end. And he wasn't: he never was. . . .

She heard the radio as she climbed the stairs, and her insides
contracted in a spasm of disgust. "The same thing," she thought,
"the same darned thing. Why can't it be different for once, just for
once?" With her shoulder she pushed open the door. It closed behind
her with a bang; but Anna, sleeping in her chair as usual, hardly
stirred.

Laura put her books down on the dresser, then switched the dial
of the radio to "off" with a hard, vicious twist of her fingers. Crossing
the room she opened the closet, hung up her coat, and slammed the
door hard, thinking, "So what if it wakes her? I hope it does!" But
it didn't.

On the way to the rear of the apartment she glanced briefly at her
mother. In the wheel chair Anna slumped like an abandoned rag
doll. Her peroxide hair, showing gray and brown at the roots where
it was parted, fell over her forehead. Her chin was on her breast, and
from one corner of her mouth a trickle of spittle trailed to the collar
of the shabby brown dress. The green sweater she wore was open; it
hung about her thin shoulders in rumpled folds, and from its sleeves
her skinny wrists and the fingers tipped with bright red nails pro-
truded like claws of a chicken, clutching the worn arms of the chair.
Passing her, Laura repressed an exclamation of contempt.

In the kitchen Laura poured herself a glass of milk and stood
drinking it by the drain. When she had finished, she rinsed the glass
under the tap. It fell from her hand and shattered against the floor.

"Is that you, Laura?" Anna called.

"Yeah."

"Come here. I want you to do something for me."

Laura sighed. "O.K. As soon as I clean up this mess."

She dried her hands and walked into the front room. "What is it?" she asked.

Anna motioned with her head. "Over there, on the dresser," she said. "The check from the relief came. I wrote out the store order. You can stop on your way back and give the janitor the rent."

"All right," Laura said wearily. She took her coat from the closet. At the door to the hall she paused and turned to face Anna, who was already fumbling with the radio dial. "Anything else?" she asked, playing out their bimonthly game.

Anna smiled. "Yes," she said. "I didn't put it on the store list, but if they have some of those chocolate-covered caramels I like . . ."

Laura nodded and closed the door. Music from the radio chased her downstairs.

When she returned, laden with packages, she stopped in the bedroom only momentarily to turn down the volume of the radio. "The least you can do is play it quietly," she muttered. "I could hear it a block away."

In the kitchen, still wearing her coat, she disposed of the groceries.

"Did you get everything, Laura?" Anna called.

"Yeah."

"Pay the rent?"

"Uh-huh."

"Did they have any of those caramels?"

This time Laura didn't answer. Somewhere, deep inside, the low-burning flame of hate flickered to a new height.

"Laura!" Anna called.

"What d'you want?" the girl shouted angrily.

"I asked if you got my candy."

About to reply, Laura's gaze fell to the remaining package on the porcelain-topped kitchen table. It seemed to hypnotize her, holding her eyes fast and drawing her hand toward its curled neck. Slowly her fingers untwisted the bag and plunged inside. When they emerged, they carried two squares of candy to her mouth. Without tasting, she chewed and swallowed rapidly.

Behind her Laura heard the shuffle of wheels. She turned to find

Anna crossing the threshold of the bedroom. Snatching up the bag, the girl hurried into the dining room and faced her mother across the oval table.

"D'you have the candy?" Anna asked.

Laura nodded and held up the sack.

"Give it here," Anna said, extending her hand.

Laura shook her head and put the hand with the paper bag behind her back. Puzzled, Anna sent her chair around the table toward the girl, who waited until her mother came near, then moved quickly to the opposite side, placing the table between them again.

"What kind of nonsense is this?" Anna asked. In reply, Laura put another piece of candy in her mouth.

"Laura!" Anna demanded. "Give me my candy!" She gripped the wheels of her chair and spun them forward. It raced around the table after the girl, who skipped lightly before it. Three times Anna circled the table, chasing the elusive figure that regarded her with narrowed eyes. Exhausted, finally, she stopped. Across from her, Laura stuffed more candy into her mouth and chewed violently.

"Laura," Anna panted, "what's got into you? Why are you doing this?"

Laura took the bag from behind her back and held it temptingly over the table. "If you want it so bad," she said, breathing hard, "come get it." She shook the bag triumphantly. "See," she said, "it's almost all gone. You'd better hurry."

Inside, at the very core of her being, the flame was leaping. A warm glow of exultation swept through her, filling her body with a sense of power and setting her nerves on fire. She felt like laughing, like screaming, like dancing madly. In her mouth the taste of chocolate was intoxicating.

Her mother whimpered. "Give me the candy. . . . Please, Laura."

Laura held the bag high. "Come and get it!" she screamed, and backed away slowly toward the front room.

Anna spun her chair in pursuit. By the time she reached the bedroom, Laura was at the door. She waited until her mother's chair came close, then she whirled and ran through, pulling the door behind her with a loud crash.

Leaning against the banister, Laura listened to the thud of Anna's fists against the wood and her sobs of angry frustration. Hardly conscious of her actions, she crammed the remaining candies into her mouth. Then, from deep in her body, a wave of laughter surged upward. She tried to stop it, but it broke through in a crazy tide of hilarity. The sound of this joyless mirth rebounded from the stair well and echoed from the ceiling of the narrow hallway—as it was to echo, thereafter, along with the sound of footsteps and falling rain, in her dreams. . . .

The weeks following the crucial hours I have just described were very difficult ones for Laura. As she worked through the guilt-laden memories now released from repression, her self-regard, never at any time very high, fell lower and lower. Bitterly, she told the ugly rosary of her pathetic past, not sparing herself (or me) the slightest detail. In a confessional mood, she recited all her faults of behavior—toward her family, her friends, her teachers, her associates—throughout the years. Under the influence of newly acquired but undigested insights the pattern of her sessions with me changed. No longer did she find it necessary to pour out the acid of her hate and contempt, to vilify and condemn me and the world for our lack of love for her. Now she swung the pendulum to the other side: everyone had been too nice to her, too tolerant; she didn't deserve anyone's good opinion, particularly mine.

In keeping with her new mood, Laura also changed the style of her life. She became rigidly ascetic in her dress, adopted a strict diet, gave up smoking, drinking, cosmetics, dancing and all other ordinary amusements. The decision to surrender the novel joys of sex with her lover, Ben, was hard to make, but, tight-lipped and grim with determination, she declared her intention to him and stuck by her word.

For my part, in these weeks of confession and penitential repentance I remained silent and still permissive, revealing nothing of my own thoughts or feelings. I neither commented on the "sins" Laura recounted nor the expiatory measures she employed to discharge them. Instead, as I listened, I tried to reformulate her neurosis in terms of the dynamic information available to us at that point. Naturally, I saw through the recent shift in analytic content and behavior: it was, of course, but a variant of the old design, only implemented by conscious, deliberate techniques. Fundamentally, Laura was still Laura. That she now chose to destroy herself and her relationships in a more circumspect and less obvious fashion; that the weapons she now turned upon herself were regarded—at least by the world outside the analytic chamber—in the highest terms, altered not one whit the basic fact that the core of her neurosis, despite our work, remained intact. Laura, in short, was still profoundly disturbed, still a martyr to secret desires that had not been plumbed.

She did not think so—nor did her friends. As a matter of fact, they were astonished at what they called her "progress," and word reached me that my reputation in Baltimore—an intimate city where who is going to which analyst is always a lively topic at parties— had soared to new heights. And, indeed, to the casual observer Laura seemed improved. In the curious jargon of the analytic sophisticate, she was "making an adjustment." Her rigorous diet, her severity of manner and dress, her renunciation of all fleshly joys and amusements, her sobriety and devotion to "serious" pursuits, above all her maintenance of a "good" relationship with the eligible Ben (*without sex*, it was whispered)—these were taken as tokens of far-reaching and permanent alterations in personality due to the "miracle" of psychoanalysis. Those with whom she came in contact during this time of course never bothered to peer beneath the mask of public personality she wore. They were content to take her at face value. Because she no longer disrupted their gatherings with demonstrations of her well-known "bitchiness," because she no longer thrust her problems on them or called for their help in times of distress, they felt relieved in their consciences about her. In brief, without laboring the point, so long as Laura disturbed no one else and kept her misery to herself, and so long as she represented to her associates the passive surrender to the mass ideal each one of them so desperately but fruitlessly sought, just so long were they impressed by the "new look" that Laura wore.

But we knew, Laura and I, that the battle had yet to be joined, for only we knew what went on behind the closed doors of 907 in the Latrobe Building. In this room the masks fell away: either they were discarded because here they could not hide the truth, or they were taken from her by the soft persuasion of continuous self-examination with insight. The first to go was the last she had assumed: the defensive mask of self-abnegation.

The time came when I found it necessary to call a halt to Laura's daily *mea culpas*, to put a stop to the marathon of confession she had entered at the beginning of her second year with me. Three factors influenced my decision to force her, at last, off the new course her analysis had taken. The first and most important of these was my perception of the danger implicit in this program of never-ending self-denunciation. As she searched her memory for fresh evidence of guilt, I could see how overwhelmed she was becoming by the enormity of her past behavior. Try as she might, I knew she could never salve her conscience by the penitential acts and renunciations she invented, and I feared the outcome of a prolonged contest between contrition and atonement: it could only lead to the further debility of her ego, to a progressive lowering of self-esteem which might wind up at a point I dared not think about.

The second and hardly less important reason why I felt I had to urge Laura away from this attempt to shrive herself in the manner she chose was the simple fact of its unproductiveness for therapy. As I have already said, this psychic gambit of self-abnegation only substituted one set of neurotic symptoms for another and left the basic pathological structure untouched. Moreover, it provided precisely the same kind of neurotic satisfaction she had been securing all along by her old techniques. The martyrdom she now suffered by her own hand was equivalent to the self-pity formerly induced by the rejection she had unconsciously arranged to obtain from others. And while it is true that she no longer exercised hate, hostility and aggressive contempt outwardly, it was only the direction in which these negative elements were discharged that had been altered: they remained.

Finally, my decision was also influenced by sheer fatigue and boredom with what I knew to be only an act, a disguise of behavior and attitude adopted to squeeze the last ounce of neurotic gratification from me and the entire world which, by psychic extension from love-withholding parents, she viewed as rejective and denying. To tell the truth, I became tired of the "new" Laura, weary of her pious pretenses, and a trifle nauseated with the holier-than-thou manner she assumed. And while this was the least of my reasons for doing what I did, I hold it chiefly responsible for the almost fatal error in timing I committed when I finally acted on an otherwise carefully weighed decision to eject my patient from the analytic rut in which she was, literally, wallowing.

The session that precipitated the near catastrophe took place on a Thursday afternoon. Laura was the last patient I was to see that day, since I was taking the Congressional Limited to New York where I was scheduled to conduct a seminar that night and give a lecture on Friday. I was looking forward to the trip which, for me, represented a holiday from work and the first break in routine in many months. Something of this mood of impatience to get going and pleasurable anticipation must have been communicated to Laura, for she began her hour with a hardly disguised criticism of my manner and appearance.

"Somehow," she said after composing herself on the couch, "somehow you seem different today."

"I do?"

"Yes." She turned to look at me. "Maybe it's because of the way you're dressed. . . . That's a new suit, isn't it?"

"No," I said, "I've worn it before."

"I don't remember ever seeing it." She resumed her usual position. "Anyway, you look nice."

"Thank you"

"I like to see people look nice," she continued. "When a person gets all dressed up, it makes them feel better. I think it's because they think other people will judge them on the basis of their outer appearance—and if the outer appearance is pleasing and nice, people will think what's behind is pleasing and nice, too—and being thought of that way makes you feel better. Don't you think so?"

I was lost in the convolutions of this platitude, but its inference was pretty clear.

"What exactly are you getting at?" I asked.

She shrugged. "It's not important," she said. "Just a thought..." There was a moment of silence, then, "Oh!" she exclaimed. "I know why you're all dressed up.... Today's the day you go to New York, isn't it?"

"That's right," I said.

"That means I won't see you on Saturday, doesn't it?"

"Yes. I won't be back until Monday."

"Is the lecture on Saturday?"

"No, the lecture's tomorrow, Friday."

"—But you're going to stay over until Monday.... Well, I think the rest will do you good. You need it. I think everyone needs to kick up his heels once in a while, just get away, have some fun and forget everything—if he can."

The dig at my irresponsibility toward my patients, particularly Laura, and the implication that I was going to New York to participate in some kind of orgy, were not lost on me.

"I hate to miss an hour," Laura continued in the same melancholy tone she had been using since this meeting began. "Especially now. I feel I really need to come here now. There's so much to talk about."

"In that case," I said, "you should take more advantage of the time you're here. For example, you're not using this hour very well, are you?"

"Perhaps not," she said. "It's just that I feel this is the wrong time for you to be going away."

"Now look here, Laura," I said. "You've known about missing the Saturday hour for more than a week. Please don't pretend it's a surprise to you. And, besides, it's only one hour."

"I know," she sighed. "I know. But it feels like you're going away forever.... What if I should need you?"

"I don't think you will.... But if you should, you can call my home or the office here and they'll put you in touch with me."

I lit a cigarette and waited for her to go on. With the first inhalation, however, I began to cough. Laura again turned around.

"Can I get you something?" she asked. "A glass of water?"

"No, thank you," I answered.

"That cough of yours worries me," she said when the spasm had passed and I was once more quiet. "You should give up smoking. I did, you know. It's been two months since I had a cigarette. And my cough's all gone. I think that's the best of it—no more coughing. I feel fine. You should really try it."

I continued to smoke in silence, wondering where she would take this theme. Before long, I found out.

"It wasn't easy. The first two weeks were agony, but I determined not to give in. After all, I had a reason. . . ."

"To stop coughing?" I suggested, permitting myself the small satisfaction of retaliating for her deliberate provocation of the past half hour.

"Of course not!" she exclaimed. "You know very well I had good reasons for giving up smoking—and other things too."

"What were they?" I asked.

"You of all people should know," she said.

"Tell me."

"Well—it's just that I want to be a better person. If you've been listening to everything I've said these past weeks you know how I used to behave. Now I want to make amends for it, to be different, better. . . ."

"And you think giving up smoking and so on will make you a better person?"

She fell silent. Glancing over at her, I noticed the rigidity of her body. Her hands, until now held loosely on her lap, were clenched into fists. I looked at my watch and cursed myself for a fool. Only ten minutes left and a train to catch! Why had I let myself rise to the bait? Why had I permitted this to come up now, when it couldn't be handled? Was there any way out, any way to avoid the storm I had assisted her to brew? I put my trust in the gods that care for idiots and took a deep breath.

"Well?" I asked.

"Nothing I do is right," she said hollowly. "There's no use trying. I just make it worse."

"What are you talking about?

"Myself," she said. "Myself and the mess I make of everything. I try to do what's right—but I never can. I think I'm working it all out—but I'm not. I'm just getting in deeper and deeper. It's too much for me, too much. . . ."

When the hour ended, I rose and held the door open for her.

"I'll see you Monday," I said.

Her eyes were glistening. "Have a good time," she sighed.

On the train to New York I thought about Laura and the hour just ended, reviewing it word for word and wondering just where I had made my mistake. That I had committed a serious error I had no doubt, and it hardly needed Laura's abrupt change of mood to bring this to my attention. To mobilize guilt and anxiety just prior to a recess in therapy is in itself unwise. In this instance I had compounded the blunder by losing control over myself and responding, as I seldom do in the treatment situation, to criticism and provocation. I asked myself—had she touched some peculiarly sensitive chord in me? Am I so susceptible to faultfinding? Have I, all unaware, become especially tender on the subject of my incessant smoking? my cough? my responsibility to my patients? my appearance? Or was it, as I suspected then and am sure of now, that I had made the decision to contrive a directional change in Laura's analysis but had been incited to violate the timetable of therapy by an unexpected display of the fatuousness that had become her prevailing defense?

That evening I had dinner with friends and conducted the scheduled seminar, after which many of us gathered for a series of nightcaps and further discussion in a colleague's home. I had forgotten all about Laura by the time I returned to my hotel, and when the desk clerk gave me a message to call a certain long-distance operator in Baltimore, I thought it could concern only something personal at home or a communication from my office. I was surprised when Laura's voice came over the wire.

"Dr. Lindner?"

"Yes, Laura. What is it?"

"I've been trying to get you for hours."

"I'm sorry. Is something wrong?"

"I don't know. I just wanted to talk with you."

"What about?"

"About the way I feel . . ."

"How do you feel?"

"Scared."

"Scared of what?"

"I don't know. Just scared, I guess. Of nothing in particular—just everything . . . I don't like being alone."

"But you're alone most other nights, aren't you?" I asked.

"Yes . . . but somehow it's different tonight."

"Why?"

"Well, for one thing, you're not in Baltimore."

The line was silent as I waited for her to continue.

"And then," she said, "I think you're angry with me."

"Why do you think that?"

"The way I acted this afternoon. It was mean of me, I know. But I couldn't help it. Something was egging me on."

"What was it?"

"I don't know. I haven't figured it out. Something . . ."

"We'll talk about it Monday," I said.

More silence. I thought I heard noises as if she were crying.

"Do you forgive me?" she sobbed.

"We'll review the whole hour on Monday," I said, seeking a way out of this awkward situation. "Right now you'd better get to bed."

"All right," she said meekly. "I'm sorry I bothered you."

"No bother at all," I said. "Good night, Laura"—and hung up with relief.

I gave the lecture on Friday afternoon, and when it was over returned to my room for a nap before beginning my holiday with dinner in a favorite restaurant and a long-anticipated evening at the theater. In the quiet room, I bathed and lay down for a peaceful interlude of sleep. Hardly had I begun to doze when the phone rang. It was my wife, calling from Baltimore. Laura, she said, had slashed her wrists: I had better come home—quick. . . .

The doctor and I sat in the corner of the room, talking in whispers. On the bed, heavily sedated, Laura breathed noisily. Even in the dim light the pallor of her face was discernible, and I could see a faint white line edging her lips. On the blanket her hands lay limply. The white bandages at her wrists forced themselves accusingly on my attention. From time to time her hands twitched.

"I doubt that it was a serious attempt," the physician was saying, "although of course you never know. It's harder than you think, trying to get out that way. You've really got to mean it—you've got to mean it enough to saw away hard to get down where it counts. I don't think she tried very hard. The cut on the left wrist is fairly deep, but not deep enough, and the ones on the right wrist are superficial. There wasn't a hell of a lot of blood, either."

"I understand you got there awfully fast," I said.

"Pretty fast," he replied. "What happened was this: Right after she slashed herself she began screaming. A neighbor ran in and had the good sense to call me immediately. My office is in the same building, on the first floor, and I happened to be there at the time. I rushed upstairs, took a look at the cuts and saw they weren't too bad——"

"They were made with a razor blade, weren't they?" I interrupted.

"Yes," he said, and then continued, "so I slapped a couple of tourniquets on, phoned the hospital that I was sending her in, then called the ambulance. I followed it here to Sinai. In the Accident Room they cleaned her up and had her wrists sutured by the time I arrived. She was still quite excited, so I decided to put her in for a day or two. I gave her a shot of morphine and sent her upstairs."

"Who called my home?" I asked.

He shrugged. "I don't know. Before the ambulance came, her neighbor called Laura's sister and told her what happened and what I was going to do. I think the sister tried to get hold of you."

"I guess so," I said. "She knows Laura's in treatment with me."

"I don't envy you," he said. "She's a lulu."

"Why do you say that?"

He shrugged and motioned toward the bed with a wave of his hand. "This kind of business, for one thing. Then the way she carried on until the shot took effect."

"What did she do?"

"Oh," he said vaguely, "she kept screaming and throwing herself around. Pretty wild." He stood up. "I don't think you've got anything to worry about as far as her physical condition goes, though. Maybe a little groggy, that's all."

"I'm very grateful to you," I said.

"Not at all," he said on his way from the room. "There'll be some business with the police tomorrow. If you need me, just call."

Laura had her hour on Saturday—in the hospital. During it and many subsequent sessions we worked out the reasons for her extravagant, self-destructive gesture. As the physician had observed, her act was hardly more than a dramatic demonstration without serious intent, although in the way of such things it could well have miscarried to a less fortunate conclusion. Its immediate purpose was to recall me from my holiday and to reawaken the sympathetic attention she believed herself to have prejudiced by her hostile provocativeness on Thursday. But the whole affair, we learned subsequently, had much deeper roots.

The motivation behind Laura's attempt at suicide was twofold. Unconsciously, it represented an effort to re-enact, with a more satisfying outcome, the desertion of her father; and, at the same time, it served the function of providing extreme penance for so-called "sins" of behavior and thought-crimes between the ages of twelve and twenty-four. So far as the first of these strange motivations is concerned, it is understandable how Laura interpreted my brief interruption of therapy as an abandonment similar to that abrupt and permanent earlier departure of her father. This time, however, as indicated by the phone call to my hotel on the night I left, she believed herself to have been at least in part responsible for it, to have driven him (in the person of the analyst) away. To call him back, her distraught mind conceived the suicidal act, which was nothing less than a frenzied effort—planned, so it appeared, but not executed, more than a decade before—to repeat the original drama but insure a different and more cordial ending.

The mad act was also powered dynamically by the fantastic arithmetic of confession and penance that Laura, like some demented accountant, had invented to discharge her guilty memories. As I had feared when the pattern became clear to me, the mental balance sheet she was keeping with her hourly testament of culpability and the increasing asceticism of her life could never be stabilized. Self-abnegation had to lead to a martyrdom of some kind. My effort to prevent this miscarried—not because it was misconceived, but because it was so sloppily executed. My own unconscious needs—the residual infantilisms and immaturities within me—in this case subverted judgment and betrayed me into the commission of a timing error that could have cost Laura's life.

We both profited from this terrible experience, and in the end, it proved to have been something of a boon to each of us. I, of course, would have preferred to learn my lesson otherwise. As for Laura, she made a rapid recovery and returned to the analysis much sobered by her encounter with death. Apart from all else, the episode provided her with many genuine and useful insights, not the least of which were those that led her to abandon her false asceticism and to stop playing the role of the "well-analyzed," "adjusted" paragon among her friends.

The events just described furnished us with vast quantities of material for analysis in subsequent months. Particularly as it referred directly to the situation in psychoanalysis known technically as the "transference neurosis"—or the reflection in therapy of former patterns of relationship with early, significant figures in the life of the patient—the suicidal gesture Laura made led to an even deeper investigation of her existing neurotic attitudes and behavior. And as we dealt with this topic of transference—the organic core of every therapeutic enterprise; as we followed its meandering course through our sessions together, Laura rapidly made new and substantial gains. With every increase in her understanding another rich facet of personality was disclosed, and the burden of distress she had borne for so long became lighter and lighter.

The metamorphosis of Laura was a fascinating thing to observe. I, as the human instrument of changes that were taking place in her, was immensely gratified. Nevertheless, my pleasure and pride were incomplete, for I remained annoyingly aware that we had yet to find the explanation for the single remaining symptom that had so far evaded the influence of therapy. No progress at all had been made against the strange complaint which brought her into treatment: the seizures of uncontrollable hunger, the furious eating, and their dreadful effects.

I had my own theory about this stubborn symptom and was often tempted to follow the suggestion of a certain "school" of psychoanalysis and communicate my ideas to Laura. However, because I felt—and still feel—that such technique is theoretically unjustified—a reflection of the therapist's insecurity and impatience rather than a well-reasoned approach to the problems of psychotherapy—because I felt this way, I determined to curb my eagerness to bring my interpretations on her. In adherence to methods in which I have been trained, therefore, I held my tongue and waited developments. Fortunately, they were not long in appearing; and when they did arrive, in one mighty tide of insight my patient's being was purged of the mental debris that had made her existence a purgatory.

Laura was seldom late for appointments, nor had she ever missed one without canceling for good cause well in advance. On this day, therefore, when she failed to appear at the appointed time I grew somewhat anxious. As the minutes passed, my concern mounted. Finally, after a half hour had sped and there was still no sign of Laura, I asked my secretary to call her apartment. There was no answer.

During the afternoon, caught up in work with other patients, I gave only a few passing thoughts to Laura's neglect to keep her hour or to inform me she would be absent. When I reminded myself of it at the close of the day, I tried, in a casual way, to recall her previous session and examine it for some clue to this unusual delinquency. Since none came readily, I pushed the matter from my mind and prepared to leave the office.

We were in the corridor awaiting the elevator when we heard the telephone. I was minded to let it ring, but Jeanne, more compulsive in such matters than I, insisted on returning to answer. While I held the elevator, she re-entered the office. A few moments later she reappeared, shrugging her shoulders in answer to my question.

"Must have been a wrong number," she said. "When I answered all I heard was a funny noise and then the line went dead."

I arrived home shortly after six o'clock and dressed to receive the guests who were coming for dinner. While in the shower, I heard the ringing of the telephone, which my wife answered. On emerging from the bathroom, I asked her who had called.

"That was the queerest thing," she said. "The party on the other end sounded like a drunk and I couldn't make out a word."

During dinner I was haunted by a sense of unease. While attending to the lively conversation going on around me, and participating in it as usual, near the edges of consciousness something nagged uncomfortably. I cannot say that I connected the two mysterious calls with Laura and her absence from the hour that day, but I am sure they contributed to the vague and fitful feeling I experienced. In any case, when the telephone again rang while we were having our coffee, I sprang from my place and rushed to answer it myself.

I lifted the receiver and said, "Hello?" Over the wire, in response, came a gurgling, throaty noise which, even in retrospect, defies comparison with any sound I have ever heard. Unmistakably produced by the human voice, it had a gasping, breathless quality, yet somehow seemed animal in nature. It produced a series of meaningless syllables, urgent in tone but unidentifiable.

"Who is this?" I demanded.

There was a pause, then, laboriously, I heard the first long-drawn syllable of her name.

"Laura!" I said. "Where are you?"

Again the pause, followed by an effortful intake of breath and its expiration as though through a hollow tube: "Home . . ."

"Is something wrong?"

It seemed to come easier this time.

"Eat-ing."

"Since when?"

". . . Don't—know."

"How d'you feel?" I asked, aware of the absurdity of the question but desperately at a loss to know what else to say.

"Aw-ful . . . No—more—food . . . Hun-gry . . ."

My mind raced. What could I do? What was there to do?

"Help—me," she said—and I heard the click of the instrument as it fell into its cradle.

"Laura," I said. "Wait!"—But the connection had been broken and my words echoed in my own ears. Hastily, I hung up and searched through the telephone directory for her number. My fingers spun the dial. After an interval, I heard the shrill buzz of her phone. Insistently, it repeated itself over and over. There was no answer.

I knew, then, what I had to do. Excusing myself from our guests, I got my car and drove to where Laura lived. On the way there, I thought about what some of my colleagues would say of what I was doing. No doubt they would be appalled by such a breach of orthodoxy and speak pontifically of "counter-transference," my "anxiety" at Laura's "acting out," and other violations of strict procedure. Well, let them. To me, psychoanalysis is a vital art that demands more of its practitioners than the clever exercise of their brains. Into its practice also goes the heart, and there are occasions when genuine human feelings take precedence over the rituals and dogmas of the craft.

I searched the mailboxes in the vestibule for Laura's name, then ran up the stairs to the second floor. In front of her door I paused and put my ear against the metal frame to listen. I heard nothing.

I pushed the button. Somewhere inside a chime sounded. A minute passed while I waited impatiently. I rang again, depressing the button forcefully time after time. Still no one came to the door. Finally, I turned the knob with one hand and pounded the panel with the flat of the other. In the silence that followed, I heard the noise of something heavy crashing to the floor, then the sibilant shuffling of feet.

I put my mouth close to the crack where door met frame.

"Laura!" I called. "Open the door!"

Listening closely, I heard what sounded like sobs and faint moaning, then a voice that slowly pronounced the words, "Go—away."

I shook the knob violently. "Open up!" I commanded. "Let me in!"

The knob turned in my hand and the door opened. I pushed

against it, but a chain on the jamb caught and held. In the dim light
of the hallway, against the darkness inside, something white shone.
It was Laura's face, but she withdrew it quickly.

"Go—away," she said in a thick voice.

"No."

"Please!"

She leaned against the door, trying to close it again. I put my foot
in the opening.

"Take that chain off," I said with all the authority I could muster.
"At once!"

The chain slid away and I walked into the room. It was dark, and
I could make out only vague shapes of lamps and furniture. I fumbled
along the wall for the light switch. Before my fingers found it, Laura,
who was hardly more than an indistinguishable blur of whiteness by
my side, ran past me into the room beyond.

I discovered the switch and turned on the light. In its sudden,
harsh glare I surveyed the room. The sight was shocking. Everywhere
I looked there was a litter of stained papers, torn boxes, empty bottles, open cans, broken crockery and dirty dishes. On the floor and
on the tables large puddles gleamed wetly. Bits of food—crumbs,
gnawed bones, fishheads, sodden chunks of unknown stuffs—were
strewn all about. The place looked as if the contents of a garbage
can had been emptied in it, and the stench was sickening.

I swallowed hard against a rising wave of nausea and hurried into
the room where Laura had disappeared. In the shaft of light that
came through an archway, I saw a rumpled bed, similarly piled with
rubbish. In a corner, I made out the crouching figure of Laura.

By the entrance I found the switch and pressed it. As the light
went on, Laura covered her face and shrank against the wall. I went
over to her, extending my hands.

"Come," I said. "Stand up."

She shook her head violently. I bent down and lifted her to her
feet. When she stood up, her fingers still hid her face. As gently as
I could, I pulled them away. Then I stepped back and looked at
Laura. What I saw, I will never forget.

The worst of it was her face. It was like a ceremonial mask on which some inspired maniac had depicted every corruption of the flesh. Vice was there, and gluttony, lust also, and greed. Depravity and abomination seemed to ooze from great pores that the puffed tautness of skin revealed.

I closed my eyes momentarily against this apparition of incarnate degradation. When I opened them, I saw the tears welling from holes where her eyes should have been. Hypnotized, I watched them course in thin streams down the bloated cheeks and fall on her nightgown. And then, for the first time, I saw it!

Laura was wearing a night robe of some sheer stuff that fell loosely from straps at her shoulders. Originally white, it was now soiled and stained with the evidences of her orgy. But my brain hardly registered the begrimed garment, except where it bulged below her middle in a sweeping arc, ballooning outward from her body as if she were pregnant.

I gasped with disbelief—and my hand went out automatically to touch the place where her nightgown swelled. My fingers encountered a softness that yielded to their pressure. Questioning, I raised my eyes to that caricature of a human face. It twisted into what I took for a smile. The mouth opened and closed to form a word that it labored to pronounce.

"Ba-by," Laura said.

"Ba-by?" I repeated. "Whose baby?"

"Lau-ra's ba-by . . . Lo-ok."

She bent forward drunkenly and grasped her gown by the hem. Slowly she raised the garment, lifting it until her hands were high above her head. I stared at her exposed body. There, where my fingers had probed, a pillow was strapped to her skin with long bands of adhesive.

Laura let the nightgown fall. Swaying, she smoothed it where it bulged.

"See?" she said. "Looks—real—this way."

Her hands went up to cover her face again. Now great sobs shook her, and tears poured through her fingers as she cried. I led her to the bed and sat on its edge with her, trying to order the turmoil of my thoughts while she wept. Soon the crying ceased, and she bared her face again. Once more the lost mouth worked to make words.

"I—want—a—baby," she said, and fell over on the bed—asleep. . . .

I covered Laura with a blanket and went into the other room, where I remembered seeing a telephone. There, I called a practical nurse who had worked with me previously and whom I knew would be available. Within a half hour, she arrived. I briefed her quickly: the apartment was to be cleaned and aired; when Laura awakened, the doctor who lived downstairs was to be called to examine her and advise on treatment and diet; she was to report to me regularly, and in two days she was to bring Laura to my office. Then I left.

Although the night was cold I lowered the top on my car. I drove slowly, breathing deeply of the clean air.

Two days later, while her nurse sat in the outer room, Laura and I began to put together the final pieces in the puzzle of her neurosis. As always, she had only a vague, confused memory of events during her seizure, recollecting them hazily through a fog of total intoxication. Until I recounted the episode, she had no clear remembrance of my visit and thought she had dreamed my presence in her rooms. Of the portion that concerned her pitiful imitation of pregnancy, not the slightest memorial trace remained.

It was clear that Laura's compelling desire was to have a child, that her feelings of emptiness arose from this desire, and that her convulsions of ravenous appetite were unconsciously designed to produce its illusory satisfaction. What was not immediately apparent, however, was why this natural feminine wish underwent such extravagant distortion in Laura's case, why it had become so intense, and why it had to express itself in a manner at once monstrous, occult and self-destructive.

My patient herself provided the clue to these focal enigmas when, in reconstructing the episode I had witnessed, she made a slip of the tongue so obvious in view of the facts that it hardly required interpretation.

It was about a week after the incident I have recorded. Laura and

I were reviewing it again, looking for further clues. I was intrigued by the contrivance she wore that night to simulate the appearance of a pregnant woman, and asked for details about its construction. Laura could supply none. Apparently, she said, she had fashioned it in an advanced stage of her intoxication from food.

"Was this the first time you made anything like that?" I asked.

"I don't know," she said, somewhat hesitantly. "I can't be sure. Maybe I did and destroyed the thing before I came out of the fog. It seems to me I remember finding something like you describe a couple of years ago after an attack, but I didn't know—or didn't want to know—what it was, so I just took it apart and forgot about it."

"You'd better look around the apartment carefully," I said, half joking. "Perhaps there's a spare hidden away someplace."

"I doubt it," she replied in the same mood. "I guess I have to mike a new baby every . . ." Her hand went over her mouth. "My God!" she exclaimed. "Did you hear what I just said?"

Mike was her father's name; and of course it was his baby she wanted. It was for this impossible fulfillment that Laura hungered—and now was starved no more. . . .

THE TABOO SCARF

GEORGE WEINBERG

This fascinating look into a patient's therapy, with excerpts from specific sessions, provides a picture of a therapist and patient working together to solve a painful problem. The patient, who is involved in a serious relationship with someone, is able to have sex but is not able to kiss the man she loves.

In these sessions, one can see how a talented therapist works. Dr. Weinberg provides an example of "listening with the third ear" that is described in the excerpt by Theodor Reik. He allows the patient, Maggie, the space she needs. He does not press to satisfy his own curiosity, and he listens and watches carefully to pick up the messages his patient is sending, while watching his own reactions to these messages. This genuine attention and caring Dr. Weinberg offers allow the patient to trust him, laying the groundwork for a moment where his patient takes a risk that leads to her cure.

Owing to an egg's shape, a beast banging on it from the outside will have great trouble breaking it open. But the slightest tap from inside the shell can shatter it; when the chick is ready it can pop out and get started. Nature in its selective wisdom thus favors the new generation—for instance, the unborn ostrich over a pride of lions, who can slam an egg halfway across the Serengeti without being able to open it. Nearly all the leverage is from within.

By the same token, a patient, *any* patient, tapping even lightly, can accomplish more personality change than even the best therapist working alone from the outside.

The appreciation of this is ushering in the next century of psychotherapy. The therapist is no mere surgeon, providing relief or cure to the patient lying on the couch. That picture has already given way to a new one of the patient as blocked but striving, as potentially able to identify his own feelings and to act in new ways, and ultimately as the one who must crack the shell of his own problem.

Beyond our offering warmth and insights, we must find places where each patient can tap, even gently, against the surface of his container. We encourage effort. But only by the patient's own exertions of will, by his or her acts, can real change be produced.

I saw an unforgettable example of this some years ago. Had the patient not tried something whose importance we both underestimated, she might never have made the discovery that changed her life. Beyond that, Maggie's case illustrates that as we go forward, we also go back. To hide from the future is to hide from the past— to venture ahead is to delve into both. In this sense, we either live many periods of our lives simultaneously, or we don't live any at all.

Maggie was twenty-seven, tall, attractive in an angular way, with dark, intelligent eyes. She was a graduate student in paleontology, and she loved her subject so much that I think she would have talked about it the whole hour unless I'd broken in.

She had already gone looking for fossils in the United States and was eager to travel to Africa, where, she told me, all human life began. "Though right now what I'm doing is mostly cataloging." She smiled engagingly.

Her problem was unusual.

"Doctor, I've been going with a boy for three years. I love him, but I'm terrified of marrying him. I just can't." She paused, as if gathering the courage to continue. "And something else. I know how silly this sounds. But I'm afraid to kiss him on the lips."

She looked into my eyes for anything possibly condemning but found nothing, and went on. "Some people can't have orgasms. I do, most of the time. I enjoy sexual intercourse with David—at least, I would a lot more if it wasn't for this."

She reiterated that she loved David. "But this is just impossible!"

She was becoming agitated. "He wants to marry me, but I don't see how I can. The way things are, I don't see how I can."

"He's upset too?" I asked.

"Of course he is. He was married once—for two years. He loves me. He wants to marry me, or at least he did. But I keep putting it off. I mean I said, 'Wait until September,' and that was last year. Then July. Now it's October. I'm just very afraid that if I marry him—" She stopped.

"Afraid of what?"

"I don't know. We had a terrific fight last summer. He left me in the car and took the train home alone, from Massachusetts. I really thought it was over. We didn't talk for a long time, two weeks. Then I broke down and called him. He was glad. I love David, that's what's so crazy about this, so wrong!"

"When you picture yourself married to him, what comes to mind?"

"I don't know. I've done that. I don't know. Death, maybe. I can understand why he's so upset. He's thirty-seven. He really wants to have a family, and he's a wonderful person."

She sighed deeply.

"You've had this problem before?" I asked her.

"From the time we started. He tried to kiss me goodnight, the first night. I couldn't. And even after that, I just couldn't."

"I mean with other men."

"Well, I've always had the problem—I guess you'd call it a phobia. But I never realized how severe it was."

In the past she'd imagined that she just wasn't fond enough of the man. "But I love David."

Near the end of the session, she asked me, "What do you think my chances are?"

"I don't know for sure," I told her. "Probably good. But we're going to have to dig."

Only after she was gone did I realize that I'd drawn that metaphor from her own calling, though in sessions to come I sometimes did this deliberately, to summon her exuberance.

But digging wouldn't be so easy, as I learned the next time. There was something else unusual here. Maggie could remember virtually nothing about her life before she was ten.

When, at a recent birthday party for her mother, an aunt showed her photos of the frame house the family had lived in, it was barely familiar. She had only an indistinct memory of trees peering into her bedroom window and of her father being downstairs. She was told that she would run over to him when he got home at night, that she would take his jacket and bring him a shot of bourbon, and that he loved her. But even this was hearsay.

In his photos he was handsome. She knew that he was a powerful union leader, and that he had provided well for the family. They'd lived in Weston, Connecticut, quiet, friendly, more rural than neighboring Westport. According to her mother, they would all go to Westport for Sunday brunch—she and her parents, and her mother's parents, who lived in Fairfield, a half hour away.

It had been a paradise, but then her father left, suddenly and forever.

Maggie and her mother had quickly relocated to a dingy downtown sector of Fairfield, not far from her grandparents, and they strove hard. She recalled her mother sitting her down in the new, smaller kitchen. Her mother had said, "It's up to us now. We have each other and that's more than enough. We'll do fine."

And in a sense they did. Her mother took a job as a saleswoman, and from then on it was urban life. Maggie saw more of her grandparents than of her mother, who was off working much of the time and came home exhausted. But she knew that her mother was toiling for her welfare, and she felt taken care of.

Remarkably, her amnesia covered the first period of her life, in Weston, and seemed nonexistent after that. That it conformed so precisely with that phase, touching nothing else, argued strongly that it was psychogenic. It could hardly be that all her powers of observation and retention had suddenly developed on the day they moved to Fairfield, and yet her memory of the new apartment, of the friends she made, of begging permission to stay overnight with one, of the local school was excellent—she was, if anything, more detailed and precise in her retention of these experiences than most adults are.

She could vividly recall her grandfather's taking her to New York City on a few occasions. Once they went to a ball game that he wanted to see, and she fell asleep. But another time he took her to the Museum of Natural History, and the sight of the dinosaurs on the first floor was something she never forgot. "He saw how fascinated I was and bought me a big, colored picture book on the subject."

Especially graphic to Maggie was a cartoon in *The New Yorker* that appeared when she was eleven. Two scientists had pieced together the foot, up to the knee, of some gigantic prehistoric creature. One of them, looking at the random array of bones remaining on the floor, was saying to the other, "Well, I'm willing to say the hell with it if you are."

Maggie told me that she'd found this cartoon a riot and had kept the page. She smiled when telling me the caption, and I could not help wondering if it expressed a part of her own thinking, an impulse not to reconstruct, that might dovetail with her not remembering.

Later, when I mentioned to a colleague that Maggie's amnesia "fit her first decade like a glove," my mind free-associated to so-called "glove anesthesia," in which the person experiences numbness and sometimes total paralysis of the hand up to the wrist with no other symptom. True neurological damage would never impair only the hand and nothing else; it would follow certain pathways called "dermatones," and thus involve not only the hand but the arm. For this reason, we can always diagnose glove anesthesia as psychosomatic. Numbness of the whole hand—and only the hand—attests to the use of will.

Similarly, the fact that one period of Maggie's life was utterly blanketed by "forgetfulness," while the rest was wholly available to her, was altogether too neat to allow any explanation other than a psychogenic one. The evidence seemed strong that Maggie could not remember because she unconsciously chose not to.

Because her amnesia "gloved" the era of her father's presence in her life, I especially wondered about him. Any information about how Maggie had perceived him or felt about him when he was around promised to be valuable. Indeed, even random facts about him were welcome at this stage—whatever we learned might be suggestive since up to now we'd had virtually nothing to go on.

My best information, it seemed, would have to come from another source. I would have to study how Maggie behaved with me. Though she could remember nothing about her father, she had spent hundreds of formative hours with him. She had developed through him some sense-of-herself-in-his-presence, that is, a sense-of-herself-in-a-man's-presence, and that had led her to some theory about what men are like and about how she should behave around them.

Almost surely, she would reveal those early formed beliefs in her dealings with me. There would be some commonality between her reaction to that primary man in her life and her reaction to me. Perhaps I could uncover at least something of her picture of her father from the way she perceived me—and acted with me.

Studying the so-called transference to learn about a patient's father or mother is a common technique relying on this transfer of reaction. If we are distrusted, we may suspect that the patient distrusted a parent. The patient who constantly repeats himself to us possibly had a parent who didn't listen. The patient who always anticipates harsh judgments from us may have gotten them from one or both parents. Reasoning backward, we can often infer what a patient thought of a parent from how the patient perceives us and treats us.

Usually, of course, the therapist has the patient's memories to compare with his own experience of the patient. In this case, however, having only Maggie's treatment of me to start with, I would have to reason entirely backward, trying to ascertain from it how she might have perceived her father. I would have no corroboration for this backward inference—at least not for a while. So far, the transference was all I had.

At first I imagined that I was seeing nothing in the way she dealt with me. Maggie's mode of treating me could be best described as polite and factual. She always arrived on the dot and was never curt with me. She never joked. She asked me for nothing, except at times for my opinion as to whether she could be cured. She simply came, and talked, and left. Only slowly did I realize that what I had initially taken as nonresponse toward me on Maggie's part was a very real response—namely one of extreme caution.

It might follow that she had treated her father with the same deference and conformity, that she had kept him at the same respectful distance, that she had admired him but never kidded with him or taken any kind of liberty. If so, and if this early acquired formality of hers had been adopted as a defense against closeness, why had she adopted it? What had she been afraid of? Was she guarding against a love for her father that felt illicit, or against encouraging his love? I wondered if anything had taken place between them that had motivated this guardedness.

Any such inferences of mine had, of course, to remain only a hypothesis. Her diplomacy with me might have a simpler, more recent explanation. I had seen many graduate students like Maggie become overly deferential in dealing with their professors, who make the ultimate decision about whether they get their degree. Perhaps Maggie's diplomacy with me was merely an extension of a daily style that she'd adopted at Columbia's department of paleontology.

I decided that, though she didn't remember her early life, I would at least get her to tell me everything she'd been told about it by other family members. Over the next few weeks I asked her a great number of questions.

Maggie told me that she had no idea why her father left. Only one thing was certain—that he hadn't wanted to go and that it had been completely her mother's choice. After leaving, he'd tried desperately to come back, but her mother had remained adamant.

Maggie told me, "My grandfather said that in the beginning, my father used to call every day and beg her to let him return. Sometimes twice a day. But she wouldn't even talk to him."

"Really!"

"Yes. Even after he left Connecticut to live in Chicago, he used to tell my grandfather he'd come back in a minute to see me if she would let him. Even if my mother wouldn't talk to him, he'd come back to see me."

"I wonder why she was so strong on the subject."

"She even gave up his financial support, because then he would have had the legal right to see me."

"Why did she throw him out?"

"I don't know."

"You must have thought about it. What speculations did you make? What crossed your mind?"

"My mother's sometimes very strange. All at once she just couldn't stand him. That's what my grandfather said. She just wanted no part of him, and he left. He left like a man."

She said this glibly, almost proudly, as if she'd been over it often, as if she were reciting a foregone conclusion. But I could tell that a lot of emotion was still bound up in her simple narrative, that perhaps Maggie suspected more than she wished to disclose. Maybe he'd been caught with another woman, but I had no evidence, and I surely didn't want to venture such a guess.

During the next few weeks, she went on to portray her mother as close-lipped, honest, and given to a life of stoic resignation. If the woman, now in her sixties, enjoyed anything, she certainly didn't let Maggie know. She had only a few friends—women—including a cousin whom she went on vacations with. Maggie felt sure that there had never been another man in her mother's life; she hadn't even dated anyone.

As a girl, Maggie would sometimes ask her mother if she was ever going to remarry. Her mother would snap, "I don't have time to waste on another man. And besides, I've never met a man good enough for my daughter."

"I used to be glad," Maggie told me. "Now I worry about her being alone in old age. But she's not an easy woman."

That seemed like an understatement.

"And even if she had wanted to marry again," Maggie explained, "because she's a devout Catholic, I don't think she could have without a lot of hullabaloo."

"And you never heard from your father again," I said, partly by way of summary.

"Never. My mother wouldn't let him contact me."

She said this so emotionally that I brought the subject up again the next week, in case there was more to it.

"He tried to come back?"

This time she didn't respond, which I took to mean that the answer was, decisively, no.

The next two months yielded little. Her early life seemed like a lost city that, if we could even glimpse it, could tell us an enormous amount about her contemporary life—in particular, about her symptoms.

I decided to change my approach. Instead of continuing to inquire about her past, I began looking into her *attitude* toward the "forgetfulness" itself.

"Does it trouble you that you can't remember those early days in Weston?"

"I guess it does."

Her words said yes, but she sounded almost blithe about having lost touch with those first ten years. Such indifference, if I read Maggie correctly, provided virtually clinching evidence that she really didn't want to remember that early period—that she was forgetting it by a strong act of will.

The more I discussed it with her, the surer I became that I was seeing what the nineteenth-century psychiatrist, Pierre Janet, termed *"la belle indifference."* Janet was the first to identify such indifference as a telltale sign that the person is producing his seeming incapacity by an act of will. The sufferer is getting something he secretly wants out of the disability, be it paralysis or numbness, for instance—or here, in Maggie's case, memory failure.

I had worked with Maggie for three months and now was certain that, in her "loss" of the past, she was unconsciously achieving a desired effect. And by that time I also felt almost certain that her amnesia had to be related to the inhibitions—against kissing and marriage—that had driven her to seek my help. Maggie's was one of those rare and classic cases in which "lifting the veil of amnesia" would, indeed, prove crucial and perhaps tantamount to her resolving her symptoms. . . .

She began the session by talking about her grandfather. "I guess my relationship with Grandpa was the best one I ever had with a man. He always lit up when he saw me, and we trusted each other completely. I think we both felt misunderstood. I even loved his polished bald head. I used to rub it with a cloth and we'd both laugh."

She went on to say that "when Grandma Dorothy died it was sad, but I could live with it, she did a lot of nagging. But when Julian passed away, I lost something tremendous."

I wondered why she'd decided to talk about her grandparents so much that day, but it seemed best not to ask. I had a strong sense that she was headed somewhere and, very possibly, she herself didn't know where.

She said, "Grandpa was never himself when he was with her. She was very scowling and critical."

"Critical of what?"

"Of where he took me. Like to a football game when it was cold, or to his office. Or when he talked about wines to me. She was really tough. She scowled all the time and broke in on him if he was telling a story."

"What do you mean?"

"I mean we were having a big Thanksgiving dinner. A lot of people were over there, I think I know who they were, I'm not sure. And he was starting to tell a story, like, 'So I was driving up the West Side Highway at about forty-five—' and she'd break in, real tough, nasty. 'You were not, Julian. You were going sixty!' It might not even have been relevant to his story. And he'd look so sad, and he'd stop and he'd never finish the story. He'd just quit and then wipe his face with a napkin and excuse himself from the table."

"What did you do?"

"Maybe sit there if my mother wouldn't let me get up. Or maybe, I think that day, I followed him into the study. He'd show me the wine labels that he was importing, red and gold with pictures, like big stamps. They were pretty. And he'd say, 'Maggie, this one's really good.' We were outcasts, now that I think of it."

"So, in a way, he was really like a father to you, wasn't he?"

"Yes. Maybe because his marriage was so bad. But he really loved me. I was everything to him, everything to Julian. He used to brag about me to the people he worked with, to the truckers and stuff. I didn't appreciate him at the time."

In other words, I thought, the first two marriages she'd witnessed, the only ones for a long time, had both been variations of hell. I recalled her response a while ago, when I'd asked her what being married had made her think of—she'd replied, "death." Her father might as well have been dead.

I think she saw the beneficent look in my eyes as she talked about her grandfather.

But then she suddenly corrected me. "No. You said he was like a father. But he wasn't. He was never like my father. I always thought about my real father, out there, somewhere, thinking about me."

This was new, and I was pleased to receive it.

"You thought about him a lot, Maggie?" I asked her.

"All the time. When I got a top spelling grade. When I put on a fancy polka-dot dress, I remember, to go to my friend Paula's party. Other times. A lot of times. I guess I wanted him to know what I was doing, how well I did, all the time."

"Too bad he didn't," I chimed in.

"But he did!"

Could I have heard her correctly? No, that was impossible.

"Say that again," I asked her.

She moved quickly and nervously, and color came to her cheeks. Half-choking, she repeated, "But he did."

I would have thought it was her imagination, but her eyes were moist with tears, and she seemed unable to talk.

I handed her the box of tissues, and she wiped her face with them but did a lousy job. I waited for her to compose herself.

"This was the big secret between my grandfather and me. I promised him all my life I wouldn't tell. All his life. That he wouldn't tell, and that I wouldn't tell. I mean that we wouldn't tell my mother or Dorothy."

She looked at me plaintively, her eyes glistening with tears.

I got the unspoken message and assured her. "Maggie, I promise you I'll never talk about this. Not to your mother or to anyone. You know that. But I promise you again."

She nodded.

"Anyhow, Grandpa kept in touch with Daddy. Daddy insisted. No matter what my mother said, he had to know what was happening with me. He used to call my grandfather at the office. He couldn't call me. He was afraid I'd say something, I was so young. He said we'd be together, he'd meet me when I grew up."

"He was living in Chicago?"

"Yes, I didn't know his address. But he had a big union job there. Grandpa knew it, but he told me he gave Daddy his word not to give it to me. So Mother wouldn't get it. If mother knew, we would be ruined. Grandpa used to tell me that all the time. He'd call me aside and remind me. He used to whisper, 'Don't forget our secret.' Sometimes when we were alone, especially if I looked sad, he'd say, 'Hey, Maggie, how's our secret?' and I guess I'd cheer up and I'd smile. Or maybe he'd just put his finger to his lips, that was the signal, I'd do the same thing. We even did it in front of Dorothy and my mother at the table, and we'd know."

"Did you ask if you could talk to your father?"

"No. He told me I couldn't. But Daddy would always send me a birthday card, care of my grandfather. I could see the address. He couldn't mail them directly, naturally."

"How come you didn't tell me all this before?" I asked Maggie.

"I guess I didn't trust you. But now I do. I guess I felt funny about it. Oh yeah, he used to send me Christmas cards too."

"What would they say?"

"They were very beautiful. But very simple. Like, 'I love you, Maggie.' Or 'I'm always thinking about you, Maggie.' Once he sent me a note, 'Congratulations on getting three A's and a B in school, and have a great summer. You worked hard. You deserve it.'"

"That must have meant a lot."

"A lot? It was everything. My mother didn't know a damn thing about school, or my homework, except that I had to go there and do it. Oh yeah, I used to ask my grandfather, 'How come Daddy knows so much about me?' and he'd wink. He was a wonderful man, Julian. Once he went to Chicago on business and talked to my father."

She stopped abruptly, her face crimsoned and she almost lost her balance. She was sobbing profusely.

It crossed my mind that all that emotion missing during our first four months and then some was here, coursing through her all at once, as she remembered.

She told me, "When Julian went to Chicago . . . he had dinner with Daddy. . . . And Daddy said he wanted to see me. . . . I was fourteen. He hadn't seen me in years. . . . But Grandpa said, 'You can't. That's the deal. You promised my daughter—that's my mother—if you come to New York to see Maggie, and mess up her life, I'll shoot you.' "

"My God."

"I was so upset. I didn't talk to Grandpa for a month, maybe a whole month. No, maybe it wasn't that long. He was so sad. But finally we became friends. He said he had to do it for me. If there was trouble, he'd lose touch with my father altogether."

"You were kind to forgive him."

A half smile broke through. "Yes, well, Grandpa bought me a dress and said Daddy had sent him the money for it. But I don't believe it. I think Grandpa just bought it. But I guess I'll never know."

"And after your grandfather died, how old were you when he died?"

"Seventeen. After that my father couldn't contact me, not directly. I guess that was the deal. So I lost two people at once, two men, two real people. . . ."

She was all tears now, her body had gone limp. And I knew that she would say no more. Our time was up, and I suggested that she come in the next day, instead of waiting.

Heroically, she stood up and said, "Thanks, I don't have to, though. I'm glad I told you."

. . .

Perhaps because David could see how much Maggie was suffering and how hard she was trying, he softened a great deal. For the time being, at least, he dropped his deadlines with Maggie. That helped considerably. David's becoming so patient with her made Maggie herself more impatient than ever for cure.

It wasn't simply that she'd been opposing him in the past. She wasn't negative, in that sense. But while he'd been hammering at her to change, she'd conceived of her task as having to change for *him*. Now she was assuming the burden much more as her own.

I could see that in her present state of mind, she would leave few stones unturned. But I also knew that this feeling of urgency on her part was temporary. One bad evening and David might lose his control, and Maggie her hopefulness. I was eager to find something she could do—almost anything, soon—that might teach us more before that inevitable setback.

In retrospect, I think that a sense of this being an optimum time for me to exhort her, and for her to delve into herself, accounted for the single session in which we finally broke through the shell.

It was unusually cold for early November. Flakes of snow eddied under the gray sky and were starting to cover the heavily trafficked streets. Several of my out-of-town patients had canceled late-afternoon sessions that day, being snowed in, and there was a general feeling in the city of people wanting to go home early and stay there.

Unlike my other patients, who layered themselves with sweaters under heavy coats, Maggie seemed to enjoy defying the elements. She had on a well-tailored beige coat that was belted at the middle; it had a huge fur collar that left her neck very exposed. As she hung up the coat on the rack in my hallway, it crossed my mind that she must be cold but I didn't say anything.

The session was full of subject matter, mostly her studies.

When it was over and we walked to the door, we noticed a sumptuous red-and-gold scarf lying on the couch in my waiting room.

I commented that it was a shame that my previous patient had left it, she must be cold, and then mentioned how pretty it was.

Maggie didn't say anything, she just scrunched up her face.

"Maggie," I asked, "you don't like the colors?"

I had a sense of her pulling back as if they were the colors of a poisonous reptile.

"I hate scarves. I never wear them."

"Really?"

She'd spoken with such finality that I was taken aback. Trying to soften her attitude, she added, "I just don't like wearing anything around my neck."

I remembered her battle with David over the necklace that she had turned into a bracelet, and I had the natural impulse to let the whole thing go. I felt like closing the office and going home. Besides, I had a personal rule that once a patient left my office, even if I did choose to follow that person to my waiting room, the session was over. I was no longer the person's therapist out there.

But I suddenly had a fierce impulse to push further. In retrospect, I think I sensed that Maggie's quiet negation of scarves had a mega-ton of force behind it, and that made me curious.

"Maggie, why don't you try it on? The woman who comes here ahead of you couldn't care less. I'm sure of that."

Maggie knew her by sight. More than once they'd exchanged pleasantries in my waiting room.

"I know, but I hate them."

"Maggie, then don't," I said. "But I almost get the sense you're afraid of that scarf. Anything you're afraid of is probably worth doing, just so we don't widen the circle of those fears that you hate yourself for—"

She headed toward the scarf, picked it up, and then draped it around her neck, so that the ends fell loosely on her shoulders. "This is the first time in I don't know when . . ." she said blithely. And then she collapsed onto my couch, the scarf still draped over her shoulders.

For an instant, by the glaze of her eyes, I thought she'd had an epileptic seizure, or passed out entirely. "I'm sick. Very sick," she said. And then she repeated flatly, "Doctor, help me. I'm sick. Very sick."

I removed the scarf at once, but it made no difference. She seemed dazed. "Oh, dear God, help me!" she said. She was addressing no one in particular, at least no one present.

I sat down in a chair across from her.

"I'm sick. I'm very sick," she repeated. "I remembered something, I don't know if it really happened. No, it couldn't have. Oh my God, dear God, please help me."

I just waited. As a child, she'd told me, she was religious. However, I'd never heard her say the word "God" before.

She went on. "A fat guy, Blecker, stopped him. Oh, thank God for Blecker."

I looked at her but didn't want to disturb her memories, even by asking who Blecker was.

Her return look was acknowledging. "Blecker was Daddy's body-guard. A giant. He used to go to work with Daddy. He used to sit outside the house. Oh, thank God he was there. Oh, thank God he was there! I remember the screaming and screaming." She stopped.

"Who was screaming?" I asked.

"Me. I was screaming and screaming. He was choking her. With a scarf, like that one. Not red. She was wearing it. We burned it. Grandpa and me. We burned it when he was gone. Could I have some water?"

"Of course!"

As I rushed out to get some, I was struck by how incredibly dry she seemed. She hadn't shed a tear. She was in shock. No, she was more like someone being choked.

She gulped the water down. "My daddy was, he was *choking* her with the scarf. She couldn't scream. She couldn't say anything. Screaming and screaming, I was screaming and screaming, and Blecker came running in. He thought something had happened to Daddy, and he saw and he shouted, 'Stop, Harry. *Stop.*' I thought Daddy was going to kiss her. I think he was. He put his hands on her cheeks, the way he used to, he was so tender. The way he used to kiss me when I went to sleep. But he was strangling her and she fell down. He was strangling her with the *scarf*! He didn't know what he was doing."

She looked up at me as if to ask, Could I take it? Was it acceptable that she was saying all this? Were things safe now?

At least that was what I must have thought because I said, "It's all right, Maggie. It's all right now. Tell me whatever you want."

"And Blecker picked up the big glass table, the whole gigantic glass table, and he smashed it on my daddy, on his back, and Daddy let go." She breathed, reliving the relief, the recognition that it was over.

"My daddy was sitting in a chair. He was dazed, that was the last time I saw him. And I started to run to my mother, she was lying on the floor, and Blecker picked me up and he threw me in the bedroom, on the bed. And he must have locked the door, I don't know. And then Mommy came in and said, 'Maggie, I'm all right. You're all right. Don't worry.'

"And the next day they told me Daddy and Blecker were gone. My mother was gone too. She went to the hospital, but Grandpa said she'd be fine, it was just a checkup. I asked him, 'Is Daddy coming back?' and he said, 'I don't think so.'

"I remembered Grandpa and I went into the living room. It was a cold winter day, like now, and we lit a fire, and the glass table was cracked down the middle, and I saw the scarf on it, and I cried, and Grandpa picked me up and said, 'No more scarf. No more scarf.' And I was crying. And he put it in the fire and we watched it burn. We watched it burn up. And Daddy was gone."

"That was the last you ever saw of him? I mean actually saw him?" She nodded yes.

She felt sheepish. I thought it was because she thought she'd presumed upon me with all that emotion. And I said, not knowing what else to say, "It's all right, Maggie."

But she clarified. "I've been so unfair to Mommy."

"I'll be home tonight," I told her. "If you want to call, you can." This time she took my number, just in case. . . .

What made Maggie one of those rare children who at the time utterly refuse to face what has happened to them? Her father's attempted strangulation of her mother just before he left, the horror of it to Maggie, was probably a factor.

And those around Maggie took special pains to reinforce her forgetfulness. Neither her mother nor her grandmother had any impulse to remind her of life in Weston, her life before her father left. Untutored in psychology and deniers of reality themselves, they never considered that such pervasive denial as hers could have harmful effects. They treated her as if what is forgotten is gone.

As for her grandfather, Maggie's mother was certainly apt in describing him as a dreamer. Although well-intended, he was the architect of a ruse that reached the proportions of a life-lie. Over the years, Maggie had lived with the falsehood he had contrived and had attempted in every way she could have to sustain it.

Together, Maggie and I studied her methods of supporting the lie her grandfather had bequeathed her. Not only was this the best means of weakening it, but as patients become conscious of their methods of bolstering falsehoods, they delude themselves less. Denials thrive in darkness, and we wanted all the light we could get.

While growing up, Maggie had come upon many evidences of the truth, which she had found ways of discounting. Her family's very relocation to Fairfield was a reminder that they had much less money than they used to, and that her father wasn't contributing. Her telling friends that they'd relocated for her to go to a better school substituted for that reminder. Her father, she would often explain, was on extended business in Chicago, where he was a very important man. This presentation also reinforced her own fantasy that her family would do anything for her and that they were close-knit, even though her father was away. It helped her forget that her father was never coming back.

As with most untruths, and especially a life-lie, the need for constant surveillance to stamp out reminders of the reality is the chief cost. For Maggie, these reminders were everywhere. No wonder she thought of death when she thought about marriage.

Because marriage meant strangulation, she would tell her girlfriends that she was never getting married. "I'm going to be a career woman, instead," she would say in high school.

Years later, she remembered, she felt great disappointment when a close woman friend of hers announced her engagement. Maggie had rationalized this as dismay over discovering that her friend wasn't as serious about her career as Maggie had hoped.

Kissing was a desperate reminder of what had happened, one that she'd worked hard to banish from her life. Even more than marriage, "a kiss on the lips" meant to her "the kiss of death." The loss of voice, the loss of freedom, the loss of life, were, not surprisingly, all bound up in the kiss. She did her best to be sure that no one kissed her on the lips.

She remembered having been very distraught the year after her father left when her girlfriends would talk about kissing. They would ask her tauntingly if she'd ever kissed a boy and once when she'd told them no, a friend had said, "I'll show you how to do it." Maggie had fled in horror. For many years, she'd refused to date, and when she did go places with boys, she was careful to choose the shyest, the least aggressive, and if possible even a boy who was physically weaker than she.

And that waterskiing story her grandfather used to tell, in which Maggie's father couldn't find the word "decapitated," was far more loaded than either Maggie or her grandfather imagined. She would beg her grandfather to tell the story, which she described as so funny that it made her sick. I could see why it did. Though she loved hearing anything about her father, the story itself was a stern reminder of the last day she ever saw him, in that it linked her father with strangling.

I got her to tell me that little anecdote many, many times, which she did quiveringly, until finally she could relate it to me without a trace of discomfort.

IRVIN D. YALOM

There are patients a therapist looks forward to seeing and those he or she en-dures. At different points in the course of therapy, those feelings may change. In this chapter from *Love's Executioner,* Dr. Yalom finds it difficult to tolerate Elva, a patient whose negativity reminds him of his mother. Yet, ultimately, he shares with this patient the "best hour of therapy" he ever gave.

How does this happen? After prior negative feelings toward Elva, his openness to his patient's sense of humor allows him to react with genuine glee to a com-ment she makes, and the relationship takes a turn. Elva, sensing that she is appreciated, opens up and shares more of herself. Then, Dr. Yalom shares his own feelings about the issues that they (and most people) fear—aging, loss, and death. Elva is touched by his humanness and his honesty, and the groundwork is laid for a creative moment that is illuminating for both patient and therapist.

I greeted Elva in my waiting room, and together we walked the short distance to my office. Something had happened. She was different today, her gait labored, discouraged, dispirited. For the last few weeks there had been a bounce in her steps, but today she once again resembled the forlorn, plodding woman I had first met eight months ago. I remember her first words then: "I think I need help. Life doesn't seem worth living. My husband's been dead for a year now, but things aren't getting any better. Maybe I'm a slow learner."

But she hadn't proved to be a slow learner. In fact, therapy had progressed remarkably well—maybe it had been going too easily. What could have set her back like this?

Sitting down, Elva sighed and said, "I never thought it would happen to me."

She had been robbed. From her description it seemed an ordinary purse snatching. The thief, no doubt, spotted her in a Monterey seaside restaurant and saw her pay the check in cash for three friends—elderly widows all. He must have followed her into the parking lot and, his footsteps muffled by the roaring of the waves, sprinted up and, without breaking stride, ripped her purse away and leaped into his nearby car.

Elva, despite her swollen legs, hustled back into the restaurant to call for help, but of course it was too late. A few hours later, the police found her empty purse dangling on a roadside bush.

Three hundred dollars meant a lot to her, and for a few days Elva was preoccupied by the money she had lost. That concern gradually evaporated and in its place was left a bitter residue—a residue expressed by the phrase "I never thought it would happen to me." Along with her purse and her three hundred dollars, an illusion was snatched away from Elva—the illusion of personal specialness. She had always lived in the privileged circle, outside the unpleasantness, the nasty inconveniences visited on ordinary people—those swarming masses of the tabloids and newscasts who are forever being robbed or maimed.

The robbery changed everything. Gone was the coziness, the softness in her life; gone was the safety. Her home had always beckoned her with its cushions, gardens, comforters, and deep carpets. Now she saw locks, doors, burglar alarms, and telephones. She had always walked her dog every morning at six. The morning stillness now seemed menacing. She and her dog stopped and listened for danger.

None of this is remarkable. Elva had been traumatized and now suffered from commonplace post-traumatic stress. After an accident or an assault, most people tend to feel unsafe, to have a reduced startle threshold, and to be hypervigilant. Eventually time erodes the memory of the event, and victims gradually return to their prior, trusting state.

But for Elva it was more than a simple assault. Her world view was fractured. She had often claimed, "As long as a person has eyes, ears, and a mouth, I can cultivate their friendship." But no longer. She had lost her belief in benevolence, in her personal invulnerability. She felt stripped, ordinary, unprotected. The true impact of that robbery was to shatter illusion and to confirm, in brutal fashion, her husband's death.

Of course, she knew that Albert was dead. Dead and in his grave for over a year and a half. She had taken the ritualized widow walk— through the cancer diagnosis; the awful, retching, temporizing chemotherapy; their last visit together to Carmel; their last drive down El Camino Real; the hospital bed at home; the funeral; the paperwork; the ever-dwindling dinner invitations; the widow and widower's clubs; the long, lonely nights. The whole necrotic catastrophe.

Yet, despite all this, Elva had retained her feeling of Albert's continued existence and thereby of her persisting safety and specialness. She had continued to live "as if," as if the world were safe, as if Albert were there, back in the workshop next to the garage.

Mind you, I do not speak of delusion. Rationally, Elva knew Albert was gone, but still she lived her routine, everyday life behind a veil of illusion which numbed the pain and softened the glare of the knowing. Over forty years ago, she had made a contract with life whose explicit genesis and terms had been eroded by time but whose basic nature was clear: Albert would take care of Elva forever. Upon this unconscious premise, Elva had built her entire assumptive world—a world featuring safety and benevolent paternalism.

Albert was a fixer. He had been a roofer, an auto mechanic, a general handyman, a contractor; he could fix anything. Attracted by a newspaper or magazine photograph of a piece of furniture or some gadget, he would proceed to replicate it in his workshop. I, who have always been hopelessly inept in a workshop, listened in fascination. Forty-one years of living with a fixer is powerfully comforting. It was not hard to understand why Elva clung to the feeling that Albert was still there, out back in the workshop looking out for her, fixing things. How could she give it up? Why should she? That memory, reinforced by forty-one years of experience, had spun a cocoon around Elva that shielded her from reality—that is, until her purse was snatched.

Upon first meeting Elva eight months before, I could find little to love in her. She was a stubby, unattractive woman, part gnome, part sprite, part toad, and each of those parts ill tempered. I was transfixed by her facial plasticity: she winked, grimaced, and popped her eyes either singly or in duet. Her brow seemed alive with great washboard furrows. Her tongue, always visible, changed radically in size as it darted in and out or circled her moist, rubbery, pulsating lips. I remember amusing myself, almost laughing aloud, by imagining introducing her to patients on long-term tranquilizer medication who had developed tardive dyskinesia (a drug-induced abnormality of facial musculature). The patients would, within seconds, become deeply offended because they would believe Elva to be mocking them.

But what I really disliked about Elva was her anger. She dripped with rage and, in our first few hours together, had something vicious to say about everyone she knew—save, of course, Albert. She hated the friends who no longer invited her. She hated those who did not put her at ease. Inclusion or exclusion, it was all the same to her: she found something to hate in everyone. She hated the doctors who had told her that Albert was doomed. She hated even more those who offered false hope.

Those hours were hard for me. I had spent too many hours in my youth silently hating my mother's vicious tongue. I remember the games of imagination I played as a child trying to invent the existence of someone she did not hate: A kindly aunt? A grandfather who told her stories? An older playmate who defended her? But I never found anyone. Save, of course, my father, and he was really part of her, her mouthpiece, her animus, her creation who (according to Asimov's first law of robotics) could not turn against his maker—despite my prayers that he would once—just once, please, Dad—pop her.

All I could do with Elva was to hold on, hear her out, somehow endure the hour, and use all my ingenuity to find something supportive to say—usually some vapid comment about how hard it must be for her to carry around that much anger. At times I, almost mischievously, inquired about others of her family circle. Surely there must be someone who warranted respect. But no one was spared. Her son? She said his elevator "didn't go to the top floor." He was "absent": even when he was there, he was "absent." And her daughter-in-law? In Elva's words, "a GAP"—gentile American princess. When driving home, her son would call his wife on his automobile telephone to say he wanted dinner right away. No problem. She could do it. Nine minutes, Elva reminded me, was all the time required for the GAP to cook dinner—to "nuke" a slim gourmet TV dinner in the microwave.

Everyone had a nickname. Her granddaughter, "Sleeping Beauty" (she whispered with an enormous wink and a nod), had two bathrooms—two, mind you. Her housekeeper, whom she had hired to attenuate her loneliness, was "Looney Tunes," and so dumb that she tried to hide her smoking by exhaling the smoke down the flushing toilet. Her pretentious bridge partner was "Dame May Whitey" (and Dame May Whitey was spry-minded compared with the rest, with all the Alzheimer zombies and burned-out drunks who, according to Elva, constituted the bridge-playing population of San Francisco).

But somehow, despite her rancor and my dislike of her and the evocation of my mother, we got through these sessions. I endured my irritation, got a little closer, resolved my countertransference by disentangling my mother from Elva, and slowly, very slowly, began to warm to her.

I think the turning point came one day when she plopped herself in my chair with a "Whew! I'm tired." In response to my raised eyebrows, she explained she had just played eighteen holes of golf with her twenty-year-old nephew. (Elva was sixty, four foot eleven, and at least one hundred sixty pounds.)

"How'd you do?" I inquired cheerily, keeping up my side of the conversation.

Elva bent forward, holding her hand to her mouth as though to exclude someone in the room, showed me a remarkable number of enormous teeth, and said, "I whomped the shit out of him!"

It struck me as wonderfully funny and I started to laugh, and laughed until my eyes filled with tears. Elva liked my laughing. She told me later it was the first spontaneous act from Herr Doctor Professor (so that was my nickname!), and she laughed with me. After that we got along famously. I began to appreciate Elva—her marvelous sense of humor, her intelligence, her drollness. She had led a rich, eventful life. We were similar in many ways. Like me, she had made the big generational jump. My parents arrived in the United States in their twenties, penniless immigrants from Russia. Her parents had been poor Irish immigrants, and she had straddled the gap between the Irish tenements of South Boston and the duplicate bridge tournaments of Nob Hill in San Francisco.

At the beginning of therapy, an hour with Elva meant hard work. I trudged when I went to fetch her from the waiting room. But after a couple of months, all that changed. I looked forward to our time together. None of our hours passed without a good laugh. My secretary said she always could tell by my smile that I had seen Elva that day.

We met weekly for several months, and therapy proceeded well, as it usually does when therapist and patient enjoy each other. We talked about her widowhood, her changed social role, her fear of being alone, her sadness at never being physically touched. But, above all, we talked about her anger—about how it had driven away her family and her friends. Gradually she let it go; she grew softer and more gentle. Her tales of Looney Tunes, Sleeping Beauty, Dame May Whitey, and the Alzheimer bridge brigade grew less bitter. Rapprochements occurred; as her anger receded, family and friends reappeared in her life. She had been doing so well that, just before the time of the purse snatching, I had been considering raising the question of termination.

But when she was robbed, she felt as though she were starting all over again. Most of all, the robbery illuminated her ordinariness, her "I never thought it would happen to me" reflecting the loss of belief in her personal specialness. Of course, she was still special in that she had special qualities and gifts, that she had a unique life history, that no one who had ever lived was just like her. That's the rational side of specialness. But we (some more than others) also have an irrational sense of specialness. It is one of our chief methods of denying death, and the part of our mind whose task it is to mollify death terror generates the irrational belief that we are invulnerable—that unpleasant things like aging and death may be the lot of others but not our lot, that we exist beyond law, beyond human and biological destiny.

Although Elva responded to the purse snatching in ways that *seemed* irrational (for example, proclaiming that she wasn't fit to live on earth, being afraid to leave her house), it was clear that she was *really* suffering from the stripping away of irrationality. That sense of specialness, of being charmed, of being the exception, of being eternally protected—all those self-deceptions that had served her so well suddenly lost their persuasiveness. She saw through her own illusions, and what illusion had shielded now lay before her, bare and terrible.

Her grief wound was now fully exposed. This was the time, I thought, to open it wide, to debride it, and to allow it to heal straight and true.

"When you say you never thought it would happen to you, I know just what you mean," I said. "It's so hard for me, too, to accept that all these afflictions—aging, loss, death—are going to happen to me, too."

Elva nodded, her tightened brow showing that she was surprised at my saying anything personal about myself.

"You must feel that if Albert were alive, this would never have happened to you." I ignored her flip response that if Albert were alive she wouldn't have been taking those three old hens to lunch. "So the robbery brings home the fact that he's really gone."

Her eyes filled with tears, but I felt I had the right, the mandate, to continue. "You knew that before, I know. But part of you didn't. Now you really know that he's dead. He's not in the yard. He's not out back in the workshop. He's not anywhere. Except in your memories."

Elva was really crying now, and her stubby frame heaved with sobs for several minutes. She had never done that before with me. I sat there and wondered, "Now what do I do?" But my instincts luckily led me to what proved to be an inspired gambit. My eyes lit upon her purse—that same ripped-off, much-abused purse; and I said, "Bad luck is one thing, but aren't you asking for it carrying around something that large?" Elva, plucky as ever, did not fail to call attention to my overstuffed pockets and the clutter on the table next to my chair. She pronounced the purse "medium-sized."

"Any larger," I responded, "and you'd need a luggage carrier to move it around."

"Besides," she said, ignoring my jibe, "I need everything in it."

"You've got to be joking! Let's see!"

Getting into the spirit of it, Elva hoisted her purse onto my table, opened its jaws wide, and began to empty it. The first items fetched forth were three empty doggie bags.

"Need two extra ones in case of an emergency?" I asked.

Elva chuckled and continued to disembowel the purse. Together we inspected and discussed each item. Elva conceded that three packets of Kleenex and twelve pens (plus three pencil stubs) were indeed superfluous, but held firm about two bottles of cologne and three hairbrushes, and dismissed, with an imperious flick of her hand, my challenge to her large flashlight, bulky notepads, and huge sheaf of photographs.

We quarreled over everything. The roll of fifty dimes. Three bags of candies (low-calorie, of course). She giggled at my question: "Do you believe, Elva, that the more of these you eat, the thinner you will become?" A plastic sack of old orange peels ("You never know, Elva, when these will come in handy"). A bunch of knitting needles ("Six needles in search of a sweater," I thought). A bag of sourdough starter. Half of a paperback Stephen King novel (Elva threw away sections of pages as she read them: "They weren't worth keeping," she explained). A small stapler ("Elva, this is crazy!"). Three pairs of sunglasses. And, tucked away into the innermost corners, assorted coins, paper clips, nail clippers, pieces of emery board, and some substance that looked suspiciously like lint.

When the great bag had finally yielded all, Elva and I stared in wonderment at the contents set out in rows on my table. We were sorry the bag was empty and that the emptying was over. She turned and smiled, and we looked tenderly at each other. It was an extraordinarily intimate moment. In a way no patient had ever done before, she showed me everything. And I had accepted everything and asked for even more. I followed her into her every nook and crevice, awed that one old woman's purse could serve as a vehicle for both isolation and intimacy: the absolute isolation that is integral to existence and the intimacy that dispels the dread, if not the fact, of isolation.

That was a transforming hour. Our time of intimacy—call it love, call it love making—was redemptive. In that one hour, Elva moved from a position of forsakenness to one of trust. She came alive and was persuaded, once more, of her capacity for intimacy.

I think it was the best hour of therapy I ever gave.

WHEN NIETZSCHE WEPT

IRVIN D. YALOM

In this fictionalized version of the encounter between Josef Breuer, a friend and mentor of Freud, and philosopher Friedrich Nietzsche, Breuer convinces Nietzsche to become his therapist. But Breuer is playing a dangerous game. He hopes that the reversal of roles will enable the difficult Nietzsche to open up and delve into his own problems. In sessions before the one described in this excerpt, Nietzsche has stubbornly applied behavior modification techniques in an attempt to help Breuer rid himself of his obsessions with a former patient. But now Breuer is forced to admit that he indeed does need help, and the breakthrough provokes a genuine and honest exchange that allows the therapy to take a new course.

Nietzsche then begins to use Breuer's methods of "chimneysweeping": saying anything and everything that comes to mind about a subject. As the two men move closer, emotionally and philosophically, they experience a clarity that illuminates the meaning of Breuer's obsession with the former patient and allows Nietzsche to begin to discover his own pain.

"We're not getting anywhere, Friedrich. I'm getting worse."

Nietzsche, who had been writing at his desk, had not heard Breuer enter. Now he turned around, opened his mouth to speak, yet remained silent.

"Do I startle you, Friedrich? It must be confusing to have your physician enter your room and complain that he is worse! Especially when he is impeccably attired and carries his black medical bag with professional assurance!

"But, trust me, my outward appearance is all deception. Underneath, my clothes are wet, my shirt clings to my skin. This obsession with Bertha—it's a whirlpool in my mind. It sucks up my every decent thought!

"I don't blame *you*!" Breuer sat down next to the desk. "Our lack of progress is *my* fault. It was I who urged you to attack the obsession directly. You're right—we do not go deep enough. We merely trim leaves when we should be uprooting the weed."

"Yes, we uproot nothing!" Nietzsche replied. "We must reconsider our approach. I, too, feel discouraged. Our last sessions have been false and superficial. Look at what we tried to do: to discipline your thoughts, to control your behavior! Thought training and behavior shaping! These methods are not for the human realm! Ach, we're not animal trainers!"

"Yes, yes! After the last session I felt like a bear being trained to stand and dance."

"Precisely! A teacher should be a raiser of men. Instead, in the last few meetings, I've lowered you and myself as well. We cannot approach human concerns with animal methods."

Nietzsche rose and gestured toward the fireplace, the waiting chairs. "Shall we?" It occurred to Breuer, as he took his seat, that though the future "doctors of despair" might discard traditional medical tools—stethoscope, otoscope, ophthalmoscope—they would in time develop their own accoutrements, beginning with two comfortable fireside chairs.

"So," Breuer began, "let's return to where we were before this ill-advised direct campaign upon my obsession. You had advanced a theory that Bertha is a diversion, not a cause, and that the real center of my *Angst* is my fear of death and godlessness. Maybe so! I think you may be right! Certainly it's true that my obsession about Bertha keeps me pasted to the surface of things, leaving me no time for deeper or darker thoughts.

"Yet, Friedrich, I don't find your explanation entirely satisfying. First, there's still the riddle of 'Why Bertha?' Of all the possible ways to defend myself against *Angst*, why choose this particular, stupid obsession? Why not some *other* method, some *other* fantasy?

"Second, you say Bertha is merely a diversion to misdirect my attention from my core *Angst*. Yet 'diversion' is a pale word. It's not enough to explain the *power* of my obsession. Thinking about Bertha is preternaturally compelling; it contains some hidden, powerful meaning."

"*Meaning!*" Nietzsche slapped his hand sharply against the arm of his chair. "Exactly! I've been thinking along similar lines since you left yesterday. Your final word, 'meaning,' may be the key. Perhaps our mistake from the beginning has been to neglect the *meaning* of your obsession. You claimed you cured each of Bertha's hysterical symptoms by discovering its origin. And also that this 'origin' method was not relevant to your own case because the origin of your Bertha obsession was already known—having begun after you met her and intensifying after you stopped seeing her.

"But perhaps," Nietzsche continued, "you've been using the wrong word. Perhaps what matters is not the *origin*—that is, the first appearance of symptoms—but the *meaning* of a symptom! Perhaps you were mistaken. Perhaps you cured Bertha by discovering not the origin, but the meaning of each symptom! *Perhaps*"—here Nietzsche almost whispered as if he were conveying a secret of great significance—"*perhaps symptoms are messengers of a meaning and will vanish only when their message is comprehended.* If so, our next step is obvious: if we are to conquer the symptoms, we must determine what the Bertha obsession *means* to you!"

What next? Breuer wondered. How does one go about discovering the *meaning* of an obsession? He was affected by Nietzsche's excitement and awaited instructions. But Nietzsche had settled back in his chair, taken out his comb, and begun to groom his mustache. Breuer grew tense and cranky.

"Well, Friedrich? I'm waiting!" He rubbed his chest, breathing deeply. "This tension here, in my chest, grows every minute I sit here. Soon it will explode. I can't reason it away. Tell me how to start! How can I discover a meaning that I myself have concealed?"

"Don't try to discover or solve anything!" Nietzsche responded, still combing his mustache. "That will be my job! Your job is just to chimneysweep. Talk about what Bertha *means* to you."

"Haven't I already talked too much about her? Shall I wallow once again in my Bertha ruminations? You've heard them all—touching her, undressing her, caressing her, my house on fire, everyone dead, eloping to America. Do you really want to hear all that garbage again?" Getting up abruptly, Breuer paced back and forth behind Nietzsche's chair.

Nietzsche continued to speak in a calm and measured manner. "It's the *tenacity* of your obsession that intrigues me. Like a barnacle clinging to its rock. Can we not, Josef, just for a moment, pry it away and peer underneath? Chimneysweep for me, I say! Chimneysweep about this question: What would life—your life—be like without Bertha? Just talk. Don't try to make sense, even to make sentences. Say anything that comes to your mind!"

"I can't. I'm wound up, I'm a coiled spring."

"Stop pacing. Close your eyes and try to describe what you see on the back of your eyelids. Just let the thoughts flow—don't control them."

Breuer stopped behind Nietzsche's chair and clutched its back. His eyes closed, he rocked to and fro, as his father had when he prayed, and slowly began to mumble his thoughts:

"A life without Bertha—a charcoal life, no colors—calipers—scales—funerary marbles—everything decided, now and for always—I'd be here, you'd find me here—always! Right here, this spot, with this medical bag, in these clothes, with this face which, day by day, will grow darker and more gaunt."

Breuer breathed deep, feeling less agitated, and sat down. "Life without Bertha?—What else?—I'm a scientist, but science has no color. One should only *work* in science, not try to live in it—I need magic—and passion—you can't live without magic. *That's* what Bertha means, *passion and magic*. Life without passion—who can live such a life?" He opened his eyes suddenly. "Can you? Can anyone?"

"Please chimneysweep about passion and living," Nietzsche prodded him.

"One of my patients is a midwife," Breuer went on. "She's old, wizened, alone. Her heart is failing. But still she's passionate about living. Once I asked her about the source of her passion. She said it was that moment between lifting a silent newborn and giving it the slap of life. She was renewed, she said, by immersion in that moment of mystery, that moment that straddles existence and oblivion."

"And *you*, Josef?"

"I'm like that midwife! I want to be close to mystery. My passion for Bertha isn't natural—it's supernatural, I know that—but I need magic. I can't live in black and white."

"We all need passion, Josef," Nietzsche said. "Dionysian passion *is* life. But does passion have to be magical and debasing? Can't one find a way to be the *master* of passion?

"Let me tell you about a Buddhist monk I met last year in the Engadine. He lives a spare life. He meditates half his waking hours and spends weeks without exchanging a word with anyone. His diet is simple, only a single meal a day, whatever he can beg, perhaps only an apple. But he meditates upon that apple until it's bursting with richness, succulence, and crispness. By the end of the day, he *passionately* anticipates his meal. The point is, Josef, you don't have to relinquish passion. *But you have to change your conditions for passion.*"

Breuer nodded.

"Keep going," Nietzsche urged. "Chimneysweep more about Bertha—what she means to you."

Breuer closed his eyes. "I see myself running with her. Running away. Bertha means *escape*—dangerous escape!"

"How so?"

"Bertha is danger. Before her, I lived within the rules. Today I flirt with the limits of those rules—perhaps that's what the midwife meant. I think about exploding my life, sacrificing my career, committing adultery, losing my family, emigrating, beginning life again with Bertha." Breuer slapped himself lightly on the head. "Stupid! Stupid! I know I'll never do it!"

"But there's a lure to this dangerous teeter-tottering on the edge?"

"A lure? I don't know. I can't answer that. I don't like danger! If there's a lure, it's not danger—I think the lure is *escape*, not from danger but *from safety*. Maybe I've lived too safely!"

"Maybe, Josef, living safely *is* dangerous. Dangerous and deadly."

"Living safely *is* dangerous." Breuer mumbled the words to himself several times. "Living safely *is* dangerous. Living safely *is* dangerous. A powerful thought, Friedrich. So is that the meaning of Bertha: to escape the dangerously deadly life! Is Bertha my freedom wish—my escape from the trap of time?"

"Perhaps from the trap of *your* time, your historical moment. But, Josef," he said solemnly, "do not make the mistake of thinking she will lead you out of time! Time cannot be broken; that is our greatest burden. And our greatest challenge is to live *in spite of* that burden."

For once, Breuer did not protest Nietzsche's assumption of his philosopher's tone. This philosophizing was different. He didn't know what to *do* with Nietzsche's words, but he knew they reached him, moved him.

"Be assured," he said, "I have no dreams of immortality. The life I want to escape is the life of the eighteen eighty-two Viennese medical bourgeoisie. Others, I know, envy my life—but I dread it. Dread its sameness and predictability. Dread it so much that sometimes I think of my life as a death sentence. Do you know what I mean, Friedrich?"

Nietzsche nodded. "Do you remember asking me, perhaps the first time we talked, whether there were any advantages to having migraine? It was a good question. It helped me think about my life differently. And do you remember my answer? That my migraine forced me to resign my university professorship? Everyone—family, friends, even colleagues—lamented my misfortune, and I am certain history will record that Nietzsche's illness tragically ended his career. But not so! The reverse is true! The professorship at the University of Basel was *my* death sentence. It sentenced me to the hollow life of the academy and to spend the rest of my days providing for the economic support of my mother and sister. I was fatally trapped."

"And then, Friedrich, migraine—the great liberator—descended upon you!"

"Not so different is it, Josef, from this obsession that descends upon you? Perhaps we are more alike than we think!"

Breuer closed his eyes. How good to feel so close to Nietzsche. Tears welled up; he pretended a coughing fit in order to turn his head away.

"Let us continue," said Nietzsche impassively. "We're making progress. We understand that Bertha represents passion, mystery, dangerous escape. What else, Josef? What other meanings are packed into her?"

"Beauty! Bertha's beauty is an important part of the mystery. Here, I brought this for you to see."

He opened his bag and held out a photograph. Putting on his thick glasses, Nietzsche walked to the window to inspect it in better light. Bertha, clothed from head to toe in black, was dressed for riding. Her jacket constricted her: a double row of small buttons, stretching from her tiny waist to her chin, struggled to contain her mighty bosom. Her left hand daintily clasped both her skirt and a long riding whip. From her other hand, gloves dangled. Her nose was forceful, her hair short and severe; and on it perched an insouciant black cap. Her eyes were large and dark. She did not trouble to look into the camera, but stared far into the distance.

"A formidable woman, Josef," said Nietzsche, returning the photograph and sitting down again. "Yes, she has great beauty—but I don't like women who carry whips."

"Beauty," Breuer said, "is an important part of Bertha's meaning. I'm easily captured by such beauty. More easily than most men, I think. Beauty is a mystery. I hardly know how to speak about it, but a woman who has a certain combination of flesh, breasts, ears, large dark eyes, nose, lips—especially lips—simply awes me. This sounds stupid, but I almost believe such women have superhuman powers!"

"To do what?"

"It's too stupid!" Breuer hid his face in his hands.

"Just chimneysweep, Josef. Suspend your judgment—and speak! You have my word I do not judge you!"

"I can't put it into language."

"Try to finish this sentence: 'In the presence of Bertha's beauty, I feel—' "

" 'In the presence of Bertha's beauty, I feel—I feel—' What do I feel? I feel I'm in the bowels of the earth—in the center of existence. I'm just where I should be. I'm in the place where there are no questions about life or purpose—the center—the place of safety. Her beauty offers infinite safety." He lifted his head. "See, I tell you this makes no sense!"

"Go on," said Nietzsche imperturbably.

"For me to be captured, the woman must have a certain look. It's an adoring look—I can see it in my mind now—wide-open, glistening eyes, lips closed in an affectionate half-smile. She seems to be saying—oh, I don't know——"

"Continue, Josef, please! Keep imagining the smile! Can you still see it?"

Breuer closed his eyes and nodded.

"What does it say to you?"

"It says, 'You're adorable. *Anything* you do is all right. Oh, you darling, you get out of control, but one expects that of a boy.' Now I see her turning to the other women around her, and she says, 'Isn't he something? Isn't he dear? I'll take him into my arms and comfort him.' "

"Can you say more about that smile?"

"It says to me I can play, do whatever I want. I can get into trouble—but, no matter what, she'll continue to be delighted by me, to find me adorable."

"Does the smile have a personal history for you, Josef?"

"What do you mean?"

"Reach back. Does your memory contain such a smile?"

Breuer shook his head. "No, no memories."

"You answer too quickly!" Nietzsche insisted. "You started to shake your head before I finished my question. Search! Just keep watching that smile in your mind's eye and see what comes."

Breuer closed his eyes and gazed at the scroll of his memory. "I've seen Mathilde give that smile to our son, Johannes. Also, when I

was ten or eleven, I was infatuated by a girl named Mary Gomperz—
she gave me that smile! That exact smile! I was desolate when her
family moved away. I haven't seen her for thirty years, yet I still
dream about Mary."

"Who else? Have you forgotten your mother's smile?"

"Haven't I told you? My mother died when I was four. She was
only twenty-eight, and she died after giving birth to my younger
brother. I am told she was beautiful, but I have no memories of her,
not one."

"And your wife? Does Mathilde have that magical smile?"

"No. Of *that* I can be certain. Mathilde is beautiful, but her smile
has no power. I know it's stupid to think that Mary, at age ten, has
power, while Mathilde has none. But that's the way I experience it. In
our marriage it is *I* who have power over *her*, and it is she who desires
my protection. No, Mathilde has no magic, I don't know why."

"Magic requires darkness and mystery," Nietzsche said. "Perhaps
her mystery has been annihilated by the familiarity of fourteen years
of marriage. Do you know her too well? Perhaps you cannot bear the
truth of a relationship to a beautiful woman."

"I begin to think I need another word than beauty. Mathilde has
all the components of beauty. She has the aesthetics, but not the
power, of beauty. Perhaps you're right—it is too familiar. Too often
I see the flesh and blood under the skin. Another factor is that there's
no competition; no other men have ever been in Mathilde's life. It
was an arranged marriage."

"It puzzles me that you would want competition, Josef. Just a few
days ago, you spoke of dreading it."

"I want competition, and I don't. Remember, you said I didn't have
to make sense. I'm just expressing words as they occur to me. Let me
see—let me collect my thoughts—*Yes*, the woman of beauty has more
power if she is desired by other men. But such a woman is too dangerous—she will scald me. Maybe Bertha is the perfect compromise—
she's not yet fully formed! She is beauty in embryo, still incomplete."

"So," Nietzsche asked, "she's safer because she has no other men
competing for her?"

"That's not quite it. She's safer because I have the inside track.

Any man would want her, but I can easily defeat competitors. She is—or, rather, was—completely dependent on me. For weeks she refused to eat unless I personally fed her every meal.

"Naturally, as her physician, I deplored my patient's regression. Tsk, tsk, I clucked my tongue. Tsk, tsk, what a pity! I expressed my professional concern to her family, but secretly, as a man—and I'd never admit this to anyone but you—*I relished my conquest*. When she told me, one day, that she had dreamed of me, I was ecstatic. What a victory—to enter her innermost chamber, a place where no other man had ever gained entry! And since dream images do not die, it was a place where I would endure forever!"

"So, Josef, you win the competition without having had to compete!"

"Yes, that is another meaning of Bertha—*safe contest, certain victory*. But a beautiful woman *without* safety—that is something else." Breuer fell silent.

"Keep going, Josef. Where do your thoughts go now?"

"I was thinking about an unsafe woman, a fully formed beauty about Bertha's age who came to see me in my office a couple of weeks ago, a woman to whom many men have paid homage. I was charmed by her—and terrified! I was so unable to oppose her that I could not keep her waiting and saw her out of turn before my other patients. And when she made an inappropriate medical request of me, it was all I could do to resist her wishes."

"Ah, I know that dilemma," said Nietzsche. "The most desirable woman is the most frightening one. And not, of course, because of what she is, but because of what we make of her. Very sad!"

"Sad, Friedrich?"

"Sad for the woman who is never known, and sad, too, for the man. I know that sadness."

"You, too, have known a Bertha?"

"No, but I have known a woman like that other patient you describe—the one who cannot be denied."

Lou Salomé, thought Breuer. Lou Salomé, without a doubt! At *last*, he speaks of her! Though reluctant to relinquish the focus on himself, Breuer nonetheless pressed the inquiry.

"So, Friedrich, what happened to that lady you could not deny?"

Nietzsche hesitated, then took out his watch. "We have struck a rich vein today—who knows, perhaps a rich vein for both of us. But we are running out of time and I am certain you still have much to say. Please continue to tell me what Bertha means to you."

Breuer knew that Nietzsche was closer than ever before to disclosing his own problems. Perhaps a gentle inquiry at this point would have been all that was necessary. Yet when he heard Nietzsche prod him again: "Don't stop: your ideas are flowing," Breuer was only too glad to continue.

"I lament the complexity of the double life, the secret life. Yet I treasure it. The surface bourgeois life is deadly—it's too visible, one can see the end too clearly and all the acts, leading right to the end. It sounds mad, I know, but the double life is an additional life. It holds the promise of a lifetime extended."

Nietzsche nodded. "You feel that time devours the possibilities of the surface life, whereas the secret life is inexhaustible?"

"Yes, that's not exactly what I said, but it's what I mean. Another thing, perhaps the most important thing, is the ineffable feeling I had when I was with Bertha or that I have now when I think about her. Bliss! That's the closest word."

"I've always believed, Josef, that we are more in love with desire than with the desired!"

" 'More in love with desire than with the desired!' " Breuer repeated. "Please give me some paper. I want to remember that."

Nietzsche tore a sheet from the back of his notebook and waited while Breuer wrote the line, folded the paper, and put it in his jacket pocket.

"And another thing," Breuer continued, "Bertha eases my aloneness. As far back as I can remember, I've been frightened by the empty spaces inside of me. And my aloneness has nothing to do with the presence, or absence, of people. Do you know what I mean?"

"Ach, who could understand you better? At times I think I'm the most alone man in existence. And, like you, it has nothing to do with the presence of others—in fact, I hate others who rob me of my solitude and yet do not truly offer me company."

"What do you mean, Friedrich? How do they not offer company?"

"By not holding dear the things I hold dear! Sometimes I gaze so far into life that I suddenly look around and see that no one has accompanied me, and that my sole companion is time."

"I'm not sure if my aloneness is like yours. Perhaps I've never dared to enter it as deeply as you."

"Perhaps," Nietzsche suggested, "Bertha stops you from entering it more deeply."

"I don't think I want to enter it more. In fact, *I feel grateful to Bertha for removing my loneliness.* That's *another* thing she means to me. In the last two years, I've never been alone—Bertha was always there at her home, or in the hospital, waiting for my visit. And now she's always inside of me, also waiting."

"You attribute to Bertha something that is your own achievement."

"What do you mean?"

"That you're still as alone as before, as alone as each person is sentenced to be. You've manufactured your own icon and then are warmed by its company. *Perhaps you are more religious than you think!*"

"But," Breuer replied, "in a sense she is always there. Or *was,* for a year and a half. Bad as it was, that was the best, the most vital, time of my life. I saw her every day, I thought about her all the time, I dreamed about her at night."

"You told me of one time she was *not* there, Josef—in that dream that keeps returning. How does it go—that you're searching for her——?"

"It begins with something fearful happening. The ground starts to liquefy under my feet, and I search for Bertha and cannot find her——"

"Yes, I'm convinced there is some important clue in that dream. What was the fearful event that happened—the ground opening up?"

Breuer nodded.

"Why, Josef, at that moment, should you search for Bertha? To protect her? Or for her to protect you?"

There was a long silence. Twice Breuer snapped his head back as though to order himself to attention. "I can't go further. It's astounding, but my mind won't work anymore. Never have I felt so fatigued. It's only midmorning, but I feel as though I've been laboring without stop for days and days."

"I feel it, too. Hard work today."

"But the right work, I think. Now I must go. Until tomorrow, Friedrich."

EXCERPTS FROM DR. BREUER'S CASE NOTES ON ECKHARDT MÜLLER, 15 DECEMBER, 1882

Can it have been only a few days ago that I pleaded with Nietzsche to reveal himself? Today, finally, he was ready, eager. He wanted to tell me that he felt trapped by his university career, that he resented supporting his mother and sister, that he was lonely and suffered because of a beautiful woman.

Yes, finally, he wanted to reveal himself to me. And yet, it's quite astounding—I did not encourage him. It was not that I had no desire to listen. No, worse than that! I resented his talking! I resented his intruding upon my time!

Was it only two weeks ago I tried to manipulate him into revealing some tiny scrap of himself, that I complained to Max and Frau Becker about his secretiveness, that I bent my ear to his lips to hear him say, "Help me, help me," that I promised him, "Count on me"?

Why, then, was I willing to disregard him today? Have I grown greedy? This counseling process—the longer it goes, the less I understand it. Yet it is compelling. More and more, I think about my talks with Nietzsche; sometimes they even interrupt a Bertha fantasy. These sessions have become the center of my day. I feel greedy for my time and often can hardly wait until our next one. Is that why I let Nietzsche put me off today?

In the future—who knows when, maybe fifty years hence?— this talking treatment could become commonplace. "Angst doctors" will become a standard speciality. And medical schools— or perhaps philosophy departments—will train them.

What should the curriculum of the future "Angst doctor" contain? At present, I can be certain of one essential course: "re-

lationship"! That's where the complexity arises. Just as surgeons must first learn anatomy, the future "Angst doctor" must first understand the relationship between the one who counsels and the one who is counseled. And, if I am to contribute to the science of such counseling, I must learn to observe the counseling relationship just as objectively as I observe the pigeon's brain.

Observing a relationship is not easy when I myself am part of it. Still, I note several striking trends.

I used to be critical of Nietzsche, but no longer. On the contrary, I now cherish his every word and, day by day, grow more convinced that he can help me.

I used to believe I could help him. No longer. I have little to offer him. He has everything to offer me.

I used to compete with him, to devise chess traps for him. No longer! His insight is extraordinary. His intellect soars. I gaze at him as a hen at a hawk. Do I revere him too much! Do I want him to soar above me? Perhaps that is why I do not want to hear him talk. Perhaps I do not want to know of his pain, his fallibility.

I used to think about how to "handle" him. No longer! Often I feel great surges of warmth toward him. That's a change. Once I compared our situation to Robert's training his kitten: "Stand back, let him drink his milk. Later he'll let you touch him." Today, midway through our talk, another image flitted through my mind: two tiger-striped kittens, head touching head, lapping milk from the same bowl.

Another strange thing. Why did I mention that a "fully formed beauty" recently visited my office? Do I want him to learn of my meeting with Lou Salomé? Was I flirting with danger? Silently teasing him? Trying to drive a wedge between us?

And why did Nietzsche say he doesn't like women with whips? He must have been referring to that picture of Lou Salomé that he doesn't know I saw. He must realize his feelings for her are not so different from my feelings toward Bertha. So, was he silently teasing me? A little private joke? Here we are, two men trying to be honest with one another—yet both prodded by the imp of duplicity.

Another new insight! What Nietzsche is to me, I was to Bertha. She magnified my wisdom, revered my every word, cherished our sessions, could scarcely wait until the next—indeed, prevailed upon me to see her twice daily!

And the more blatantly she idolized me, the more I imbued her with power. She was the anodyne for all my anguish. Her merest glance cured my loneliness. She gave my life purpose and significance. Her simple smile anointed me as desirable, granted me absolution for all bestial impulses. A strange love: we each bask in the radiance of one another's magic!

Yet I grow more hopeful. There is power in my dialogue with Nietzsche, and I am convinced that this power is not illusory.

Strange that, only hours later, I have forgotten much of our discussion. A strange forgetting, not like the evaporation of an ordinary coffeehouse conversation. Could there be such a thing as an active forgetting—forgetting something not because it is unimportant, but because it is too important?

I wrote down one shocking phrase: "We are more in love with desire than with the desired."

And another: "Living safely is dangerous." Nietzsche says that my entire bürgherlich life has been lived dangerously. I think he means I am in danger of losing my true self, or of not becoming who I am. But who am I?

ABOUT THE THERAPEUTIC RELATIONSHIP

ERICH FROMM

According to Erich Fromm, the relationship between the therapist and the patient (the analysand) *is* the therapy. In this relationship, the facade that one presents in many conventional relationships must be replaced by "authenticity." As a result, it becomes more difficult to repress feelings, and the patient can be relieved of the pressure that is caused by the energy it takes to represses those feelings.

As the patient says whatever comes to mind, the therapist responds by telling the patient what he has heard—which may be quite different. Rather than analyzing and interpreting what the patient says, the therapist finds something in himself that allows him to connect with the patient, to find a common ground.

Fromm believes that the talents of a good therapist are measured in personal qualities, and this requires training in the humanities, for there are universal human qualities to be found through the study of literature, mythology, and religion. Ultimately, Fromm questions the value of medical training as a requirement for psychotherapeutic practice.

THE RELATION BETWEEN ANALYST AND ANALYSAND

It is not enough to describe the relation between analyst and analysand as an interaction. There is an interaction, but between a prison guard and a prisoner there is an interaction, too. Skinner has gone in his book *Beyond Freedom and Dignity* (1971) so far to state that the man who is tortured controls the torturer as much as the torturer controls him, because by his shouts of pain he tells the torturer what means to apply. In a perverse way, one might say in a certain sense Skinner is right, but only in a very absurd sense, because essentially the torturer controls his sacrifice and there is indeed some interaction, but it is negligible, as far as the question is concerned about who controls whom.

I don't want to compare the family situation with that of the torturer and the tortured, but I am mentioning this drastic example to question the concept of interaction. It's perfectly true, the interaction is there, but in any interaction you have to raise one question. Who is the one in this interaction who has the power to force the other one? Is it an interaction of equals or is it an interaction of unequals who basically cannot fight on the same level? The academic sociological concept of interaction implies a great danger. It is purely formalistic; that is to say, the interaction is wherever two people interact.

One has to determine whether the quality of interaction is one of equality or one of control, of greater force by the one who can force the other to act as he wishes. A classic expression for this question is to be found in international and also in civil treaties. If a very strong power makes an alliance with a very small power, it is phrased in terms of an alliance; that is to say, even the annexation is phrased in terms of a treaty of equals. But what is certain in these treaties is that *de facto* all the rights, except usually language, are to a greater power—but formally it is a treaty. The same old story in business—and the Roman law called that a *societas leonina*, a Lion Society: a big firm makes an association, a contract of fusion with small firms. Legally it reads as if the two make a free contract, but in fact the big firm simply takes over the small firm; but this is not expressed in these legal terms, it is expressed that the two are perfectly free to make a contract while the small firm is not free at all. That interaction of itself is not enough. This interaction is too formal; although it's real enough, it's too abstract. What matters in all human rela-

tionships is primarily the relatively free unjealous power of two partners.

In this respect I have a different experience from that of Freud—
actually I have both experiences because I have been trained at an
orthodox Freudian institute in Berlin, and practiced as an orthodox
Freudian analyst for about ten years until I became more and more
dissatisfied with what I experienced. I noticed I became bored during the hour. The main difference is to be seen in the following:
Freud saw the whole analytic situation as a laboratory situation;
here was a patient who is an object; the analyst as a laboratory man
watches what comes out of the mouth of this object. Then he draws
all sorts of conclusions, gives back to the patient whatever he sees.
In this respect I am also on the opposite side of Dr. Rogers. I think
the whole expression "client-centered therapy" is kind of strange
because every therapy has to be client-centered. If the analyst is
such a narcissist that he cannot be centered on the client, he really
shouldn't do the job he is doing. I don't think client-centered therapy, which is something self-evident, means just mirroring, on the
contrary.

What do I do? I listen to the patient and then I say to him: "Look,
what we are doing here is the following. You tell me whatever comes
to your mind. That will not always be easy; sometimes you will not
want to tell me. All I ask you in that case is to say that there is
something you won't tell me, because I don't want to put any more
pressure on you that you have to do things. Probably in your life you
have been told much too often that you have to do something. All
right, but I would appreciate it if you would tell me that you are
leaving out something. So I listen to you. And while I am listening
I have responses which are the responses of a trained instrument, I
just am trained in this. So what you tell me makes me hear certain
things and I tell you what I hear, which is quite different from what
you are telling me or intended to tell me. And then you tell me how
you respond to my response. And in this way we communicate. I
respond to you, you respond to my response, and we see where we
are going." I am very active in this.

I don't interpret; I don't even use the word interpretation. I say what I hear. Let us say the patient will tell me that he is afraid of me and he will tell me a particular situation, and what I "hear" is that he is terribly envious; let us say he is an oral-sadistic, exploitative character and he would really like to take everything I have. If I have the occasion to see this from a dream, from a gesture, from free associations, then I tell him: "Now, look here, I gather from this, that, and the other that you are really afraid of me because you don't want me to know that you want to eat me up." I try to call his attention to something he is not aware of. The whole point here is that there are some analysts, Rogers most extremely so, some Freudian analysts less extremely so, who believe the patient should find it himself. But I think that prolongs the process tremendously; it is long enough and difficult enough anyway. What happened? There are certain things in the patient which he represses; and he represses them for good reasons; he doesn't want to be aware of them; he is afraid of being aware of them. If I sit there and wait for hours and months and years perhaps, until these resistances are broken through, I waste time for the patient.

I am doing the same thing that Freud does in dream interpretation. The dream may be a harmless dream, and yet what Freud says is, this dream really says you want to kill me. I do that with other things, too. I tell the patient what I see and then I analyze the patient's resistance to what I am saying. Or, if there is not much resistance, then the patient will feel it, but I am very aware of the fact that intellectualization doesn't help a bit, in fact it makes everything impossible. What matters is whether the patient can feel what I am referring to.

Spinoza has said knowledge of the truth in itself changes nothing unless it is also an affective knowledge. This holds true for all psychoanalysis. You may analyze and find out that you suffer from a depression because as a child you were neglected by your mother. You can find that out and believe that until doomsday and it'll not do you the slightest good. Maybe that's exaggerated, it may be a little help, you know the reason but it's like the exorcism of the devil. You say, "That's the devil," and if you have done that for many years by the way of suggestion, eventually if the patient feels he has ex-

orcised the devil—and the mother who rejected him is the devil—
then he may eventually feel less depressed if the depression was not
so serious. To know what is repressed means really to experience it
here, not only in thought but to fully feel it. This kind of experience
has in itself a very relieving effect. It is not the question of explaining
something: "This is because—," but of really feeling. In the kind of
an X-ray you feel in depth: here I am depressed. If you really feel it,
that promotes the idea to do something to clear the depression and
you can come to the next stage where you maybe feel: "I am really
furious and I punish my wife with my depression." On the other
hand, the person may be so sick or the depression may be so severe
that even that does not help.

PRECONDITIONS OF THE PSYCHOANALYST

For every psychoanalytic work there is one important aspect: the
personal qualities of the analyst. The primary thing here is his experience and his understanding of another human being. Many analysts become analysts because they feel very inhibited to reach
human beings, to relate to human beings, and in the role of an
analyst they feel protected, especially if they sit behind the couch.
But it is not only that. It is also very important that the analyst is
not afraid of his own unconscious and therefore he is not afraid to
open up the patient's unconscious and that he is not embarrassed
about it.

This leads me to what you might call the humanistic promise of
my therapeutic work: There is nothing human which is alien to us.
Everything is in me. I am a little child, I am a grown up, I am a
murderer, and I am a saint. I am narcissistic, and I am destructive.
There is nothing in the patient which I do not have in me. And
only inasmuch as I can muster within myself those experiences which
the patient is telling me about, either explicitly or implicitly, only if
they arouse and echo within myself can I know what the patient is
talking about and can I give him back what he is really talking about.
Then something very strange happens: the patient will not have the
feeling I am talking *about* him or her, nor that I talk down to him
or her, but the patient will feel that I am talking about something

which we both share. The Old Testament says: "Love the stranger, because you have been strangers in Egypt and therefore you know the soul of the stranger." [Deut. 10:19]

One knows another person only inasmuch as one has experienced the same. To be analyzed oneself means nothing else but to be open to the totality of human experience which is good and bad, which is everything. I heard a sentence from Dr. Buber recently about Adolf Eichmann, that he could not have any particular sympathy with him although he was against the trial, because he found nothing of Eichmann in him. Now, that I find an impossible statement. I find the Eichmann in myself, I find everything in myself; I find also the saint in myself, if you please.

If I am analyzed that means really—not that I have discovered some childish traumata, this or the others primarily—it means that I have made myself open, that there is a constant openness to all the irrationality within myself, and therefore I can understand my patient. I don't have to look for them. They are there. Yet my patient analyzes me all the time. The best analysis I ever had is as an analyst and not as a patient, because inasmuch as I try to respond to the patient and to understand, to feel what goes on in this man or woman, I have to look into myself and to mobilize those very irrational things which the patient is talking about. If the patient is frightened and I repress my own fright I will never understand the patient. If the patient is a receptive character and I cannot mobilize that in me which is receptive or was receptive but is still there, at least in a small dose, I will never understand it.

The training curriculum of psychoanalysts should include the study of history, history of religion, mythology, symbolism, philosophy, that is to say all of the main products of the human mind. Instead of that, today officially the requirement is that he studies psychology and has a doctor's degree in psychology. Well, I think that is—and I am sure many psychologists agree with me—simply a waste of time. They do it only because they are forced to do it, because otherwise they do not get the degree which the state recognizes, that is a condition for their being licensed as psychotherapists. In academic psychology, which you study in universities, you hear practically nothing about men in the sense in which psychoanalysis deals with men in order to understand their motivations, to understand their problems; at best you have something like behaviorism, which by definition excludes the understanding of man, basically, because it really emphasizes all that we have to study in the behavior of man and how this behavior is manipulated.

The analyst should not be naive; that is to say, he should know the world as it is and should be critical toward what happens. How can one be critical about the psyche of another person, about his consciousness, if one is not at the same time critical about the general consciousness and the forces which are real in the world? I do not believe one can. I do not believe that truth is divisible, that one can see the truth in personal matters but be blind in all other matters. One can see the truth to some extent in personal matters, but one can never see it if one's mind is half blinded. If one's mind is completely awake and open, then indeed he can see whether it's a person or whether it's society, whether it's the situation or anything, or whether it's art.

One has to be critical and to see what is behind the appearances. I do believe that one cannot understand a person, an individual, unless one is critical and understands the forces of society which have molded this person, which have made this person what he or she is. To stop at the story of the family is just not enough. For the full understanding of the patient it is not enough either. He will also only be fully aware of who he is if he is aware of the whole social situation in which he lives, all the pressures and all the factors which have their impact on him. I do believe that psychoanalysis is essentially a method of critical thought, and to think critically is indeed very difficult because it is in conflict with one's advantages. No one is particularly promoted for thinking and being critical. Nobody has any advantage for it, except maybe in the long run.

In my opinion social analysis and personal analysis cannot really be separated. They are part of the critical view of the reality of human life. Perhaps it is much more useful to the understanding of psychoanalysis to read Balzac than it is to read psychological literature. Reading Balzac trains one better in the understanding of man

in analysis than all the analytic forces in the world, because Balzac
was a great artist who was able to write case histories, but with what
richness, with what wealth, really going down to the unconscious
motivations of people and showing them in their interrelations to
the social situation. That was the attempt of Balzac: he wanted to
write the character of the French middle class of his time. If one is
really interested in man and in his unconscious, don't read the text-
books, read Balzac, read Dostoyevsky, read Kafka. There you learn
something about man, much more than in psychoanalytic literature
(including my own books). There one finds a wealth of deep insight,
and that is what psychoanalysis could do, should do with regard to
individuals.

What people and especially analysts today ought to learn first of
all is to see the distinction between authenticity and façade. Actually
that sense is greatly weakened today. Most people take words for
reality; that's already a crazy, insane confusion. But I think also most
people do not see the difference between façade and the authentic,
although unconsciously they do. You can often find a dream in which
a person has seen a man in the daytime and he thought he was very
nice and he liked him, and then he has a dream in which he sees
this person as a murderer, or a thief, which simply meant subliminally
he was aware that this man is dishonest. But in his consciousness he
was not aware while he saw him. Of course, you don't assume somebody is a murderer—I don't mean realistically murderer, but in his
intentions—or that somebody is destructive unless we have proven
it, or maybe the man said something to him and so he was flattered.
In our dreams we are usually honest, much more honest than we are
in the daytime, because we are not influenced by events from the
outside.

DEALING WITH THE PATIENT

[To begin a therapeutic relation, mutual trust must be presupposed.
If a patient asks me whether I trust him, I shall answer:] "I trust you
at the moment but I have no reason to trust you and you have no
reason to trust me. Let's see what happens, whether we can trust
each other after a while when we have had some contact." If I'd

said: "Of course I trust you!" I would be lying. How can I trust him unless he is a very exceptional person? Sometimes I trust a person after seeing him or her five minutes. Sometimes I know definitely I don't trust somebody. That's then too bad because that's no basis for analysis.

Not to start analysis depends on many things. If I have an impression that I don't trust this person, but I still see there is something in which he or she could change, I might tell him or her that I really don't find him or her very trustworthy but still I think maybe there is something. Or if that is not the case, I would find some reason without offending him or her, to say that I don't think we are very well prepared to work together, he (or she) had better go to somebody else.

I would never say to anybody in the world—and I have never said so—that he or she could not be analyzed or he or she could not be helped. I am deeply convinced that that is a statement for which nobody can be responsible. I am not God and there is no way of knowing definitely if a person is hopeless or not. My own judgment can be that he or she is, but how can I trust my own judgment to that extent that I would speak a verdict about that person and say somebody else could not help him? So I have never ended an initial interview or any initial work with this statement. If I have felt I was not in a position to work with that person, I have tried to send him or her to somebody else—and this I did not as an excuse but because I deeply believe it is my obligation to give him or her any chance he or she has, and my judgment is certainly not enough to base such a vital decision on.

As far as reducing dependency is concerned, that is a matter of dosage in every case. If you have a patient who is a near schizophrenic with an extreme—what I would call—symbiotic attachment to his or her analyst, in which the person feels absolutely lost, if he or she does not have that unshakeable or unbreakable tie with the host person, you will find in many pre-schizophrenic or schizophrenic patients that there is a symbiotic relationship to the mother or father figure. That is the moment where they should be confronted with the necessity to stand on their own feet—although there might be the danger of a psychotic breakdown. In a symbiotic relationship, I would put it this way: the process of individuation has not occurred in spite of the fact that the person is beyond adolescence.

Freud believed that by examining, by studying the depth of a person, his insight into the processes going on in his very depth should lead to a change in his personality, to a cure of symptoms. I like to call attention to the fact of how extraordinary this idea was, especially if you consider the present time, and some people said so even then, many years ago—to devote that much time to one person is not in the contemporary mood. On the contrary, since everything has to be done in a hurry, the most important objection to analysis is it still takes so much time.

Quite surely a bad analysis should be as short as possible, but a deep and effective analysis should last as long as necessary. Naturally one should try methods to make it last no longer than necessary but the idea that it is worthwhile to devote that attention for hundreds and hundreds of hours to one person is in itself, I would say, an expression of a deep humanism in Freud. The reason that a psychoanalysis takes too long in itself is not a reason against it, and if one presents it as a social problem, it is a sheer rationalization. That is to say, one really rationalizes one's ideas that a person doesn't deserve that much attention, that that person is not that important. One rationalizes that by presenting a viewpoint, a social viewpoint, that only the ones that are better off get this treatment.

The idea that the patient must pay for the treatment, otherwise he can't get well, is like the opposite of what the Gospel says, the rich will never go to Heaven. I think it's plain nonsense. Because the real question is what effort somebody makes; for a very rich person paying for the treatment means absolutely nothing. In fact, it's a deduction from taxes which is always desirable. So if a person shows no interest whether he pays or doesn't pay, that's the only criterion, and it's a very self-serving rationalization that he has to pay—the more he pays, the quicker he gets well, because he makes more of a sacrifice. It's the thinking really of modern times, that what you pay for you value most, and what you don't pay for you value little. If you pay much then you may value analysis even less because you are accustomed to buying. That's a fact. People don't value, particularly when they have money; they don't value particularly what they buy.

[In regard to group psychotherapy] I am very suspicious, but I have to say I have never done group therapy and probably precisely because I dislike it tremendously. I just dislike the idea of one person talking intimately about himself in front of ten other people. I couldn't stand it. I also have the suspicion that this is the psychoanalysis for the man who cannot pay twenty-five dollars, but if ten get together, you pay fifty and that's fine.

Actually I can imagine that especially for adolescents group therapy might be very useful. If they are not very sick, have similar problems, it might help them to see that they have common problems and on a superficial basis with some good teaching, some good advice, I think their problems might be alleviated and it is a very good thing. But I do not think it is in any way a substitute for psychoanalysis. Psychoanalysis is a method which is so individualized and so personal that I don't think it lends itself to the method of group-therapy. I am in this respect an individualist and an old-fashioned man.

I believe that atmosphere which we are seeing today, reduces privacy more and more for the sake of common chatter and leads to an anti-human and anti-humanist attitude. I don't think it is conducive to any good therapy except in very specific cases where I do not want more. The statement that the relation to the patient is artificial—that doesn't impress me. A love relationship between two people is also artificial because they don't make love in society and their most intimate hour is not shared by ten other people. I think there is a lot of rationalization in an age in which privacy gets lost more and more.

A SHINING AFFLICTION

ANNIE G. ROGERS

The therapist in this true story is Annie Rogers, a psychology intern treating Ben, a severely disturbed boy. The excerpt describes their first session.

Rogers is a talented and particularly intuitive therapist. Part of her talent rests on her ability both to allow the patient the space he needs without involving herself in his struggle and to maintain enough distance so that he can express himself freely. She is rewarded in this first session with a small measure of intimacy from Ben, a major achievement in light of his relationships until this moment and the seriousness of his illness.

Rogers shows us the session and her thought processes as the session proceeds. At the end we read her summary of the session, which shows her compassionate and insightful reading of the boy's behavior. Finally, she describes the clinical listening process, the "listening with the third ear" that allows her to communicate with and relate to Ben.

Ben walks rapidly down the hall ahead of me, his dark head bobbing up and down with the stiffness of his gait, then turns to walk backwards, regarding me warily. "Would you like to unlock the door?" I ask, offering him my keys. He takes them, unlocks the door and walks inside the playroom. He does not speak. He goes to the blackboard

and erases the scribbles another child has made, picks up two puppets, then a ball of clay, examining and discarding each toy. He
kneels on the floor and throws the puppets behind him, saying, "We
need this one, and this one, and this." He leaves them strewn on
the floor and pulls a game off the toy shelves, the game of Sorry.

"I know this game," he says.

"You know that game and you will play it," I state back simply.

He sets up the red and blue players on the game board. I wonder
to myself if he knows the rules.

He does not invite me to play, but plays the game aloud. He picks
up the top card. "Five," he reads, and moves his blue player in five
leaps around the board and into "home." "I am the blue and I am
going to win." Then he picks another card, a nine, and moves the
red player exactly nine spaces, counting each one aloud. "Three,"
and the blue player makes three huge leaps into "home." Within
eight moves he has "won" the game.

"I won!" he announces to me.

"You made up your own rules so your player would win the game,"
I clarify.

He looks at me, studying me, then bends and picks up a puppet
and throws it into the corner by the sink, and looks at me to see my
response.

"You can play by your own rules here," I say, wondering if he
thought my comment was an admonition. Then he picks up the
puppets one by one and throws them forcefully into the corner, and
turns again to look for my reaction.

Is he trying to provoke me? Showing me his anger for my comment? Trying to find my rules and limits? I don't know, but I feel it
is important for me not to enter into a power struggle. I want him
to experience his *own* control and lack of control and his *own* feelings.

"You wanted to throw all those puppets, and you did!" I say.

I hear screaming in the hall and fast footsteps and then a child's
body thuds abruptly against the closed door. Ben startles, and looks
directly at me for the first time.

"What's that?" he says.

"That is a little boy who is hurting a lot and he ran into our door."

Ben raises his index finger and absently touches his lower lip, which I see for the first time is cut and slightly swollen. "How did you hurt your lip?" I ask. He looks surprised.

"I hit it," he says.

"How did you hit it, Ben?"

He stands for a moment, his blue eyes unfocused, as if in a trance, then walks over to the paints.

I sit back, literally sitting on my hands to stop myself from inter-fering with his attempt to set up the paints. He unscrews paint lids, spilling, pours water, spilling, and dribbles color from the brush as he begins to paint.

"There is an apron in the drawer to keep it off your shirt," I tell him. Ben reaches in for the apron, using it only to wipe his hands. He makes several swift strokes with the blue paint, then paints a red splotch over the blue.

I lean over to look and ask, "What is that, Ben?"

"A bird that's got his tail caught on fire." He blots it out in black paint, as if to erase it, and says, "Don't distract me."

"You would like me to be quiet?"

"You're distracting me."

And I was! I sit back in silence as he covers the page with black paint. I wonder how he's come to know a word like *distract* in his five short years. He looks up at me.

"Can I put the clay on the paper and cut through it?"

I rephrase it: "You would like to see how that works?"

He nods and goes to get the clay from the lowest toy shelf, then simply sits on the floor, facing away from me toward the shelves. Very still. He twists around and gives me a single clear bark. At a loss, I inquire back, "Woof?" He gives a small, whimpering series of barks. "The puppy dog is sad?" I guess. He growls and barks loudly. "And the puppy is mad now." He barks more loudly and howls and I see his first smile, showing his straight baby teeth. His eyes do not smile.

He whimpers again, then begins to convey a stuffed bear to the corner by picking it up between his teeth and crawling there on all fours. He crawls back to the toy shelves and sorts through a box of small plastic toys, removing six marbles and putting them on the floor next to the chair where I sit. He bends over and puts a marble in his mouth, then nudges my hand with his nose. I open it and he spits the small wet marble carefully into my hand. In this manner he "gives" me all six marbles. Then he barks for them and I give them back. He repeats the entire process again, then leans up against my leg as he fingers the other toys in the box. He crawls over to the sink and raises himself up, climbing into the chair in front of it, and barks. He looks at the paper towels within his reach, and then at me.

"Oh," I say, "the puppy dog wants *me* to give him towels to wipe the paint off, hmm?"

I give him several wet towels and he wipes his hands. It is time to leave. We both know this. I don't need to say it. In silence I accompany him down the hall to rejoin his class.

Ben has made eloquent statements about himself in play today. First he tries to show me that he has complete control over his invisible game partner, and that he cannot bear to lose. When I see this and comment, "You made up your own rules so your player would win the game," Ben makes an attempt for control again by trying to provoke a reaction from me by throwing the puppets. Or perhaps he is simply frustrated with me. Or he may be showing me his anger at my comment.

But I have observed him in his classroom, in the hall, in the cafeteria, trying to provoke a reaction from others in exactly this way, so this seems to me an explanation worth trusting for a bit. He would walk up to an older boy and kick out, or deliberately knock over his milk, or shout into an adult's shocked face, "Shut up, fuck-face!" and nearly always get the same reliable response: someone else would take charge of him, at times physically restraining him as he struggles, biting, banging his head, seemingly impervious to pain. In this "out of control" state, Ben uncannily holds a great deal of power. His attempts to control through lack of control ironically mean that he has to sacrifice the experience of himself—just Ben—and that he cannot freely choose to be himself with other children and with adults.

I want to show Ben that he can have an effect on me, that he can choose to be himself with me, and make things happen between us. Insofar as possible, I want to follow his wants and needs, and not impose restrictions unless he begins to hurt himself or me physically. Behind the overt need to control, Ben is asking a haunting question, one seldom heard by adults: "Can I test the width and breadth of who I am, in my anger, my messiness, my babyishness *and* in my real competence, and will you let me be?" My efforts to read his behavior and let him be, with his reminder, "Don't distract me," pay off in the first physical and emotional contact between us. While Ben is testing my ability to interpret his feelings in his barking, he is also making use of the information I give back to him. Through this process of hearing his feelings named aloud for him, he is able to make himself vulnerable in his gift of six marbles, spat so carefully into my waiting hand, and to lean against me in relief as if to say: "This is who I am when I'm being me."

As I play with Ben, I listen "with a third ear," I listen for what's under the surface of his words and play. This depends upon paying attention to both Ben and myself. I notice and take in his words, the pitch and tone of his voice, his gestures, his movements toward and away from me. I attend to my feelings, and especially to those moments just before and just after I respond to him. In the absence of Ben's response to what I say or do I cannot know if I have heard him. But fortunately he is quite clear. When he is painting and I keep talking to him, for example, he says, "You are distracting me!" In his puppy dog play, he barks and growls, and I guess, "The puppy dog is mad?" This isn't a difficult interpretation, but I watch Ben for his response, and he affirms it, barking and growing louder, then rewarding me with his first smile. Within this circle of attention we surprise one another, and then Ben leans up against my leg and gives me his gift of six wet marbles.

This "clinical" listening I am learning also carries particular risks. Were I to listen to Ben as if I already knew the meaning "behind" his words and actions, looking to find some validation of a scheme I have already become invested in, I would no longer hear him. I would shut him out of the present, and nothing could get through to me then. If I claimed that kind of authority with any consistency, how could he correct me? On the other hand, I cannot abandon the meanings I bring to Ben's play. After all, I spend a great deal of my time, in supervision, thinking about the meanings of his play; it's part of my training to learn how to think symbolically about the ways children play. This training is a foundation for what I do when I am with Ben. But my training isn't the only source of my knowledge.

THERAPY

STEVEN SCHWARTZ

Therapy is a novel about the effect that a therapist's patients and personal life have on his ability to do his job. The realm of feelings that a patient presents to a therapist range from sexual feelings to feelings of hatred that drive the patient to try to undermine the therapist.

In this excerpt, the patient, Maureen, has found her therapist, Cap's, most vulnerable point and aimed squarely at it in an attempt to hurt him. She has called him a "plodder," the exact word his father had used to describe him and the characterization he had spent his life trying to disprove.

How did Maureen know where to aim her verbal hit? In spite of the therapist's attempts to remain anonymous, most patients do pick up a great deal about the therapist during the course of hours and hours spent together.

Maureen Kels sat in his office, in black stockings and black knit skirt, her feet pulled under her on the couch. She lit a cigarette.

"Maureen—"

"Sorry. I keep forgetting where I am. Seventy-five dollars an hour, and it doesn't even entitle me to enjoy a cigarette." She stood up and dropped the cigarette in the coffee mug on his desk. It sizzled in the dregs. The mug was his favorite; she somehow knew this, he guessed.

She was his most difficult client; he'd braced himself for the visit. He'd intended to relax first by taking his lunch hour, but his sessions with Julian and Sable had gone over and set him behind.

"What's been going on?" asked Cap. He noted that Maureen hadn't said a word about his new son. Cap knew by now, after working with her for two years, that the lapse was no oversight but a conscious omission. The baby would mean more if she could make a silent issue out of it. They'd eventually get around to both her jealousy and her resentment of him for having his own child now. It was going to be the theme of the month, he could see, with all his clients.

She'd turned thirty-six just recently, had never been married, and had no promising prospects (though many affairs). She insisted she wasn't interested in having children, but nevertheless she had found a reason to walk out on the session when he first told her that Wallis was pregnant.

"I'm not really here today."

"Oh?" said Cap. "Who am I talking to?"

"My answering service." A dig at his refusal to give out his home number. He made clients use the answering service, though he encouraged them to call if necessary. It was the only way he and Wallis could get any peace. If clients needed him quickly, they could place an emergency call. Maureen had told him it was humiliating to make an emergency call, to tell some flunky answering-service operator "This is an emergency," just so he'd call her back right away. "What about all your 'unconditional positive regard'?" she'd asked. Unconditional positive regard doesn't mean being invincible, he'd explained. Even therapists have limits, especially therapists, and his acceptance of her was unconditional within those limits. "Oh, Casper," she'd said, the only one who called him Casper, having seen his full name (everyone thought Cap was short for Kaplan) on his doctoral degree, which hung on the back of his closet door—he'd found her in there "looking around" one day after he'd gone down the hall to get some tea. "Unconditional within limits. Sounds like 'minor emergency.' A nice oxymoron if I've ever heard one." Maureen was a professor in the environmental economics department at the university. She'd grown up on a farm near Port Arthur, Texas, where her parents had been pecan growers. They'd been poor, preoccupied with the farm, which was always losing money. On more than one occasion she'd told him she'd gone into economics as a means of understanding their poverty and had never figured it out. "Maybe we can think of some more," Maureen had said. "Unconditional prevaricator. Wait! That's not an oxymoron that's hyperbole. I mean, there's nothing unconditional about the lines you hand me, is there? They're all based on my good, solid payment for such insults. If I'm fool enough to hand over seventy-five bucks a week for horse poop like 'unconditional within limits,' then I can't really blame anyone but myself."

He stuck with her. Rode her anger, a bull out of the chute. Her pattern was to sabotage relationships with men when she became frightened of being too emotionally involved. After a grace period, when she could be charming (Cap had seen this side, and he never knew what he would get in the therapy), she'd find her lover's weakness and step on it, on her way out the door. He'd confronted her about her pattern of dropping men before they had the chance to drop her.

"Has it occurred to you," she fired back, "that the behavior you claim is my defense against being rejected is simply my waking up to what losers most men are? Hmm?"

By the time she came to Cap, she had already been through four therapists, two in Pierre, two in other places where she'd lived. It was hard, almost impossible at times, to sidestep her attacks and not take them personally. It helped to know that she would have found something wrong—anything—about his character in order to undermine their work. He knew the two other therapists in town, both male, whom she'd seen for a short period. One had flat-out told her, after two sessions, that he couldn't work with her. ("You're just figuring that out, Sherlock?" she'd said as her exit line, leaving him with a fine-tipped, personalized dart.) And the other, whose intelligence and critical acumen were irreproachable—he was a recognized scholar in his field—she had informed, "Physically—well, this shouldn't matter, but it does to me: I mean, I have some issues around sexuality—physically, I just can't take you seriously. You're like talking to a pudgy little brother." She'd left. A Denver therapist, prior to these two, had been "overtly simple-natured" and lacked "the requisite darkness." Only her first therapist, from Minneapolis, was truly a gem, a man who had "tuned me up and turned me on—healed my body-body split the minute he opened his gorgeous mouth," but he'd died.

She'd done the same with Cap, compared him to the idealized, if conveniently dead, therapist, while checking him off the list like others she'd found wanting. But it had not been his appearance that she'd maligned. Indeed, as she reported frequently, she often masturbated fantasizing about him. He was keeping the flames going down below. That was worth the price of admission alone, since nothing else he did earned it . . . by the way, did he ever masturbate over her? ("No," he told her honestly, knowing that if he avoided the question she'd think otherwise.)

She'd tried insulting him in small ways at first: his bad taste in office furniture ("Neat—my grandmother has a lamp like that with a cute doily underneath it"); his choice of teas ("Umm, Lipton, how original"); his clothes ("That shirt would go well with elephant bells"); his voice ("You stutter sometimes, did you know that?"); his sex life ("Can't have kids or can't manage it?"); even his choice of magazines and of soap in the bathroom ("Irish Spring, how . . . pungent").

Through with the petty insults, she went for the bigger stuff. Once when he'd asked her why she found it difficult to sustain a healthy reciprocity with a man, she'd said, "Wow. 'Sustain a healthy reciprocity.' I wish I could talk like that. Will you teach me to speak like a social scientist, Casper?" He'd meant simply to ask her what happened inside when someone paid her a compliment, told her he liked or loved her. He admitted the stuffy jargon, but she wouldn't let him forget it. "Why can't that man sustain a paradigmatic, intergalactic, oceanic copulation?" she'd said, complaining about one of her lovers, who suffered from premature ejaculation and on whom she wasted no sympathy, as she did on no man. "I bet you wouldn't have all that wordiness of yours in bed, Cap dear, would you?"

It took her a year to get him. Her sensor had worked overtime. Finally, she found it. It was a spring day. He'd just come back from enjoying a walk across the street at Skookum Park, stopping there to eat his lunch. He'd been glad when they'd changed her appointment slot to two P.M., so he could take a lunch break first. A full stomach, some exercises—a quick game of racquetball with Dick—it helped him to face the afternoon, especially on Wednesdays, with Maureen. He'd been feeling pretty good, satisfied with the progress he'd been making with clients (Maureen excepted), happy about where they lived, guiltless about being so far from his parents, resigned to having no children, and resigned about his brother, Allan, who was thirty-seven, schizophrenic, and still lived with Cap's parents in Philadelphia. Cap was explaining something to her, a little awkwardly—distracted by the nice day, the budding lilacs, the apple tree in crisp white blossom outside his window, the sudden sharpness of a Western spring born from a winter with windchill temperatures of twenty-five below—explaining a concept of parental introjects, when she interrupted him: "You're a plodder, aren't you?" He'd frozen, stunned. He could see in her eyes, the soft, almost tender and solicitous way that she'd said it, that she knew she'd found the key, turned gold back to lead, the prince back to the frog, pecked at the warty, ugly bottom of her man. Bingo.

FINAL ANALYSIS

ROBERT U. AKERET

Tales from a Traveling Couch is Robert Akeret's collection of stories about patients he visits twenty years after their therapy has ended. He is curious about how the therapy affected them—about whether they are satisfied with their lives and to what extent his work has helped them. It is not exactly a scientific experiment after so many years. All of the patients had a world of intervening experiences and relationships that affected their behavior and their lives. In this epilogue of the book, Akeret reviews what he has learned about each patient and is comforted by the fact that they have all made "epic journeys" that allowed their lives to progress in the face of obstacles along the way, and that he shared part of that journey with them.

> *Presume not that I am the thing I was.*
> —WILLIAM SHAKESPEARE, *Henry IV, Part II*

I have been sitting in my office for over a week now, waiting to come to rest. My traveling couch continues to swoop back and forth in time and place as I try to make sense of my journey. I feel exalted, humbled, inspired, confused.

In my absence the mail has piled up on my desk. One colleague sent me a *New Yorker* cartoon which shows a patient on a couch saying to her therapist, "Well, I do have this recurring dream that one day I might see some results."

Ah, yes, results. This trip was not simply the self-indulgence of a sexagenarian with an extravagant appetite for story endings; it was a pilgrimage for answers: Did I actually provide lasting help for my patients? Did they find the lives they were seeking? Was life sweeter, fuller than it would have been if we had never encountered one another?

Crucial questions. Impossible questions.

Also in my pile of correspondence is an article by Frederick Crews that a friend clipped from the *New York Review of Books*. It starts like this:

> That psychoanalysis, as a mode of treatment, has been ex-
> periencing a long institutional decline is no longer in serious
> dispute. Nor is the reason: though some patients claim to
> have acquired profound insight and even alterations of per-
> sonality, in the aggregate psychoanalysis has proved to be an
> indifferently successful and vastly inefficient method of re-
> moving neurotic symptoms. It is also the method that is least
> likely to be "over when it is over." The experience of un-
> dergoing intensive analysis may have genuine value as a form
> of extended meditation, but it seems to provide many more
> converts than cures.

Beneath the article I find a substantial packet of heated replies and counterreplies that the article engendered in the pages of that magazine for months thereafter: psychotherapists angrily defending their turf; Professor Crews attacking them as pseudo-scientists without a clue to the protocols of the scientific method. Strangely none of this touches me. I have no illusions that this enterprise of mine was a scientific experiment.

The truth is, none of the scientific methods for judging the results of therapy mean much to me either, though for a very simple and quite possibly naïve reason: because I do not believe individual lives are comparable. I do not believe that any experiment that compares the results of Person A, who has been in therapy, with Person B, who has not been in therapy, with Person C, who has been in "placebo" therapy, can yield data that will be meaningful to me. This is because no matter how similar Persons A, B, and C may be, in terms of their presenting problems and personalities, I shall always be struck by their differences—the differences that make each of them unique, the differences that will stay with them throughout their lives.

To whom would I compare Naomi? To another woman who copes with pathologically low self-esteem by adopting an alternative identity? Would any alternative identity do, or would it have to be as a flamenco dancer? And if so, would it have to be as a flamenco dancer who is escaping from an abusive childhood at the hands of a self-loathing mother? Would anything less than these similarities miss what is absolutely essential about Naomi? Would anything less be able to account for her unique abilities to cope and change? And who would be my "control" for Charles? Would simply another zoophilic do, or would it have to be another man who lusts after a polar bear? Who for Seth? Who for Sasha?

For better or for worse, I have always thought of psychotherapy more as an art than a science and of myself as more of a lyrical therapist than a doctrinaire theoretician. So I am inclined to evaluate the results of my work in the same ways I would evaluate other artwork: subjectively, intuitively, aesthetically—with imagination and leaps of faith. But even within this slippery context, I still want to know the same thing that the scientist does: whether or not therapy did help my patients to lead "better" lives—*whatever that means.*

One thing it can mean is that a patient reports that he *feels* better after therapy and that he continued to feel that way generally in the years that followed. That, for example, Naomi was freed from her feelings of self-hate for the rest of her life; that Seth was able to leave his stultifying depressions behind him; that Mary was no longer overcome by feelings of rage and guilt.

None of these three patients was able to report a "perfect cure" to me in this sense. Naomi had a relapse wherein she suffered her mother's abuse for eight more years, during which those awful feelings of self-hatred returned to torture her. And Seth, after decades of feeling increasingly stronger, happier, and more positive, was suddenly overcome by a terrible depression—what he called a "divine blight"—which only the passage of time was able to heal. Of these three patients, only Mary was able to say that the feelings that had brought her into my office in the first place—the rage at being treated as an inferior in her family, the guilt over "willing" her father's death—had left her for good after therapy. Yet even Mary admitted that deep in her heart she would forever long for a loving father. She did not believe that therapy could ever quell *that* feeling of emptiness. No, none of them lived completely happily ever after.

But the operative word is *generally*—and these three patients reported *generally* feeling much better in their lives following therapy than they had in the years leading up to therapy. No, there are no controls with which to compare these resulting feelings; I cannot say for sure that any or all of these three individuals would not have felt better simply with the passage of time, with what used to be called quite reasonably "growing out" of a bad patch of life. I can only go by the gut response that these patients and I shared: that therapy was somehow responsible for their generally feeling so much better.

Yet I certainly cannot say that of the other two patients I visited; neither Charles nor Sasha felt significantly better when I saw them these many years later than they had felt when I first encountered them. Sasha now suffered from feelings of extreme loneliness and despair; he took antidepressants to get through the day; he was toying with suicide, albeit as much for literary reasons as to escape his depression. And Charles, too, felt lonely and somewhat benumbed. "Crazy" as Charles had been when I first saw him, he was more passionate then than now, more passionately in love and hence, I believe, more passionately alive. The same could be said about Sasha in the midst of his extramarital affairs—passionate, full of feelings. Of course, both were in a more passionate stage of life then. But to be fair, there is the distinct possibility that it was therapy itself that at least robbed Charles of his strongest and deepest feelings, robbed him of feelings in the name of personal survival.

Sasha would be the first to differentiate between "feeling good" and "passionately feeling." For him, "feeling good" is banal, insignificant stuff compared with the feelings of the passionately lived life. From his existential point of view, it is better to be passionately miserable than to be mindlessly blissful. Many psychotherapists passionately agree with Sasha; to them, simply "feeling good" smacks of Brave New Worldism, especially in this age when "mood brighteners" like Prozac and Zoloft are being substituted for depth therapy. One of the side benefits of Prozac is that it has forced those of us who practice "talk" therapy to define more closely what it is that we are trying to do if it is not just to make our patients feel better.

When Fromm posited biophilia as the goal of therapy, he was not talking about simply feeling good. Biophilia represents feeling *fully alive*, being more able to participate in a full range of emotions (including grief, compassion, and sorrow as well as exaltation, passion, and joy) and being able to live productively. It suggests an awareness of life's possibilities and an attitude of hope and love toward all of life. Biophilia's opposite, necrophilia, represents an attitude of despair and negation, a withdrawal from life, and a mode of being that defeats life's possibilities.

By this standard, of the five patients I visited, Seth probably traveled the farthest from necrophilia toward biophilia in the course of therapy and thereafter. (I suppose it is no coincidence that Seth is the one patient of this group whom I worked with under Fromm's guidance.) When I first encountered Seth, he fantasized about himself as a mechanical object; when I saw him decades later in New Mexico, he was surely one of the most centered, life-embracing people I have ever met. At one point during our long Albuquerque night together, I asked Seth if he thought there were any experiences in his life that he believes would have been denied him if he had not undergone therapy, and he answered, "*All* of my experiences after therapy were made possible by it." Even Seth's staggering midlife descent into depression, deathly as it was, ultimately was experienced by him as a response to becoming more fully alive at a time when he was not yet ready for it—"opening the windows" too quickly. I can imagine Seth's response to Professor Crews's dismissal of analysis as merely "a form of extended meditation": *"My God, what could be more enriching than an extended meditation?"*

On Fromm's necrophilia-biophilia scale, Mary seems an indisputable winner, too. She entered therapy in a deep depression that was only relieved by bursts of anger and other acting out, and she left therapy feeling strong and loving, happily committed to both her work and her family of creation. When I visited Mary in Northern California, I found a woman not only filled with love for life but dedicated to passing that love along, taking her place in what she viewed as the "chain reaction" of loving care. She had clearly attained Fromm's therapeutic goal of a "loving attitude" toward life. This should not be construed as some saccharine greeting card ideal; rather, it is the logical conclusion of the existential syllogism that to live fully, one must love life.

Naomi fared well by Fromm's criteria, too. She arrived in my City College cubicle feeling alienated and dead, and she left feeling vibrant and confident—albeit vibrant and confident *as someone else!* In the years that followed, she had briefly fallen back under the spell of her necrophilic mother, and even when I visited her in Florida, she was still unable to embrace completely her native identity as a Jew. But from what I experienced of her that day, Naomi was living life to the fullest, not retreating from it. What could be better testament to biophilia than when she joyfully declared to me, "Isn't it wonderful . . . the way you can be so many people in one lifetime?"

I am sure there are many therapists who would call that statement "insane," the ravings of a woman with multiple personality disorder. Not me. I call it a declaration of love of life. And I'd like to think that Fromm would call it that, too.

One particularly elusive criterion for how well a course of therapy has worked is whether or not it effected a "core change" in the patient's personality. Fromm was alluding to this when he compared "re-forming" a patient's behavior with repairing a slum: "If you make a few repairs here and there in a slum, it's still a slum."

Sometimes I can put my finger on this distinction; sometimes I cannot. What constitutes the continuous "core" self has bedeviled philosophers and psychologists since the Greeks. I do know that when Sasha wanted me just to do a little "tinkering," that felt wrong; I believed that we would have to go deeper than that to effect any meaningful change in his life. And one thing I can say without a shred of doubt is that Naomi had an indisputable core change: She changed identities. Or is that too much of a change?

In a book I read on the plane back from Paris, I came across a reference to a case of Milton Erickson's in which an energetic young patient insisted that he was Jesus Christ; Erickson's treatment was to find the young man a job as a carpenter. Perhaps Erickson was practicing the ultimate in Christ-inspired therapy: He was not judging his patient, just facilitating his self-realization. But he was not giving him any personal insight.

One thing that psychotherapy can do that Prozac can never do is provide a patient with knowledge of himself. Fromm wrote that psychoanalysis should be seen "not as a therapy, but as an instrument for self understanding . . . an instrument in the art of living. . . ."

This knowledge would include the salient themes of one's life, an identification of one's true desires and the conflicts that surround them, the differences between difficulties created by external reality and those created by internal fantasy.

But self-knowledge in itself is no guarantee that a person will feel better or even change destructive patterns of behavior. All we have to do is think of Sasha to realize that, although, of course, Sasha believed that therapy had done him a world of good.

For me, this goes to the nitty-gritty of the question of what it means for a patient to get better. Whose notion of "better"—mine or the patient's? The therapist Carl Rogers warned that "it is a dangerous philosophy to assume the right to be the self-appointed authority on what is best for someone else." And Dr. Szasz put it even more bluntly, "Therapy is like religion: there should be a free choice."

But if I allow my patients to pick their own therapeutic goal, when can I feel confident that they are ready to make this choice? In the depths of depression? At the height of mania?

My personal answer is another murky one: Patients are ready to make this decision at the point when they know themselves well enough to understand that decision's implications. But after that Szasz is right: Free choice must reign.

In thirty-five years of practicing psychotherapy, no one has tested me more formidably on this issue than Sasha Alexandrovich. Even now, after visiting him in Paris, I remain conflicted. Above all, Sasha's goal in therapy was to get back to creating art. He succeeded in this fabulously, and he makes a convincing case that he owes it all to his therapy with me; the subject of his art is himself; therapy revealed himself to himself in a way that he was able to transform into art. Thus, by his own lights, therapy was wonderfully successful. But this makes me think of Crews's assertion that therapy has won "more converts than cures." Sasha was converted to the psychoanalytic framework for understanding himself and others, yet his life seems untouched by this understanding. And Sasha's life pains me deeply. It seems necrophilic in the extreme: He treats himself as an object with his pills and injections; he cannot truly love another human being; he loves life so little that he would sacrifice it for the sake of a good book. By Fromm's standards, therapy has failed miserably with Sasha.

Or has it? If, for Sasha, creating transcendent art is the ultimate in being aware and alive, who am I to say that he is necrophilic? Shouldn't I rather say that his necrophilic life feeds his biophilic art and that art is the life he has chosen?

But I will never be completely comfortable with that idea. God help me, if Sasha does write *Diary of a Suicide*, I know I will feel that I failed him.

It is just the opposite that pains me about Charles. I am quite sure that I helped him save his biological life; without that, of course, he would have had nothing. But I was unable to help him find a very satisfying life to replace the passionate (albeit suicidal) one that I turned him away from. I did not have enough time for more than crisis intervention with Charles. I wish I could have given him more. But honestly, I am not sure how much more I could have given him.

And that brings me to my ultimate question: How can I know if I am responsible for whatever gains my patients made in their lives? That is to say, even if I were absolutely clear on what "getting better" meant, how could I be sure that therapy was the cause and not something else?

Seth provides an interesting case in point. Between the last time I saw him in 1968 and when I visited him twenty-six years later, he had immersed himself in a good two dozen varieties of therapy and spiritual growth programs, ranging from Rolfing to vision quests. What, if anything, in his therapy with me can be credited for the tremendous changes he made in his life?

I asked him that question at one point in my visit. Seth laughed and said, "They *all* deserve credit, and so does every person I have met, for that matter. I am the sum of all my experiences. But my therapy with you set me on this path, and for that I am eternally grateful."

I want very much to believe him, of course.

Citing a study of therapy outcomes done by Lester Luborsky, Professor Crews raises the question of how much we can credit the particular content of therapy with whatever "cure" follows it. Crews says, "No doubt it is motivationally useful for each of the myriad extant psychotherapies to offer its clients some structure of belief—whether it be about undoing infantile repression, contacting the inner child, surrendering to the collective unconscious, or reliving previous incarnations—but as Luborsky understood, such notions are window dressing for the more mundane and mildly effective process of renting a solicitous helper."

I should rage against this kind of attack, I know, but I do not. Maybe I am getting old and running low on passionate anger. But I like to think that my love for my patients is finally maturing to the point where it does not really matter to me who or what takes the credit for their cure. I am just so very grateful and happy to see them living satisfying lives no matter what the reason.

Truth to tell, I would not really mind if Professor Crews proved that the therapy I gave my patients turned out to be nothing more than some handholding and a sympathetic ear, the simple work of a "solicitous helper." Actually I would take great pride in that. I think I do it well.

As I look back over my follow-up journey, something Seth said comes to mind. "You're greedy to find out if what you dedicated your whole life to has amounted to anything."

Well, I do feel I made a difference. I sometimes wonder if in the coming century psychotherapy will be viewed as some kind of arcane witchcraft, a clumsy and attenuated method of transformation and self-knowledge that my grandchildren will think of in the same way that I now think of exorcisms. Yet not even this thought upsets me. I keep thinking of the time when Mary's son, Jared, asked me, "So, what's the verdict? Does therapy work?" And Mal answered for me, "Maybe it only works when it works."

That, in the end, is all I could have asked for.

The couch finally settles in my office. I find myself remembering something Fromm once said to me: "I see each patient as the hero of an epic poem."

I have always liked that idea, but I don't believe I fully understood it until I took my journey. Until now I did not appreciate the sheer epic proportions of a person's life. The mere fact that in spite of all the obstacles they faced, Naomi and Charles and Seth and Mary and Sasha could make their ways from youth into middle age touches me deeply. I have returned from my travels awed by the capacity of Man to survive; that, in itself, strikes me as heroic. And nothing that therapy can or cannot do compares with it.

About the Contributors

ROBERT U. AKERET received a Ph.D. in psychology from Columbia University and trained with Rollo May and Erich Fromm at the William Alanson White Institute, where he received his certificate in psychoanalysis. He is the author of *Tales from a Traveling Couch*, *Photoanalysis*, *Not by Words Alone*, and *Family Tales, Family Wisdom*.

GAIL ALBERT received a Ph.D. in experimental psychology from Johns Hopkins University. In addition to her private practice, she serves as the executive director of the Project for Psychiatric Outreach to the Homeless in New York City. She is the author of *On the Couch* and *Matters of Chance*.

MARK EPSTEIN is a graduate of Harvard College and Harvard Medical School. He lives in New York City, where he is in private practice and is a consulting editor to *Tricycle: The Buddhist Review*. He is the author of *Thoughts Without a Thinker*.

ERICH FROMM was a German psychoanalyst and author who immigrated to the United States in 1934 soon after the Nazis assumed power. In his early career he was a follower of Sigmund Freud, but he separated himself by proposing that neuroses can result from the influences of culture and society, not just from innate drives. He wrote many books, including *Escape from Freedom*, *Man for Himself*, *The Art of Loving*, and *Psychoanalysis and Religion*. *The Art of Listening* was published posthumously from his writings about his approach to psychotherapy.

LESTON HAVENS received a B.A. from Williams College and an M.D. from Cornell University. He taught psychiatry at Harvard Medical School and is now director of residency training at Cambridge Hospital in Massachusetts. He is the author of *A Safe Place*, *Learning to Be Human*, and *Coming to Life*.

A. M. HOMES teaches at Columbia University and lives in New York City. She is the author of *A Country of Mothers*, *Jack*, and *The Safety of Objects*.

ROBERT LINDNER was a professor of psychology at Lehigh University and chief of the Psychiatric-Psychological Division of the Federal Penitentiary at Lewisburg, Pennsylvania. *The Fifty-Minute Hour* was a stunning success and the first book of its kind—a popular retelling of extraordinary psychiatric case histories. It served as a precursor to current books by writers such as Oliver Sacks. Lindner was also the author of *Rebel Without a Cause*, *Stone Walls*, and *Prescription for Rebellion*.

JANET MALCOLM, a former staff writer at *The New Yorker*, has written a number of books, including *Psychoanalysis: The Impossible Profession* and *In the Freud Archives*.

THEODOR REIK, one of Freud's earliest and most brilliant students, was a lay psychoanalyst who practiced in Berlin and Holland. He eventually moved to New York, where he set up a training group. His many books include *Listening with the Third Ear*, *The Search Within*, *Of Love and Lust*, *The Compulsion to Confess*, and *Creation of Woman*.

ANNIE G. ROGERS, a Ph.D. in psychology, wrote *A Shining Affliction* about her first patient when she was a psychology intern. While she was treating the child, her own childhood abuse came to the surface, and she suffered a breakdown that led to her absence from work for a period of time. She has a private practice with children in Massachusetts and teaches at the Harvard Graduate School of Education. She is coauthor of *Women, Girls, and Psychotherapy: Reframing Resistance*.

STEVEN SCHWARTZ is the author of *Therapy*, *To Leningrad in Winter*, and *Lives of the Fathers*. He lives in Fort Collins, Colorado.

SAMUEL SHEM (a pseudonym of Dr. Stephen Bergman) graduated from Harvard College, was a Rhodes Scholar at Balliol College, Oxford, and received his medical training at Harvard Medical School. In addition to *Fine*, he is the author of *House of God* and *Mount Misery*, both comic novels about the experiences of doctors in training.

HERBERT S. STREAN received a doctoral degree in social work from Columbia University. He has held a distinguished professorial position at Rutgers University